Sandy Dennis

ALSO BY PETER SHELLEY
AND FROM McFARLAND

Australian Horror Films, 1973–2010 (2012)

Jules Dassin: The Life and Films (2011)

*Frances Farmer: The Life and Films
of a Troubled Star* (2011)

*Grande Dame Guignol Cinema: A History
of Hag Horror from* Baby Jane *to* Mother (2009)

Sandy Dennis
The Life and Films

PETER SHELLEY

McFarland & Company, Inc., Publishers
Jefferson, North Carolina, and London

LIBRARY OF CONGRESS CATALOGUING-IN-PUBLICATION DATA

Shelley, Peter, 1962–
Sandy Dennis : the life and films / Peter Shelley.
  p. cm.
Includes bibliographical references and index.

ISBN 978-0-7864-7197-3 (softcover : acid free paper) ∞
ISBN 978-1-4766-0589-0 (ebook)

1. Farmer, Frances, 1913–1970.
2. Actors—United States—Biography.
3. Motion picture actors and actresses—United States—Biography.
I. Title.
PN2287.D386S54 2014   791.43'028'092—dc23   [B]   2013042384

BRITISH LIBRARY CATALOGUING DATA ARE AVAILABLE

© 2014 Peter Shelley. All rights reserved

No part of this book may be reproduced or transmitted in any form or by any means, electronic or mechanical, including photocopying or recording, or by any information storage and retrieval system, without permission in writing from the publisher.

Front cover: Sandy Dennis, circa 1966 (Photofest)

Manufactured in the United States of America

*McFarland & Company, Inc., Publishers
Box 611, Jefferson, North Carolina 28640
www.mcfarlandpub.com*

Table of Contents

Acknowledgments vii
Preface 1
Introduction 5

THE FILMS

Splendor in the Grass (1961)	49
The Three Sisters (1966)	57
Who's Afraid of Virginia Woolf? (1966)	60
Up the Down Staircase (1967)	69
The Fox (1968)	74
Sweet November (1968)	81
That Cold Day in the Park (1969)	85
Thank You All Very Much (1969)	93
The Out of Towners (1970)	98
Mr. Sycamore (1975)	103
God Told Me To (1976)	106
Nasty Habits (1977)	110
The Four Seasons (1981)	113
Come Back to the 5 & Dime Jimmy Dean, Jimmy Dean (1982)	118
Another Woman (1988)	126
976-Evil (1988)	136
Parents (1989)	144
The Indian Runner (1991)	149

TELEVISION

The Guiding Light (1956)	157
Naked City (1962)	157
Naked City (1963)	160
The Fugitive (1963)	162

v

Arrest and Trial (1964)	164
Mr. Broadway (1964)	167
A Hatful of Rain (1968)	168
The Man Who Wanted to Live Forever (1970)	170
Something Evil (1972)	172
Police Story (1978)	176
Perfect Gentlemen (1978)	180
Wilson's Reward (1980)	183
Young People's Specials, "The Trouble with Mother" (1985)	184
The Execution (1985)	185
The Love Boat (1985)	189
Alfred Hitchcock Presents, "Gigolo" (1985)	190
The Equalizer (1986)	194

Appendix: Theater Credits   199
Bibliography   209
Index   223

Acknowledgments

Thanks to Barry Lowe for his continuing financial and moral support. Additionally, thanks go to Kath Perry, Chris Lewis, Catherine Alfred, and Stewart South.

Preface

The first time I saw Sandy Dennis was in *Who's Afraid of Virginia Woolf?* and her oddness seemed to confirm Pauline Kael's notorious quip from her review of *The Fox* that Dennis had made an acting style out of post-nasal drip. That viewing was probably on television; as a teenage movie fan in the 1970s, I would guess the first time I saw Dennis in the cinema was in *The Four Seasons.* In the ensemble cast of Alan Alda's comedy she was marginalized, but in her few scenes I agreed once again with Kael, who wrote that Dennis was the only one she cared about.

It's typical of Hollywood's short-term memory that, despite having won the 1967 Best Supporting Actress Academy Award for her role in *Who's Afraid of Virginia Woolf?*, Dennis may now be forgotten by all but the most ardent of film followers. Following the notion that an actress' professional life only has five years of success, her *New York Times* obituary noted that she was "never able to match the dazzling successes of her earlier years in terms of either public acclaim or favorable reviews."

In his 1972 book *The Great Movie Stars: The International Years*, David Shipman quotes *The London Evening Standard* of 1968 on Dennis: "It was symptomatic of the change in Hollywood that [she] could become a star as she is — mousy, buck-toothed, and plain — without anyone trying to transform her into Natalie Wood." Shipman wrote that in 1968 she seemed bound for major stardom, though at the time of his writing, the matter was "rather in doubt."

Tennessee Williams had a more positive view of Dennis, as stated in his 1982 conversation with James Grissom. Perhaps thinking more of her theater work than her cinematic accomplishments, Williams wrote the following: "There is a cottage industry alive and well in analyzing and dissecting this actress, and I understand the interest, even as I fail to understand the underlying goals of so many of the analysts."

If Dennis *is* remembered, she is generally grouped with Geraldine Page and Kim Stanley. This is because they were two fellow actresses who utilized Actors Studio nervous tics and offbeat mannerisms to represent Method-realism in their acting styles. However, this grouping is rather misleading, since Dennis was not a contemporary of Page and Stanley in films or the theater. Kim Stanley emerged in the American theater of the late 1940s and Page in the early 1950s, and Dennis would not make her official Broadway debut until 1957. Dennis would appear in scenes with Page in *Nasty Habits* (1977), though Page received higher billing, and all three actresses can be seen together in *The Three Sisters* (1966).

In terms of movie stardom, the three enjoyed varying degrees of success. Page would win the Best Actress Academy Award for *The Trip to Bountiful* (1985), although her other leading film roles were few. Only the horror title *What Ever Happened to Aunt Alice?* (1969),

Happy as the Grass Was Green (1973), and *The Trip to Bountiful* saw her top-billed. Stanley was only top-billed twice in film, in *The Goddess* (1958) and *Séance on a Wet Afternoon* (1964).

Dennis had more leading roles in film — *Up the Down Staircase* (1967), *The Fox* (1968), *Sweet November* (1968), *That Cold Day in the Park* (1969), *Thank You All Very Much* (1969), and the later *Come Back to the 5 & Dime Jimmy Dean, Jimmy Dean* (1982) — although, like the other two, she was unable to maintain this position in her career. Foster Hirsh, in his book *A Method to Their Madness*, claims that Dennis, perhaps even more than Page and Stanley, was too specialized to sustain general audience acceptance, turning her into a "sideshow rather than a mainstream attraction."

The fact that none of the three could be considered conventional beauties possibly also played a part. And then there is the age factor. Stanley was thirty-three by the time she made *The Goddess*. Page was thirty-seven when she starred in *Summer and Smoke* (1961) and thirty-eight when she made *Sweet Bird of Youth* (1962). Although these were leading roles, for both of which she was nominated for the Best Actress Academy Award, Page was not top-billed in either. Dennis was thirty when she scored the lead in *Up the Down Staircase*.

Hollywood is a notoriously youth-oriented town, with a woman in her early twenties deemed to be the most attractive. The fact that an actress might be more skilled because of her experience does not seem to matter, apart from exceptional circumstances. So while the three honed their craft in theater and on television, they were unable to capture Hollywood's interest until later, and it probably cost them.

The association of the three actresses also provides a point of comparison in that, of the three, Dennis could be the most quirky in performance style, a style that could both attract and repel audiences. While some detractors called her "Dennis the Menace," her admirers insisted that Sandy was dandy. Her many mannerisms included stuttering and word repetition, speaking in broken sentences and with a nasal whine, slurring, whispering, throat gulps, nervous giggles and laughing, a teeth-baring smile, eye blinking and twitches and eye-closing, tongue-poking and sliding, lip-biting, hand-gesturing (including pointing, a hand to the forehead, and a hand to the mouth), head-shaking and a wrinkling of the chin.

These accumulated effects are certainly what make her so distinctive and unforgettable. In 1967, in *The New York Times*, Broadway critic Walter Kerr wrote of her "habit" of "speaking onstage as though sentences were poor crippled things that couldn't cross a street without making three false starts from the curb." Dennis herself would address the issue of her mannerisms in an interview with Jerry Parker dated April 1973: "I am not mannered. There are times when I use that [sniffles and stammers and fluttering hands], and then I use it to the fullest degree. But then it is deliberate and planned. But I have that reputation and I will have it because the critics refuse to give it up. It's their problem."

Included in their review of *Mr. Sycamore* in *The Motion Picture Guide* is a comment by Jay Robert Nash and Stanley Ralph Ross about Dennis' film career and her acting style: "When she first came on the screen her nervous and quirky mannerisms were thought to be a breakthrough in realistic acting. But she's done that same sort of irritating thing through her career and audiences saw that's just about *all* she does." This reads as reductive of Dennis' acting ability and appeal. However, Nash and Ross may have a point about the audience's supposed loss of interest in seeing her, considering the roles she would later assay.

As of the writing of this book there are only two existing biographies of Sandy Dennis. One is her own autobiography, which was published posthumously and makes few references to her career and her private life. The second is a chapter in Boze Hadleigh's *Hollywood Lesbians*, where Hadleigh provides a four-page biography and then a fifteen-page interview he conducted with her. There are also small references to *Come Back to the 5 & Dime Jimmy Dean, Jimmy Dean*; *Who's Afraid of Virginia Woolf?*; *Up the Down Staircase*; and *The Fox*.

This book, then, is an attempt to provide an appreciation of Dennis for her film and television work. Her stage work is also covered in a brief biographical chapter to give context to her life and the film and television work that has been recorded for prosperity. For the biographical chapter I have applied the following rule for the information I have accessed. Any statement of fact is supported by common agreement in the accessed sources, with variations recorded according to the differing source. For each of Dennis' films, made-for-TV movies and television appearances, I have created its own chapter.

I have viewed all of her available titles to accurately describe the content and give my critical evaluation and assessment. As some of the titles are not available commercially, I have accessed prints from auctions and collectors, and therefore not judged the quality of photography too harshly in these sometimes less than ideal copies.

Regrettably, there are some titles I could not access. These are the made-for-TV movies *A Hatful of Rain* (1968) and *Wilson's Reward* (1980), the *Young People's Specials* TV show episode "The Trouble with Mother" (1985), and *The Love Boat* TV show episode "Roommates/Heartbreaker/Out of the Blue" (1985). For these chapters I have gathered as much information as possible, including any form of synopsis I could find. Since *A Hatful of Rain* and *Wilson's Reward* are both remakes, I have used the synopsis of the originals under the assumption that the teleplays have kept the same narratives.

For what I have viewed, I have commented on Dennis' performance, as well as made observations on the title's narrative, and filmmaking technique and style. I do not have the agenda of a biased fan, so I do not hesitate to point out elements that are disappointing or that I find downright bad, as well as praising things that I find worthy.

Each chapter includes a cast and crew filmography taken from the actual film, with transcribed spelling (e.g., *The Out of Towners*, although the film is often known as *The Out-of-Towners*). For *Edward Albee's Who's Afraid of Virginia Woolf?*, *Anton Chekov's The Three Sisters*, and *D.H. Lawrence's The Fox* I have dropped the credited author's name before the title. *976-EVIL* is referred to as *976-Evil*. The *Alfred Hitchcock Presents* TV episode known as "Arthur, or the Gigolo" is shortened here to "Gigolo." I have noted alternate titles. I have used the American title *Thank You All Very Much* for *A Touch of Love*, which was the title used for release in the United Kingdom.

Listings are supplemented by information from the *Internet Movie Database*, *Turner Classic Movies*, and the *Internet Theatre Database*, although sometimes the less-than-ideal copies of material made the confirmation of some contributors impossible. The chapters also provide a plot synopsis, make mention of any songs, the filming dates of the production and any location sites, the release or screening date, any publicity taglines, period and contemporary reviews, information about remakes, and the VHS or DVD availability.

The release dates listed are those for the United States (e.g., the *Internet Movie Database* indicates *The Fox* is from 1967 because it was first released in Canada, but it didn't make its United States debut until 1968). Some exact release dates are unknown (e.g., *The Three Sisters*, so the *Internet Movie Database* 1966 date is used). I also provide any behind the scenes information. To supplement chapters I have provided complimentary imagery, with portraits of Dennis, stills, and posters where possible.

I hope my study of the film and television work of Sandy Dennis is as satisfying for my readers as it has been for me, and that my book encourages others to seek out and find all I have found, and more.

Introduction

Sandy Dennis was born Sandra Dale Dennis on April 27, 1937, in Hastings, Nebraska, at the Mary Lanning Hospital. Nebraska is the state of origin of many famous show business people, including Fred Astaire, Marlon Brando, Montgomery Clift, James Coburn, Henry Fonda, Dorothy McGuire, and Robert Taylor. Ted Sorensen, another Nebraskan refugee and ex–White House aide, was quoted in a *Time* magazine article on Dennis dated September 1, 1967: "The state is old, outmoded, a place to come from or a place to die."

Dennis was the daughter of railway postal clerk Jack Dennis, who was said to have an IQ of 160, and his secretary wife, Yvonne Hopps, who worked at the Lincoln School of Commerce. Sandy Dennis had an older brother, Frank, although his date of birth is unknown, who would become a consulting engineer in Des Moines. The family lived in the same house up until 1941, which was located two blocks from her grandparents: Frank, a traveling salesman for a flour and feed company, and Fannie Dennis. That same year the family moved to a smaller, more affordable house on the lot adjacent to their previous one.

Dennis had started dance classes at Flavia Waters Dance Class for Infants and was preparing for a recital, where she would be in tap shoes and dress as part of the American flag. The *Time* magazine article quotes her saying she was kicked out of tap-dancing class at the age of three because, "All I wanted to do was stand in front of the mirror and look at myself in my Uncle Sam suit." But the recital would never be, because in the summer of 1942 the Dennises moved forty miles away to a new house in Kenesaw. Jack had also been working as a driver for the Debus Baking Company in Hastings, so after the move to Kenesaw he would stay with his parents during the week to be close to the bakery. In her memoirs, Dennis writes that the Kenesaw house also brought a new dog, a stray called Skippy. He was a wire-haired black and white terrier who became Yvonne's and stayed with the family for eighteen years.

In 1944 the family moved back to a house on the south side of Hastings, near Yvonne's parents, and Jack left to serve in the army during World War II. Dennis attended Abraham Lincoln Elementary School (called Lincoln Capital Grammar in other sources), and Frank went to Hastings High. Jack returned from service, and in 1946 the family moved again. This time they went to Lincoln, where Dennis finished high school, presumably at Lincoln High.

Some sources claim that Frank was in the same graduating class as television talk show host Dick Cavett. Since Cavett was born in 1936, one might guess Frank's age as approximately the same, which would make him only one year older than Dennis. However, a photograph of her and Frank on the Sandy Dennis Foundation website makes it appears that Frank was much older. A 1953 Lincoln High Yearbook shows a picture of Dennis as a sophomore and Cavett as a junior.

In an article in *The Pittsburgh Press* dated March 21, 1982, Ed Blank says that Cavett was in the year ahead of Dennis and quotes her as saying Cavett "was the one on the debating team who had the most incredible low voice in the whole world." Blank also quotes Cavett recalling Dennis as being "very shy, very anonymous."

Time quotes Cavett, described as her classmate, as saying that Dennis was so anonymous "she managed to get from class to class without going through the halls." He was cast opposite her in the junior play. "Sandy was so moving that I forgot my lines and ended up ad-libbing something from Noel Coward." In Boze Haldeigh's book *Hollywood Lesbians*, Dennis says she knew Cavett "slightly, but not intimately." The *After Dark* interview confirms Dennis' low social profile at Lincoln High: "I was not very forward. I was just very ordinary. I didn't take part in most things, and I was not the most popular girl. I was just sort of non-existent."

Dennis' paternal grandmother Fannie died in 1951 at age 73 following a long illness, and her grandfather, Frank, died unexpectedly in 1953. Neither had lived to see Dennis act on stage, a desire apparently born after she watched the Philco Television Playhouse production of Horton Foote's play *A Young Lady of Property*, broadcast by NBC on April 5, 1953. She would describe seeing this show as "a moment of truth." It starred Kim Stanley and Joanne Woodward, and was directed by Vincent Donehue (also known as Vincent J. Donehue and Vincent Donahue).

In his article on Dennis in *Theater Week* dated March 23, 1992, Michael Buckley quotes Foote saying of Dennis: "What makes her special is a sense of individuality she brings to her performance. The great ones have it. Geraldine Page, Kim Stanley, Sandy Dennis." Dennis played leading roles in high school and also appeared with the Lincoln Community Theater Group, now located in Damariscotta, Maine.

In the October 24, 1976, interview in *The Pittsburgh Press* with William A. Raidy, Dennis says the first amateur productions of plays she saw were *Uncle Tom's Cabin* and *Peter Pan* as a young girl. She also talks of seeing her first professional production in Colorado when she was eleven. It was *The Time of the Cuckoo* and starred Shirley Booth. Dennis was so impressed that she mailed Booth a St. Christopher medal; though she never heard back about it, Dennis knew from then on what she wanted to do with her life.

In the *After Dark* interview Dennis said, "I never wanted to be a nurse or a teacher or any of those other things little girls always want to be. As far back as I can remember, I wanted to be an actress." Other sources say she spent her childhood wanting to be Margaret O'Brien and her adolescence wanting to be Gloria Grahame. Of O'Brien, Dennis stated, "I dreamed all my life of being another O'Brien. I thought it was so unfair that I didn't have parents, like Margaret's, who would take me to Hollywood. Now that I've been there, I don't know..." Other actresses she is said to have modeled herself on were Bette Davis and Alexis Smith. She also enjoyed the movie performances of Julie Harris in *The Member of the Wedding* (1952), which she saw fifteen times, and Audrey Hepburn in *Roman Holiday* (1953), which she went to see nine times.

In her interview with Lenore Nicklin in the *Sydney Morning Herald*, dated September 19, 1972, Dennis corrects a story that her father paid $5,000 to have her teeth straightened. She says he couldn't afford $5,000, and so, "I just wore a lot of bands for about three years." *Time* says the orthodontia cost $3,000. However, in her interview with Rex Reed in *The New York Times* on June 19, 1966, Dennis tells him that her father *did* pay the $5,000. And her teeth still stuck out.

At school she is said to have acted in and directed plays and skits. Dennis described herself as a "terrible tyrant" and said she made everyone's costumes from crepe paper. *Time* magazine reports that she made a public appearance in the third grade when she adapted a Cinderella-based drama, junking the script on the eve of the performance (of which she was director and leading lady). In junior high school she went on stage in something called *Hatchet Hannah*, froze and walked right off.

In high school Dennis wrote poetry and was a voracious reader, although the *Time* article says she became a reader long before she got to school, and "gobbled six or seven books a week." She especially liked Shakespeare (which she is reported to have recited into a tape recorder her parents gave her) and the Nebraskan novelist Willa Cather. At high school she also joined the pep club, but despised her cheerleader's orange beanie and socks. Her mother says Dennis would get sick on the days there were football games and never saw one of them.

She also acted in productions of the Lincoln Community Theatre. It is reported that she auditioned for the title role in their production of *Time Out for Ginger*. When she won the part she told them she didn't want it, preferring to play the thirty-five-year-old female lead in *The Rainmaker*, which the company planning to do later that year. They gave her the part. Tom Killen in *After Dark* says that Dennis won the company's Best Actress award for her performance. In her interview with Julie Wirz for *The Hour*, dated January 22, 1981, Dennis says the play she first auditioned for was *The Crucible*, and that she got a part in the production that was to be held in a church. She also says she got the role in *The Rainmaker* despite the company's policy that an actor could only do one play a season.

Dennis graduated from Lincoln High in 1955 and was a college student at both Nebraska Wesleyan University and the University of Nebraska, spending one semester at each, supposedly to appease her parents. She then dropped out to join a summer stock company in New London, New Hampshire, after having been invited by its director, Norman Ledger. She played the supporting role of Jane in William Douglas Home's *The Reluctant Debutante* at the Westport Country Playhouse, Connecticut, for a one-week engagement. The production was directed by Walt Witcover, and the stars were Ruth Chatterton and Arthur Treacher.

In what may have been her first critical review, the July 9, 1957, *Norwalk Hour* wrote of her: "Miss Dennis has beauty and talent and shows a finesse and timing a seasoned trouper would envy.... She almost steals the show several times." She would later play the role again in a mostly student production at the University of Akron Theatre in November 1957.

At nineteen years of age, Dennis decided to pursue her acting career in New York, with a tiny stake from her family. In a 1965 *St. Petersburg Press* interview with Lloyd Shearer, she says her parents would also send her one hundred dollars a month. She shared a coldwater East 13th Street flat with a girlfriend, paying half the rent of twenty-six dollars a month. *Time* paints a bleak picture of this time, reporting that Dennis collected unemployment insurance and had to contend with "roaches that rattled the dishes" of her flat.

She studied with Uta Hagen, Lee Grant and Herbert Berghof at the Herbert Berghof Studio, and Lee Strasberg at the Actors Studio. Her Herbert Berghof fellow students were said to be Anne Bancroft and Gene Wilder, and Dennis would later teach at the school in 1989. In the *Time* magazine profile, Berghof is quoted as saying: "From the beginning, she knew how to find in each character she played the story that was original and new and worth telling."

Within months Dennis had won her first professional role — as the thirteen-year-old Hilde in Henrik Ibsen's *The Lady from the Sea* at the Off Broadway Tempo Theatre. In an April 15, 1973, interview with *The Tuscaloosa News*, she says she got the role after a man stopped her in the street and asked if she was an actress. That man happened to be the play's producer/director, William Gyime. Other sources state that Dennis was stopped as she window-shopped on MacDougall Street in Greenwich Village.

In the *Village Voice* review of the production, dated December 12, 1956, Jerry Tallmer said of her: "The teenage Miss Dennis reaches some really fine subtle notes." Dennis says she was paid forty-five dollars a week to do the show. The production ran for three weeks, and doing it got her an agent, Arnold Hosquith. He helped her get the next stage job, playing the part of the high school girl Elma Duckworth in a production of William Inge's play *Bus Stop* at the Royal Poinciana Playhouse in Palm Beach, Florida.

In Dennis' memoirs, the writer of the introduction, Doug Taylor, mentions the production. He says it starred his future wife, Barbara Baxley, who would go on to play Dennis' mother in the national tour of the William Inge drama *The Dark at the Top of the Stairs*. Taylor reports that when Dennis tried out for the role of Elma, whom Taylor calls Alma, she claimed she had played the part before. However, Baxley could tell after watching Dennis for two minutes that this was a lie. Baxley apparently thought she was perfect for the part, however, despite her inexperience. Taylor says Baxley surreptitiously guided Dennis' movements with whispered instructions and secret signals, unbeknownst to the director.

The *Time* article includes a photograph of Dennis in *Tender Trap*, dated 1956, although it does not give the name of the theater or city where she performed. Meanwhile, she landed a role on the television soap opera *The Guiding Light*, playing Alice Holden from May to June 1956.

Dennis made her Broadway debut as a replacement understudy for the roles of Flirt Conroy and Reenie Flood in *The Dark at the Top of the Stairs*. The play was directed by Elia Kazan and opened at the Music Box Theatre in New York on December 5, 1957. It ran until January 17, 1959. The play starred Eileen Heckart, Pat Hingle, and Teresa Wright, with Evans as the original Flirt Conroy and Judith Robinson as the original Reenie Flood. It had an out-of-town tryout at the Schubert Theatre in New Haven, Connecticut, from November 7 to 9, 1957, before heading to Broadway. *Time* says Dennis was so desperate to go on in one of the parts that she would report in with the pun, "Dennis, anyone?"

Dennis' observation of Eileen Heckart may have resulted in the younger actress appropriating a gesture that Heckart often used. This is the pointing mannerism (though Heckart would not use it in *Up the Down Staircase*, in which the actresses appear together). The mannerism may have come from both actresses having studied with Herbert Berghof. Or perhaps it was something learned by Dennis at the Actors Studio, since another Actors Studio student, Joanne Woodward, uses it liberally as the gesture of a Southern woman in her Oscar-winning film *The Three Faces of Eve* (1957).

Dennis and Heckart can be linked in another way. In his book *Good Dames: Virtue in the Cinema*, James Robert Parish provides a description of the parts Heckart often played, which can be equated with Dennis and her roles. Parish says Heckart was frequently the "pathetic lonelyheart ... whose heartrending sadness pulled at the viewer's sympathy." He also characterizes Heckart as a "homebody" with "woebegone looks and a Midwestern demeanor."

In *Up the Down Staircase* (1967), Sylvia Barrett (Dennis) receives solace from fellow school teacher Henrietta Pastorfield (Eileen Heckart).

When making the comparison between the screen success of Dennis and Heckart, one also has to take into account the age factor. Dennis began working in television and films in her twenties, while Heckart didn't start until she was in her thirties. Presumably because of her age, Heckart's persona would remain that of the spinster or mother, and she never played a romantic leading lady.

Like Dennis, Heckart would win her only Academy Award in a supporting role for *Butterflies Are Free* (1972). She kept working until she was seventy-nine, primarily on television and in occasional film supporting roles, as well as on the stage. It is interesting to ponder whether Dennis would have also continued to do so if her life had not ended at fifty-four.

While she was the understudy in *The Dark at the Top of the Stairs*, Dennis began a relationship with fellow understudy Gerald S. O'Loughlin. They would live together for seven years in New York. The actor would be reunited with her for the made-for-TV movie *Wilson's Reward* in 1980. In a May 20, 1980, interview with the *Tri City Herald*, O'Loughlin says that his drinking problem contributed to their breakup. *Time* says another contributing factor was that Dennis had fallen in love with a prominent and married star, although unnamed.

Tuesday Weld was the original understudy for the two parts in the play. It is said that Dennis replaced Weld late in the season's run after Weld went to Hollywood, though other sources say Dennis was the understudy for a year before she had the opportunity to play a part.

Dennis also played Reenie Flood in the play's national tour, which starred Barbara Baxley, Audrey Christie (who would later play Freda Loomis in Dennis' film *Splendor in the Grass*), and George L. Smith. In 1976 *Pittsburgh Press* interview, Dennis says she heard about *The Dark at the Top of the Stairs* from actress Baxley, who was a friend of Inge's. Baxley is quoted in the 1976 *After Dark* magazine interview saying, "There she was, fat and shy and sensitive, and you could see she had this great talent, but she didn't know anything."

Some of the tour included the Playhouse Theatre in Wilmington, Delaware, from January 21 to 24, 1959; the Hanna Theatre in Cleveland, Ohio, from February 19, 1959; the American Theatre in St. Louis, Missouri, for a one-week engagement beginning March 30, 1959; the Erlanger Theatre in Chicago for four weeks from April 6, 1959; the Pabst in Milwaukee, Wisconsin, to May 16; and the Coconut Grove Playhouse in Miami, Florida, where the play ran from May 18 to May 30, 1959.

After the tour, Dennis appeared as Anne Frank in *The Diary of Anne Frank* at the Totem Pole Playhouse, Pennsylvania, for a one-week engagement in July 1959. The production was directed by Cliff Clothren, and co-starred William Putch and Margot Stevenson. She returned to New York to play Mordeen in John Steinbeck's play *Burning Bright* at the Off Broadway Theatre East. The production was directed by Matt Cimber and ran from October 16, 1959, with a cast that included Philip Keneally, Clifford David and Leon B. Stevens.

In his *Village Voice* review dated October 21, Michael Smith wrote of Dennis' "complex tensions." In *The New York Times* review, dated October 17, Lewis Funke describes her as "wispy and attractive and indicates sensitivity as an actress. But she also is awkward in this role, and entirely too mannered in her delivery."

Dennis followed this with another supporting role in a production of the Thomas W. Phipps play *Motel* at the Wilbur Theatre in Boston in January 1960. The cast included Siobhan McKenna, Richard Easton, George Mathews, and Joe Ponazecki. Back at New York's Off Broadway Grace Protestant Episcopal Church, Dennis was top-billed as Sister Gabrielle. She played a seventeenth-century nun in Henry de Montherlant's *Port Royal*, performed on April 24 and May 1, 1960. The production was directed by Herbert Berghof and also starred Uta Hagen, Jenny Egan, Joan Matthiessen, Olga Bellin, and Betty Sinclair. Dennis' studies with Hagen no doubt enabled her involvement. In *The New York Times* review, dated April 26, Arthur Gelb wrote that in a small role Dennis gave a "provocative performance."

Sometime between April and August 1960 she completed the supporting role of Kay in her film debut, *Splendor in the Grass*, directed by Elia Kazan. No doubt the fact that Kazan had been the director of *The Dark at the Top of the Stairs*, and that both plays were by William Inge, aided her casting. However, in an article by Rex Reed in *The New York Times* dated June 19, 1966, Dennis says Kazan never paid any attention to her because her part was so tiny and she was "such a kid then." The film starred Natalie Wood, Warren Beatty and Pat Hingle, and was released on October 19, 1961.

Dennis' next Broadway role was that of Millicent Bishop in Robert L. Joseph's *Face of a Hero* at the Eugene O'Neill Theatre. The production was directed by Alexander Mackendrick, and starred Dennis' future *The Out of Towners* film co-star Jack Lemmon, as well as Edward Asner, Betsy Blair, and Albert Dekker. The show opened on October 20 and ran until November 19, 1960.

Still from *Splendor in the Grass* (1961), Dennis' feature film debut. At the New Year's Eve party are (left to right in the foreground) Wilma "Deanie" Loomis (Natalie Wood), Kay (Dennis), and Bud Stamper (Warren Beatty).

In his *New York Times* review, dated October 21, 1960, Howard Taubman did not mention Dennis' performance in her supporting role. She is said to have played a pathetic, pregnant waif murdered by a playboy. *Time* quotes Lemmon saying that "if Sandy had been playing my role, we'd probably still be running."

She would be one of the recipients of the 1961 Theatre World Award, along with such notables as Joan Hackett and Robert Goulet, although her award was not for any particular performance. However, Dennis would wait another year before again appearing on Broadway. The character was another teenager, Ann Howard, in Grahame Greene's *The Complaisant Lover* at the Ethel Barrymore Theatre. The show was directed by Glen Byam Shaw and ran from November 1, 1961, to January 27, 1962. Her co-stars were Michael Redgrave, Googie Withers, and Gene Wilder. The production appeared to have had an out-of-town tryout in Hartford, Connecticut, in October.

When it opened in New York it was reviewed by Howard Taubman in *The New York Times* on November 2, 1961. All Taubman could say of Dennis was that she was "pretty." In the *New York Herald-Tribune*, Walter Kerr called her a "charmer with a face like fresh mint." It is reported that half way through the first act on opening night on Broadway, her petticoat started to fall off because the elastic of her half-slip gave way. The audience was startled and amused, since they noticed it falling before she did. When she became aware of the problem she didn't miss a line, and simply stepped behind a couch and removed it. In response, the house erupted with applause. Michael Redgrave would speak of her "obvious star quality."

Dennis made her first appearance on television on the ABC special *Music for a New Year's Night*, broadcast on January 1, 1961. She appeared as one of seven young performers referred to as the "Class of '61." The other six were folk singer Casey Anderson, pop singer Marilyn Cooper, dancer-singer Pat Finley, operatic baritone Ronald Reitan, soprano Benita Valente, and ballet dancer Edward Vilella. Kitty Carlisle hosted the show.

Dennis next played the sensitive social worker Sandra Markowitz in Herb Gardner's comedy *A Thousand Clowns* at the Eugene O'Neill Theatre. The production ran from April 5, 1962, to April 13, 1963, and was directed by Fred Coe. Her co-stars were Jason Robards, Gene Saks and William Daniels. The show apparently had an out-of-town tryout in Boston in March.

In his *New York Times* review dated April 6, 1962, Howard Taubman wrote about Dennis' "admirable comic timing." Her performance would win her the 1963 Tony for Best Featured Actress in a Play, and it was said that the success of the play allowed her to buy linoleum for her kitchen.

Still from the ABC television show *Music for a New Year's Night — Class of 1961*. It was Dennis' first appearance on television.

In the *New York Herald-Tribune*, Walter Kerr made what would become a famous remark about her: "Let me tell you about Sandy Dennis. There should be one in every home." Reportedly, Shirley Knight had been offered the part of Sandra but had to turn it down due to a film commitment. This dynamic would be repeated later when Shirley was unavailable to repeat her Broadway stage performance in *The Three Sisters* in the disastrous London production and the film version, roles taken by Dennis.

During the run of the play, she filmed a guest appearance in an episode of the ABC television series *Naked City* entitled "Idylls of a Running Back," broadcast on September 26, 1962. The episode also featured her *A Thousand Clowns* co-star William Daniels. In her 1976 *After Dark* magazine interview, Dennis said that in 1962 she had resigned from a role on television rather than wear a padded bra, though it is not known what the role was. At this time she also signed a deal with Seven Arts to make films, although they would never offer her one.

In an interview with Bob Thomas for *Miami News*, dated June 6, 1967, Dennis would talk of her first adventures in Hollywood. She was told to report for an interview for a Bob Hope picture at MGM. They tried to glamorize her, and the hairdresser teased her hair into a mammoth production. She combed it down to a normal size.

Finally she told the director she didn't think she was right for the picture. He told her to have lunch in the commissary and then go home.

The next time Dennis decided she should be more cooperative. She was sent to Warner Brothers to test for *Ensign Pulver* with Robert Walker. The director, Joshua Logan, told her: "We want you just as you are." But when she reported for the test, he turned up with a foundation garment and falsies. Logan told her Warner wanted her this way. The garment had ribs that cut into her stomach when she sat down. Dennis says the falsies were so large she couldn't see her feet. "The test was so bad nobody wanted to talk about it." She slunk back to New York.

This experience was also covered in her *After Dark* interview, in which Dennis adds that she was up for the role of a nurse in *Ensign Pulver*, perhaps that of Nurse Scotty (ultimately played by Millie Perkins). She says the role went to "some ninety-pound thing." It is notable that her companion of the time, Gerald O'Loughlin (later known as Gerald S. O'Loughlin), appeared in a supporting role in the film. Dennis had reportedly told Logan about turning down the television role where she was asked to wear padding. He told her, "Don't worry, honey. It doesn't matter if you have a shape like a pear. You'll be just great for this part."

In this interview Dennis says "someone," not Logan, brought the girdle and the falsies to her to wear. The falsies were the old-fashioned foam-rubber type, not the type with the padding sewn into the bra. She told Tom Killen in the interview: "There are times when you have to give in, and I decided that this was one of them." So she put on the falsies, which were very uncomfortable. "The tits were sticking out front like balloons and I looked absolutely ridiculous. And of course I didn't get the part."

Another film she lost out on was the movie version of *A Thousand Clowns*, directed by Fred Coe and released in 1965. Her part was taken by Barbara Harris. This was particularly disappointing since Jason Robards, William Daniels, Gene Saks and Barry Gordon all repeated their stage roles for the film, as well as director Fred Coe. In an article in *The New York Times* by Eugene Archer, dated June 14, 1964, it was stated that Dennis was unable to do the film because of her commitment to *Any Wednesday*. This notion was confirmed by Jason Robards in an interview in *The Pittsburgh Press* dated February 5, 1966. However, since *Any Wednesday* would open in February 1964, it would seem that by June she would have been free in the daytime to do the film, particularly as it was shot in New York and not in Hollywood.

In March 1964 Hedda Hopper, in *The Hartford Courant*, reported that Steve McQueen had announced he would star in the film version of *Any Wednesday* with Dennis, and that filming would begin in April. However, that did not come to pass. In her Hollywood column dated April 22, 1964, Sheilah Graham reported that Dennis refused to make a screen test for the part. The actress believed no one else had been asked to test for the part and that they had seen how she looked on television. "I felt it was a lack of confidence in me."

In her December 22, 1966, article for *The Miami News*, Sheilah reported that the film producers had decided to go with Harris rather than Dennis. Dennis said she was very unhappy that she didn't get it. She had expected to do so, which implies that she would have made herself available, and that the producers just didn't want her. The producers of the film were Fred Coe, Herb Gardner and Ralph Rosenblum. The Broadway play was produced by Coe and Arthur Cantor. The film was released on December 13, 1965.

A Thousand Clowns co-star Jason Robards introduced Dennis to jazz saxophonist and composer Gerry Mulligan, and he became her new companion. Mulligan would go on to compose the title song for the film *A Thousand Clowns*. Dennis and he lived together in a five-bedroom apartment on the Upper West Side and also had a home in Weston, Connecticut. It is said she married him after only knowing him for two weeks. They are reported to have wed in June 1965, and although Dennis is quoted as referring to him as her husband, other sources deny they were ever married. In his article for *The Milwaukee Sentinel*, dated February 26, 1977, Earl Wilson said that Dennis and Mulligan went through the fiction that they were married for ten years and didn't reveal the truth until after the couple broke up in 1976. Wilson quotes Dennis saying, "I don't remember whether the subject ever came up. We didn't tell everybody we were just living together because that wasn't in fashion then as it is now. I didn't want to get married."

She would reflect on her relationship with Mulligan for a *People* magazine interview on March 13, 1989. Asked why she was attracted to him, she replied, "There is nothing, not one f——— thing I can think of. What the hell did I know about jazz? Staying up all night blowing a trumpet is not interesting to me." Dennis would say she found Mulligan a very handsome man, but that's about how deep her feelings went. In the interview she revealed that she and Mulligan pretended they were wed when she became pregnant in 1965. She later miscarried and was candid about how little she was affected by the loss. "If I'd been a mother, I would have loved the child, but I just didn't have any connection with it when I was pregnant.... I never ever wanted children. It would have been like having an elephant."

Time reported that Dennis was tone-deaf, ignorant of jazz, and that the only records she owned were by Andy Williams. Mulligan was quoted as saying, "She's a kid who had a fear of music laid on her as a child. She's just now learning to relax." In a 1968 *Life* article by Wayne Warga, she would describe the kind of modern jazz that Mulligan pioneered as "a whole lot of damn racket." It was reported that he did his composing at home at an electric piano equipped with earphones so that only he could hear.

Warga also gave some insight into the Dennis/Mulligan domestic situation when he reported that they had two telephones, one for each of them. Dennis let her answering service take her calls, but when she was at home she would answer *his* calls, "carefully writing down his schedule like a secretary." They had a live-in maid who was there to manage the animals, and she would do the household chores.

Time also reported that Dennis lived with Mulligan, five dogs and twenty-one stray cats at the Weston home. Her love of cats would continue throughout her life, and even be incorporated into some of her later acting roles. When Sandy's mother divorced her father in 1967, she joined the Weston home. In an interview with Sheilah Graham in *The Pittsburgh Press*, dated December 17, 1967, Dennis said that her cat collection began eight years before when she rescued a cat from a boy in the street who was hurting it. That cat was Jennifer. She found the second, a Siamese named Maggie, while working on *Who's Afraid of Virginia Woolf?* The third was an Abyssinian named Elizabeth after Elizabeth Taylor. When the cats had kittens, what was three soon became twenty-nine.

On April 24, 1963, Dennis' second guest appearance on the TV show *Naked City* was aired. The episode was entitled "Carrier." She would also be seen in two more TV show guest appearances: *The Fugitive* episode entitled "The Side of the Mountain," broadcast on October 1, 1963, and the *Arrest and Trial* episode entitled "Somewhat Lower Than the Angels," broadcast on February 2, 1964. These latter two shows were filmed in Hollywood, as opposed to *Naked City*, filmed in New York.

Her next appearance on Broadway was as Ellen Gordon in the Muriel Resnick comedy

Any Wednesday at the Music Box Theatre, which opened on February 18, 1964, and ran until June 26, 1966. The show would move to the George Abbott Theatre for its run from February 15 to June 26, 1966. It was directed by Henry Kaplan, and co-starred Don Porter, Gene Hackman (who would later co-star with Dennis in the 1988 film *Another Woman*), and Rosemary Murphy. It is said that the show's tryout was calamitous. Before it opened on Broadway it had gone through one leading man (Michael Rennie), five directors, and thirteen endings, with the thirteenth tried on opening night. The show also had a record five co-producers. However, it became a sleeper smash.

In *The New York Times*, dated February 19, 1964, Howard Taubman wrote that Dennis made the play. He described her as having a "cool, wayward effervescence." Taubman also said: "She invests this creature with an open-eyed wonder that can change suddenly into wry shrewdness with deadly comic effect." She would win her second Tony Award for Best Actress in a Play for her performance.

However, Dennis would not appear in the film version of *Any Wednesday* either. That part would go to Jane Fonda, who co-starred with Jason Robards in the Don Porter role, Dean Jones in the Gene Hackman role, and Rosemary Murphy recreating her Broadway role. It was announced in April 1965 that Warner Bros. wanted Dennis for the film, and that it would also star Frank Sinatra and Elizabeth Ashley.

In her interview with Sheilah Graham in *The Pittsburgh Press*, dated December 11, 1966, she would say it was a pregnancy that lost her the role, although she would also lose the baby. The *Time* article confirms that she had a miscarriage during the filming of *Who's Afraid of Virginia Woolf?* The film of *Any Wednesday* was released on October 30, 1966. In her June 7, 1967, interview Dennis also commented she had no regrets about losing the film, since, "I played the role long enough."

Time reports that her run of the play was problematic, which may have cost her the movie role. "It was the most horrible year of my life," she is quoted as saying, and also the time "when everything seemed to go wrong." She had broken up with Gerald O'Loughlin and fallen in love with someone else, but before the show had even opened she was sick of it. In her *After Dark* interview Dennis would say she didn't really know what she was doing.

During the run, *Time* says she would improvise "to an indulgent and irresponsible extreme." One night in the middle of a love scene someone in the audience sneezed, and instantly Dennis called out, "God bless you." On other nights she would get into coughing matches with the audiences or wave goodbye to those she saw leaving early. She had learned from *A Thousand Clowns* co-star Jason Robards to jigger with the script, and some nights the play would finish thirty minutes earlier than usual because of her "revisions." The show's best known props were balloons, and she might shoot down those that floated to the ceiling with an air rifle. It is said that co-stars Murphy and Hackman refused to speak to Dennis offstage.

On March 1, 1964, there appeared a one-page article on her in *The New York Times* by Joanne Stang entitled "Sweet Success." On May 24, 1964, Dennis was photographed for the *Chicago Tribune* with her Best Dramatic Actress Tony award for *Any Wednesday*, with Alec Guinness (who won the Best Dramatic Actor award for *Dylan*), Carol Channing (who won Top Female Musical Star for *Hello, Dolly!*), and Bert Lahr (who won Top Male Musical Star for *Foxy*). On June 4, 1964, there appeared a one-page article on her in *The New York Post* by Jerry Tallmer entitled "Closeup: Tony Winner."

In the *Look* magazine edition of June 16, 1964, there was an article on Dennis entitled "Any Wednesday's Sandy," which promoted the stage play. The text describes the play's character as a "tootsie of vast daffiness" but added the following: "Miss Dennis does not look the part. She acts, and her skills at that craft are so lavish that she makes simple old-fashioned sex appeal seem woefully insufficient." Describing the actress' real life, the article included the observation that she eats apples on the streets, accompanied by a photograph of her doing just that while holding a dog. Other photographs show her at home sipping coffee by a sink full of dishes, and partially obscured behind tights hung to dry. Three photographs have her running through how she passes out on stage in a key moment as she sits on a chair, Dennis checking the play's lines with Gene Hackman and Muriel Resnick, and she and with Gerry O'Loughlin on a walk in the park. Dennis stands on a bench as he stands on the ground next to her smoking a cigarette. She smiles, but he does not. Gerry is spelled "Jerry" in the text and is said to be the man in her private life at this time.

On June 28, 1964, Dennis was photographed backstage at *Any Wednesday* with Don Porter and Lynda Bird Johnson, the daughter of the President. During the Broadway run, Dennis would make another TV guest appearance. This time it was on the show *Mr. Broadway*, filmed in New York. The episode was entitled "Don't Mention My Name in Sheboygan," and it was broadcast on November 7, 1964.

In March 1965 it was announced that Dennis had signed to do the film version of Edward Albee's Broadway play *Who's Afraid of Virginia Woolf?* It was scheduled to start production in June. However, filming would take place from July 26 to December 13, 1965. Directed by Mike Nichols, it also starred Elizabeth Taylor, Richard Burton, and George Segal. The film was released on June 22, 1966. In March 1965 there appeared an article on Dennis in the magazine *Holiday* by Russell Hoban and entitled "The Antic Arts: The New Ingenue."

Anton Chekhov's *The Three Sisters* was produced by the Actors Studio and ran at the Morosco Theatre from June 22 to October 3, 1964. It was directed by Lee Strasberg, and the cast included Kim Stanley as Masha, Geraldine Page as Olga, and Shirley Knight as Irina, as well as Barbara Baxley, Kevin McCarthy, James Olson, Robert Loggia, and Luther Adler. Kim Stanley left the production before the end of the run. Peggy Feury stepped in to play Olga, and Geraldine Page replaced Stanley as Masha. However, Stanley made herself available to film the production on videotape in late October 1964 by Paul Bogart for TV as an Actors Studio fundraiser. The available video calls the film *Anton Chekov's The Three Sisters*, and in it Dennis plays Irina, while Shelley Winters replaces Barbara Baxley as Natasha. It reportedly saw release in 1966, and then again in 1977, with the popularity of producer Ely Landau's American Film Theatre series.

The Broadway production was invited to go to London for the 1965 World Theatre Festival at the Aldwych Theatre for two weeks, from May 13 to May 22, 1965. Kevin McCarthy pulled out because he did not want to work with Stanley again, and was replaced by George C. Scott. The Actors Studio actually brought two productions to London, the other being James Baldwin's *Blues for Mister Charlie*, which starred Al Freeman, Jr. and was directed by Burgess Meredith. It ran from May 3 to May 12.

In his book *A Method to Their Madness*, Foster Hirsh reports that Strasberg held rehearsals with the new cast before they left for London. At one he yelled at Dennis in front of the entire company, as she delivered Irina's speech at the end of Act One. Strasberg objected to her mannerisms, saying, "My God. What are you doing up there? Are you trying to ruin my play?" Dennis reportedly paused, then told him, "You can't speak to me this way. I'm a human being." When the company came to London the feeling was that they were under-rehearsed. This wasn't helped by the fact that Kim Stanley had arrived later than the others because she had refused to fly and had sailed across. The cast was given a tennis court and an armory to rehearse in, rather than a proper rehearsal room.

By the time they were allowed into the Aldwych, they didn't have enough time to adjust the blocking to this different sized area, which had a steep space between the stage and the first row as big as the stage itself. The lighting also had to be adjusted, and there was a problem with costume fittings. There was only one dress rehearsal, and Tamara Daykarhanova fell and broke her arm. Additionally, the British had a different interpretation of Chekhov than the Americans, since the British saw the characters as aristocrats. The first show began late, and the stage management were lax in advising the actors of their cues, so that the three-hour-and-ten-minute show actually ran for four hours.

The show is described by Hirsch as one of the legendary disasters of the modern theater. The audience booed the actors, calling out, "Yankees, go home!" When Irina said, "It has been a terrible evening," someone in the audience called out, "It sure has." This caused the whole audience to laugh in an uproar. At the curtain call, the actors were hooted and hollered at, and things were thrown. There were hyena laughs and boos. For some reason the stage manager kept raising the curtain, so the humiliation was endured for eight curtain calls until the actors left the stage. Reviews were ferocious.

In *The Observer*, Penelope Gilliat wrote that Dennis was "ludicrous and painful."

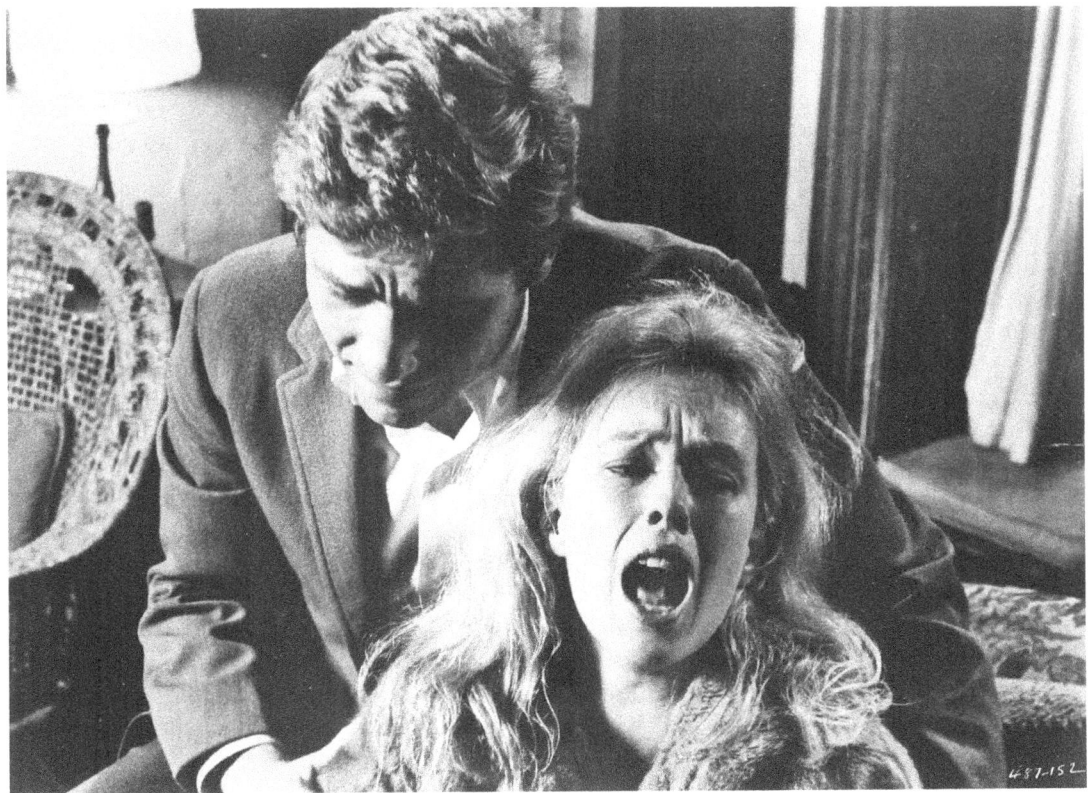

From left, Nick (George Segal) comforts the distraught Honey (Dennis) in *Who's Afraid of Virginia Woolf?* (1966). She won the Best Supporting Actress Academy Award for her performance.

Bernard Levin of the *Daily Mail* wrote, "Miss Dennis has one trick: Saying 'I-er-I-ah' for the first person singular pronoun." Foster Hirsch quotes playwright Meade Roberts (who had seen and loved the New York production) as noting that Dennis stammered continuously, had a silly Marilyn Monroe hairdo, and holes in her shawl.

Lee Strasberg agreed with the critics about what went wrong. He felt the performance fell apart, but that it was no one's fault. Strasberg would confess he didn't want to go to London to begin with. He thought if the original company had gone, it would have been different.

Dennis followed this disaster with triumph. She returned to Hollywood to make *Who's Afraid of Virginia Woolf*, and her performance would win her the Best Supporting Actress Academy Award. She was unable to accept the award in person at the Santa Monica Civic Auditorium in Los Angeles on April 10, 1967, since she was shooting the film *Sweet November* in New York at the time.

Dennis was photographed that night at a restaurant in New York after the win was announced. It was reported that she heard about her award because there was a television set tuned into the broadcasting at the restaurant. The award was accepted by Mike Nichols on her behalf. In an article in the *Herald-Journal* by Peer J. Oppenheimer, dated May 17, 1968, Dennis says another reason she didn't attend was her fear of flying. Her non-appearance resulted in her being accused of being anti–Hollywood and anti-awards. In the interview she said if she was ever nominated again, she would go to avoid the same criticism.

Interviewed on June 7, 1967, Dennis would say her decision not to go to the awards show was also influenced by the shooting of *Sweet November*. She said the company was two or three days behind schedule, and that she was needed because she was in every shot (an exaggeration, as there are some scenes in the film in which she does not appear). Dennis also stated that she thought the company would have given her the time off to go to the awards if she had asked, but that she didn't want to ask.

In the pressbook for *Sweet November* she offered further opinions on the Academy Award. She didn't want to think she would win, so that if she hadn't she wouldn't have been disappointed. Dennis was honored to have received the nomination, but critical of the awards. She thought all the nominees should be considered winners, since they were good enough to be nominated in the first place.

In an interview with Rebecca Moorehouse for the *Sarasota Journal*, dated March 3, 1971, Dennis talked more about the Oscar, saying, "The Oscar happened to me but it never interested me." She was embarrassed when her name went up on the marquees as, "Sandy Dennis, Oscar-winner, Best Supporting Actress." The article says that she was having dinner with her business agent on the night of the awards ceremony and she had asked him, "'If I win, can I buy a set of the Encyclopedia Britannica?' I'd always wanted one. I got the set, it comes with a bookcase, and Oscar is on top of that bookcase."

After *Who's Afraid of Virginia Woolf?* Dennis was deluged with film offers, the majority of them for heavy dramatic parts. This was despite her thinking that she had first gained attention on stage for her performance in comedies, and considering the role of Honey to be a very funny part. "She was sort of semi-tragic, but also very funny," she told Tom Killen in *After Dark*. "But everybody took it so very seriously, so then in films I got a lot of serious roles."

Dennis began her second film for Warner Bros. It was *Up the Down Staircase*, directed by Robert Mulligan, and co-starring Patrick Bedford and Eileen Heckart. Dennis played the leading role of Sylvia Barrett, an English teacher at an inner-city New York high school. Filmed in New York from June to August 1966, it would be released on July 19, 1967.

Earl Wilson reported on October 22, 1966, that a film biopic of Carole Lombard had been proposed for Dennis, though nothing ever came of it.

In the *Life* article on Dennis by Wayne Warga, he reports that *Who's Afraid of Virginia Woolf?* "shot her abruptly" into the ranks of the ten biggest female box-office attractions. Tom Killen in *After Dark* says she was now able to command one hundred thousand dollars per picture. She could easily have allowed herself to be cast in well-paying but unchallenging roles. However, Killen continues, this was not for her. "The Midwestern forthrightness and desire to challenge herself won out."

Dennis traveled to Canada for the filming of Mark Rydell's adaptation of the D.H. Lawrence novella *The Fox*. Shooting took place from January to March 1967. She played the leading role of Jill Banford. The film was first released in Canada on December 13, 1967, and in the United States on February 7, 1968.

Dennis returned to New York for her next film, *Sweet November*, shot from late March to May 1967. She would play opposite Anthony Newley and Theodore Bikel in this romantic comedy for director Robert Ellis Miller, which was released on February 8, 1968. The film's pressbook reports that during filming her Connecticut home was hit with a pet population explosion. She received word that her thirteen cats had suddenly been increased by twenty kittens, and that two of her twelve dogs had produced litters totaling thirteen puppies. "The animals must have thrown a wild party after I left," she said.

On April 11, 1967, Dennis was photographed by the *Chicago Tribune* being kissed by Gerry Mulligan, congratulating her on her Oscar win. On June 16 she was a presenter at the 20th Annual Tony Awards in New York. In June 1967 there appeared an article on her in the magazine *Seventeen* entitled, "Anyone You Know?" In an article in *The Miami News*, dated December 22, 1966, by Sheilah Graham, it was reported that Dennis had pulled out of the play *Daphne in Cottage D* because schedules conflicted with the making of *Sweet November*. She had wanted to do both, but thought that if she did the play and it was a hit, that would make it impossible for her to do the film. However, the problem was solved when the play's production was postponed, which allowed Dennis to film both *Sweet November* and *The Fox* before it.

On June 7, 1967, in the *Miami News*, Sheilah Graham reported that Dennis had been studying Russian. This was in preparation for her trip to Moscow for the Moscow International Film Festival, where *Up the Down Staircase* was to be screened as the official United States entry. On July 10, 1967, she arrived with Gerry Mulligan. Also in attendance were Jack Valenti, the president of the Motion Picture Association of America, Sandra Dee and Jennifer Jones. On July 11 *The New York Times* reported that a screening of the film at the Kremlin Palace of Congress was attended by five thousand people, who gave a ninety-second round of applause to the film and the actress as she waved.

On July 14 *The New York Times* reported that

Dennis as Jill Banford in *The Fox* (1968).

Mulligan had played a six-hour impromptu jam session for one-hundred-and-fifty musicians and their friends at a Soviet youth club in Gorky Street. Dennis is reported to have been in attendance. She was unable to stay for the awards ceremony, where she won the Best Actress medal (the first American to do so). She shared the award with Grynet Molvig, the star of the Swedish film *Prinsessan* (aka *The Princess*, 1966). However, Valenti presented her with the award on August 2, 1967, at the Harvard Club in New York.

On September 1, 1967, *Time* magazine put Dennis on their cover, calling her "The Star in the $7 Dress." The image was a sketch rather than a photograph (the name of the artist remains unknown). The article, with no author named, appeared in the Show Business section and was subtitled "Talent Without Tinsel." There were photographs of her at the 1964 Tony ceremony, at the Moscow Film Festival, in *Who's Afraid of Virginia Woolf?* and *A Thousand Clowns* and *Any Wednesday*, of her father and mother, of Sandy in *Tender Trap*, and of Mulligan with her and two cats at home.

On September 23, 1967, Dennis was photographed wearing a babushka and surrounded by people at the opening of the Southeast Baltimore playground, an anti-poverty project for neighborhood children.

Her next Broadway role would be in the much-delayed *Daphne in Cottage D*. Originally scheduled to open November 30, 1966, at the Music Box, it was first postponed until February 1967, supposedly because of a lack of leading men who could begin rehearsals in October. William Daniels was sought for the role, but a TV commitment conflicted with the schedule. As reported in *The New York Times* by Sam Zolotow on September 27, 1966, producer Michael Ellis interviewed sixty actors and auditioned twenty-five but was not satisfied, and that delay cost him $24,000 in theater guarantees. The play was next scheduled for October 11, 1967, at the Cort Theatre, and then delayed again until October 15.

Dennis starred as the title character in the Stephen Levi play which ran at the Longacre Theatre from October 15 to November 18, 1967. The play was directed by Martin Fried, whom she had known as the stage manager of the Actors Studio production of *The Three Sisters*. He was married at the time to Brenda Vaccaro, who would become Dennis' best friend. The play co-starred her *A Thousand Clowns* and *Naked City* co-star William Daniels.

In *Time*, Dennis said she had been waiting two years to do *Daphne in Cottage D*, the first to be produced by this playwright, and she also contributed funds for its backing. At this time it was reported that she could earn more making films, but she said she preferred doing plays. "Standing around waiting for sets to be lit and scenes to be shot is a bore. I'd do plays all the time but there really aren't that many good ones around." In *Theater Week* Michael Buckley reported that Dennis completely controlled the production, directing it and rewriting the script.

Dennis played the suicidal wife of Joseph, a movie star who has just run over his son in a driveway accident. The production opened in out-of-town tryouts in Cincinnati, Boston (on September 3 for two weeks at the Wilbur Theatre), and Baltimore (for three weeks at the Morris A. Mechanic Theater from September 18). Clive Barnes in *The New York Times*, on October 16, 1967, wrote that Dennis "provides a considerable, even memorable performance," and she "wrings more pity out of the role than you would have thought possible."

A.D. Coleman in *The Village Voice*, on October 26, 1967, was less kind. Asking what makes her so appropriate in her present position as a "cultural Typhoid Mary, spreading the zeitgeist with a brace and tearful snuffle," he assessed her performance in the play as follows: "Miss Dennis misses — by a wide margin — the mark of a true actress, who takes from the character in order to give to the play; she is more a leech, sucking the lifeblood from the play in order to give the audience Sandy Dennis."

Walter Kerr, in an article for *The New York Times* dated November 5, 1967, did an about-face on his famous comment in the *New York Herald-Tribune* reviewing *Any Wednesday* ("Let me tell you about Sandy Dennis"). Now he wrote the following: "She has developed a habit of treating sentences as though they were poor crippled things that couldn't cross the street without making three false starts from the curb, breaking in midflight, shying back in terror, starting over bravely, hesitating in the middle of traffic.... What she's doing is jaytalking and it's illegal."

In December 1967 Dennis taped the made-for-TV movie version of *A Hatful of Rain*, broadcast March 3, 1968. Filmed in London, the telefilm was a remake of the Fred Zinnemann 1957 feature about a Korean War veteran's morphine addiction (which starred Don Murray, Eva Marie Saint, Anthony Franciosa, and Dennis' old partner, Gerald S. O'Loughlin, in a supporting role). This new version was directed by John Llewellyn Moxley, and co-starred Michael Parks as the veteran and Peter Falk in the Anthony Franciosa role.

The *Life* magazine edition of February 9, 1968, featured an article on Dennis by Wayne Warga entitled "Girl with a Good Grip on Chaos." The title refers to her career success in the face of the supposed anarchy around her. In the article she says she had wanted to be photographed in front of a room full of books, all in alphabetical order, and looking beautiful in the latest clothes. However, after three attempts, it just didn't work. Her bookshelves were filled with books and other things in all kinds of order, and around her are twenty-five cats, six dogs, and a husband. The latter refers to Gerry Mulligan, whom the article says Dennis secretly wed in 1965. The couple is pictured together with two cats in a photograph similar to one in the *Time* article of 1967. Here they are dressed differently, however, and Gerry sits on the bed with her and a dog and a cat (in the *Time* picture he sat on a chair next to the bed). Other photographs for the article show Dennis at home with her favorite cat, Maxwell, perched on her left shoulder, and in costume with "splayed legs and mobile mouth" as she awaits a performance of *Daphne in D Cottage*.

The text describes Dennis as, in spite of the uproar around her, knowing exactly what she is doing. "Amid the chaos she creates, she is always in control. She has willed herself to control all around her — and she has a powerful will." Warga attributes to Dennis a sharp intelligence, an unfailing theatrical instinct and a self-confidence that permeates everything she does. He also says she is inclined towards inelegant language and four-letter words, and "gets away with it because she always looks the innocent." The article mentions her habit of belching, which she had demonstrated when filming *Who's Afraid of Virginia Woolf?* and says she did it whenever rehearsing. "She politely excuses herself the first time, but before long she is lost in concentration and the belches are bounding up to the second balcony." She explains, "I can't help it. Rehearsing gives me gas."

Warga quotes Dennis on her mannerisms, some of which he says are "stuttering, hand-waving, and constant fiddling with her hair." He notes that some are adroitly used but get on some people's nerves. She tells him that some of them are really her, and others are for the part. Dennis confesses she could stop them, but the idea of just standing around on the stage is very unappealing to her, as she thinks it would be to the audience. "They want movement. And so do I, so I move."

Warga also opines that she is seemingly accessible to both men and women because in her acting she blends "little girl charm with her improvised mannerisms." He adds that being "soft and cuddly" avoids any "outright sexuality."

On April 10, 1968, Dennis made a guest appearance on the BBC-TV talk show *Late Night Line-Up*, and on April 21 she was again a presenter at the Tony Awards. She is also credited as appearing in a twenty-minute short for Mike Nichols called *Teach Me!* (1968). Nothing else is known about it.

Her next film role was in *That Cold Day in the Park* for director Robert Altman, who would later direct her in the 1982 stage play *Come Back to the 5 & Dime Jimmy Dean, Jimmy Dean* and the subsequent screen version. *Cold Day* was shot in Vancouver, Canada, from October to December 1968 and released June 8, 1969. Dennis played lonely spinster Frances Austen, and co-starred with Michael Burns and Susan Benton. Some sources say that Altman had first wanted to make a film of the John Haas novel *Petulia* with Dennis, but that she preferred *That Cold Day in the Park*. *Petulia* would be made by Richard Lester in 1968, with Julie Christie as the title character, an unhappily married socialite.

In the pressbook for *That Cold Day in the Park* there is an article on Dennis which quotes Russell Hoban from *Holiday* magazine on the best way to describe her on screen. Hoban claims that in the hearts of small and large boys everywhere she has filled the aching void left by the demise of Santa Claus. He describes her as "the child-woman who dotes on candied apples and ferry rides, knows Bach and Shakespeare, Dixieland and William Butler

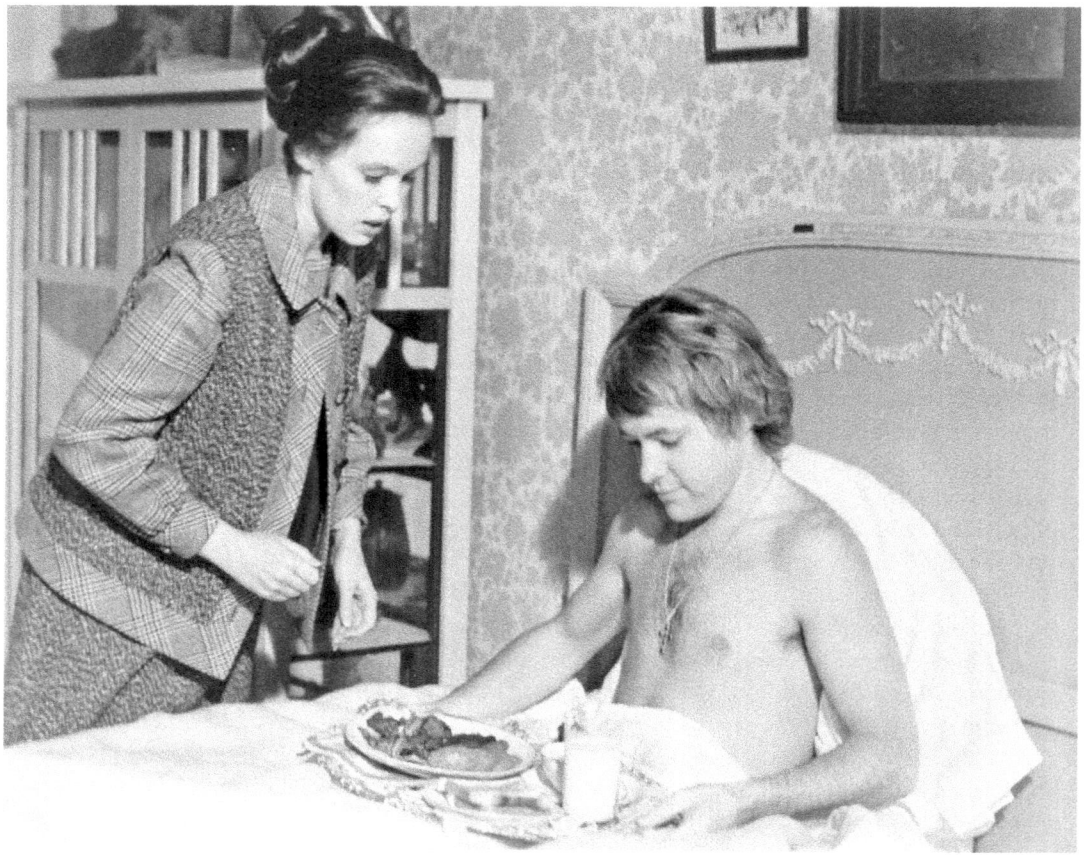

In *That Cold Day in the Park* (1969), Frances Austin (Dennis) serves breakfast in bed to her guest The Boy (Michael Burns).

Yeats, is touchingly virtuous but altogether willing, and is a cheap date but a rich experience." The article also quoted Dennis on her preference for working on the stage. "Performances can be made in a movie. Sometimes I do a good one and it's badly cut. So what I have tried to maintain is disappointing. No one can do that to me in a theatre."

In her interview with Les Wedman for *The Sun*, dated October 16, 1968, Dennis said that she had been offered *That Cold in the Park* one year earlier, and that it was scheduled to be filmed in London. After a survey trip to Vancouver the producers decided it was a preferable location for this film. The location was also envisaged for the planned follow-up title, *Images* (1972), also to be directed by Altman. That film, however, would end up being shot in Ireland. *Images* is another title that sources say Altman considered Dennis for. The part of the schizophrenic housewife Cathryn would be played by Susannah York, however. Dennis said she expected Gerry Mulligan to visit her while she was in Canada.

In early 1969 — the exact dates are unknown — she went to England to make her next film. Called *A Touch of Love* in Britain, it was released in the United States as *Thank You All Very Much* on August 18, 1969. Dennis played the unmarried and pregnant Rosamund Stacey. Directed by Waris Hussein, the film co-starred Ian McKellen and Eleanor Bron.

Dennis then returned to the United States to make her next picture, *The Out Of Towners*. Filmed in New York and Boston, from April to August 1969, it was directed by Arthur Hiller and co-starred Jack Lemmon. Dennis played Gwen, the wife of Lemmon's George

Rosamund Stacey (Dennis) and George Matthews (Ian McKellen) in *Thank You All Very Much* (1969).

Kellerman, who accompanied her husband to New York for a job interview. The film was released on May 28, 1970.

Dennis went back to Canada for the filming of a made-for-TV movie, *The Man Who Wanted to Live Forever*, from May 19 to June 28, 1970. It was broadcast in the United States on December 15, 1970. The thriller was directed by John Trent, and co-starred Stuart Whitman and Burl Ives. Dennis played Dr. Enid Bingham.

On August 13, 1970, she returned to the stage, opening at the Ivanhoe Theatre in Chicago in William Inge's play *Bus Stop*, playing Cherie, opposite Ben Piazza. The season ran for six weeks. Dennis returned to Broadway for the role of Teresa Phillips in the Alan Ayckbourn farce *How the Other Half Loves*, which ran at the Royale Theatre from March 29 to June 26, 1971. Directed by Gene Saks, the play co-starred Phil Silvers and Richard Mulligan. The plot centers on two neighbors who discover their spouses are having affairs with each other. The production saw out-of-town tryouts in Washington on February 23 and at the Wilbur Theatre in Boston on March 18. There are no reviews available for the Broadway opening. During the play's run Sandy made a guest appearance on the David Frost TV talk show on May 12 with her *How the Other Half Lives* co-star Phil Silvers, which was shot in New York.

The Paul Zindel play *And Miss Reardon Drinks a Little* received a Broadway run at the Morosco Theatre from February 25 to May 29, 1971. Directed by Melvin Bernhardt, starred Julie Harris as Anna Reardon and Estelle Parsons as Catherine Reardon. Harris continued with the play from June 30 to July 2 in Boston, but Dennis took over the role of Anna in Boston from July 3 to 10. She continued to tour with the play. From July 29 it was one week at the Westport Playhouse in Connecticut, with Salome Jens playing Catherine. From August 2 to 7 it was at the Cape Playhouse in Boston, August 9 to 14 at the Lakewood Theatre in Maine, and from August 11 to 16, 1971, at the Ivoryton Playhouse in Connecticut.

For the run at the Chicago Civic Theater from January 18, 1972, to February 27, Betty Garrett replaced Salome Jens as Catherine. Frank Savino was also part of this cast. The tour continued with a run from March 22 to April 1 at the Parker Playhouse in Fort Lauderdale, Florida. For the run at the Hyde Park Playhouse in New York from July 10, Barbara Baxley played Catherine. In his introduction to Dennis' memoirs, Doug Taylor reports that she appeared in a summer tour of the play in 1972 with Barbara Baxley, who was his wife at the time.

On May 16, 1972, Dennis was awarded the Strawhat (aka Straw Hat) Achievement Best Actress award for the summer 1971 season. The awards were given by the Council of Stock Theaters, comprising major summer theaters associated with Faberge, the cosmetic company. The ceremony was held as a luncheon at the Tavern-on-the-Green, restaurant and Dennis was given her award by Cary Grant.

She returned to television for the made-for-TV movie *Something Evil*, filmed from November to December 1971 in Hollywood. Dennis led a cast that included Darren McGavin, Ralph Bellamy, and Jeff Corey. Directed by Steven Spielberg, the show was broadcast on January 21, 1972.

Dennis accompanied Mulligan when the Dave Brubeck group went on tour for two months in the fall of 1972, stopping in Japan, Denmark and Australia, where she was interviewed on September 19.

Dennis' first spoken word LP was released in 1972 on the Caedmon label. Entitled *Young and Female*, it featured selected biographies from the book by Pat Ross. Ross' book was published by Ballantine Books and Random House the same year and was subtitled

"Turning Points in the Lives of 8 American Women." These women were Shirley MacLaine, Shirley Chisholm, Dorothy Day, Emily Hahn, Margaret Singer, Althea Gibson, Edna Ferber, and Margaret Bourke-White. The LP also sported selections read by Eileen Heckart and Claudia McNeil.

Upon her return to New York, Dennis went into rehearsal for her next Broadway play. She played Hannah Heywood in *Let Me Hear You Smile*, a comedy by Leonora Thuna and Harry Cauley, and directed by Cauley. The production was staged at the Biltmore Theatre. It only ran for eight previews and closed on opening night, January 16, 1973. Dennis played Hannah at three ages: ten, forty-eight and sixty-nine. Clive Barnes reviewed the play for *The New York Times* on January 17. He said of her, "Three chances and she missed every one of them. All she was sweet and smiling Sandy Dennis, fondling her mannerisms as if they were precious jade."

In March 1973 Dennis performed in Bob Randall's play *6Rms Riv Vu* at the Parker Playhouse in Fort Lauderdale, Florida, the Royal Poinciana Playhouse in Palm Beach, and the Cocoanut Grove in Miami. Dennis played Anne Miller, a married woman who contemplates an affair with a publicity copywriter when they are trapped together in a Manhattan apartment they have come to view. Her co-star was Leonard Nimoy, and the director was Jerry Adler.

On June 18, 1973, she was photographed with two of her cats for the *Chicago Tribune*. She next went to Chicago to play Blanche DuBois in Tennessee Williams' play *A Streetcar Named Desire* at the Ivanhoe Theatre from July 5 to August 26, 1973. The play was directed by George Keathley, and co-starred David Wilson and James Broderick as Mitch. In an interview with Vicki Salloum that appeared in *The Palm Beach Daily News* on January 15, 1976, Dennis would say that Williams was her favorite playwright. "My god, he's a genius. His language is beautiful and never gets in your way. I get angry when people say he's in a 15-year drought. If the man never did anything else in the world, he's done enough for a lifetime."

As noted in James Grissom's blog *Follies of God*, Williams would write in 1982 of her under the heading "Sandy Dennis: A Willful Intent to Grow." The title is explained by Williams saying of her, "Sandy has an admirable and willful intent to grow and to change. I admire that. I admire her." His first encounters with her in minor plays showed a concentration and a sense of detail that he found extraordinary.

Of her playing two of his characters—Blanche and Maggie—Williams says that he would never see her or think of her in them. She reportedly told him, "I want that experience. I want demands placed on me." Williams says that while her lineaments were entirely wrong for Maggie, her understanding of that woman surpassed that of Barbara Bel Geddes, who had assayed the role in the original Broadway production in 1955–56.

Williams thought Dennis seemed to understand the ache of rejection and the struggle for financial and amatory security. The playwright found her take on Blanche extraordinary, though he considered her too young for the part at the time she played it. She was aged thirty-six, but Williams thought she still looked in her twenties, with her Alice-in-Wonderland forehead adding to her youthful presentation. He would say that Dennis' grasp of the fight in which Blanche finds herself—the search for friendly coffers—was visceral and brilliant.

Williams also thought she would have made a brilliant Amanda Wingfield, the faded Southern belle from *The Glass Menagerie*. He also regretted she didn't get to play his high-strung, unmarried minister's daughter, Alma Winemiller, in *Summer and Smoke*.

Williams believed Dennis to be terribly smart and curious, and reasoned that that was why her comedic performances were so good. He also praised her lack of vanity, a quality he thought rare in actresses. His conversations with her he described as vertiginous affairs. He said her mind flew about as wildly as his own, but her face was grave and still. He would describe her face as lovely and fawn-like. Williams thought Dennis was always in thought and always poised for flight. "Sandy gives freely with her opinions and her thoughts, and she is a magpie. Ask her about anything and you'll go on a marvelous trip." Williams also liked the actress because he felt she was as uncomfortable in most social situations as he.

On December 19, 1973, Dennis made the first of what would be two guest television appearances on the family game show "*What's My Line?*," filmed in New York. Here she was the mystery guest to Larry Blyden's moderator. The panelists were Arlene Francis, Soupy Sales, Gene Shalit, and Dana Wynter. Dennis is credited as an "Academy Award Winner," and she wore a brown pants suit with her brunette hair down to her elbows. As the panelists tried to guess her identity from questions asked of her, her voice was not immediately recognizable to them.

She revealed mannerisms like poking her tongue out and licking her lips. She stuttered in hesitation when asked if she was known for her work on Broadway. Dennis nodded her head, gestured with her hands in reaction to Sales' grasping for words, smiled, fussed with her hair, and laughed when she was identified by Arlene Francis. The panelists were surprised that Dennis did not attempt to disguise her voice, presumably a tactic used by other mystery guests, though in the end this didn't help them. Larry Blyden told how she had won the Academy Award for *Who's Afraid of Virginia Woolf?* and Tonys for *A Thousand Clowns* and *Any Wednesday*, and said, "I guess by now you are a champ."

Dennis confessed she was trying to do an English accent to disguise her voice from the panelists, but found it very hard with "Yes" and "No." When Gene Shalit told her he thought she was English, she replied, "Aw, that's very nice." Larry Blyden asked her if winning prizes had changed her life, and she answered, "It's very hard to get work after you win any sort of prize." Blyden agreed, saying that after he won a Tony two years prior, after working constantly in the theater for twenty-five years, he wasn't offered one job. In response to this Dennis threw her head back and laughed and clapped her hands. When the panelists ask why she did that, she offered an explanation: "I think people continually like to discover people, so once you've been discovered two or three times you've really had it."

Blyden asked her if living with Mulligan ever interfered with her work preparation at home, or vice versa. Dennis said her house was not that big, but that he had a room of his own and nobody got to go into it except to bring his breakfast or dinner trays. When she commented that she had lots of cats, Gene Shalit asked her how many, and she replied, "A lot." Dennis said the cats didn't get to go into Mulligan's room. She said he played the piano when he worked, but it was not a distraction to her. Blyden asked her if Mulligan had ever written a song for her as a present, and she said, "No, but maybe he will."

When asked by Blyden what she was doing next, Dennis advised that she just finished making *Mr. Sycamore* in California. She said she didn't know the release date but listed her co-stars and described the plot. Blyden asked her if she could do anything she wanted to do, what would it be. She replied, "Retire, with money." He also posed the question with the assumption that she was in a position to do whatever she wanted, which he later admitted was a false assumption. He asked Dennis if she found she did things to make a living. She answered, "All the time. All the time I do it, because I have to make a living." Blyden followed up by asking her how she made it clear to people that an artist is also somebody who makes a living. She replied: "Well I don't know. That's a very good question. I suppose people always assume that you make a lot of money, which you don't really, and of course the government takes a lot of what you do make. I'm sure people are aware of that, even on a much smaller scale than people who make a great deal of money." Blyden ended by telling Dennis, "You're so gifted and you're so bright; thank you for coming on the show," and shaking her hand. She got up and shook the hand of each panelist.

On July 11, 1973, Dennis was photographed in a series of poses by Walter Kale for the *Chicago Tribune*. She wore pants and a jacket at home with her black cat Broadway Charlie and other cats. She reportedly had forty-two other felines. Dennis is quoted as saying that she acquired most of them "by sheer pain," and that the overflow goes to her mother, who has twenty-two. Some of the photographs were reprinted on July 18, 1973, and April 10, 1977. For the latter, a photo caption indicated that many of her feline friends are named after characters, such as Wilma of the Buck Rogers comic strip. Another, a fat, bizarre cat, was named Octavia.

On January 11, 1974, a review appeared by Ann Walker in *The Leader Post* about an episode of the Canadian TV show *Witness to Yesterday* in which Dennis played Joan of Arc. The show's premise had host Patrick Watson interviewing an historical figure about their accomplishments. The script was written by Laurier La Pierre. Joan was asked questions like, "Do you believe in God?" "Were you a virgin?" "Did you have normal sexual feelings?" and "Is it possible you are not sane?" An article in the *Edmonton Journal*, dated April 27, 1974, by Paul King reported that when Dennis came to the set to shoot the episode she put the script aside and insisted on ad-libbing it entirely on her own.

Dennis at home with two of her cats on July 11, 1973.

Ann Walker wrote that Dennis "provided a somewhat unconvincing portrayal. [Her] Joan comes across as being humble, reticent, almost apologetic for the acts which she had inspired, and broken of her firebrand spirit." There is no existing footage of the episode.

In the *Ottawa Citizen* on January 10, 1974, Frank Penn wrote that Sandy's appearance as Joan was "an impersonation in itself enough to overload the credulity of even the most persuasive viewer," and described her as "Sandy of Arc." Bill Musselwhite in *The Calgary Herald*, on January 7, 1974, wrote: "Sandy Dennis is not a bad actress but she inevitably comes across as spineless, simpy, and limp."

From March 7 to 17, 1974, Dennis starred as Billie Dawn in Garson Kanin's comedy *Born Yesterday* at the Pellman Theatre in Milwaukee. Her co-star was Gary Merrill, and the director was Stephen Porter. In *The Milwaukee Sentinel*, dated March 7, 1974, Dean Jensen wrote, "Sandy Dennis does not blot out the memory of Judy Holliday. Rather Miss Dennis has put her own very distinctive stamp on the role. She's both uproarious and altogether fetching to watch and hear." The production also enjoyed a one-week engagement at the Ogunquit Playhouse in Maine from July 9, as well as playing at the Westport Country Playhouse in Connecticut.

In March Dennis appeared in Hastings with the University of Nebraska Orchestra as part of the Willa Cather Centennial Festival. She narrated poems and passages written by Cather.

From May 6 to June 30, 1974, she returned to the Ivanhoe Theatre for Terrence Rattigan's play *Separate Tables*, which was directed by George Keathley, and co-starred James Broderick and Delphi Lawrence. Dennis played the dual roles of Anne Shankland and Sybil Railton-Bell. Some sources claim she appeared in a production of the play *The Gin Game* in 1974, but this cannot be verified.

The actress returned to Broadway in the role of Eva, a would-be suicide, in the Alan Ayckbourn comedy *Absurd Person Singular*. After a tryout at the Westport Country Playhouse in Westport, Connecticut, from August 26 to 31, 1974, the show opened at the Music Box Theatre on October 8, 1974. It ran until March 6, 1976, was directed by Eric Thompson, and co-starred Geraldine Page, Larry Blyden, Richard Kiley, Tony Roberts, and Carole Shelley. Dennis would not stay for the whole run, being replaced by Carol Lynley on June 26, 1975, and then Betsy von Furstenberg on January 12, 1976.

In *The New York Times*, dated October 9, Clive Barnes wrote that Dennis was "fiercely implacable." In *The New York Times*, dated October 20, Walter Kerr enthused: "Miss Dennis, hallelujah, has shed her mannerisms and has never put her stricken-Madonna face to more endearingly convulsing use." In the *After Dark* interview, she advised that the play was her first on Broadway for three years because she didn't have any offers after her last appearance. She was offered *Absurd Person Singular* by the Theatre Guild, and only agreed to do it because she liked the part, she needed the money, and she wanted to work again with Geraldine "Gerry" Page.

In his book on his mother Eileen Heckart, *Just Outside the Spotlight*, Luke Yankee reported that Heckart had previously used the same dressing room in the Music Box Theatre that Dennis inhabited. Heckart had played in the thriller *Veronica's Room* from October 22 to December 29, 1973. Yankee reports that his mother commented, "If I have to give up this gorgeous dressing room so quickly, I'm glad that it's at least going to someone who will appreciate it." Yankee also reports that a few months later he and Heckart went backstage to see Dennis after an Actors Benefit performance of her show. She is said to have hugged Heckart and thanked her for the dressing room. He also notes that Dennis called Heckart

"Eileen" and not "Heckie," which was a nickname other people called her but which she disliked.

On December 29, 1974, Dennis was photographed for the *Chicago Tribune* with British actress Carole Shelley, her co-star in *Absurd Person Singular*, in Dennis' dressing room, reading a book on astrology together.

Dennis' second spoken-word LP was reportedly released in 1974 on the Caedmon label, although some sources give it a 1971 year of release and others 1975. It was entitled *Pioneer Women: Selections from Their Journals*. The stories were read by her and Eileen Heckart. The four-sided LP comprised the stories from the journals of daughter Elenore Plaisted, missionary wife Mary Richardson Walker, army wife Martha Summerhayes, and homesteader Elinore Pruitt Stewart.

In the March 24, 1975, issue of *New York Magazine*, Dennis was one of a number of celebrities photographed by Lynn Karlin with their cats, for an article entitled "The Only Perfect Relationship in This Fickle World." Under the heading "Cats in the Belfry," Sandy was photographed holding a large dish of food in her kitchen, surrounded by twelve felines. The cats were identified as Octavia, Charity, Amanda, Ursula, Peaches, Roma, Jenny, Jess, Mama Sophie, Maggie, Hannibal, and Alexander. Dennis reported that she owned twenty-eight cats and a dog named Bathsheba, and that five of the felines slept with her.

On July 14, 1975, she was the star of the radio drama series *CBS Radio Mystery Theatre* in the episode entitled "Snake in the Grass." Her co-stars were Ralph Bell, Robert Dryden, and Arnold Stang. The episode was written by Sam Dann, and produced, directed and hosted by Himan Brown. The show was sponsored by Budweiser and Sine-Off, and ran for forty-three minutes. It was repeated on November 16, 1975.

The plot concerns Augusta Sanderson, professor of agriculture at a northwest university town. She has discovered a new species of purple clover to be used as nutrient feed grass for Himalayan goat's milk. Augusta is arrested by police detective Novak for the shooting murder of her colleague, Doctor Eugene Everett Howells. The motive is said to be that he has robbed her of her discovery. Novak learns Augusta has been framed by the Himalayan Aly, the younger brother of the Crown Prince "Shorty" Lutuf. Novak arrests Aly and then proposes to Augusta, providing a cornball conclusion to a tale that added an exotic flavor to its police procedural structure.

Dennis' performance is mostly

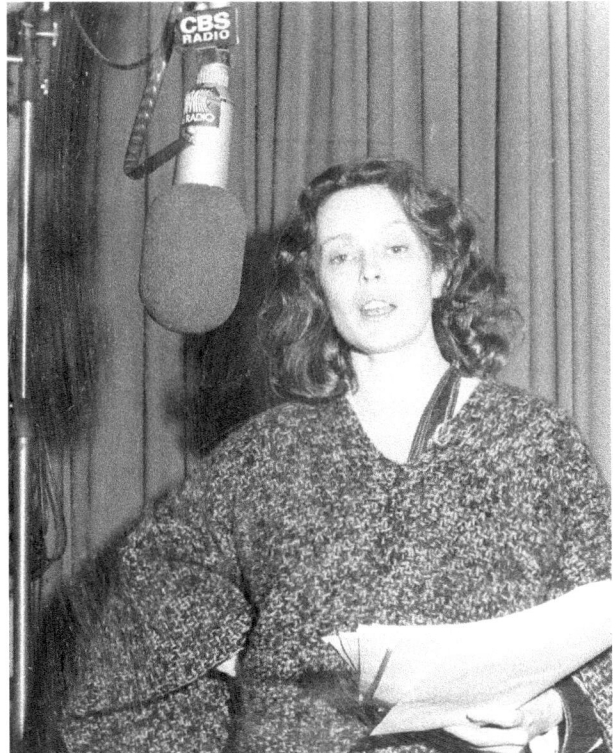

Dennis recording the *CBS Radio Mystery Theatre* episode "Snake in the Grass" in July 1975.

free of stuttering, with her trademark stammering only surfacing when a nervous Augusta is being interrogated by Novak. He tells her she gave the credit to Howells rather than any other authority on agriculture because she was in love with him. She responds, "That's ... that's ... that's..." before she admits she *was* in love with him. When Lutuf and Aly deny knowing her, she stutters, "I can't be ... I..." When Novak decides to place her under arrest, she stammers, "What, uh ... what does one bring to a jail?"

On October 17 Dennis made her second guest appearance on the TV show "*What's My Line?*"— this time as a panelist. She was reported to have broken up with Mulligan in April 1975. In an interview in *The Beaver County Times* with Earl Wilson, dated February 10, 1976, she said, "One day I think we stopped liking each other. The time came for me to say, 'Excuse me.'" In the *People* interview dated August 23, 1976, Dennis said they had split two years prior. She also commented, "I have always remained friends with people I've had relationships with. Gerry probably least of all."

During Dennis' "*What's My Line?*" appearance in December 1973 she revealed that she had just shot her return to film, the comedy *Mr. Sycamore*. It finally saw release on December 12, 1975. It was directed by Pancho Kohner and co-starred Jason Robards and Jean Simmons. Dennis played the part of Jane Gwilt, the wife of Robards' character, a man who decides he'd rather be a tree.

She took on the role of Maggie in Tennessee Williams' *Cat on a Hot Tin Roof* in a summer tour of a production that co-starred David Selby (as Brick) and Ronald Bishop. Among the stops were the Corning Summer Theatre in New York, the Ogunquit Playhouse in Maine, the Westport County Playhouse in Connecticut, the Candlewood Theatre in Connecticut (August 11 to 16), and the Arlington Park Theatre in Illinois (September 25 to November 9). In *The Lewiston Evening Journal* on August 19, 1975, Lisa Giguere wrote that Dennis "does an excellent job as far as she goes. But she doesn't go far enough. Her portrayal is completely lacking in sensuality, though the frustration, the restlessness and desperation are there."

In the *After Dark* article, Tom Killen questioned whether the actress was miscast in *Cat on a Hot Tin Roof*, by having a farm girl from Nebraska playing the feline Southern belle Maggie. She commented, "It was a challenge. I had no preconceptions about the character at all. All I can say is that my approach was different." Killen reported that the play enjoyed a sell-out season but the critics were divided. Some thought Dennis gave a very credible, interesting, and diverting performance. Others said she failed to convey even minimally the brassy, calculating nature of the character.

Dennis shot her two scenes in the Larry Cohen–directed horror film *God Told Me To* (1976) in November 1975 in New York. The film had begun production in New York in September 1975, with the St. Patrick's Day parade filmed live by Cohen in March of that year. Dennis played a supporting role in the movie, with the leading role played by Tony Lo Bianco, and other supporting parts filled by Deborah Raffin and Sylvia Sidney. The film was first released on November 21, 1976, then re-released as *Demon* in March 1977.

On November 3, 1975, Dennis was photographed with a three-and-half-month-old Siberian tiger in front of a collection box for Capital Fund, to raise money for new additions to Lincoln Park Zoo.

The Bernard Slade comedy *Same Time, Next Year* had run at the Brooks Atkinson Theatre from March 14, 1975, to May 16, 1978, and then transferred to the Ambassador Theatre for the remainder of the run to September 3, 1978. The production was directed by Gene Saks and starred Charles Grodin and Ellen Burstyn as Doris. Dennis is said by some sources to have played Doris on Broadway from March 8 to May 30, 1977, co-starring Ted Bessell. However, several reports make these dates questionable. An article in *The New York Times* dated June 7, 1976, reported that she was to join the play on June 21, 1976, replacing Loretta Swit (who had replaced Ellen Burstyn). In *Theater Week* Michael Buckely said Dennis played the role for eleven months in 1976, nine opposite Ted Bessell and two opposite Don Murray.

In *The New York Times* on July 9, 1976, John Corry interviewed Dennis in an Italian restaurant. She told him she based her interpretation of Doris on an Italian friend named Brenda. "I've used what she does, some of her behavior." Perhaps her friend is actually Brenda Vaccaro, since in *People* Vaccaro is described as her best friend. In the article, Vaccaro tells the story of when she was broke in 1968 Dennis sent her an unsolicited check for two thousand dollars. Brenda was able to return the favor in 1973 when Dennis was broke and Brenda lent her two thousand dollars.

In *The New York Times* interview Dennis also commented on the consideration of her acting mannerisms for the play. "I've been criticized for being mannered and so I keep Doris down." Additionally, she commented on the differences between herself and the character. "Doris is sentimental and romantic. I don't have a romantic bone in my body. When I am playing her I sometimes think how can anyone believe this? But people do believe it and sometimes I see them cry. I'm amazed."

The New York Times, on July 29, 1976, reported that on July 25 Dennis held a cat auction in front of the Brooks Atkinson Theatre, where she was performing in the play. The auction was organized in conjunction with the Humane Society and the Bide-a-Wee association, connected to the Bide-a-Wee animal shelter in the city. Seventeen cats were placed in homes, and donations totaled eight hundred fifty-five dollars. Dennis was quoted as saying she herself was taking home one cat to add to her current twenty-plus.

On August 5, 1975, Marilyn Beck in *The Miami News* wrote about the casting of the film version of the play Dennis was currently starring in. She was not being considered for the film, according to producer Stephen Bach, because, he said, "I'm afraid her days of important film stardom might be over." Bach would not end up producing the film, which was released in 1978, with Ellen Burstyn in the role of Doris opposite Alan Alda, and was directed by Dennis' *Up the Down Staircase* director Robert Mulligan.

Dennis made her first of two appearances on the children's TV show *Captain Kangaroo* on February 3, 1976, which was filmed in New York. Dennis can be seen in a 1976 montage introduction to the show, saying, "Good Morning, Captain," and nodding her head in footage viewed on YouTube.

In the March 1976 edition of the magazine *After Dark*, Dennis was interviewed by Tom Killen to publicize her appearance in *Absurd Person Singular* on Broadway. Accompanying the article were pictures of her in the show alone, and with Tony Roberts and Fritz Weaver, as well as stills from *Who's Afraid of Virginia Woolf?* and *God Told Me To* (then known as *Whispers*). In the interview she spoke about her image as an actress: "I've never really taken to that glamorous star routine. It would be terrific if it all was something that I was part of, but I have never been a part of it. You see, a lot of that is California, and that way of life really bores me." Dennis would describe herself to Killen as being antisocial.

In an article by Jack O'Brien for the *Sarasota Journal*, dated September 10, 1976, she was described as the star of the play *Same Time, Next Year* in New York. William Raidy's interview with her for *The Pittsburgh Press*, dated October 24, 1976, reports she was then

On the set of the TV show *Captain Kangaroo*, with Bob Keeshan, on January 9, 1976.

doing the Broadway show. An interview in *People* magazine, dated August 23, 1976, and conducted by Maria Vespa, also has her doing the play at the time.

On September 3, 1976, Earl Wilson of *The Milwaukee Sentinel* interviewed Ted Bessell. Wilson reported the actor was currently starring on Broadway in the play with Dennis and was scheduled to continue to do so until February 1977. It is believed that Don Murray replaced Bessell on March 8, 1977. In the interview with Bessell he reported that the play opened with Dennis naked under a bed sheet. He also said that, after learning she had thirty-two cats, he asked her, "Suppose you were involved with a man who doesn't like even two cats?" She reportedly answered, "Oh, the man goes."

On September 27, 1976, Dennis was photographed with the seventy-eight-thousand-five-hundred-dollar "Sphere of the Zodiac" at the Steuben Glass showroom in New York. It was reported in the *Chicago Tribune* article that she had a great interest in astrology.

In the *Pittsburgh Press* October 24, 1976, interview Dennis indicated that she had completed the film *Nasty Habits*, a comedy directed by Michael Lindsay-Hogg and starring Glenda Jackson. Dennis played a supporting role, along with Melina Mercouri, Geraldine Page, and Susan Penhaligon. The film was shot on location in Pennsylvania and at the Elstree Studios in England, and released on March 8, 1977.

The People interview also reported that Dennis was currently being sued by her ex-manager for eighty-six thousand dollars he says he advanced her for investments, and that she owed the Internal Revenue Service thirty-six thousand dollars. This supported her comment in *The Tuscaloosa News* interview of April 15, 1973, that she had to work to pay back taxes. The *People* article included three pictures of Dennis — with five cats at her Connecticut home, holding Toby the cat at a New York sale, and backstage with Ted Bessell for *Same Time, Next Year*.

On October 1, 1976, she joined Zoe Caldwell and June Havoc as one of the celebrity guests at the First Celebrity Luncheon of Friends of the American Shakespeare Theatre at Rolling Hill Country Club in Wilton, Connecticut.

Dennis did a summer 1977 tour of the George S. Kaufman and Edna Ferber play *The Royal Family*, playing Broadway star Julie Cavendish. From June 20 to July 3 she was at the Playhouse on the Mall in New Jersey. From July 12 to 15 it was the Pocomo Playhouse in Pennsylvania. From July 18 to 23 she played the Cape Playhouse in Massachusetts. From July 25 to July 30 she was at the Westport Country Playhouse in Connecticut, co-starring with Cathleen Nesbitt (playing her mother, Fanny). From August 1 to 6 Dennis played the North Shore Music Theater in Massachusetts. From August 15 to 20 she was

Dennis as Sister Winfred in *Nasty Habits* (1977).

at the Ogunquit Playhouse in Maine, with Gale Sondergaard playing Fanny. Writing in *The Lewiston Evening Journal* on August 16, Nancy Grape said of her in the show: "Dennis has grown from a slip of a girl to a majestic figure of a woman. She shows flashes of earthy humor that light up the stage, and she projects a genuineness that is the height of her craft." The tour continued, with the show being produced from August 22 to 27, 1977, at the Cape Playhouse in Dennis, Massachusetts, and from August 29 to September 3 at the Falmouth Playhouse in Massachusetts.

Dennis next appeared on stage in Noel Coward's play *Fallen Angels* at the Royal Poinciana Playhouse in Florida from January 30 to February 4, 1978. Her co-star was Jean Marsh. Dennis would also do the show at the Paper Mill Playhouse in New Jersey from February 13 to March 5, 1978. Another play she performed at the Paper Mill Playhouse was Lillian Hellman's *The Little Foxes*, with Geraldine Page and Rip Torn, from March 22 to April 2, 1978.

Dennis returned to television for a guest appearance on the TV show *Police Story* in an episode entitled "Day of Terror ... Night of Fear." She played Sharon Bristol, a travel agent who became one of a group of hostages taken by bank robbers. The episode was directed by E. Arthur Kean, and co-starred Chad Everett and Bruce Davison. Shot in Hollywood in October 1977, it was broadcast on March 4, 1978.

She was also part of the made-for-TV movie *Perfect Gentlemen*, a comic crime drama directed by Jackie Cooper. It also starred Lauren Bacall, Ruth Gordon and Lisa Pelikan, and was filmed in Hollywood from October 27 to November 1977. The movie was broadcast on March 14, 1978. Dennis made her second appearance on *Captain Kangaroo* on February 12, 1978.

It is said that director Robert Altman wanted her for the female lead of earth mother

Sheila Shea for his comedy *A Perfect Couple* (1979), and that he had written it for her. She had allegedly brought five cats at a time to script-readings, which proved to be a problem for her co-star Paul Dooley. Dooley was briefly hospitalized because of his allergy to cats, and Dennis lost the role. Shelley Duvall was next offered the role but turned it down because she had begun production on *The Shining* (1980) in May 1978. The part was then rewritten and accepted by Marta Heflin, who had appeared in Altman's previous film *A Wedding* (1978). The film would be released on April 6, 1979. Heflin would go on to play a small part in both the Broadway and film versions of Altman's *Come Back to the 5 & Dime Jimmy Dean, Jimmy Dean*, both starring Dennis.

From February 16, 1979, Dennis appeared in a production of the Tennessee Williams play *Eccentricities of a Nightingale* at the Long Beach Auditorium in California. It was part of the Long Beach Theater Festival, which ran from September 1978. The play co-starred Perry King and Nan Martin, and was directed by Michael Flanagan. There is a photograph on The Sandy Dennis Foundation site of her with Tennessee Williams, dated March 1980 and said to be taken during the play's run.

She would return to the play *Same Time, Next Year* from August 14 to 25, 1979, at the John Drew Theatre in New Hampton; from August 27 to September 1 at the Ogunquit Playhouse in Maine, co-starring Charles Kimbrough; and from October 20 to November 3 at the Fox Theatre in Los Angeles. She also did the play in Canada from November 20 to December 21, 1980, at the Stage West Theatre in Winnipeg, with Canadian actor Ted Follows.

On September 14, 1980, Dennis is reported to have attended a Barbara Cook concert at Carnegie Hall. Also in attendance were Eric Roberts, Madeline Kahn and Karen Valentine. Cook had replaced Dennis in *Any Wednesday* in 1965 during its Broadway run.

Dennis played the leading role in the made-for-TV movie *Wilson's Reward*, which was directed by Patrick O'Neal, and co-starred her former companion Gerald S. O'Loughlin and Fred Morsell. Dennis played the part of Martha James, a missionary in the West Indies of the 1920s. The show was broadcast on June 21, 1980. It was filmed on the island of Bonaire in the Netherlands Antilles, located off the coast of Venezuela.

In 1980 Dennis started a relationship with Eric Roberts, almost twenty years her junior. Roberts advised in his interview in *The Advocate*, dated February 6, 1996, that the relationship lasted for six years, while other sources say it was five. It was reported in the *Boston Globe* by Kevin Kelly, on October 4, 1981, that she came into his life after she saw him on television in *Paul's Case*, a 1980 made-for-TV movie which screened on February 11. It was based on a story by Willa Cather, known to be one of the actresses'

A publicity portrait used for Dennis' stage appearance in *Same Time, Next Year* (circa 1977).

favorite writers. Dennis called William Treusch, who also represented her as a personal manager, and invited Roberts to her house to talk about acting.

It was reported that Dennis and Roberts never lived in the same house together. Rather, he stayed in an adjoining house because of his dislike of her myriad cats. When asked about him in the March 13, 1989, *People* interview, she would say, "Eric was a very pretty boy. That's about how deep my feelings went." Her affair with Roberts almost ended tragically in June 1981, when he left her home in a Jeep and crashed into a tree down the road. Roberts was in a coma for seventy-two hours. The night of the accident, Dennis said, "He left with my dog, and I relaxed for the first time that night because he had been such a pain in the ass. I have no idea how the accident happened. I'm just glad the dog came back safe."

In a *People* interview with Roberts by Deirdre Donahue, dated September 9, 1985, Roberts would tell his version of the event. "'I tried to climb a tree in a CJ-5 [brand name for his Jeep],' he said. Leaving the Connecticut house of Sandy Dennis, he hopped into his door-less Jeep for a ride with her German shepherd. The dog leaned out too far. Roberts released the steering wheel to get a hold on the wayward pooch and ended up in a coma for three days."

Dennis said Eric left her when he fell in love with a younger woman, yet she claims the departure brought more relief than bitterness. "It's always slightly tragic when someone leaves you for somebody else, but a great burden was off my shoulders. I've picked the wrong guys in the past, and having a guy around drives me crazy anyway. I can never understand that moment when you get into bed and there's another person there who is going to intrude on your life."

The Actors Memoirs page on The Sandy Dennis Foundation website features a quote from Roberts: "From Sandy's performance in *Virginia Wolfe* to *The Out of Towners*, who comes to mind with more range? Nobody I can think of. And she was a very nice lady." Dennis reportedly would have no more romantic relationships. Roberts addressed the rumors of Dennis being a lesbian in his interview with Gerry Kroll in *The Advocate*. The actor said she had told him about her lesbian relationships during their time together. When asked if he thought she was bisexual, Roberts replied that she "appreciated the beauty of women. But Sandy also liked and appreciated what a very, very young man could do to a woman, I suppose."

Dennis returned to feature films with a supporting role in Alan Alda's romantic comedy *The Four Seasons*. Directed by and starring Alda, the picture also featured Carol Burnett, Rita Moreno, Jack Warden, Len Cariou and Bess Armstrong. Shot in California, Georgia, New York, Vermont, Virginia, and the Virgin Islands, it was released on May 22, 1981. Dennis played Anne Callan, a photographer fixated on vegetables. An article in *The Virgin Islands Daily News* reported Alda shooting on location from April 25, 1980, and suggested that filming of the other locations had been completed. Since Dennis does not appear in the Virgin Islands sequences, it is assumed that her scenes had already been completed. Earl Wilson's article in the *Toledo Blade*, dated March 5, 1980, quoted Alda as saying that he was in rehearsal for the film at the time but had not begun shooting. A March 25, 1980, squib in *The Leader Post* reported the film had begun production in New York.

In January 1981 Dennis began rehearsals on the David Florey play *Sisters*, with Brenda Vaccaro, but when the director fell ill, work was stopped. It was hoped that the production could go ahead later in the year, but this did not come to pass. From January 30 to February 1, Dennis returned to the part of Doris in *Same Time, Next Year* for a fundraiser at the Palace Performing Arts Theater in New Haven. Her co-star was Doug Taylor, who was also the credited director.

She was invited to appear in a drama class production of Jean Anouilh's verse play *The Lady's Not for Burning* at St. Edward's University in Austin, Texas. It was directed by Noel Harrison. In her interview with Ed Blank in *The Pittsburgh Press*, dated March 21, 1982, she said she accepted the invitation because it was a play she had always wanted to do, and that she used to work on speeches from it when she first came to New York.

Dennis returned to Broadway in the role of Sally Stern in the George Furth comedy *The Supporting Cast*. It ran at the Biltmore Theatre for only 36 performances, from August 6 to September 5, 1981. The director was Gene Saks, and Sandy's co-stars were Betty Garrett, Jack Gilford, Hope Lange, and Joyce Van Patten. She played the unhappy wife of a Washington congressman, one of the friends of a female writer who has published a book about celebrity spouses with thinly-veiled characters based on her friends. The narrative is complicated by the fact the friends are trapped together in a Los Angeles beach house that is threatened by a forest fire, a landslide and earthquakes. Although Hope Lange played the lead (as the writer), Dennis had probably the liveliest part, since she got to play stoned and drunk, had an offstage fall into the sea (thought to be suicide), and is carried back onto the stage before physically attacking the writer in the second act.

Dennis was photographed at the premiere party with Mary Tyler Moore and Sir Gordon White, and also with Dorothy Loudon at the Milford Plaza Hotel. The production had an out-of-town tryout on July 6 at the Kennedy Center's Eisenhower Theatre in Washington, where it received bad reviews. Dennis, however, was praised by *The Washington Post* as a "virtuoso of caricature." In *The New York Times*, dated August 7, 1981, Mel Gussow wrote, "Miss Dennis is an expert at this sort of comic pathos. We smile through her tears. She is easily the funniest member [of the cast]."

On August 16, 1981, Walter Kerr in *The New York Times* wrote another review of the play, describing Sandy as "professionally game." In *New York Magazine*, John Simon wrote on August 24 about Dennis: "It is one thing to enact an occasional neurotic, but quite another to have made a career out of exuding a condition that should be beheld only by advanced students of clinical psychology, and then only behind carefully locked doors."

A video recording exists from the first preview of the production on August 3 and is available at some libraries in the United States via the worldcat.org website. It remains the only footage to capture the effectiveness of Dennis performing live on stage. The 130-minute play itself is ordinary, with some occasionally funny lines and busy direction.

Dennis gives a broadly comic performance, employing a loud voice for her drunken character and slapstick for the running gag of a sliding glass door that people keep walking into (and also when she physically attacks Hope Lange — twice). Her acting also incorporates some of her trademark mannerisms, like stuttering, laughing, pointing, gesturing, and fiddling with her clothes. In the first act she wears glasses and has her hair up, but in the second she wears no glasses and has her hair down. Dennis enlivens the second act with her late return, when it appears that, unlike the other friends, she is not angry about the book. She scores the best moment of the show when an extended laughing fit precedes her attack upon Lange.

Dennis is said to have been with Eric Roberts in October 1981 in Boston for out-of-town tryouts for the Bill C. Davis play *Mass Appeal*. He had performed the role of seminarian Mark Dolson in an Off Broadway run in 1980, but would withdraw from the production before it got to Broadway and be replaced by Michael O'Keefe. Roberts' withdrawal was reportedly based on the medical problems he experienced from the June car accident. Late that month Dennis and Roberts were also seen in New York at a party for the head of the William Morris Agency, Arnold Stiefel, at the Park Lane hotel.

Ed Graczyk's play *Come Back to the 5 & Dime Jimmy Dean, Jimmy Dean* had first been produced by the Players Theatre of Columbus, Ohio, in September 1976, directed by the writer. Another production was done by the Alliance Theater Company of Atlanta around March or April 1977. This production starred Fanny Flagg in the part of Sissy. Dennis was initially attached to an Off Broadway production of the play in 1980, according to an article in *The New York Times* dated February 19, 1980.

This troubled production was held at the Hudson Guild Theatre and directed by Barbara Loden. Loden is said to have taken over the role Dennis vacated. The head of the Guild, David Heefner, was the play's original director but was replaced by Loden. The season is reported to have run from February 27 to March 30, but critics were not invited to review it. The cast included Fannie Flagg, Margaret Hilton, Barbara Loden, Maida Meyers, Judith Roberts, Peggy Cosgrave, Linda Kampley and Gregory Berdger.

Apparently plans were afoot to transfer the production to Broadway, and it was thought that a bad review would have hurt that chance. Reportedly there was work still being done on the play, which was being changed from three acts to two, and there was the possibility that some of the actors were to be replaced. The company also said the early closing of the production was due to an impending transit strike. The play was listed as having run from April 7, 1980, until May 4 at the Hudson Guild, with stars Loden and Fannie Flagg.

Director Robert Altman was attracted to the material and acquired the rights to the play because he wanted to make it into a film as well as direct the stage version. Shelley Duvall was considered for one of the stage roles, though Altman finally decided against her. Rehearsals began at the St. Clements Theater for a Broadway production to star Dennis as Mona, Cher in her Broadway debut as Sissy, and Karen Black as Joanne.

Sources differ as to when rehearsals began. Some say it was February 1, 1982; but the *New York Magazine* article, which describes the rehearsal process, is also dated February 1, 1982, suggesting rehearsal was already underway. The book *The First Time*, by Jeff Coplon and Cher, describes how Cher went to Altman's apartment in New York's Central Park South, where he was going to have the play read by her, Sudie Bond, Dennis, Karen Black and Kathy Bates.

The Sandy Dennis Foundation website page of Actors' Memories features a quote from Bates about Dennis. Undated, it does not specify whether it was said at the time of the Broadway play or the film version. However, Bates describes Dennis as the great peacemaker of the group. "She was the solid one with her feet on the ground, which was interesting to me at the time, because she had such an ethereal quality as an actress." Bates also remembered her wonderful sense of humor and her gorgeous hair. She also comments, "I think she was still seeing Eric Roberts at the time and we were all very jealous."

Cher read for both the characters of Joe and Sissy. However, she thought she was awful either way. Later Dennis would confide to Cher that she thought Cher's read was about the worst she'd ever witnessed. Dennis added, "You were fascinating. I could not take my eyes off you. It was like looking at a train wreck. That's just how bad you were." Altman still gave Cher the part of Sissy.

Cher reportedly bonded with Dennis, referring to her as "my f— k around friend." In her interview with Ed Blank in *The Pittsburgh Press* on March 21, 1982, Dennis spoke of her admiration for Cher: "She's very loose and naturalistic and has tremendous charisma on stage. She's the most interesting actor I've worked with in a long time."

A strain developed during rehearsals between Dennis and Karen Black when Sandy, to solve a blocking problem, said to Black, "Tell me what you want me to do. I can do anything

Candid photograph of the lead cast and director of the stage production *Come Back to the 5 & Dime Jimmy Dean, Jimmy Dean* (1982) during rehearsal. From left is Karen Black, Dennis, Cher, and Robert Altman.

you like." In response, Black said, "So can I." Altman teased Dennis with the comment, "Let Sandy act — she'll feel better."

Dennis commented on Altman's unstudied way of working on a play, where he doesn't ask actors to dissect their characters: "I don't like reading the play until you want to scream. Altman has cast this show very well — when you do that, you don't have to interfere, because everyone has a sense of her own character." Sandy admitted she hadn't got a handle on her character yet, and remarked, "See me in five years," though she reportedly seemed sanguine.

Despite the reported friction, Karen Black said of Dennis (on the Sandy Dennis Foundation website page of Actors' Memories): "Sandy was the most amazing actress: spellbinding. The audience would hang on her every pause. I will never forget her."

The play had three weeks of previews and was so popular people had to be turned away every night. Cher said Dennis was "so great and funny and giving as an actress," and gave her the dressing room Elizabeth Taylor had used in the same theater the previous year for *The Little Foxes*.

The production opened at the Martin Beck Theatre on February 18 (and ran until April 14, 1982). When the first-act curtain fell, Cher said she went to Dennis' dressing room and told her she didn't think she could go back on. Dennis told her, "Why don't you just try it for a little while, and then you can decide. Don't worry, you'll get through this." Cher got through the second act, her fear overcome. The opening night supper party was held in Woolworths, the original five and dime store, on the corner of 5th Avenue and 34th Street in New York.

In *The New York Times* on February 19, Frank Rich wrote, "Miss Dennis either runs on her sentences incoherently or scrambles them with false starts, jerky internal word repetitions and teeth-baring snorts." In *New York Magazine* on March 1, 1982, John Simon wrote of Altman, "What director in his right mind would let Sandy Dennis make rancid mincemeat of the key role?" Simon describes Dennis as "one of those totally unpalatable actresses who becomes critics darlings, and who are forthwith encouraged to indulge themselves in their excesses to even greater acclaim. [She] started out as a seemingly normal actress years ago then switched to a kind of kookiness that rapidly changed into this irreversible and always identical stage persona of someone hanging on by her teeth to the last fraying shred of sanity."

During the run Cher learned to improvise some lines. She said Dennis could easily cope with it—"She could catch anything you threw at her and throw it right back." The playwright had a problem with this improvisation, but when Altman saw that Cher's ad libs earned laughs, he told her to keep them in. Graczyk acquiesced, recognizing the value of a good laugh.

In the play, at one point Cher's character Sissy makes sandwiches. One of the other actresses reportedly complained to Altman about this action, considering it "too alive." When Dennis heard about the objection, she commented, "F**k them. You just keep making your little sandwiches." Cher told Dennis she was concerned that she wasn't good every night, and worried when she couldn't always cry in her climactic scene. The older actress replied, "Am I supposed to feel sorry for you? If you're brilliant, you'll be good three nights a week."

According to Gerard Plecki's book on Altman, the production closed at Graczyk's request rather than because of poor box office sales. This idea is supported by the statement Dennis made in her March 21, 1982, interview with Ed Blank that she would be disappointed when Cher would have to leave the play in June, suggesting there was an expectation of the show having a long run. The play would be Dennis' last Broadway appearance.

Using the Broadway set, Altman shot the play on Super -16mm film. Some sources claim it was only filmed strictly for cable television, but Altman maintains he always wanted it to be shown in cinemas. To that end he blew the 16mm up to 35mm, and the film was screened at festivals in Montreal, Venice and Toronto before receiving an official release on November 12, 1982.

Dennis would tour in *The Supporting Cast* in the summer of 1982. She would appear in the play with Patty Cosgrove, Barbara Rush and June Dayton at the Westport Country Playhouse from June 28 to July 3. The show was directed by Tom Troupe. Fran Sikorski, in *The Redding Pilot* on July 1, wrote that Sandy plays a role "she is most at-home with and is an incredible neurotic." The tour continued at the North Shore Music Theatre from July 10, the Cape Playhouse from July 26 to 31, 1982, the Falmouth Playhouse from August 2 to 7, and the Ogunquit Playhouse from August 16 to 21, 1982. Dennis would also do the play for Stage West in Canada from November 11 to 13, 1983.

From May 4 to 29, 1983, Dennis appeared Off Broadway as Sophia Bowsky, the disenfranchised wife of a city newspaper editor, in Thomas Babe's play *Buried Inside Extra* at the Joseph Papp Public Theater. The production was directed by Papp, and co-starred Dixie

Carter, Hal Holbrook, Vincent Gardenia, and William Converse-Roberts. *Buried Inside Extra* was one of two plays inaugurating the New York Shakespeare Festival's Public Theater Program with London's Royal Court Theater, and as such it was planned to go to London in the summer after the New York run. The season had been originally announced to open in New York on April 12 and close on May 29 so it could open in London on June 13 for six weeks. An article in *The New York Times* about the postponement, dated April 25, 1983, said it was due to "script revisions."

The London production coming to New York in exchange was Caryl Churchill's *Top Girls*, which played concurrently with *Buried Inside Extra*. The latter's American cast included Kathryn Grody, Sara Botsford, Polly Draper, and Linda Hunt, who took over after the British cast went home in February after having been in New York since December 1982.

In *The New York Times* on May 5, 1983, Frank Rich reviewed *Buried Inside Extra* but made no specific mention of Dennis' performance. However, in *The Pittsburgh Press*, dated May 14, Ed Blank wrote that she was on stage for just twelve and a half minutes, but her performance is a "tour de force almost worth suffering the play to see."

In May Dennis attended a concert by Chicago singer Bonnie Koloc at the Manhattan club The Other End. She is reported to have sat with actor John Heard and Bob Dylan. Koloc claims, in an interview in *New York Magazine* dated May 16, that she had known the actress for years. The interview says the singer sat with Dennis and her friends after the set, though Dylan had left early.

Buried Inside Extra opened at the Royal Court on June 17, 1983. London critics were not kind to it. John Barber of *The Daily Telegraph* wrote: "Miss Dennis's single scene was worth all the rest of the evening put together."

In the *Sarasota Herald-Tribune* of January 23, 1984, Liz Smith reported that Dennis was scheduled to make a guest appearance on the TV show *St. Elsewhere* in an episode written by John Ford Noonan. She was to co-star with Eva LaGallienne and Brenda Vaccaro; however, this appearance did not happen. LaGallienne and Vaccaro did appear in an episode of the show written by Noonan entitled "The Women," broadcast on March 28, 1984, with Blythe Danner playing the part that Dennis might have assayed.

Dennis did appear as Helen Hanff in a production of *84 Charing Cross Road* for Calgary's Stage West Theater Restaurant, opposite Donal Donnely. The play was directed by William Fisher, and it ran in January and February 1984. Writing in *The Calgary Herald* on January 25, Michael Burn opined, "[She has an] uncanny ability for baring the soul of her characters with a precise blending of gestures and words. Dennis bristles with sarcasm and wit."

She also appeared at a screening of *Who's Afraid of Virginia Woolf?* for a late-night dialogue at the Plaza Theatre in February. Eric Roberts accompanied her. Dennis appeared in summer stock in John Pielmeier's play *Agnes of God* as the psychiatrist Martha Livingstone. From June 25 to 30 she played at the Westport Country Playhouse, co-starring with Geraldine Page and Deirdre O'Connell in a production directed by Frank Marino. In *The Ridgefield Press* on June 28, 1984, Fran Sikorski wrote that she "has problems with her role early in the play, but surmounts them skilfully, crafting the role of the psychiatrist for dramatic end." The production also went to the Cape Playhouse, although the dates are unknown. Other sources claim Dennis also appeared in the play with Peggy Cass and Susan Strasberg.

On January 14, 1985, the made-for-TV movie *The Execution* was broadcast, in which Dennis had a supporting role as Elsa Spahn. Dennis played one of a group of five women who survived a Nazi concentration camp and who decide to execute the man who was their doctor and tormentor at the camp. Co-starring Loretta Swit, Jessica Walter, Barbara Barrie, Valerie Harper and Rip Torn, the movie was directed by Paul Wendkos and filmed in September 1984.

Dennis was next on stage playing Jessie Cates in Marsha Norman's *'Night, Mother* opposite Eileen Heckart as her mother Thelma. The show was at the Westport Country Playhouse from September 10 to 15, 1985. Nancy Marchand was previously announced to play the part of Thelma in a season to run September 9 to 14. The production was directed by Burry Fredrik. Dennis and Heckart met in 1957 for the Broadway production of *Dark at the Top of the Stairs* and also appeared together in the film *Up the Down Staircase*. Both said they would agree to take the play on tour if they were asked.

Interviewed by Leila Crane for *The Hour* on September 9, Dennis commented on the role: "This is very much like me and how I behave. I live with my mother and this is how I deal with things. Our life is similar, without the suicide angle." She was also interviewed by Fran Sikorski for *The Ridgefield Press* on September 12, 1985. Dennis said, "I don't feel that this is one of my most challenging roles. My mother always said that from the day I was brought to her at birth, I pulled two window shades down over my eyes. The character in the play is very much like me." Reviewing the play in *The Hour* on September 12, 1985, Leila Crane wrote, "Miss Dennis handles the pain of the role with sustained control."

On September 14 the Westport Playhouse held a pre-show champagne reception for her and Eileen Heckart as a benefit for the Wellesley College Benefit Fund.

On December 7, 1985, Dennis was one of the guest stars in an episode of the TV show *The Love Boat* entitled "Roommates/Heartbreaker/Out of the Blue." She played Gina Caldwell, who pursues Cabot Fairfield, a multimillionaire played by Harvey Korman. Filmed in Hollywood, the episode was directed by Richard A. Wells.

On December 15, 1985, Dennis guest-starred in the episode of the TV show *Alfred Hitchcock Presents* entitled "Arthur, or the Gigolo." In it she plays Helen, who has married a gigolo, Arthur, who does not like her pet cats. Brad Davis played Arthur. The episode was directed by Thomas Carter. It was filmed in September 1985.

In 1985 Dennis was top-billed in "The Trouble with Mother," an episode of the syndicated family TV show *Young People's Specials*. As Patricia Benson, she was the mother of Laurie, a thirteen-year-old girl who sees herself as a feminist and her mother as merely a housewife. The episode co-starred Jennifer Ginsberg, Amy Parker and Robert Elkins, and was written and directed by Tom G. Robertson. The broadcast date is unknown.

On January 15, 1986, Dennis made a guest appearance on the TV show *The Equalizer* in an episode entitled "Out of the Past." She played Kay Wesley, the ex-wife of the series' lead, Robert McCall, who asks him to help her when her new husband is threatened by a vengeful ex-con. Co-starring were Edward Woodward, Stephen McHattie, Barry Primus and Brad Dourif. Filmed in New York, the episode was directed by Richard Compton.

Actress Elizabeth Ashley went to Edmonton, Canada, to appear with Dennis for two months in a dinner theater play at Stage West. However, Ashley made news headlines on March 8, 1986, when she was arrested at the Edmonton International Airport in Canada at 1:30 A.M. and charged with two counts of narcotics possession. Ashely and Dennis were also scheduled to appear together in a tour of the John Ford Noonan play *A Coupla White Chicks Sitting Around Talking*.

Dennis was reportedly a replacement for Susan Anton, and she played the part of the cookie-baking, conservative, designer-clothed housewife Maude Mix. The part required her to dye her hair blonde. An article in the *Schenectady Gazette* by Eleanor Koblenz, dated April 14, 1986, reports that Dennis had rehearsed with the show's understudy, Polly Burke, while Dennis was still in Canada. The tour started with a show at the American Theatre in St. Louis, Missouri, from March 11 to 17. It then continued at the Morris A. Mechanic Theatre in Baltimore, Maryland, from March 21 to April 12, 1986; at the Proctor Theatre in Albany, New York, from April 15 to 18; and at the Parker Playhouse in Fort Lauderdale, Florida, from May 6 to 11.

Dennis returned to the Paul Zindel play *And Miss Reardon Drinks a Little*, with Anne Meara and directed by Larry Arrick. It performed at the Cape Playhouse from August 11 to 16, and at the Westport Country Playhouse from August 18 to 23, 1986. On April 26, 1987, Dennis appeared for an interview with Brian Linehan on the Canadian TV show *City Lights*.

She next took on the role of Florence Unger, the uptight nitpicker in Neil Simon's *The Odd Couple*. This female take on his famous play had run on Broadway from June 11, 1985, to February 23, 1986, starring Rita Moreno as Olive and Sally Struthers as Florence. In November 1986 Dennis played opposite Jo Anne Worley in Detroit. From March 6 to May 10, 1987, her co-star was Stella Stevens as Olive at Stage West Dinner Theatre in Canada. Kaye Ballard joined Dennis at the Pocono Playhouse in Mountainhome, Pennsylvania, from August 18 to September 4, 1988, and they were directed by Judith Haskell.

Reviewing the show for *The Morning Call*, John Flautz wrote that "Dennis dithers and shakes out her bag of vocal tricks," but acknowledges that the actresses "together find every conceivable laugh in Simon's script." Dennis and Ballard continued at the Bucks County Playhouse in Philadelphia from September 7 to 25, 1988. That run would be her last appearance on stage.

In 1987 Dennis attended the Employee's Giving Campaign at St. Vincent's Health Center in Bridgeport, Connecticut. From October 14, 1988, she could be seen in the supporting film role of the actress Claire in Woody Allen's *Another Woman*, starring Gene Rowlands. It was shot in New York and New Jersey in November 1987.

A month before that she had played a supporting role as Aunt Lucy in Robert Englund's Hollywood horror movie *976-Evil*. The film starred Stephen Geoffreys and Patrick O'Bryan, and was released on March 24, 1989. Dennis also appeared in the supporting role of school teacher Millie Dew in *Parents*, shot in Ontario, Canada, from August to October 1987. The film was directed by Bob Balaban and released on January 27, 1989.

In September 1990 she was in Omaha, Nebraska, shooting the supporting role of Mrs. Roberts in Sean Penn's film *The Indian Runner*. It starred David Morse and Viggo Mortensen, and was released on September 20, 1991. This would be her last screen appearance. Dennis was interviewed on location at the time, advising that she would rather read a book than go see a film or to the theater. She also commented that her favorite of her own films was *Thank You All Very Much*.

By this time Dennis had been diagnosed with ovarian cancer. One source says she was diagnosed in August 1990, while others maintain it was earlier. In his introduction to her memoirs, Doug Taylor says she was diagnosed in 1989 but then also says she was recovering from her first cancer operation in 1987. In his book *Hollywood Lesbians*, Boze Hadleigh says he did not meet with Dennis after 1990, and he says she retreated inside her Connecticut home with her pets because she was a solitary and private person.

According to the March 16, 1992, *People* magazine article about her death, she was undergoing chemotherapy while shooting *The Indian Runner*. The article also revealed that Dennis' father died around this time. Perhaps because there was no project to publicize, and also because she wanted to keep her illness quiet, there are no interviews with her to be found from this time. However, while battling the cancer she was also writing her memoirs, which would be published posthumously. Dennis having the cancer would be stated by Joanne Woodward in her foreword.

Doug Taylor says that despite her illness, Dennis continued to work whenever possible. She taught acting at the Herbert Berghof Studios in New York. He quotes a story she told him of the day when Liv Ullmann observed one of her classes. Two students were presenting a scene from *A Doll's House*. Dennis says they didn't have the scene, and after taking her direction, the more she worked with them the worse it became. Ullmann apparently sat slumped in her chair, staring at the actors. Dennis described it as a teacher's ultimate nightmare.

Sandy endured three operations, and was then so sick she was unable to teach, clean her house or care for her animals. Sources report that Sandy Dennis died on Monday, March 2, 1992, in Westport, Connecticut. She was fifty-four years old. There is some question as to the exact day she died. Obituaries have her friend Doris Elliott confirm the actress' death as late Tuesday, March 3. Elliott says she was informed by Dennis' agent, Bill Tresch, of her death on the Monday, but that she didn't know exactly when she had died.

The afterword to *A Personal Memoir* indicates that Dennis died in the early spring of 1992. She was at home in her bed, as she wanted to be. Two close friends, her dog, and several cats were nearby. One of the cats was Christian, whom she estimated to be twenty-one years old and who she referred to as "the quiet old man." The afterword says that Dennis' shallow breathing ceased in the still hours before dawn. Christian slept on the pillow beside her. When she died, the cat raised his head, stood up, opened his mouth, and uttered a silent meow.

Her body was cremated, and her remains interred inside mausoleum number three in Lincoln Memorial Park, Lancaster County, Nebraska. The inscription on her grave reads "Actress." She was survived by her mother Yvonne, her brother Frank, three dogs and thirty-three cats.

In 1994, Boze Hadleigh's *Hollywood Lesbians* was published by Barricade Books. A picture of Dennis appears on the cover, which features images of the ten ladies interviewed. The others are Barbara Stanwyck, Marjorie Main, Nancy Culp, Patsy Kelly, Agnes Moorehead, Edith Head, Dorothy Arzner, Capucine, and Judith Anderson.

In his introduction, Hadleigh says he had sent copies of his previous book, *Conversations with My Elders*, a collection of interviews with gay men of film, to some of the actresses in *Hollywood Lesbians*. He claims Dennis relished *Conversations with My Elders*. He says she was a friend before he formally interviewed her for the book, and he had met her through writer Robert La Guardia.

Hadleigh doesn't specifically name her as a lesbian, and neither does she in her interview with him. He says associates reported that Dennis was asexual. She confesses that she had had affairs with both men and women. When he questions her use of "they" when she asks about lesbians, she responds with giggles and puts her finger to her lips. Read into that what you may.

Dennis tells Hadleigh about how she was once asked by a lesbian gossip columnist if she was lesbian or bi. She says she found the question intimate and personal, and thought, "Who is she to ask me this and expect me to tell her." Dennis also pointed out the irony of the question, coming from the columnist who, Dennis said, "was always denying it herself, even though she lives with ... It's ... augh!"

The interview also has her commenting on the changing nature of her stardom: "I went from supporting roles into being the main event, and then to supporting roles again. They'll offer me a nothing role, and they seriously expect me to take it. I should be grateful, right?" She continues, "If I hadn't gone from supporting to something bigger, it wouldn't be like this. I could work more." Hadleigh also records Dennis' repeated use of the word "Ow" as an interjection.

In 1997, *Sandy Dennis: A Personal Memoir* was released by Papier-Mache Press and copyrighted to the Estate of Sandra Dale Dennis. In honor of her compassion for homeless animals and the comfort they provide to people, Papier-Mache donated a portion of the proceeds from the book's sale to Delta Society — people helping animals and animals helping people. Small, at seventy-seven pages, the book was co-edited by Louise Ladd and Doug Taylor, and featured the foreword by Joanne Woodward.

Doug Taylor also wrote an introduction. Woodward describes Dennis' writing as having "an almost Emily Dickensian sensibility," and comments on her elegant and dainty sense of humor. Woodward also relates to Dennis' relationship with cats, since Woodward too likes cats. Doug Taylor is a playwright, actor, and director. He had played opposite Dennis in *Same Time, Next Year*, and they took turns directing each other. Taylor would also direct a one-act play based on the memoirs, entitled *Images Stored in Dusty Places*, at the Hastings Community Theatre.

In his introduction, Taylor tells how he had been a friend of Dennis' for thirty years. He had met her at a prerehearsal gathering for her first major Broadway role. This was presumably 1962 and the play was *A Thousand Clowns*. He was at the apartment of Barbara Baxley, who was to become his wife and who had played Dennis' mother in the national tour of *The Dark at the Top of the Stairs*.

Dennis had come to Baxley to borrow a dress, and Taylor saw how she dressed in clothes that did little to enhance her attractiveness. She also wore no makeup, and her hair was ill-kempt. However, when she emerged wearing a black form-fitting wool dress, Taylor saw a transformation. To Taylor's regret, she would choose a more sedate two-piece almond outfit with a pleated skirt to wear instead.

Taylor writes about going to Dennis' empty house after her death and finding in a manila folder a chapter of her manuscript in the bottom drawer of a file cabinet. The pages were handwritten on yellow, legal-sized notepaper. He doesn't remember when she had first told him she was writing a book, only when she had commented in her house one day, "I've been writing." Taylor assumed she had planned to publish a book of photographs she had taken. But she corrected him by saying it was a book.

Dennis let him read the two chapters she had completed, and after he did, Taylor proposed sending them to a literary agent. However, she wanted to finish more chapters first. She was apparently a slow writer and had given the new chapters to a friend of hers to type. As the friend had gone away, Dennis was prepared to wait for the pages. Taylor found the completed manuscript when he searched deeper into the cabinet drawers.

After sending it to professional writer and editor Louse Ladd, it was then forwarded to her agent, Mary Jack Wald. Louise Ladd was also an actress and had been directed by Dennis in a female version of *The Odd Couple*. Wald encouraged the manuscript be submitted to publishers, and after five years it was finally published on April 27, 1997. This would have been her sixtieth birthday.

The twelve chapters describe moments in Dennis' life: childhood memories, dreams, her love of cats and other animals, repeated encounters with death, her family, falling in love, and her own mortality once she was diagnosed with cancer. There is also some mention of her career: her fondness for one stage set of an unnamed show, her admiration of an unnamed actress, and tap dance classes and a recital she was removed from as a child. Additionally, Gerry Mulligan and Eric Roberts are named in passing (first names only).

In "Circle of Soft Light" Dennis writes about her forty cats, how she obtained some, and the household damage they could cause. For instance, Paula Carlene had been found as a kitten eleven years prior during a hurricane outside a hotel room in Florida. When Dennis moved to an apartment that had been prepared for her for her ten-week stay, she would eventually acquire eight cats. Another of these felines she would name Momma. Yet another cat was found tied securely in a heavy nylon laundry bag in a dumpster and rescued.

While in Florida she says she made a plea for neutering and spaying cats on a local TV interview show. A note was later left for her which read, "Put your money where your mouth is." Other cats mentioned are Mary Frances, Bonnie, and Octavia. So is her golden retriever, Lady.

In the chapter titled "Unreserved Love," Dennis tells how she always awakens between three and four every morning. She writes about playing the radio for company in the first room she did not have to share in a house in Nebraska. She remembers 1941 when she was age four, when her family moved house. She also remembers how the new house brought Skippy the dog, and the Fourth of July picnic at Crystal Lake. The chapter also covers the death of the aged dog.

In "Thirty-Seven Acres of Woods" she writes about a house she lived in for fourteen years, twenty-two years ago. Her theater dresser, Mary, came to live with her in the house for fifteen years as a housekeeper and her "hook on the world." Dennis admits that Mary was the only person she loved without reservation, and that Mary left her before the actress died.

In "Days of Promise" Dennis recalls her first memories of her father (returning a baby bird to its nest in a tree) and sticking her brother's beebees up her nose. She also recalls the deaths of her Aunt Adrienne, Uncle George, her grandmother, and her grandfather when she was thirteen.

In the chapter "When Colors Ache," Dennis writes about her cats Gabby and Willis. They and she and the two dogs Lady and Billy all walk through the destroyed woods in the spring. The land is being cleared so that new houses can be built, and she cries. She recalls doing a play when she was young with a set that was a Midwestern house in the 1920s. Dennis says she did the play for over a year, so it is presumably *The Dark at the Top of the Stairs*.

She met a man whom she fell in love with and stayed in love for many years. She writes that she spent three years of her life in the theater on 45th Street, where at nineteen she stood in the back of the audience and watched an actress who took her breath away. The actress would become her friend. When the set was emptied at the end of the run of the first play, Dennis cried for the loss of the house, as she would cry over the disappearance of the trees.

In "The House I Never Left" she describes the summer when she was four and the family moved forty miles from the town where she was born. She moved to a house she says she lived in until her death.

In "Saint-Malo," it is May 1974, and Dennis is in a hotel with Gerry Mulligan in France. This chapter includes an italicized section written in the third person. It is autumn and the couple described having previously been in Stockholm. Now the woman knows their violent relationship must end, although not for a few more years.

In "The Laura Ashley Lady" she works in her garden at six-thirty in the morning, accompanied by her dog Lady and later some of her cats. We learn Dennis has a niece named Pam. She recalls a fall day in Denmark when she saw the remains of a burial boat, and the natural history museum in her home town that held Indian remains. Years later in England she visited a museum and laughed at the carefully labeled specimen of petrified dog feces.

In her garden Dennis imagines herself as a Laura Ashley lady, although she is dressed in tennis shoes, sweatpants and a ragged t-shirt. She picks flowers. Then, when the noise of the trucks and wood chewers start, she retreats to the lawn at the back of her house. In the garden that used to be there she grew pumpkins. Eric (presumably Eric Roberts) grew sunflowers. Then Dennis recalls the slaughter of the birds by her cats. She waved her arms and screamed obscenities at the cats, but to no avail. Her house seemed to fill with the dead and the half-dead, with flapping wings and hooded eyes.

In "Then I Will Remember" she finds a dead cat on the road and buries it in her backyard garden. She recalls the other pets she has buried — Little Boy and her sister Little Girl, Bobbie, Octavia, Eric's kittens.

In "From These Windows" she reports she is writing again after months of inactivity. She identifies herself as age fifty-two, making the time of writing the fall of 1989. She ponders her secret nature.

She knows she is dying of ovarian cancer, and she had been previously bedbound for a month from her illness, but she also knows it is not yet time to go. She isn't afraid and doesn't want to die before finishing things. She reports that she is due to have another operation in November and then more chemotherapy.

In the last chapter, "Another Spring," it is April. Dennis is bedbound again and has a colostomy bag. She reports she has a great map of scars and holes across her stomach from the surgeries. She writes of her blind cat Jake, who came to her last fall. She thinks there is a strong possibility she will escape death, although she wants to explore her feelings about it rather than hide from them as she has been doing.

At the end of the chapter is written her name as if in her handwriting. In the first "S" is drawn the eyes, mouth, whiskers and ears of a cat.

The book's cover is a photograph of Dennis with a cat on her shoulder taken by Marianne Barcellona for the 1989 *People* magazine article. Inside are other undated photographs of her taken by Walton C. Ferris Sr. and Chandler Davis, and one taken at St. Vincent's Medical Center (where she is surrounded by women in clown costumes). There are childhood photographs courtesy of Frank Dennis, more from *People* magazine, and some from the UPI/Corbis-Bettman Archive. Doug Taylor reports that he could find few pictures of Dennis offstage in her files or anywhere in her house. However, he did find portraits of her as a child in her mother's room, in the back of an otherwise empty drawer.

In *Publishers Weekly* on April 28, 1997, the book was reviewed as "Lovely and unexpected ... apart from the occasional amateurish touch, Dennis reveals herself as a gifted natural writer." For *Western North Carolina Woman*, Kerry Lee Daniel wrote that the book was "lyrical, poetic and often funny." Daniel also writes that she met Dennis in 1969, and that her performance in *The Fox* helped Daniel come out as a lesbian.

Hoping to write an article on her, Daniel found the actress listed in the Westport, Connecticut, telephone book. She spoke to Dennis' mother, who told her she was out of the country, and Yvonne Dennis invited Daniel to visit. Daniel spent time with Yvonne and the menagerie of cats. The next year, when Daniel was visiting her aunt and uncle who also lived in Westport, she dropped by the house and saw Dennis, who came outside to see whose car had parked.

Sandy had been told by her mother about Daniel's visit, and Daniel was invited to visit for the weekend. Daniel wrote, "I observed her gestures and halting speech patterns, amazed at how much the real life Sandy Dennis resembled the characters she played. Or was it the other way around?" Daniel had a hunch that the actress had won acting prizes by being herself. She also wrote that while she knew many critics found the mannerisms annoying, Daniel loved the quirkiness. "It was part of her charm." The writer said after that weekend she stayed in touch with Dennis, eventually spending another weekend at her home. However, she was shocked to hear of her death on the radio.

The book was also reviewed from an animal lover's perspective on the website *Animal People* in July 1997. Approaching the book "with the skepticism of an old cat toward a new dog," the reviewer concluded, "Cats seem to have interested Dennis far more than either her distinguished stage career or her personal relationships, which she keeps remarkably discreet. Though this is indeed a highly personal memoir, cats are the only creatures Dennis kissed and told about."

In 2007 a film was released entitled *Confessions of a Superhero*. This was a documentary by Matt Ogens about Hollywood street characters who pose for photographs with tourists in the forecourt of Grauman's Chinese Theatre on Hollywood Boulevard. One of its subjects was Christopher Lloyd Dennis, who claims to be the son of the actress and dresses as Superman. Ogens questions Frank Dennis, niece Pam and her husband Ryk about the claim. Pam and Ryk deny it is true, while Frank remains silent. Christopher Dennis' claim that he was told by his mother on her deathbed to pursue acting is also denied by Pam.

Ogens' documentary shows Sandy Dennis' burial place, as well as scenes from *The Out of Towners*, specifically the one in which she and Jack Lemmon find a lost boy in Central Park. This scene is juxtaposed with Christopher Dennis talking about how he was a "wild child." He says his mother placed him in shelters and group homes, and put him up for adoption when he was seventeen, and that he was disassociated from his birth family.

He does not identify his father, only saying the man was not married to his mother. This may be a reference to Gerry Mulligan, whom Christopher Dennis actually resembles. Ogens confronts Christopher with the notion that people have denied his claim, but he defends it by saying his mother was a private person. Amusingly, Christopher goes on to tell Ogens how he had to stop taking drugs when he was young because it made him delusional.

A six-foot-four lanky man who is an aspiring actor, Christopher Dennis says he was born in Los Angeles (although his age is not disclosed). He is presented as a sweet person and not as aggressive about getting paid tips for being photographed like others, some of whom get into trouble with the police over it. There is irony in Ogens showing Christopher Dennis' psychology student girlfriend, Bonnie, who will become his wife at the end of the documentary. Bonnie, with her blinking eyes and odd manner, resembles Sandy Dennis more than Christopher does; he looks more like Christopher Reeve, which he trades on.

In 2005 The Sandy Dennis Foundation was founded, with a mission to "memorialize the accomplishments of the late Sandy Dennis, to perpetuate her commitment to education and the performing arts, to promote cultural activities, and to encourage theatrical education, performances, and professionals." The website devotes pages to Dennis' film, theater and television work, and provides photos and actors' memories of the star.

On October 29, 2012, Louis Virtel on the website *AfterElton* wrote an article entitled "Which Pop Culture 'Sandy' Should Be the Face of Hurricane Sandy?" After Sandra Bullock, Sandy Denny, Sandy Ollson from *Grease* (Olivia Newton-John), and Sandy Duncan, Sandy Dennis was chosen as the number one candidate. Virtel would write that was because "She IS a hurricane. And her most famous line of dialogue (from *Who's Afraid of Virginia Woolf?*) is itself the goal of any noble hurricane: "Violence! Violence!"

He noted that "everything about Sandy Dennis is hurricane-worthy," and asked us to consider the following facts. She is a blustery, brandy-powered whirlwind in *Who's Afraid of Virginia Woolf?* She has a torrid lesbian affair that ends with devastation in *The Fox*. She even gets all wet with Jack Lemmon in *The Out of Towners*. She oozes anxious energy (like all good weather phenomena). And she is mad enough to be the biggest self-declared celebrity cat lady of all time.

Hurricane Sandy devastated portions of the Caribbean, mid–Atlantic, and Northeastern United States, and resulted in two-hundred-and-fifty-three fatalities. While the idea of comparing the impact of Hollywood actresses to a tropical cyclone may be seen as trivializing a natural disaster, it does demonstrate that Sandy Dennis is not completely forgotten, at least by Hollywood bloggers.

THE FILMS

Splendor in the Grass (1961)

CREW: Warner Bros. Pictures presents an Elia Kazan Production for Newton Productions, Inc. Elia Kazan (Director); William Inge, Charles H. Maguire (Associate Producers); William Inge (Screenplay); Boris Kaufman (Photography); David Amram (Music); Gene Milford (Editor); Richard Sylbert (Production Design); Anna Hill Johnstone (Costumes); Edward Johnstone, Richard Vorisek (Sound); Gene Callahan (Set Decorator); George Tapps (Choreographer); Robert Jiras (Makeup); Willis Hanchett (Hair). Filmed on location at Staten Island, Long Island, High Falls, and Horace Mann High School, Riverdale, and at the Filmway Studios from April to August 1960. Color, 119 minutes.

CAST: Natalie Wood (Wilma "Deanie" Loomis); Pat Hingle (Ace Stamper); Audrey Christie (Mrs. Freda Loomis); Barbara Loden (Virginia "Ginny" Stamper); Zohra Lampert (Angelina); Warren Beatty (Bud Stamper); Fred Stewart (Del Loomis); Joanna Roos (Mrs. Stamper); John McGovern (Doc Smiley); Jan Norris (Juanita Howard); Martine Bartlett (Miss Metcalf); Gary Lockwood (Allen "Toots" Tuttle); Sandy Dennis (Kay); Crystal Field (Hazel); Marla Adams (June); Lynn Loring (Carolyn); Phyllis Diller (Texas Guinan); Sean Garrison (Glenn). Uncredited: Jim Antonio, Lou Antonio (Oil Field Workers at Party); Godfrey Cambridge (Chauffeur); Carlos Cortés; Robert Downing; Andrew Duggan (Trailer Narrator); Ivor Francis (Doctor Judd); Hoke Howell; William Inge (Reverend Whitman); Phoebe Mackay (Maid); Charles Matthews; Charles Robinson (Johnny Masterson); Eugene Roche (Private Detective); Mark Slade (Rusty).

SYNOPSIS: In 1928 in Southeast Kansas, high school students Wilma "Deanie" Loomis and Bud Stamper are in love, but Deanie is unwilling to give up her virginity. Bud breaks up with Deanie and has sex with her classmate, Juanita Howard. When Deanie learns what Bud has done, she has a mental breakdown. She goes to the school dance and offers herself to Bud. He rejects her, and she tries to drown herself. She is sent to an asylum, and Bud goes to Yale. Two years later, Deanie is released from the asylum and visits Bud, who is now married and runs a cattle ranch. Deanie leaves to marry Johnny Masterson and live in Chicago.

NOTES: This overlong and overblown movie marks Dennis' feature film debut. Playing the supporting part of Kay, she appears in eight scenes but has little dialogue. Her performance is free of most of the later mannerisms she'd become known for, although she does employ her buck-toothed smile here.

Her best scene is perhaps the Bon Voyage Grads dance sequence, which is the last time we see her in the narrative. She dances with Bud, and the act is informed by her previous scene. Kay, Hazel and June look out of the school classroom window. Kay states, "I don't care if his father is making my folks rich, I hate Bud Stamper," after we see how Deanie is upset by the fact of Bud having had sex with Juanita. When Hazel tells her, "You'd take a date with him in a minute if he asked you," Kay replies, "I would not." To Hazel's further comment "Oh, you know you would," Kay says, "I absolutely would not." Her stance is seemingly confirmed when she sees Bud approaching the three girls and they all look to him. When he says "Hi," all three girls look away without answering. However, when we next see Kay with Bud at the dance, we see how her resolve has weakened.

Inge, however, redeems what can be viewed as Kay's hypocrisy by having her go to

Deanie when she sees her, with Kay asking Toots to dance with her so that Deanie can go to Bud. Kazan presents this with the camera on Dennis' back, providing a close-up of her only after she sees Deanie dancing with Bud to show Kay's feelings. However, a two-shot of Kay and Bud dancing prior to this reveals how happy Kay is that he is dancing with her.

Kay's first appearance has her walking down the school corridor behind Deanie. We then see her in class sitting with Hazel and June, and Kay smiles at Deanie being late for class (the rest of class laughs when Deanie is scolded for being late by Miss Metcalf). Kay breathes out in reaction to Miss Metcalf to express her dislike of her.

When the class discussion covers *The Knights of the Round Table* and Juanita says, "They looked on women as very pure," Kay comments, "They wouldn't look on her as very pure." This is a reference to Juanita as a bad girl, with her apparently dyed hair and flapper outfit, including beads and a headband. Juanita's introduction, in which she excuses herself to Bud in French, suggests that Juanita is more sophisticated than the other schoolgirls. A later scene will confirm the idea of Juanita as a "bad" girl when the boys in the shower room speak of her as being known for putting out. After Kay's outburst, Miss Metcalf warns that any more similar behavior will result in the culprit being sent to the principal, and we get a reaction shot of Kay looking afraid.

Kay is next seen at the New Year's Eve party. She tells Deanie and Bud that she has lost her date, Arnold, and asks Bud to look for him. Kazan frames Dennis in between Natalie Wood and Warren Beatty, but our view of her is obscured since in front of Kay is a toy oil tower with champagne gushing out of it. There is no follow-up to Bud's attempted search for Arnold, and Arnold as a character remains unidentified, which is an indication of how unimportant he is in the narrative. It follows that Kay's love life is equally unimportant, and her losing a boy that she had presumably come to the dance with is a confirmation of the idea of Kay being a plain and unwanted girl.

Kay is among the row of girls in the audience at Bud's basketball game. However, her next appearance is very interesting for her character. We see Deanie walk the

Poster for *Splendor in the Grass* (1961).

school corridor, saying hello to people. When she comes to the classroom door, we see Kay standing next to Juanita and another girl standing opposite them with her back to the camera. Since this comes after we know that Juanita has had sex with Bud, the emphasis is on Deanie's reaction. What is interesting is that Kay does not look at Deanie when she appears in the doorway. Deanie says hello to the opposite girl, perhaps not yet seeing Kay. In response, Kay says hello, perhaps thinking Deanie had spoken to her. Deanie seemingly ignores Kay's hello, and we see Kay's disappointment in being ignored.

Kay portrayed as a presumably good girl is an example of the sexual politics of the narrative, which hinges on whether Deanie is a good or bad girl. Freda Loomis expresses the sexual double standard when she tells Deanie, "Your father never laid a hand on me until we were married. Then I just gave in because a wife has to. A woman doesn't enjoy those things the way a man does. She just lets her husband come near her in order to have children." This comment is amusing in light of Freda's own situation, given how grotesque her husband Del has become. One reading of why Deanie has a mental breakdown is that she is too much of a good girl, and her mental problems stem from her sexual frustration. Bud is able to gain release from his sexual frustrations by having sex with the bad girl Juanita, since Deanie, as the good girl, refuses to have sex with him.

When Deanie wears a red flapper dress with garters to the Bon Voyage Grads dance for her date with Toots, she attempts to pass as a bad girl. Even her cutting her hair shorter can be read as an attempt to change her good girl image. Additionally, her trying to smoke at the dance is another attempt to present herself as a bad girl, since we have seen how Ginny smokes. When Deanie quickly discards the cigarette after Bud expresses his disapproval, it shows how smoking is against her true nature.

Deanie beckons Bud into a car with "I'm not a nice girl," although he doesn't believe her act. Deanie's decision to go with Toots is a reaction to Bud's rejection of her new persona, although Deanie will prove to be a nice girl after all when she rejects Toots at the waterfall. Inge actually complicates this moment by having Deanie call Toots "Bud" by mistake.

Bud's sister Ginny, ironically named Virginia, is also considered a bad girl since she has reportedly had an affair with a married man and had an abortion. Her appearance also clues us into her character since she dyes her hair, wears flapper clothes, smokes and drinks during prohibition. There is also the suggestion of incestuous feelings when she kisses her father on the lips at the New Year's Eve party. Ginny being a bad girl is also evident from the number of men she knows and kisses at the party, and the men who gather for the supposed gang-bang. Additionally, the wives of the married men are represented by one who is fat, which follows the presentation of older people as grotesques.

Freda confirms to Deanie that Ginny is a bad girl when she describes her as "boy crazy," and Kazan objectifies her twice by showing only her legs. Ginny is also defined as a bad girl by her choice of companions, whether it be the married man in Chicago, the gas station attendant Glenn (who is inarticulate but handsome), the married bootlegger Brian Stacey, and the married men she seems to know at the New Year's Eve party. Ginny is first seen with peroxided hair, then red-dyed hair for the Stamper family portrait (for which she stands provocatively with bottom sticking out while the others look dignified), and then back to peroxided blonde for the New Year's Eve Party. Ginny's bad girl stands in marked contrast to her mother, a plain woman who must have been a good girl and only had sex/children within the bounds of matrimony. Her relationship with her husband Ace is suggested by the unhappy looks she expresses and the look of contempt Ace gives his wife.

Bud choosing Angelina to marry implies that she is a good girl, though her being non–

American might exclude her from what may be an Anglo-centric whore/Madonna complex. It is possible that Bud slept with Angelina before they were married, but this remains conjectural. What is interesting is that, like the New York speakeasy dancer who resembles Deanie, Angelina also resembles Deanie in her hairstyle and comparative innocence.

Angelina being pregnant and the mother of another child, which we assume is Bud's, confirms that what we see at the film's conclusion is the resolution of his character's conflict. He now has a presumably satisfying sexual relationship, which is indicated by the kiss Bud gives Angelina after Deanie leaves. This conflict resolution also extends to his career path. Bud now lives on and works the cattle ranch that was his father's, and this has only come about after the death of Ace.

Juanita as a bad girl is given some conflicted feelings. When she is friendly to Bud, it is shown from Deanie's jealous point of view. We may not think that Juanita has genuine feelings for him, since she is dating Toots. It is her guilt feelings over seeing how disturbed Deanie is about the situation that has Juanita upset when Deanie runs out of the schoolroom.

At one point Miss Metcalf asks Deanie to explain the film's title in class, said to be from William Wordsworth's poem "Ode Intimations of Immortality (From Recollections of Early Childhood)." Deanie will again speak of it in the last scene when she leaves Bud. "Though nothing can bring back the hour of splendor in the grass, glory in the flower, we will grieve not; rather find strength in what remains behind."

We do not see Juanita again in the narrative, which is a shame, and Toots' interest in pursuing Deanie after Bud has broken up with her suggests how temporary the relationship between Toots and Juanita is.

The waterfall location for lovers is an interesting metaphor, and it is used more than once to show both the frustrated attempts at passion of Bud and Deanie, and that of Deanie and Toots. The phallic pipes we see at the waterfall location when Toots takes Deanie there underscore his sexual interest in her. It is also interesting that Deanie should use the waterfall lake in an attempt at suicide. This proves doubly ironic given Natalie Wood's known fear of water and her fateful death by drowning.

Apparently Wood had asked Kazan if she could do the scene in a controlled studio tank, but he assured her it was a very shallow lake and that her feet would always be close to the bottom. To assuage her fears, the associate producer, Charles H. Maguire, got into the water with her, just out of camera range. Kazan said that this didn't entirely reassure her, but that she did the scene and then clutched at Maguire. When she was back on dry land, Wood continued to shake with fear and then laugh hysterically with relief.

Ace having a crippled leg allows for Ace's projected desire for Bud to be an athlete. It also adds to Ace's aggression, whereby he doesn't listen when Bud tries to tell him what Bud wants for his life. This scene recalls the one between James Dean's Jim Stark and his father Frank (played by Jim Backus) in *Rebel Without a Cause* (1955, directed by Nicholas Ray) where Dean finally yells, "You're not listening to me!" The difference here is that Beatty's Bud doesn't get such an explosion, and Bud's frustrated speaking in light of Ace's constant interruptions reads as funny. Reportedly, Ace being a cripple stemmed from the fact that Pat Hingle had broken a hip and ankle after a fall down an elevator shaft prior to filming. Because Kazan wanted him for the part, it was incorporated into the character. Ace' perversity is also indicated by the smile on his face when he goes to the window of the hotel room from which he will jump after the stock market crash.

Kazan's direction of the film is uneven, but he offers some inventive touches. The performance of Pat Hingle as Ace is totally over-the-top, and there is humor in his battles with Ginny. The film's biggest laugh comes when Ace congratulates Reverend Whitman for a "Fine sermon" after we and the Reverend have seen how Ace has slept through it.

Making his film debut after false starts at Twentieth Century–Fox, Warners and MGM, Warren Beatty's performance is occasionally too self-consciously aping Marlon Brando and James Dean. In the scene where Ginny slaps Bud, Beatty's facial reaction is pure Brando, as he gives her a look of tolerated acceptance.

Two old women are shown watching Deanie and Bud at her house. The expression of the women is both jealous and judgmental, but the expectation of harmful gossip remains unfulfilled. However, a similar shot of three smiling Negro chauffeurs in the car park at the New Year's Eve party creates the expectation that Ginny will be gang-raped. The smiles of the three men suggest they know what is about to happen, and, being men, they are aroused by it. However, Ginny's reaction to the supposed gang-rape does not suggest that it was actually rape. We only see the suggestion that one man had been with her in the car where she is found by Bud, although it appears that this man is not Joe, whom Ginny had been kissing prior to being in the car.

Kazan begins the New Year's Eve party supposed gang-bang scene with the men gathering around Ginny, but regrettably uses an awful saxophone score to underline the sexual menace. What makes the score even more offensive is how it is not 1920s period music but rather 1950s jazz. The men following Ginny out to the car park continues the threat, but the expected group attack fails to materialize. Kazan again uses the awful saxophone music when Toots is in the car with Deanie at the waterfall.

Another scene carries a sexual connotation when Bud forces Deanie down to her knees, saying, "At my feet, slave." He tells her that he wants her to agree to "worship" him, to do anything he asks, and to tell him that she cannot live without him. However, the expectation of her delivering fellatio is not met, which is hardly surprising given the film was made in 1961.

Charles Robinson was cast as Johnny Masterston presumably because of his physical similarity to Beatty, so that Deanie's new romance with him harkens back to her love for Bud. The fact that Johnny should be in the asylum with Deanie makes him a less than ideal partner, especially since he too has daddy issues. It is noteworthy that we don't see him after he has been discharged.

The casting of Phyllis Diller as Texas Guinan in the New York speakeasy is disappointing, given that she only has one joke to deliver, though it is nice to see her in this milieu. Her character, as an aging flapper, is an interesting combination of bad girl and older grotesque.

The film is the only original screenplay that playwright William Inge wrote, and is said to be based on a story he heard in his past. Director Kazan would say that it is not one of his favorite films but that the last reel is his favorite last reel. He liked the ending for its bittersweet ambivalence, "that you have to accept limited happiness, because all happiness is limited, and that you must live with the sadness as well as with the joy."

A scene that was cut had Deanie jumping out of her bath after arguing with Freda and running nude down a hallway to her bedroom, with a shot of her bare legs kicking hysterically on the mattress. The scene was cut because the censors objected to the sight of Natalie Wood's bare backside. Another scene that apparently was excised was spoken about by Pat Hingle on September 21, 2006, when he gave a talk at the University of North Carolina, Wilmington. Hingle said it was included in the film's first edit but not in the final cut. He claims that Inge wrote the addition to the scene just for him, after Hingle expressed his disappointment that Ace would commit suicide. The cut scene has Ace getting the doll salesgirl from the New York speakeasy to go back to his room with him after Bud has left. Ace dictates a long suicide note about how Bud has never found happiness because he hasn't had the opportunity, since he's been following orders his entire life. Ace figures the only way to free his son so that he can make his life worthwhile is for Ace to kill himself. He opens the window and jumps out, curtains flapping slightly in the wind. The camera pans over to the bed, where the girl was taking down the note. She has fallen asleep, with only a couple of lines written on the page. Bud will never see the note explaining his father's true motive.

The silent movie that Bud, Toots and Rusty watch is *Glorious Betsy* (1928), and the actress seen in the film is Dolores Costello.

It is said that Natalie Wood initially didn't like working with Warren Beatty because she didn't think he bathed enough, something she supposed he did because scruffiness equaled Actors Studio authenticity. But then her opinion changed. When Wood remarried Robert J. Wagner in 1972, they named their yacht the *Splendour* in honor of the film, using the English spelling of "splendor" for the yacht as a symbolic gesture "to differentiate between then and now." The *Splendour* was the yacht the couple was on when Wood fell into the water and drowned off the coast of Catalina in 1981.

Diana Varsi was Kazan's first choice for the part of Deanie, but she was under contract to Twentieth Century–Fox and under suspension, and then left the movie business in March 1959 after a nervous breakdown. His second choice was Jane Fonda. In Ellis Amburn's biography of Beatty, *The Sexiest Man Alive*, the author claims that Daniel Petrie saw Fonda's test that she did with Beatty (Petrie would later direct Fonda in the made-for-TV movie *The Dollmaker*, 1984), and said that Fonda "looked like a female impersonator doing an impression of Henry Fonda." What Petrie was doing there is unknown, though presumably he was a friend of Kazan's since they were contemporaries as theater directors.

In her autobiography *My Life So Far*, Jane Fonda talks of the audition. She remembers how Kazan asked her if she thought herself ambitious before she did her piece. She thought that her answering no lost her the role. Fonda may have rationalized this answer as one that Deanie might have given, since good girls aren't supposed to be ambitious. Or perhaps she answered it as herself. But either way she could see that Kazan was not impressed.

Ellis Amburn claims that Carolyn Jones wanted the part of Deanie but was deemed unsuitable. Amburn says that Kazan also liked Lee Remick, who he had introduced in *A Face in the Crowd* (1957), but she was unavailable. Others sources state that Remick was tested but was considered too mature looking for the part, an assessment that was also made about Fonda.

William Inge suggested Natalie Wood. Sources differ as to whether Warner Bros. production chief Jack Warner wanted Wood for the role, since she too was on suspension at the time. Some say Warner offered Wood to Kazan at a discounted price because he considered her a liability at the time and wanted to turn her into an asset. Kazan supposedly thought of her as a "washed-up child star." Amburn says that Kazan thought Wood lacked the virginal aura he was after for the part. After he agreed to meet her he saw that she was "a restless chick who reminded me of the 'bad' girls in high school who looked like 'good' girls." Behind the well-mannered young wife, Kazan detected a desperate twinkle in her eyes. "I knew there was an unsatisfied hunger there. I became interested."

Other sources say that Warner supposedly tried to talk Kazan out of casting Wood, since Warner held a grudge against her for going on suspension. In his autobiography *Pieces of My Heart*, Robert Wagner says that Warner had cast Audrey Hepburn in *The Nun's Story* (1959) and Leslie Caron in the romance *Fanny* (1961) in roles that Wood should have played. Wagner says that Wood agreed to test for the role of Deanie, despite the fact that she was an established actress, and that secured her the part. In Gavin Lambert's book on Wood, he says that Warner preferred Diane McBain for the part. McBain was another Warners contract player, who had made her film debut in a supporting role in *Ice Palace* (1960). She was three years older than Wood and blonde, but not apparently to Kazan's liking.

For the role of Bud, actors considered included Dennis Hopper, Jody McCrea and Troy Donahue. Donahue was a Warner Bros. contract player, but in Robert Hofler's book about Donahue's agent Henry Wilson, Donahue is quoted as saying that Kazan refused to even meet with him. Inge suggested Beatty, whom he knew from his 1959 Broadway play *The Loss of Roses*, which would be filmed as *The Stripper*. Kazan would say that Beatty "was a little 'snotty'—I don't know a better word for how he behaved—but he was able to grow into a formidable man." According to one of the makeup artists, the crew found Beatty arrogant and didn't like him. He was given the nickname "Mental Anguish," or "M.A." for short, which crew members called him behind his back. In her book on Beatty, *A Private Man*, Suzanne Finstad writes that at the wrap party Kazan would give Beatty a hand mirror that said "Good God, Warren," a gag gift that was "self-explanatory."

Gavin Lambert claims that Wood pretended not to want to play Deanie because Warner wanted her to, since she knew Warner enjoyed ordering her into a movie she didn't want to make. Lambert says she even gave this impression to Kazan, refusing to test for the part but agreeing to an interview. She apparently came to the interview dressed unlike the way Deanie would dress to further her supposed stance, but Kazan saw through it.

Lambert reports that the film's starting date of the second week of March 1960 had to be postponed due to a Screen Actors Guild strike and that the new date was scheduled six weeks later. Warner took advantage of the strike, by suspending all his contract players, including Wood, for the duration. This negated the need for them to be paid. Robert Wagner's contract with Twentieth Century–Fox was not renewed at the time, which allowed him to stay with Wood.

One of Kazan's assistants was Mart Crowley, whose job it was to pick up Wood every day she was on call and drive her to the set. This began a life-long friendship between the two. Crowley would later achieve fame as the writer of *The Boys in the Band*, which had a successful Broadway run and then was filmed in 1970. Wood would employ Crowley as her secretary and have him move into her house.

According to Lambert, Beatty's fiancée, Joan Collins, was also on the set watching Beatty before she had to leave for Italy to make *Esther and the King* (1960).

Lambert says that Kazan's one problem with Wood came when she insisted on having MGM hairdresser Sydney Guilaroff style her hair. This is something Kazan would say was an occasion of the movie star "overtaking" the actress. Interestingly, Guilaroff receives no screen credit for his work.

Ellis Amburn claims that Kazan told Beatty that he didn't need to re-watch his screen test after filming it. He also reportedly told Beatty that he needed him to help him direct the movie, which presumably was Kazan's way of pandering to an actor. Amburn says that Beatty was known as one of "Inge's boys," an able-bodied and ambitious actor whom Inge desired and consequently promoted. The writer does not claim that Beatty slept with Inge, though he does say that Inge was known as "Warren's fairy godfather."

Amburn labels Beatty's role as "gay material," a paradox in light of his reputation for voracious heterosexuality. The idea that the sexual frustration of Deanie and Bud reflects that of Inge's "personal agony as a gay man forbidden by society to live according to his natural instincts" is perhaps a stretch. Furthermore, the notion that Inge was channeling homosexual angst into a mainstream heterosexual plot mirrors the mentality of other gay playwrights, like Tennessee Williams and Edward Albee, who inserted coded gay characters into works like *A Streetcar Named Desire* and *Who's Afraid of Virginia Wolf?* Beatty is quoted as saying as filming began, "I'm a bit scared and worried, but I'd try anything involving Bill and Gadge," (Gadge being Kazan's nickname).

Amburn also claimed that Beatty was not nominated for an Academy Award for the film because Warner preferred to put him up for Best Supporting Actor for his performance in *The Roman Spring of Mrs. Stone* (1961). Warner did so to help boost the box office of the latter title, but the decision turned out to be a tactical error, since Beatty would not score the nomination. Amburn states that Beatty was so angry at being relegated to the supporting actor position that he said he informed the Academy that he would reject the nomination if offered. This attitude would not have been appreciated from an actor in his first film role, who should have been grateful for any nomination.

In Peter Biskind's book *Star: How Warren Beatty Seduced America*, he quotes Barbara Loden saying that Beatty and Wood were jealous of each other, since each thought the other was receiving more attention from the director. She also said that Kazan was worried that the coldness between the two leads was affecting their love scenes. Kazan reportedly told Beatty, "Pretend it's Joan."

In Richard Schickel's biography of Kazan, Schickel claims that Beatty's casting was questioned by Kazan when the director saw a silent screen test Beatty had done with Jane Fonda, which was considered awful. Kazan agreed to let Beatty shoot a second test, which was more successful. Schickel also quotes Beatty saying that he had the impression that Kazan "didn't like good looking guys," which led to a rocky start. Beatty seemingly objected to Kazan's "more fussy" direction of Wood, not thinking that perhaps she may have needed more help than he. Beatty also objected to the fact that Kazan barred him from watching dailies. Kazan rationalized this dictum by saying that Beatty needed to avoid "negatives" that doing so might create.

Schickel also tells the story of how one day on set Kazan made a comment that Beatty didn't like, and Beatty replied with, "Why did you name all those names?" Kazan was shocked, but Beatty repeated the question. Beatty is quoted as saying, "It was my testosteronic desire to confront him." Kazan apparently grabbed Beatty by the arm and conducted him up three flights of stairs to Beatty's dressing room. There Kazan sat the actor down and proceeded to give his reasons. Beatty says he wasn't much interested in why, but he was impressed by the time Kazan took to offer his reasons, and the director's earnestness won him over. Beatty's comment about Kazan naming names refers to how the filmmaker, on April 11, 1952, was a cooperative witness before the House on Un-American Activities Committee and named seventeen people as communists, an act which cost him many friends in the theater and film business.

RELEASE: October 10, 1961, with the taglines "A LOVE STORY UNLIKE ANY OTHERS!!," "Its unrelenting moments, Its tragedies and splendors!" and "There is a miracle in being young ... and a fear."

REVIEWS: The picture was critically acclaimed by Bosley Crowther in *The New York Times* (October 11, 1961), *Time* magazine (October 13, 1961), and *Variety* (December 31, 1961). Pauline

Kael, in *5001 Nights at the Movies*, described it as a "Baroque primer–Freud" and "the old corn, fermented in a new way." Dennis was not mentioned in reviews.

AWARDS: William Inge (Best Screenplay Academy Award), Natalie Wood (Best Actress Academy Award nomination).

REMAKE: The film would be remade as a made-for-TV movie, directed by Richard C. Sarafian and broadcast by NBC on October 26, 1981. It starred Melissa Gilbert as Deanie, Cyril O'Reilly as Bud, Ned Beatty as Ace, Eva Marie Saint as Freda, Michelle Pfeiffer as Ginny, and Lenora May as Kay. The remake is not commercially available.

DVD: Released by Warner Home Video on February 3, 2009.

The Three Sisters (1966)

The Actors Studio/Commonwealth United Entertainment (uncredited).

CREW: The Actors Studio Theatre in association with Ely Landau Presents. As Staged for the Actors Studio Theatre on Broadway by Lee Strasberg. Paul Bogart (Director), Ely Landau (Producer), Randall Jarrell (New English Version), Will Steven Armstrong (Scenic Design), Theoni V. Aldredge, Ray Diffen (Costumes), Charles Reinhard (Photography), Lee Baygan (Makeup), Ben Berenberg (English lyrics for Russian songs), Gino Lombardo (Sound). Produced at Videotape Center, Black & White, 169 minutes.

CAST: Luther Adler (Chebutykin, Ivan Romanovich), Tamara Daykarhanova (Anfisa), Sandy Dennis (Irina Sergeyevna Prozorova), Gerald Hiken (Andrei Sergeyevich Prozorov), Robert Loggia (Solyoni, Vasili Vasilevich), Salem Ludwig (Ferapont), Kevin McCarthy (Vershinin, Alexander Ignatevich), James Olson (Tuzenbach, Nicholai Lvovich, Baron), Geraldine Page (Olga Sergeyevna Prozorova), Albert Paulsen (Kulygin, Fyodor Illich), Kim Stanley (Masha, aka Maria Sergeyevna Kulygina), Shelley Winters (Natasha, aka Natalia Ivanovna), Bill Burns (Carnival Character), John Harkins (Fedotik, Alexia Petrovich), Marcia Haufrect (Gypsy), Janice Mars (Maid and Street Musician), Mary Mercer (Maid and Carnival Character), Brooks Morton (Adjutant and Street Musician), David Paulsen (Rode, Vladimir Karlovich), Delos Smith (Officer and Bear), James Tolkan (Officer and Carnival Character), Nadyne Turney (Maid and Gypsy).

SYNOPSIS: Russia, May 1897. Olga, Masha, and Irina, the Prozorova sisters from Moscow, are living in a provincial town. It is Irina's twentieth birthday, and relatives and friends gather for a lunch. Eighteen months later it is winter and Carnival Week. Andrei Prozorova is married to Natasha. The married Masha and Lieutenant Colonel Vershinin are lovers. Solyony declares his love to Irina, but she rejects him. In spring two years later there has been a fire in the town. Baron Tuzenback proposes to Irina, and she accepts. In the fall Natasha has moved all the sisters out of their house. Solyony kills the Baron in a duel, but Irina still plans to leave town. The army departing for war causes Vershinin to leave Masha. The three sisters stand together for the last time and question life's sufferings.

NOTES: Dennis' second film appearance has the patina of a filmed Broadway play; however, this archival recording is a mixed blessing. While it captures a sense of the Actors Studio stage production, it also reveals their worst excesses in terms of ensemble performances. One must make allowances for the period technology and the budget, which limits the action to set-bound activity even when it uses the pretext of a backyard and woodland. However, director Paul Bogart is largely unsuccessful in terms of having the actors pull back their theatrical performances to deliver more naturalistic ones. Most of them appear to be yelling as if still projecting to the back row of the theater, and background activity occasionally upstages what is happening in the foreground (e.g., before lunch in Act 1 when people are talking at the table as Tuzenbach speaks with Irina, and in Act 2 when singing upstages the dialogue between Masha and Vershinin). At a running time of nearly three hours, this provides mostly tedious viewing with only momentary interest.

A blonde Dennis appears in Act 1 with her hair pulled back off her forehead but loose in the back. She is dressed in white, as opposed to Geraldine Page and Kim Stanley, who are dressed in black. In Act 2 Dennis appears with her hair piled up after Irina returns from work, and then wears a grey shawl for the remainder of the act. She wears a white shawl in Act 3, and loose strands of hair hang about her face when she enters (as if disheveled). The act ends with her hair loose when she is in bed. In Act 4 Dennis wears a white blouse and black skirt, and her hair is up again.

A still from *The Three Sisters* (1966). Standing are Masha (Kim Stanley, left) and Olga (Geraldine Page). Irina (Dennis) is seated (Photofest).

She uses her mannerisms here — smiling and laughing, touching her mouth, pointing and gesturing, stuttering, tongue-poking, eye-blinking, and head-nodding. Among the general ensemble, her Irina arranges a vase of flowers as Olga talks, laughs with Chebutykn and declares how she wants to work, teases Andrei about being a violinist lover, and tells Tuzenbach how unhappy all the sisters are. This last moment has Irina admitting she is crying, although Dennis sheds no apparent tears. She *does* supply tears for Act 4, however, when Irina hears of the death of the Baron.

Her best moments come in Act 2 when Solyoni declares his love for Irina, and Dennis expresses Irina's rejection by employing a stillness as she listens; and in Act 4 when she tells how she accepted the Baron's proposal since she knows she is no longer fated to go to Moscow. This acceptance is a turnaround from her reaction in Act 3, where Dennis goes into mannerism overdrive, gasping for breath as if having a nervous breakdown.

Kim Stanley gives perhaps the best of the three sister performances, since she supplies spurts of anger and emotion. It is fascinating to compare the mannerisms that the three female leads employ, though perhaps a bit unfair to draw comparisons between Stanley's mature acting and Dennis' novice, with Page's Olga hardly making any impression at all. What distinguishes Stanley from Page and Dennis is that she doesn't break up her sentences. Rather, she uses a deeper voice and an English-sounding accent for her enunciation. However, it is also apparent that Stanley employs a very mannered laugh and her crying in Act 4 over the leaving of Vershinin remains unconvincing. Stanley's scene with McCarthy in Act 2 displays the genuineness of feeling between Masha and Vershinin. Kevin McCarthy seems to be the best at speaking in a more naturalistic way.

Shelley Winters also uses a murmuring mannerism to express Natasha's insecurity in Act 1, and also in Act 3 for Natasha's distress at the fire. She benefits from getting to assay the play's most interesting character. It's funny that actresses tend to regard Masha as the most desirable part, since Natasha seems to be a more active character than any of the three passive sisters.

In Jon Krampner's book *Female Brando: The Legend of Kim Stanley*, he writes of the making of the film. He reports that both Kim and Shelley Winters were difficult. Kim would not come to rehearsals, and when she did she would express her dislike of some of the other actors, specifically Kevin McCarthy. This was a problem, given the romance between their characters Masha and Vershinin. She was also self-conscious and pained about her weight gain, which in itself could be contextualized by the woman of the period she was playing. She wore a corset, but it didn't help; and a shawl she was given to wear upset her (because of its obfuscating purpose).

Director Paul Bogart had trouble with Shelley's New York vocal intonations, and demonstrated an insensitivity to "status distinctions" when Shelley voiced her objection to not being asked to watch footage shot, while Kim Stanley and Geraldine Page were. Bogart is quoted as saying after a while he couldn't wait to get it over with. "If you watch it, you can see that Act 1 is very carefully made, Act 2 is a little less so, Act 3 even less so, and Act 4 is 'Hurry up, let's get out of here.'"

The Actors Studio production company had previously produced a TV show entitled *The Actors Studio*, making episodes from 1948 to 1950, and would go on to create the TV show *Inside the Actors Studio*, but *The Three Sisters* was the only film the company would produce. The production company Commonwealth United Entertainment would also present Sandy's film *That Cold Day in the Park* (1969).

RELEASE: Reportedly, it received a premiere in 1966, but not a general release until June 30, 1977. In her interview with Rex Reed on June 19, 1966, in *The New York Times*, Dennis said that the delay in the release of the film was due to Seven Arts, with whom she had signed a contract to make films but had not approved her making this one.

REVIEWS: *The Three Sisters* was critically lambasted by George Gent in *The New York Times* on January 20, 1968, and then Vincent Canby in *The New York Times* on June 30, 1977. Gent would write that "Miss Dennis was embarrassingly disconcerting with her overly familiar mannerisms of speech and hand-waving." Canby would say, "Dennis acts as if she were afraid her upper teeth were going to pop out. The recurring gesture of a hand reaching up to the mouth evokes not emotional desperation but severe orthodontic panic."

PRIOR PRODUCTIONS AND REMAKES: The play had been previously filmed many times for television, and there would be subsequent remakes as well. For instance, there was a 1964 Russian adaptation. Other versions include a British film directed by Laurence Olivier in 1970 and starring Joan Plowright as Masha, a French/Italian/German picture in 1988, a Hungarian adaptation in 1991, a Russian/American film in 1993 and a German/Russian movie in 1994. There was also an America film inspired by the play in 2005 entitled *The Sisters*.

DVD: Released on VHS by Hen's Tooth Video on July 15, 1997. Not available on DVD.

Who's Afraid of Virginia Woolf? (1966)

Warner Bros.

CREW: Mike Nichols (Director), Ernest Lehman (Producer/Screenwriter), Alex North (Music), Haskell Wexler (Photography), Sam O'Steen (Editor), Richard Sylbert (Production Design), George James Hopkins (Set Decoration), Irene Sharaff (Costumes), Gordon Bau (Makeup), Ron Berkeley (Mr. Burton's Makeup), Sydney Guilaroff (Miss Taylor's Hair), John Burt Reilly (Hair), M.A. Merrick (Sound). Uncredited: Wayne Fitzgerald (Titles), Herbert Ross (Choreographer). Black & White, 129 minutes. Filmed on location in Massachusetts and in Hollywood, from July 26, to December 13, 1965.

CAST: Elizabeth Taylor (Martha), Richard Burton (George), George Segal (Nick), Sandy Dennis (Honey). Uncredited: Agnes Flanagan (Roadhouse Waitress), Frank Flanagan (Roadhouse Manager).

SYNOPSIS: At the New England New Carthage College, associate history professor George and his wife invite the newly appointed biologist Nick and his wife Honey to their house for drinks. They will also entertain them with the parlor games "Humiliate the Host," "Get the Guests" and "Bringing Up Baby." Martha tells their guests of her sixteen-year-old child, and George seeks revenge on her. George reveals Nick's confided secret that he only married Honey because he got her pregnant, and that she had an abortion. Nick seduces Martha. George tells Martha that their son has died. Nick and Honey leave. It is revealed that the son is only a fiction and that Martha has lost tonight's games.

NOTES: Playing another supporting role, Dennis is juxtaposed with the less obviously mannered acting styles of the three other main actors, and, surprisingly, her mannerisms are less jarring here. Perhaps the company of such stars as Elizabeth Taylor and Richard Burton in an award-winning and much anticipated stage-to-screen adaptation adds to the pedigree of her appearance. And perhaps it is also the knowledge that Dennis would win the Best Supporting Actress Academy Award for her performance that makes a retrospective viewing of the film seem so special.

Her Honey is described (before she is seen) as "mousy" and "having no hips." The first comment alludes to her comparatively ordinary beauty, but the latter is undermined by the fact that Dennis is not slim-hipped. This may be due to her being pregnant at the time of filming, but it is not hidden by the shapeless dress she wears, particularly when she is shown to have wider hips than Martha in a shot with Dennis and Taylor together.

Nick describes Honey as "frail" and someone who "throws up easily," although her throwing up results from her drinking. Honey being the daughter of a preacher matches the persona of her as naïve, although she still had sex with Nick before marriage, with her supposed pregnancy being the reason he married her. The fact that it was an hysterical pregnancy adds to her persona, just as Nick marrying her as much for her money as for her being pregnant marks him as an opportunist.

Dennis is introduced with her dyed blonde hair pulled back from her forehead with a dark headband. Her hair is longer than we have seen it on screen before, halfway down her back. It will become gradually disheveled during the evening as Honey gets drunk. Dennis' performance will incorporate her standard mannerisms — stuttering, pointing and gesturing, smiling, eye closing, and head-nodding — as well as touching her chin and fiddling with her necklace. When all four go driving, Honey wears a headscarf. She will use the scarf to complement the

Poster for *Who's Afraid of Virginia Woolf?* (1966).

"interpretive" dancing she performs at the roadhouse where she "dances like the wind." Honey's hair is sans scarf and loose when she dances, and remains loose for the rest of the narrative.

Here, perhaps for the first time on television or film, Dennis is funny. When she tells George that Martha is changing her clothes because "I imagine she wants to be comfortable," and George yells, "You don't know!" Honey's fearful fleeing to Nick is comical. She is also funny when she is drunk and says, "I'd like another little nipper of Brandy, please," with her nodding her head as she says the line. Mike Nichols explains in his DVD audio commentary that "you need a comedienne for Honey, someone who is funny and annoying and still doesn't drive you crazy."

Honey's reaction to George asking if Martha has told her about their son goes from smiling to serious. Honey noticing Martha's hand on Nick's knee, as does George, expresses her jealousy. Honey laughs when Martha tells the boxing match story before screaming in reaction to George aiming his "umbrella gun" at Martha. Honey takes off her headband to let her hair loose when she asks the momentous question, "Where is your son?"

Honey, being drunk, creates context for Dennis' mannerisms, and we see her vulnerability when she says she is going to be sick from the drinking. She claps her hands in anticipation of the "violence" of George trying to stop Martha from telling the story of his novel, and also when George strangles Martha after she has told it. Dennis also expresses Honey's annoyance at Nick when he tries to stop her from dancing, and also when he tries to get her to leave the roadhouse during George's "get the guests" speech. She utters guttural cries along with "You couldn't have told them" when she realizes that Nick has told the story of her hysterical pregnancy (after George relays it as the plot of his alleged second novel). She looks vulnerable when George finds her lying in the back seat of the car parked at the house. Nichols repeats this image of Honey collapsed when she falls in front of George on the front yard. Regrettably, Nichols does not provide us with an image of Honey lying in the bathroom in what Nick describes as being similar to a fetal position.

When Honey is brought back for the final game, she hops in and carries the bottle Nick had said he had seen her drinking from earlier. When Martha talks about her son, Honey reacts by howling, "I want a child"— in opposition to her earlier proclaimed fear of childbirth. Honey expresses pain at the idea that George will tell Martha about the death of their son. Dennis supplies tears, as well as placing her hands over her ears when Martha screams in reaction to the news.

Honey is supposed to be inebriated as a reaction to the news of her false pregnancy being divulged to Martha and George. However, it is not clear whether she is aware that Nick has slept with Martha and is also upset about that. There is additional ambiguity about whether Nick has been successful in making love to Martha or whether he is the flop she has accused him of being because his potency has been affected by his drinking. The exit of Nick and Honey is presented in an arbitrary way by Nichols, since the focus is more on the shattered Martha and the victorious George.

Nichols manages to de-theatricalize the stage origins of the play somewhat by employing shock cuts, odd camera angles, hand-held camera work, out-of-focus effects, zooms (which were new to cinema technique), and extreme close-ups. The opening is lit like a horror movie, with a sense of foreboding, which the sad music undercuts. The horror movie theme is repeated in the scene of George, unseen, approaching the car before he opens the door to find Honey on the backseat.

In the DVD audio commentary, Nichols says that the opening shot of the moon was actually taken from a vampire movie, although other sources say it was from *The Letter* (1940). Nichols leaves the stagebound play behind when George and Nick walk outside the interior set to talk in the grounds in front of the house, when the foursome go to the roadhouse, and when Martha walks the grounds looking for George for an extraordinarily long three minutes as she "clinks."

Despite the Academy Awards bestowed upon Dennis and Taylor, it is Burton who gives the film's finest performance. He is the only one who makes us cry, in the scene when George realizes that Martha has slept with Nick. Burton's laughing that turns to crying is, of course, an actor's trick, but it is hard to do. He makes it work because we can feel the crying under the laughing from the beginning. Burton is believable as an academic, as is Taylor as a spoiled rich girl. He never takes a false step, and Nichols helps with the physicality that can make him seem stiff and awkward in other roles. Nichols also gives Burton the longest close-up in the film, a four-minute take for George's "bergin" speech. This is unlike the later four-minute take on Taylor for Martha's monologue about their son, which Nichols interrupts with cutaways.

Taylor's appearance as Martha may be a preview of her later real-life look, but here it reads as a façade, as much as her speaking voice and blowsy manner is a performance. The aging makeup is obviously makeup. Taylor's youthful beauty is still apparent underneath, despite the weight she reportedly gained for the part. The fright wig she wears looks like a wig, even given the context of 1960s hair styles.

Taylor uses her hands too much and over-stresses the swear words that were newly allowed in cinema. Worst of all, her Martha is so unpleasant that the role struggles against Taylor's natural likeability. This makes Martha barely funny, although Taylor does offer some good screams and impersonations. Equally, Martha's tears over the son's death and her anguish are undermined by Taylor's lack of empathy and the falseness of the situation.

The idea of George speaking Latin as Martha continues talking of their son is another theatrical contrivance that loses its impact on film. The overlapping dialogue reads as a period theatrical device that would only enter mainstream film style with Robert Altman in the late 1960s and 1970s.

Taylor and Burton seem comfortable with each other. This reveals the genuine feeling between the two characters, who will "exercise" their supposed hostility in the "games" they play during the evening, as much as it also reveals the comfort level of two actors who were a couple in real life.

George's warning to Martha about not doing "the bit about the kid" is the first reference to the plot point of their sixteen-year-old son. The idea that the boy is imaginary is one of Albee's worst theatrical devices he employees to reveal the psychological games of the couple who play with truth and illusion. George's defeat of Martha comes because he kills off the son without her permission, although it makes the drama seem like a hollow mind-game.

The play had been produced on Broadway at the Billy Rose Theatre and ran from October 13, 1962, to May 16, 1964. Directed by Alan Schneider, it starred Uta Hagen as Martha, Arthur Hill as George, George Grizzard as Nick, and Melinda Dillon as Honey. In the film's DVD special feature *A Daring Work of Raw Excellence*, Albee reports that his favorite review said, "This is a play that should be seen by dirty-minded women." The production would win Tonys for Best Play, Director, Actress, Actor and Supporting Actress. The play was selected for the 1963 Pulitzer Prize for Drama, but the Prize was withheld because of objections to the then-controversial use of profanity like "goddamn," "son-of-a-bitch," "screw you," "up yours," "great nipples," and "hump the hostess," as well as its sexual themes.

Producer Jack Warner purchased the rights to make the film version, although he had been warned that the play was unfilmable by the Motion Picture Production Code, which became the Motion Picture Association of America by 1966. Warner would bypass the Association's censorship by releasing the film with an adults-only warning that read "No one under 18 will be admitted unless accompanied by his parent." This strategy worked both to get around the Association and also to give the film added publicity.

Warner is said to have wanted Bette Davis and James Mason for the roles of Martha and George. In Shaun Considine's book *Bette & Joan: The Divine Feud*, Considine says Davis campaigned vigorously for the role. Davis is quoted as saying, "I must have it. I love those gutsy words. I told Mr. Albee that I would kill for the part." Davis said that when she heard Taylor had been given the role, "I really went into shock. Miss Taylor is a darling, but, my dear, they must be obviously making another picture." William J. Mann's book on Taylor quotes Mike Nichols on his concern over Taylor playing Martha: "It's like asking a chocolate milkshake to do the work of a double martini."

Other candidates for of Martha included Ingrid Bergman, Rosalind Russell and Patricia Neal, with Uta Hagen never even considered, despite her stage performance in the role. Mercedes McCambridge had been one of the Broadway replacements for Hagen onstage and reportedly sought the film part as well.

Hagen's George — Arthur Hill — was, however, in the running for the film, as well as stars like Cary Grant, Henry Fonda, and Peter O'Toole. In *A Daring Work of Raw Excellence*, Albee advises that Fonda was the first actor sought for the role of George, but that his agent refused to pass on the script to him. Glenn Ford is another actor that was said to have been offered the part but turned it down, feeling that it would ruin his career to play a henpecked, emasculated college professor.

Jack Lemmon was reportedly offered the role and accepted it, but then changed his mind the next day without giving any explanation. Some sources, however, claim that Lemmon was out of the running because his asking price was too high. Warren Beatty and Pamela Tiffin were considered for Nick and Honey. Connie Stevens, who was under contract to Warner at the time, reportedly sought the role of Honey, but Nichols wouldn't allow her to test for it.

Included on the Special Edition DVD are seven minutes of Dennis' screen test. It was directed by Irvin Kirshner and shot by Haskell Wexler, as indicated by the film slates shown. There are six takes of varying screen sizes, and in them all she wears the same costume — a sleeveless black dress with necklace — and her hair is held back at the front by a black headband.

She plays opposite Roddy McDowall in two scenes that are variations from the play. Honey dances for Nick and then tells him the story of how she had to introduce herself to people, which Honey tells Martha in the film. There is a third scene that does not appear in the play at all in which she asks him for a drink.

In close-up Honey tells Nick how she loves to drink Brandy. The dancing scene is shot in an extreme long shot as Nick plays a record of Beethoven's Symphony #7 in A major, op. 92, 2nd movement. She takes off her shoes and sings off-key as she dances. When he stops the music, she stops and points her hand at him, employing one of her standard hand gestures.

The next take is a medium shot in which she stops dancing after he stops the music. Dennis then points, laughs and smiles, with her eyes closing (more examples of her trademark mannerisms). The fourth take is a close-up of Honey telling the story of how she introduced herself. The fifth is a medium shot of her with Nick asking for a drink, and the sixth is an alternate take of the fourth close-up, though this time Dennis employees stuttering and word repetition.

Fred Zinnemann was the first director attached to the project, but he withdrew, reportedly preferring to make *A Man for All Seasons* (1966). Screenwriter Ernest Lehman was brought in for the screenplay adaptation, and he also insisted on being the producer. Lehman vetoed Warner's casting choices, preferring the more box office–savvy Taylor and Burton (although Taylor was twenty years too young for the part and Burton five years too old, according to Albee). According to *A Daring Work of Raw Excellence*, John Frankenheimer was also attached to the film, but Taylor had him removed because she wanted Nichols.

The book *Furious Love: Elizabeth Taylor, Richard Burton and the Marriage of a Century*, by Sam Kashner and Nancy Schoenberger, claims that after Zinnemann departed, Burton suggested Henri-Georges Clouzot. This idea was shot down by Taylor. She also reportedly objected to Frankenheimer because he insisted that his name appear above the title. In his book on Taylor, David Bret claims that she had wanted Frankenheimer, but that he would not work with Burton.

According to a 2005 interview with Edward Albee, Lehman hired himself to write the screenplay for two hundred and fifty thousand dollars. Albee says that when Nichols and Burton and Taylor read the script, they hated it. Unknown to Lehman, they changed all of the dialogue back to Albee's play, save two lines: "Hey, let's go to the roadhouse!" and "Hey, let's come back from the roadhouse!" Albee said, "Two lines for $250,000, $125,000 apiece. That's pretty good."

An article on the Turner Classic Movies database claims that Taylor had approved Arthur Hill to play George because Burton did not initially want the part. "Used to playing dashing and heroic characters, he was profoundly uncomfortable playing a wimp." However, when Burton he changed his mind, Hill was out, and Burton used his discomfort to add to the character's self-loathing. "He's not me, that moon-faced chap beaten down by a woman," the actor said.

In his book on Taylor, Alexander Walker quotes a letter Lehman wrote to Jack Warner after Taylor had told Lehman that she wanted Burton to play George. Lehman had told her that the production couldn't afford him. This was presumably after Elizabeth's 1.1 million dollar star salary. She would also receive ten percent of the gross and cast approval. Lehman also told Taylor that he thought Burton was "too strong" for the role, and that a Taylor/Burton film appeared "too rich." Taylor disagreed, saying that the role called for a great actor and one who could belt out great dialogue like no one else could. She felt Burton fit both criteria, as well as being able to suggest a man with intellectual depth.

Burton left it to Taylor to represent him because, thought Lehman, Burton was "overproud" to make a personal proposal, despite "itching" to play the part. Lehman conceded that casting Burton had the advantages of bringing in an important steadying influence on Taylor. Also, Lehman thought she would not be worrying where Burton was while she was filming. Lehman advised making the deal for Burton to Warner "if we can live with it." Warner agreed, and Burton was signed for seven-hundred-and-fifty-thousand dollars.

In *Furious Love* Lehman is quoted as saying that his decision to cast Burton was aided by the actor's appearance in *The Night of the Iguana* (1964). When he saw the lines around the block for that film, which starred Burton *without* Taylor, he imagined the lines around the block in every city of the world for a movie starring Burton *and* Taylor. The two had already appeared together in *The V.I.P.s* (1963), *Cleopatra* (1963), and *The Sandpiper* (1965), and all three films had been box office successes.

However, there was a problem with Taylor. She had initially taken a "disbiding dislike" to the shrewish character of Martha. Burton had said, "You've only to read the first lines and you know this is a great play." He had reportedly told Taylor that he thought the part of Martha could be her Hamlet, and, "You'd better play it to stop anyone else from doing it and causing a sensation." Burton did a screen test for Lehman, who still wasn't sure he was right for the part of George; and he only got it after Lehman and Warner conferred.

On the DVD audio commentary Nichols states that he knew Taylor, Burton and Segal prior to filming. He had met Burton when the actor was playing King Arthur in the musical *Camelot* on Broadway at the Majestic Theatre from December 3, 1960, to January 5, 1963. Nichols was playing in the comedy *An Evening with Mike Nichols and Elaine May* on Broadway at the John Golden Theatre in a run from October 8, 1960, to July 1, 1961. Nichols says that Burton introduced him to Taylor, whom he had met on their film *Cleopatra*. The actors had become companions before they married each other on March 15, 1964. Nichols claims he went to Rome to visit the couple during the making of the film, which was in production from September 30, 1960, to March 7, 1963. Nichols says he knew George Segal because he had worked with him on stage before. Mel Gussow, in his book on Albee, says this was off Broadway in 1964 at the New Theatre in Ann Jellicoe's play *The Knack*, which ran from May 22, 1964, to January 9, 1966.

Nichols also advises that the part of Nick had been offered to Robert Redford, whom Nichols had directed on Broadway in *Barefoot in the Park*. Nichols had turned down the opportunity to make the film version of *Barefoot* because he preferred to do *Who's Afraid of Virginia Woolf?* (although *Barefoot* would not go into production until after *Virginia Woolf* had been released). Nichols says that Redford eventually rejected the part of Nick because he did not like how the character was humiliated in the narrative and how he might be perceived as weak.

In his book on Redford, Michael Feeney Callan quotes the actor on why he turned down the part: "[He] just died in the text. I felt he started powerfully, but the author didn't know what to do with the character, so he trailed off after the first half." Nichols is quoted as saying, "I thought he could have invested some real magic in that role. I thought he had made a mistake." In their book on Redford, William Schoell and Lawrence J. Quirk make the obtuse comment that Redford's rejection of the part was probably due to his being "uncomfortable with the [play's] allegedly homosexual subtexts and references."

There was a three week rehearsal period before filming. Nichols observed that Dennis, Burton and Segal all learned the techniques of film acting from Taylor. Nichols said he worked on the adaptation. He disagreed with Lehman's wish to change the imaginary child to a real boy who had hanged himself in the hallway closet that George and Martha had sealed and papered up. Lehman also didn't want George to wear spectacles.

On the commentary, Nichols says that he was sorry to lose his favorite line from the play, Martha's witty rejoinder to a pedantic remark made by George: "Abstruse! In the sense of recondite. Don't you tell me words."

In the DVD featurette *Too Shocking for Its Time* it is said that Nichols refused to film alternate takes in which the profanities would be replaced with "clean" words. Martha's "Screw you!" as said to George when he opens the door to Nick and Honey, was changed to "Goddamn you!" via editing and another voice actress. Interestingly, "Screw you!" was restored for the original soundtrack album, a Deluxe Edition two-record set which included the entire film's dialogue. The other major phrase objected to by the Motion Picture Association of America was "Hump the Hostess," but it remained intact.

Nichols says he replaced the first director of photography, Harry Stradling Sr. Stradling said he would shoot the film in color and then de-saturate it for the black and white look the director wanted. Nichols insisted that the film had to be in black and white to protect Taylor's aging makeup, although other sources claim that Nichols objected to Stradling's ideas of "beautifying" her.

On his DVD audio commentary, replacement cinematographer Haskell Wexler says that he was hired after Jack Warner removed him from *A Fine Madness* (1966). This is because Nichols had been upset by Stradling, who had described *8 1/2* as a "piece of shit" at a screening. Nichols says that Kershner was also at the screening, which explains why he had filmed Dennis' screen test.

Wexler also states that Burton was concerned about being shot by him because he was afraid that Wexler's documentary past would make him want to expose the realism of the pock marks on Burton's face. However, this fear proved unfounded, since Wexler was just as concerned with concealing them as he was with Taylor's age makeup.

In his commentary, Nichols describes Dennis as a "brilliant, brilliant girl." She was beloved by the crew, and she herself choreographed Honey's dance. He says she was brilliant at extreme states of all kinds and always found some strange new way of coming at it that no one else had ever done before. Later Nichols thought it harmed her career because she was so eccentric. However, he felt that Dennis being unusual and unconventional was perfect for Honey.

Nichols said that her glory arose from the fact that she was funny at whatever she was playing, at least part of the time. He thought she brought to the part what great actors do — "Being inside the person and outside the person at the same time. The knife edge act of showing somebody and being somebody." He compared Dennis to Christopher Walken in that there is technique but also impulsive behavior.

In the *Life* article Dennis says that she fought with Nichols. "But whenever I said he was wrong he would yell, 'Sandy, Sandy, do it this way for me.'" She says she liked him enormously, and she would do it, "and goddammit, he's right."

In the *Talk* article Lehman says that Dennis arrived at the studio on July 6, 1965, for the table reading of the script. Lehman says he had lunch with her and Taylor, and that the women were comparing their bellies. Dennis claimed that she had a belly that made her look like a woman who had been pregnant for twelve months.

Lehman says that Burton underwent a screen test on July 16, 1966. Lehman noted in his diary on this date that Burton "looked all wrong: much too strong." Other sources attribute this quote to the alleged earlier test Burton had made for the part.

Dennis also underwent another screen test on this date, this time wearing the fur jacket and blue dress, and sans makeup. A further test had her wearing makeup. The feeling was that she looked four months pregnant, partly due to the dress and partly due to her stomach protruding. According to Lehman's diary on September 26, 1965, Dennis was indeed pregnant and in her second or third month. Apparently she had confessed this to Nichols.

On October 13 her manager told Lehman that she was due in May 1966. The manager said he would speak to her doctor about whether she could wear some kind of girdle or corset which would not injure her or the baby. In the meantime, Lehman notes that she had gained weight from over-eating. On December 20 Lehman reports that Dennis suffered a miscarriage, only two weeks after she had recorded Honey's scene crying, "I want a child."

On the commentary, Nichols stated that when asked if he liked the film, Albee replied that he didn't like the score. This is presumably because it sometimes upstaged his words. One thing that Albee reportedly had wanted but didn't get was to show the rest of the campus, since Nichols didn't feel it necessary.

Albee had wanted Bette Davis to play Martha, if only to see her parody herself from *Beyond the Forest* (1949) with the opening line, "What a dump." He was also surprised that the film was shot in black and white. In Edward Sikov's book on Davis, *Dark Victory*, Albee is quoted as saying, "Taylor was quite good, and Burton was incredible." In the end, though, he still felt that "with Mason and Davis you would have had a less flashy and ultimately deeper film."

Time reported that one of Albee's fondest memories of the movie was "the bubble of spittle on Dennis' mouth towards the end." In Philip C. Kolin's book *Conversations with Edward Albee*, he is quoted as saying, "I have a few quarrels with [her] interpretation, but they're so minor compared to what could have happened."

In the interview with Albee on the DVD of *A Delicate Balance*, he also talks about *Virginia Woolf*. He says that he had a few problems with it. He "wrote" it in color, but it was shot in black and white. This is presumably because when it was made it was absurdly thought that a serious film had to be in black and white. Only musicals or frivolous films were shot in color.

Also, Albee thinks Elizabeth Taylor did her finest screen acting in *Virginia Woolf*. Nonetheless, she was twenty years too young for the role. And Burton, who was meant to be younger than she, was clearly a lot older. When filming began, Taylor was age thirty-two and Burton was thirty-nine. Albee believes that threw the balance off. This was Albee's basic problem with the film.

In his audio commentary, Wexler advises that Dennis was "kooky and interesting," and that she formed a friendship with Taylor that saw them participating in belching contests (which Dennis always won). *Time* quoted Burton on the belching: "Gigantic belches. I mean enormous ones, like a drunken sailor. Sandy always won for number and volume." In his book on Burton, Michael Munn quotes Dennis on Taylor and Burton: "I felt that Richard wanted Elizabeth to give her very best and he really kind of helped her through the part."

Wexler says that he was aware of Burton drinking on set, though this was something that could be hidden, given George's drinking in the narrative. Wexler also points out camerawork errors and tells that he heard how he was going to be replaced on the film because it was thought to look too dark. This is something which Dr. Drew Casper, in *A Daring Work of Raw Excellence*, describes as necessary for the characters — to be "engulfed in the black night of the soul." Wexler also reports how farmers in the New England location sued Warner Bros. because they claimed their cows were upset by the night lights and didn't give as much milk.

C. David Heymann, in his book on Taylor, advises that there were production delays due to Elizabeth breaking a tooth. She took a week off, and later another several days when she injured an eye.

Wexler also comments on the notion that some people held about the play — that George and Marsha were actually homosexuals, and that's why their child was imaginary. He calls it "fashionable" and "smart," but disagrees with the theory. In his chapter on Dennis in *Hollywood Lesbians*, Boze Hadleigh asks her about this. Hadleigh thought that the claim came from a "homophobic critic." She replied that Albee and no one else agreed with this theory. Hadleigh suggested to her that the critic resented a gay playwright's success." To this, Dennis said that "heterosexuals have written most of the gay roles. Till recently."

George Segal was interviewed on June 11, 2010, by Louis Virtel for the *Movieline* website after having attended an AFI tribute to Mike Nichols. Segal commented on Dennis in the film, saying that their on-screen mania stayed on-screen. "We had a relationship of mutual respect, we really liked each other. We kept it all for the camera. And she was great. So spontaneous."

The title was obviously inspired by the song "Who's Afraid of the Big Bad Wolf?" sung in the Disney cartoon *The Three Little Pigs*, but apparently Warner Bros. was unable to secure the use of tune. When the characters sing the title phrase it is illogically set to the melody of the public domain folk song "Here We Go 'Round the Mulberry Bush."

Mad magazine published a spoof of the movie entitled "Who in Heck Is Virginia Woolf?!" in its March 1967 edition. It was written by Larry Siegel and illustrated by Mort Drucker. Martha is called Liz until the guests arrive, and they refer to her as Marcia; and

George is called Dick and then John. Nick is named Nat, and Honey is Bunny. At the beginning Dick tells Liz, "This is an Art Film, so now the Censors will have to let us talk dirty!" with the subsequent swearing replaced by dingbats. The games that are played include "House," "Pin the Tail on the Donkey," "Choke Your Partner Until He Gags and Dies," "Dirty Giant Steps," "Go to the Roadhouse for No Reason at All When We Could Do the Same Thing We're Going to Do There ... Right Here," and "Charades." When Nat asks if John and Marcia spend every night playing games, she tells him, "Tonight was something special for us! It's our Wedding Anniversary."

When Nat suggests that Bunny throw up to "get into the swing of things by doing something disgusting," both John and Marcia also encourage her. But when Bunny cannot, Marcia calls her a "Party Pooper." Here it is John who first mentions their fantasy son. Marcia states his name is Lance, and he turns out to be real. To John and Marcia's dismay, he is presented as a nerdish, conventional Harvard student whom they describe as "disgustingly wholesome" and want to kill.

RELEASE: June 22, 1966, with the taglines "You are cordially invited to George and Martha's for an evening of fun and games," "The Violet-Eyed Venus Becomes a Boozing, Tired, Greying 'Virago,'" and "Drop in for Drinks and Brace Yourself."

REVIEWS: The film was critically acclaimed by Stanley Kauffman in *The New York Times* on June 24, 1966; Edith Oliver in *The New Yorker* on July 2, 1966; and Clive Hirschhorn in *The Warner Bros. Story*. Kauffman describes Dennis as "credibly bland," and Hirschhorn labels her "superb." Oliver writes, "When a performance is as triumphant as Miss Dennis' any description seems irrelevant. It is not a matter of what she does but of what she is."

AWARDS: Elizabeth Taylor (Best Actress Academy Award, Best British Actress BAFTA), Sandy Dennis (Best Supporting Actress), Richard Sylbert (Academy Award, Best Art Direction), George James Hopkins (Academy Award, Best Set Decoration, Black and White), Haskell Wexler (Academy Award, Best Cinematography), Irene Sharaff (Academy Award, Best Costume Design, Black and White). Richard Burton (Best Actor Academy Award nomination, Best British Actor BAFTA), George Segal (Best Supporting Actor Academy Award nomination), Mike Nichols (Best Director Academy Award nomination, Best Film BAFTA), Ernest Lehman (Best Picture Academy Award nomination, Best Screenplay from Another Source Academy Award nomination).

DVD: Released by Warner Home Video on October 1, 1997. Special Edition released by Warner Home Video on December 5, 2006.

REMAKES: The film would be remade as a Dutch made-for-TV movie in 1973, a Swedish made-for-TV movie in 1985, and a Romanian made-for-TV movie in 1995.

Up the Down Staircase (1967)

Warner Bros. Pictures/Pakula-Mulligan Production/Park Place Production

CREW: Robert Mulligan (Director), Alan J. Pakula (Producer), Tad Mosel (Screenplay, based on the novel by Bel Kaufman), Fred Karlin (Music), Joseph Coffey (Photography), Folmar Blangsted (Editor), George Jenkins (Art Director), Ann Roth (Costumes), Dennis Maitland (Sound), Warner Bros. Cosmetics (Sandy Dennis' Makeup). Color, 123 minutes. Filmed June to August 1966 on location in New York.

CAST: Sandy Dennis (Sylvia Barrett), Patrick Bedford (Paul Barringer), Eileen Heckart (Henrietta Pastorfield), Ruth White (Beatrice Schacter), Jean Stapleton (Sadie Finch), Sorrell Booke (Dr. Samuel J. Bester, Principal), Roy Poole (J. J. McHabe), Florence Stanley (Ella Friedenberg), Vinnette Carroll (the Mother), Janice Mars (Miss Gordon), Loretta Leversee (Social Studies Teacher), John Callahan, Denis Fay, Otto Lomax, Martha Greenhouse (Alberta Kagan), María Landa (Carole Blanca), Robert Levine (Mr. Osborne), Elena Karam (Nurse

Frances Eagen), Francis Sternhagen (Charlotte Wolf), Candace Culkin (Linda Rosen), Lewis Wallach (Lou Martin), John Gerstad, Dan Morgan, Joey Sacks, Salvatore Rasa (Harry A. Kagan), Jeff Howard (Joe Ferone), Ellen O'Mara (Alice Blake), Jose Rodriguez (Himself), John Fantauzzi (Edward "Eddie" Williams). Uncredited: Bud Cort, Linda Gellen (Students), Merle Exit (Merle), Lance Herle (Bob Whiteside), Bel Kaufman (Teacher Talking to Mr. McHabe), Daniel Nugent (Tough Student in Miss Barrett's Class), Esther Rolle (Teacher), Esmeralda Santiago (Esmeralda), Jeffrey Walker (Student Who Shoves Miss Barrett).

SYNOPSIS: Sylvia Barrett comes to New York City's Calvin Coolidge High School as a Homeroom and English teacher. Her overcrowded class consists of forty-four mixed race students from underprivileged families. She reports student Joe Ferone when he brandishes a switchblade knife, and he later attempts to seduce her, misinterpreting her interest in him. Student Alice Blake attempts suicide after the teacher Paul Barringer ridicules the love note she gives him. Sylvia believes that she is a failure and submits her resignation. However, she withdraws it when student Jose Rodriguez tells her what being his teacher has meant to him.

NOTES: Dennis' casting as a novice teacher in her first starring role perfectly fit the seeming reticence of her persona, which might have otherwise led her to continue in supporting parts. Her gradual emergence as a leader to her class matches the actress' emergence as a leading player, without any obvious star grandstanding.

Poster for *Up the Down Staircase* (1967).

She appears with shorter, shoulder-length brown-blonde hair that she wears with a 1960s flip. Dennis uses some of her mannerisms in her performance — smiling, hair-fiddling, pointing, stuttering, eye-closing, head-nodding, tongue-poking, and touching her hand to her forehead. Her Sylvia first wears a bland flesh-colored dress that makes her almost disappear in the classroom. She later wears a dark grey/purple suit with blue blouse and a colored scarf, and she wears her hair in a black hairband.

In the staircase scene with Joe, Dennis looks beautiful in close-up, and her acting is nearly devoid of mannerisms as she looks at him. Director Robert Mulligan presents her in alternate profiles for her close-up reactions when Barringer tells her at the dance how he loves her, and when she accuses him of avoiding commitment. When Sylvia is told to report to Bester's office after Alice has jumped out the window, we see Dennis run down the hallway in her odd way.

Sylvia's vulnerability is expressed in many ways on her first day. She is bumped into by students, thought to be a student by other teachers when she attempts to catch a teacher's elevator, walked away from when she is speaking to Mr. McHabe, has her space invaded by students in her classroom as they walk behind her, and completely ignored when they talk in front of her. Her disempowerment is highlighted when she is confronted by troubled student Joe Ferone. She appears to be afraid of Joe. He intimidates her by refusing to tell her his name and making her read the class roll until she comes to his name. He also tears up the Delaney card she asks him to fill out and drops the torn pieces in front of her, then walks out of her classroom.

Sylvia is also ridiculed by the other teachers. This occurs when Paul Barringer draws a caricature of her after she tells the others in a teachers meeting, "I am so happy to be here." News of her quoting an Emily Dickinson poem with the line "brigate" that the class reacts against also makes its way around the teachers as gossip about Sylvia's failure. Barringer even disparagingly reads some of the notes from Sylvia's class suggestion box.

Sylvia's gradual empowerment begins when she buys her own supplies, like a dustpan and broom to clean up the glass from a broken window, and chalk, and she how she writes behavioral rules on the blackboard for her class. She speaks up for herself when she is called into McHabe's office over the issue of Joe, although Sylvia refuses to implicate the boy.

The tension between Sylvia and Joe is underlined when she asks him to stay behind to talk to him, and he walks out on her again. When he follows her down the staircase, Joe reveals how intelligent, eloquent and insightful he is, despite his delinquency. Sylvia shows strength by asking him for the switchblade knife he brandishes. It is another surprise that Joe hands it over to her without resistance. A further surprise comes when she asks him to accompany her to McHabe's office, which he does.

Sylvia shows a combination of fear and strength when she is followed in the street after school by some harassing boys. She stands still when she comes to Joe, who tells her, "Don't walk this block alone, Teach." She also shows compassion for Linda, who appears in class with a bruised eye. When Sylvia asks the girl if she can do anything for her, Linda tells her that she would like a school dance. Afterwards we see posters for the upcoming dance, so we assume that Sylvia has passed on Linda's request.

An implied friendship develops between Sylvia and Beatrice Schacter from them catching the bus home together and walking the neighborhood streets. There is also implied respect when Beatrice asks Sylvia to check in on her class while Beatrice is away sick.

Sylvia's eventual engagement of her class is demonstrated with her lesson on *A Tale of Two Cities*, which Dr. Bester observes, although this triumph is colored by the subplot of Alice's suicide attempt. Are we to judge Sylvia for putting off Alice wanting to talk to her and thereby leaving Alice feeling despondent enough to jump out a window? Perhaps not. But later Sylvia will admit to the school inquiry that she is to blame for not talking to Alice when the student had asked.

Sylvia does not erase "McHabe Is a Jailer" from the blackboard graffiti, knowing that Bester is coming to watch her teach and will presumably see it. When she writes "A Tale of Two Cities" on the blackboard, it is over where the "Jailer" line would have been. The scene climaxes in an extreme close-up of Dennis, her pleasure in seeing her class talking about the lesson evident on her face. The students do not leave straight after the bell rings, as we have seen them do before. Sylvia will tell McHabe that this is her class in "the sound of thinking."

Sylvia has tears in her eyes when she tells Joe, "You, Joe. 85%." This refers to his exam grade. Her quick walk away from him seems to be a protective act. The tension between

Sylvia and Joe climaxes when he comes to see her at school at 10:30 P.M. after the Welcome Parents meeting. He has decided that Sylvia's efforts to help him are based on her sexual interest in him. This also tells us of the way he relates to women. Mulligan photographs Dennis unflatteringly here, with a low camera angle and lighting that highlights the disparity in the characters' ages. This presentation of Sylvia underscores Joe's delusion, since we never think that she does have romantic feelings for him. When he tries to kiss her, Sylvia holds his face to stop him and says, "Oh, Joe. No." She expresses this is in a tender way so as to ease the judgment and rejection. However, her comment also contains the ambiguity of sexual excitement.

When Sylvia submits her resignation to Bester, he tells her that she is "a born teacher." She counters that she "can't get through to" her students. This reasoning seems unbelievable given how we have seen the change in her students' attention. However, as a plot point it leads the way to Jose's coming out at the "Silas Marner" trial. The trial is a narrative affectation, given that it is hard to believe that the students would agree to participate in such a thing. Their agreement and attention to Sylvia demonstrate the respect they have for her and is evidence that she can finally control them.

The script offers the occasional moment of humor along with the pathos. For instance, an amusing exchange occurs when Lou Martin offers to give a book report on *Macbeth*. When Sylvia asks whether the play was required reading the previous year, Lou tells her, "I aint read it before." She corrects him with, "I've never read it," to which he replies, "Me neither."

Mulligan uses hand-held camerawork and a three-hundred-and-sixty-degree camera movement as a point-of-view turn for Sylvia's first entrance into her classroom. When Joe walks out on Sylvia for the second time, Mulligan keeps the camera on Dennis' back rather than providing the expected reaction shots of her face. When Sylvia takes Joe to McHabe's office, Mulligan holds the camera outside the office and deprives us of the interior dialogue, employing music instead.

Mulligan also shows sensitivity in the presentation of Alice Blake's love for Barringer, where bad timing stops her from retrieving the love note from his letterbox. This sensitivity is in opposition to Barringer's own insensitivity in how he corrects the grammar and spelling in the note she has written, rather than considering its content. When asked about this by Bester, Barringer will say, "I didn't want to encourage a neurotic teenager." Mulligan zooms in on Dennis' silent reaction, her eyes closing and head nodding. Tellingly, the next time Barringer speaks to Sylvia she will ignore him.

Mulligan creates suspense by intercutting between Alice in Ballinger's empty classroom and Sylvia and her class. He only suggests Alice's jumping out the window without actually showing it. The score is also effective in representing Sylvia's individual character and the small-scale drama of the narrative.

Dennis was interviewed by Hal Boyle on the set of the film, and it was published in *St. Joseph's News Press* on August 31, 1966. She told Boyle that she was having a wonderful time. She said that she liked making films but still missed the hours and habits of the theater, which she was more used to. Dennis told Boyle, "Ideally, I suppose that I'd rather do only plays — and make as much money as you can making movies. But that's impossible."

In her interview with Jamie Portman for the *Ottawa Citizen*, dated January 31, 1984, Dennis reflected on the character of Sylvia: "She was very forthright who knew exactly what she was about." In Boze Hadleigh's *Hollywood Lesbians* he tells her that he found her teacher "so moving, the kind of teacher we'd all like to have had in high school." However, in her 1976 *After Dark* interview, Dennis said, "Of all my films, this is the one that I like least. It was fun making it — I'm not talking about an unpleasant experience — but I found the movie boring and uninteresting."

In his book on producer Alan J. Pakula, Jared Brown advises that the film was first screened for several national educational organizations. These included the National Congress of Parents and Teachers and the American Association of School Administrators. They conferred upon it the 1967 School Bell Award on May 15, 1967, in the hope that the public would identify with the heroine.

Mad magazine published a parody of the film in its April 1968 edition. Written by Stan Hart and illustrated by Mort Drucker, it was entitled "In the Out Exit." Sylvia Barrett is named Miss Sylvie Parrot, J. J. McHabe is McHate, and Paul Barringer is Paul Deranger. Joe Ferone is Joe Marone, and Dr. Samuel J. Bester is Dr. Bested.

The parody commented on Dennis' mannerisms by having the Henrietta Pastorfield character observe that she is twitching. Miss Parrot explains, "I'm not nervous. That's the way I act!" Henrietta responds with, "Well, cut it out! It's making me nervous!" When Joe tries to kiss Miss Parrot, he tells her, "The way your face keeps twitching, I keep missing."

It also comments on her looks. Miss Parrot tells Joe Marone, "Why won't you let me reach you! I know I can help if you'll only let me!" He asks her how she knows that, and she tells him, "Because I'm much prettier than Sidney Poitier!" Joe replies, "Er ... you wanna bet?!"

The parody also covers the plot point about Alice Blake's suicide. Here she only jumps from a first floor window and survives. The joke here is that when she jumps she says, "Mr. Deranger thinks I'm nothing more than a stupid child. Well, I'll show him I'm not stupid." After she lands she comments, "I guess I AM pretty stupid after all!"

When Miss Parrot tells Dr. Bested that she wants to leave the school, he replies, "Sorry to hear that. Our school needs teachers like you! You make the rest of us look good!" The mock-trial that Jose presides over leads to the hanging of a student, and the parody ends with Miss Parrot deciding to stay on at the school. She tells Dr. Bested, "I got to thinking how fortunate I am to be teaching in this ultra-exclusive Private School. What if I had to take a teaching assignment in one of those tough New York City Schools!?!"

RELEASE: July 19, 1967, with the taglines, "Simple words that start a war: 'Good morning. My name is Miss Barrett. I am your Home Room teacher...,'" "The year's #1 best seller picks you up and never lets you down," "The first mistake this pretty young teacher made was to get off the bus. The second was to walk into Calvin Coolidge High School for the first time. The third was to fall in love with it," and "Up the Down Staircase is the story of a girl who fell in love with a monster... (The Girl is Sylvia Barrett. Occupation: Brand new teacher)."

REVIEWS: *Up the Down Staircase* received critical acclaim from Richard Schickel in *Life* magazine on July 7, 1967, Roger Ebert in the *Chicago Sun-Times* on July 25, 1967, and Bosley Crowther in *The New York Times* on August 18, 1967. Schickel wrote that "Sandy Dennis at last fulfils the promise everyone has sensed in her." Ebert said that she gave a "quiet, natural, splendid performance." Crowther wrote, "Miss Dennis walks away with the show, giving a vivid performance of emotional range and depth." However, in *5001 Nights at the Movies*, Pauline Kael said that "Dennis, blinking as if she'd taken pills and been awakened in the middle of the night, reacts confusedly before the situations even develop."

AWARDS: Grand Prix and Best Actress co-winner at the Moscow International Film Festival.

DVD: Released by Warner Home Video on November 6, 2007.

The Fox (1968)

Warner Bros./Claridge Pictures/Motion Pictures International

CREW: Mark Rydell (Director), Raymond Stross (Producer), Howard Koch (Associate Producer), Lewis John Carlino, Howard Koch (Screenplay, based on the novella by D.H. Lawrence), Lalo Schifrin (Music), William Fraker (Photography), Thomas Stanford (Editor), Charles Bailey (Art Director), Leah Rhodes, Roger Palmer (Costumes), Ken Brooke (Makeup), Jim Keeler (Hair), Des Dollery (Sound), Don Record (Main Title and Montages). Uncredited: Steve Broidy (Executive Producer). Filmed at Studio City, Ontario, Canada, from January to March 1967.

SONGS: "That Night" (Lalo Schifrin/Norman Gimbel), sung by Sally Stevens; "Roll It Over" (Oscar Brand), sung by Anne Heywood.

CAST: Sandy Dennis (Jill Banford), Keir Dullea (Paul Renfield), Anne Heywood (Ellen March), Glyn Morris (Overstreet, Estate Agent).

SYNOPSIS: Jill Banford and Ellen March live on an isolated farm in rural Canada. A fox has been raiding their chicken coop. Ellen finds the fox in the woods but is unable to shoot it. Merchant seaman Paul Grenfel arrives in search of his grandfather, the deceased former owner of the farm. Paul stays and helps Ellen with chores. He proposes to Ellen, and she accepts. Jill is against it, and she refuses to let Paul and Ellen live on the farm. Paul kills the fox. When he goes to settle his affairs with the navy, Jill makes love to Ellen. Ellen decides she will stay with Jill. Paul returns and chops down a tree, which kills Jill when it lands on her. The farm is sold, and Paul and Ellen leave to start a life together.

NOTES: Dennis' next starring film role sees her play a woman of sexual ambiguity. While her use of mannerisms undercuts her performance, she does have moments of effective stillness and bursts of anger. The scenario that has her lose her friend to another inspires empathy for her character's loss, with the ultimate sympathy saved for her eventual fate. Dennis' scene of kissing another woman also attests to the career risks she was prepared to take in order to present controversial material.

Her hair is browner here than in *Up the Down Staircase*, and it sports blonde tips. She employs her usual mannerisms of stuttering, repeating words, head-nodding, smiling, tongue-poking, lip-biting, and eye-closing. Her laughter in the scene where Ellen is drunk and singing makes Dennis' Jill likeable.

Dennis abandons her mannerisms to offer a moment of stillness when Jill interrupts Paul and Ellen in the barn, then quickly changes from laughter to anger when she hears that Paul intends to marry Ellen. Dennis reveals Jill's anger and strength when she tells Paul that he cannot stay on at the farm if he marries Ellen. She looks vulnerable as she beseeches Paul to wait until he is settled before he takes Ellen away.

When Jill cries at seeing Paul and Ellen taking a walk at night, Dennis puts her hand to her forehead and covers her face, which blocks audience empathy for her tears. She does the same thing when Jill falls to her knees to cry when she cannot find Ellen after she goes looking for her. Dennis offers more tears when Jill talks to Ellen after Paul goes away. Her lesbian advance begins with kissing Ellen's hand, then kissing her neck, and finally kissing her on the mouth. It is telling that director Mark Rydell has the women making love clothed, whereas he had Ellen naked while she was being made love to by Paul.

There is an odd lack of empathy for Jill's fate in the tree-chopping scene. This is perhaps because of Rydell's quick cuts but also because of the implication of suicide in Jill's refusal to protect herself. Paul refusing to let Ellen go to Jill denies us any emotional reaction. However, there is some resonance to the last scene where the house's contents are emptied, since we had associated it with Jill. Perhaps Ellen's advice to Overstreet to give away her

Poster for *The Fox* (1968).

clothing tells us of Ellen's ultimate lack of feeling toward Jill in the face of her psychic domination by Paul.

Jill wears glasses to do the accounts, which adds to her look of a spinster, and she sometimes wears a hairband. The color scheme of Jill's clothes includes a red dress, cardigan and red scarf. The addition of a red cap and an orange/red sweater into Ellen's otherwise drab color scheme may be symbolic of her awakened passion. Additionally, the fox is red, and Paul has a purple/red sweater. After Jill comes to dislike Paul, the red color in her clothes is less visible. She wears her red headscarf under a hooded jacket to shop for groceries, but removes it quickly when she is home. She wears a red scarf around her neck when she searches for Ellen at night after Ellen and Paul go for a walk. Ellen's change from pants to a dress is also signaled by the use of red, since her dress and shoes are orange/red. Ellen also wears a matching headscarf when she goes walking with Paul at night.

The color red is also significant for the comb of the chicken that Paul slaughters as bait for the fox, the blood from its decapitation with an axe, and the red bullet of the gun. When Ellen sees Paul off at the train station, she wears a dress with red stockings. When she goes back to the farm we see that Jill wears a red cape. Although Ellen returns to wearing pants after Paul has left, she also wears her orange/red blouse and a red sweater. This perhaps indicates her divided psyche. Jill wears a red dress for the final scene when the tree is chopped down and she is killed. The blood from Jill's mouth is red; and the final use of red is the interior of the car in which Paul and Ellen drive away.

Paul's fur-trimmed jacket aligns him symbolically with the fox, and Ellen will tell Paul that he resembles the animal. This is apparent in the scene where he stares at her as she tries to read a book. Her staying with him rather than going to bed with Jill demonstrates her preference. Paul's alignment is also demonstrated after they hear the sounds of the foxes at night crying as they hunt, and Paul talks of how he understands the fox's will to kill. Additionally, the scene ends ambiguously when Paul asks Ellen for the second time to marry him, since it appears she acquiesces in order to make him release her from his embrace.

Paul's association with the fox is strengthened by a shot of him when he is about to chop down the tree and has warned Jill that it may fall on her. Does he want it to fall on her? He does warn her twice, so we don't really think he does. Rydell ends the film on a shot of the skinned fox hanging on the farmhouse wall, appearing to be smiling. This could be read as the fox being pleased over Paul's victory in taking Ellen away from the farm.

Gender roles between the two women are divided. Jill is the homemaker who cooks and sews, feeds the animals, shops for groceries, and does the household finances. Ellen does the manual labor, like chopping wood and mending fences. She also uses their gun, and Ellen as the huntress is extended to her reading about the behavior of the fox. Jill wears dresses and Ellen wears pants. However, Jill calling Ellen "March" is an odd masculine touch. Anne Heywood's English accent adds to Ellen's exoticism, in contrast to Jill's American ordinariness.

Jill appears to be happy with their secluded existence, whereas Ellen is frustrated and emotionally distant. Jill's frustration is demonstrated when she masturbates in the bathroom, and later when she looks at her reflection in the water in the woods and touches her breasts. Jill gives Ellen a shoulder massage, and it is apparent that the action sexually stimulates Ellen, since after a bath she masturbates alone. The two women sleep in the same bed, but there is no hint of a sexual relationship between them. They do not even kiss goodnight.

Jill's love of the animals can be paralleled with Dennis' real-life fondness for cats and dogs, although Jill is not enamored of the predatory fox (understandably so). The scene where the women have a snowball fight shows that they can have fun together, although there is an initial concern that they are more interested in that than retrieving the cow that has got out. Ellen later shows another instance of physical closeness to Jill when Jill cries and Ellen holds her in her arms and strokes her hair.

The tree on the farm is a prefiguring narrative presence. Jill twice asks Ellen to chop it down, but Ellen refuses because she thinks it is still alive. Paul cuts a branch off it to use for firewood, and Ellen has evidently finally agreed to Jill's request to take the tree down in the last scene. Jill not being strong enough to make the last chops is further evidence of her lack of masculine physical strength. However, Ellen is presumably able to do it before Paul reappears and offers to help. It is noteworthy that Paul observes that the tree is still alive. This is the reason that Ellen previously refused to chop it down. This time Ellen does not resist Jill's request, presumably as a way to make amends. Ironically, if Ellen had held to her previous stance, she would have saved Jill's life.

Paul's initial appearance interrupts Jill telling Ellen about the letter she has received from her brother, Robert. Jill is reminded of his friend Jim Collins, who one summer at a picnic on a lake followed her into the woods in a rainstorm and held her down onto the ground. She speaks of his weight on her. Her reaction is ambiguous, since it could be either that of desire or fear. Although Dennis uses her mannerisms here, she also slows down her speech, which redeems the scene (as does as the score under it).

It is narratively interesting that it is Jill who has to tell Ellen to lower the gun she holds on Paul. Ellen's caution towards him is paralleled with the apparent pleasure Jill takes in talking to him. This creates an expectation that will not be met — that Paul will have a stronger interest in Jill. Ellen making coffee for Paul and then preparing his room may suggest a change in her character. It is as if she is embracing her feminine nature more, since we assume that these are the kinds of things that Jill might do instead. However, doing them also allows Ellen to get away from Paul, which may be more to the point.

When Jill asks Paul to stay, she then asks Ellen for her permission. Ellen's indifferent answer is not a no, and so is read as a yes. This apparent indifference will be underlined at the dinner scene. Ellen collecting eggs from the chickens is an action that may be read as a masculine, opportunistic one, since we don't see her feed the chickens as we do Jill. We also see Ellen carrying two pails of coal into the house herself after refusing Paul's help.

At dinner, Ellen starts to carve the pheasant that Paul has caught and Jill has cooked, but Jill asks Paul to do the carving instead. Ellen is also indifferent to the idea of Paul doing repairs around the farm, although it is implied that this is Ellen's work.

Jill comments that having Paul with them reminds her of her brother, which would seem to preclude a romantic interest from her. Paul's behavior towards Jill seems to send mixed messages. For example, he gives her a bouquet of flowers, which can be read as a romantic gesture, although we assume that he has more interest in Ellen. The fact that he gives them to Jill and not Ellen may be just an act of kindness to keep her on his side, considering his agenda. Ellen doesn't relax around Paul until after she gets drunk. This scene also sees Ellen expressing physicality towards Jill when she holds her as she teaches her how to play the guitar. It is interesting that the song Ellen plays on her guitar and sings is one of heterosexual love, and her sarcasm to Jill about her cooking continues to express the dissatisfaction Ellen appears to feel.

Paul's proposal to Ellen is something of a narrative surprise, since we assumed that he just wanted to have sex with her. Perhaps this idea of needing to marry her to have her comes from the Lawrence novella, which is set in England in the 1910s, although the film adaptation had "modernized" the period setting. The adaptation also changed the character of Henry, who was only twenty years old, into the older Paul; and the Ellen character was called Nellie.

In the novella both women were presented as educated, refined and sexually repressed spinsters who didn't have sex with each other or anyone else. In the film it is really only Jill who can be described as educated and refined. It is the idea of Paul wanting to marry Ellen that supposedly brings out the latent lesbianism between the women, which they act on. Also, as they were women in their late twenties, the idea in the novella of a boy dealing with an older woman who he is afraid of offered a different dynamic. This age difference also makes the novella's end more resonant, since after the boy has deliberately killed the Jill character, he marries Nellie, but their relationship is unhappy. Rather than the submissive type that the film's Ellen is to Paul, the novella's Ellen is independent and unsettled, and the boy regrets having come between the two women.

In the film, after Jill learns that Paul is to marry Ellen, Jill describes him as a "drifter." Paul as a man, rather than the boy of the novella, is presented as a fantasy of every woman's dream. Except for Jill, that is. The adaptation also changes Ellen's character. Now a woman who has been living with another woman for an extended length of time, by choice, suddenly agrees to have sex with Paul. The treatment implies that she is so overwhelmed by the man that Ellen becomes an indecisive and compliant pushover, with the groundwork having been laid by the idea of Ellen already being sexually frustrated. There is even the implication that Ellen is hypnotized by Paul, demonstrated by Rydell's lighting on the faces of Paul and Ellen. There is the further implication that the reason Jill does not move away from where the tree will fall at the climax is because she too is now hypnotized by Paul's fox.

When Paul loads the gun after overhearing Jill talking about him to Ellen, the expectation is created that he will use it on Jill. However, he goes hunting for the fox instead. The fox's face appearing from its ground hole is paralleled with Paul's face, framed by the interior darkness of his fur-trimmed jacket.

In the face of her anger, Ellen accuses Jill of secretly being interested in Paul. This ambiguity is also apparent in the scene where Jill asks Paul for a favor: to wait to get settled in Vermont before he takes Ellen away. Paul replies with "You make it sound like bookkeeping. I want her and I'm going to take her." Jill offers him all her money not to take Ellen, and Paul proceeds to comment on Jill's assumed lesbian tendencies. She hasn't had a man, but is "not bad looking." Jill closes her cardigan protectively, which is a comically clichéd reaction of the threatened virgin. When he grabs her, stopping her from leaving the room, an expectation of rape is created. This expectation is not met, partly because it appears that Jill draws Paul to her with her hand that he holds. Her slapping his face when he tells her that what she needs is a man ends the possibility of consensual sex. Rydell then has Jill go off to look at herself in a mirror after Ellen's appearance interrupts the confrontation.

The dead plants on the kitchen windowsill indicate Jill's neglect of the house because of her sadness over Ellen's commitment to Paul. Ellen also points out that Jill hasn't eaten, and that her hair is tangled. Jill asks Ellen, regarding Paul, "Is he what you want?" Ellen replies, "I don't know." Ellen tells Jill that she has been happy with her, which is a surprise, since we have seen how unhappy Ellen appears to be. Additionally, Ellen explains her feelings about Paul as follows. "When I'm with him, I want to touch him, and when he holds me, I feel I'm sinking into his flesh and there's no more me. When he's not here, I don't know. I'm confused."

This issue of Ellen's self-definition is seemingly resolved after she is kissed by Jill. The women presumably make love, though this is not shown. In her letter, Ellen tells Paul about Jill: "I know her, and when we're together I seem to know myself. We have a life here, and even if it can't last, while it does it has some meaning."

Jill moving the duck away from outside the shed before Paul chops down the tree is seen as an act of kindness, since she must think the animal is in danger. This makes her refusal to move away from the same area puzzling. Perhaps it is *because* Paul warns her twice that she may be hit by the tree. She doesn't attempt to run out of the way even when Ellen calls out to her as the tree falls. Are we supposed to think that Jill is committing suicide by deliberately putting herself in the path of the tree? Is she doing it because she knows that since Paul has returned, Ellen will leave her? Perhaps.

Vito Russo, in *The Celluloid Closet*, and Dennis in her interview in *Hollywood Lesbians* state that the tree falls between Jill's legs, providing the phallic symbolism of her being penetrated as well as killed. However, a viewing of the film does not make this apparent, so that such a reading is only a projected interpretation.

Rydell uses a subjective camera for the fox's point of view when it advances on the chickens. He employs quick cuts for the attack, which includes shots of Jill screaming and Ellen with the gun. His photographing Ellen in the bathroom in multiple mirrors may suggest her divided psyche, and also the potential for duplicity which will later become apparent. Rydell pans the camera from Ellen to the fox watching her, and intercuts close-ups of the two of them as they stare at each other, providing extreme close-ups of their eyes.

Freeze-frames and red flashes are used after the women have their snowball fight. Jill lies on the ground with her mouth open, perhaps a prefiguring of her death. The sound of a horse neighing and the chickens squawking introduce the appearance of Paul, who is presented like a horror movie antagonist. There are repeated shots of his shadow passing by the house's window, and when he enters he stands in shadow. Rydell then supplies a shaft of light to show only Paul's eyes as he talks to the women, a technique he repeats for Ellen when she watches Paul as he speaks to Jill.

Rydell intercuts between Jill running to find Ellen, and Ellen and Paul making love. The suggestion of Ellen's climax is underscored by a shot of Jill falling to her knees in the snow and crying. Another reading of Jill's reaction is that she is crying because she can hear Ellen's climax.

Zooms and out-of-focus effects are also frequently used. Rydell holds the silence between Jill and Ellen for forty-two seconds when Jill returns from seeing Paul off at the train station. He includes a montage under the narration of Ellen's letter to Paul. There are superimposed images of the fox, Ellen and Jill kissing, Ellen and Paul making love, and Ellen and Jill snowball-fighting. Rydell employs low camera angles to show Paul looking at Jill and when he chops the tree, as if confirming that she will be hit by the falling trunk. A shot of Jill seen between two of the branches makes her appear like a target.

In a *Time* magazine article Keir Dullea said, "Sandy is one of the most selfless and unactressy actresses I have ever worked with." It was reported that on location the production experienced bone-chilling temperatures of twenty-five degrees below zero. The article observed that Dennis' choice of the film indicated that her "concern is not the price but the property, not her image but her interest in the work." *Time* would describe the role as "a lesbian, hardly a career booster."

In her interview with Sheilah Graham that appeared in *The Pittsburgh Press* on December 17, 1967, Dennis said that she agreed to do the film because Rydell was a friend of hers. She said yes when he called her before she had even read the script. Afterwards she went out and bought the novella and loved it. Dennis said the girl in the book was unattractive, but she saw the character as more plain than ugly. In the 1976 *After Dark* magazine interview, Rydell labeled Dennis an "emotionally fluid actress."

In *Hollywood Lesbians*, Boze Hadleigh asked her if she was advised not to take the part. She said some people did warn against it, but the feeling was that since she had won the Oscar she could get away with it. Dennis also thought that the fact that the material was D.H. Lawrence also helped, since it gave the subject the patina of classic literature. Hadleigh asked her if she was attracted to Anne Heywood, and she said she was. Dennis also told Hadleigh that she thought the characters of the two women were interesting but that the man was shallow. "I sort of felt Anne could leave me for Keir, she could experiment by having a sex-like affair with him, then come back to me. But they shouldn't have killed me off!"

The October 1967 issue of *Playboy* featured a pictorial for the film. It includes stills of Anne Heywood, Keir Dullea and Dennis, as well as nude shots of Heywood taken specifically by *Playboy*. The one still featuring Dennis shows her being kissed by Heywood, when "the gesture [of comfort] turns into an embrace of unexpected emotion."

The film is featured in the documentary *The Celluloid Closet* (1995). It shows the scene in which Paul wonders why Jill hasn't been with a man and grabs her, and later includes the sequence in which Jill is killed by the symbolic falling tree. The documentary spotlights the character of Jill as one of the "Unhappy Gay People." Arthur Laurents says that the fate of gay characters in American literature is the same as all characters that are sexually free. You must pay and suffer. "If you're a woman who commits adultery you're only put out in the storm. If you're a woman who has another woman you better go hang yourself." The documentary narration states, "By now a pattern was clear. Characters of questionable sexuality would meet a nasty end in the last reel."

In Vito Russo's source book for the documentary he writes that by Rydell making the lesbian relationship between Jill and Ellen explicit, he "exaggerates the results of that lesbian passion," and the film shows that gay relationships are inherently violent. Russo would also point out that some critics were confused by the denouement, since in the treatment Jill wore a dress and Ellen pants. He quotes Martin Gottfried, who asked in *Women's Wear Daily*, "How could the feminine one be the real lesbian?" Gottfried couldn't believe that Paul could be attracted to Ellen, "the bulldyke," over Jill, "the female lesbian." Perhaps the answer to his question was given by Pauline Kael, who described Jill as "frumpy" (a code for unattractive).

RELEASE: Released in Canada on December 13, 1967, and in the United States on February 7, 1968, with the taglines, "The Fox ... symbol of the male," and, "Between Ellen and Jill came Paul..."

REVIEWS: The picture was critically acclaimed by Renata Adler in *The New York Times* on February 8, 1968; by Roger Ebert in the *Chicago Sun-Times* on April 22, 1968; and by Clive Hirschhorn in *The Warner Bros. Story*. In *Going Steady*, Pauline Kael was less impressed, claiming that by making the material sexually explicit, the makers had diminished the story. Adler wrote that "Dennis has trouble at first with the part. [Then] her strain begins to work within the part rather than against it." Ebert said that Dennis "has a difficult role; [it] could have become ridiculous, but Miss Dennis manages it well." Kael acknowledged the actress' risk in taking the "whining" role but also wrote her famous quip: "One might uncharitably point out that she had already made an acting style out of post-nasal drip."

DVD: Released by Warner Bros. on November 17, 2009.

Sweet November (1968)

Warner Bros.—Seven Arts/Gina Productions

CREW: Robert Ellis Miller (Director), Jerry Gershwin, Elliott Kastner (Producers), Herman Raucher (Screenplay), Michel Legrand (Music), Daniel L. Fapp (Photography), James Heckert (Editor), John Lloyd (Art Director), Ralph S. Hurst (Set Decorator), Ann Roth (Costumes), Gordon Bau (Makeup), Jean Burt Reilly (Hair), Stanley Jones (Sound). Color, 113 minutes. Filmed in New York from March to May 1967.

SONG: "Sweet November" (Leslie Bricusse, Anthony Newley), sung by Anthony Newley.

CAST: Sandy Dennis (Sara Deever), Anthony Newley (Charles "Charlie" Blake), Theodore Bikel (Alonzo), Burr DeBenning (Clem Batchman), Sandy Baron (Richard Slaven), Marj Dusay (Carol), Martin West (Gordon), Virginia Vincent (Mrs. Schumacher), King Moody (Digby), Robert Gibbons (Sam Naylor). Uncredited: Francis De Sales (Executive in Charlie's Office), Norma Jean Kron (Girl Walking in Brooklyn).

SYNOPSIS: In New York City, British box manufacturer Charlie Blake meets apartment manager Sara Deever. She asks him to be her November man, to live with her so that she can fix whatever problem he has. He agrees. She has him stop work, and he writes romantic poetry. Charlie falls in love with Sara and learns that she has a terminal illness. She loves him, too, but refuses to let him stay with her once the month is up. Charlie leaves and is replaced by Sara's December man.

NOTES: In this film Dennis' hair color is more red/brown than her previous blonde/brown. She wears it loose but also sometimes tied back with a ribbon, and in ribboned pigtails. She uses the mannerisms of lip-biting, stuttering, hair-fiddling, gesturing, pointing, tongue-poking, and head-nodding. However, these mannerisms fit the character she plays. Charlie will later observe her behavior of "quick tiredness, little trembles, and uneven breathing [in sleeping]" due to her illness.

Dennis downplays the ingénue charm of Sara by expressing control-freak frustration and irritation. This is perhaps an attempt to work against the mawkish pathos of the material. She looks lovely in the scene where she and Charlie talk in bed together, and she sadly tells him how people need to be remembered. Sara's intransient existence also allows her some emotional distance. It's unsurprising that Charlie calls the love poem about her "Enigma," and the narrative shows that she does not change this attitude, despite her love for Charlie.

The actress employs stillness to good effect when Sara denies Richard another month, and a sour expression and charmless anger in reaction to Charlie's jealousy over Clem. She covers her face when she cries in reaction to Charlie storming out of the house after he refuses to talk about her December Gordon. Dennis looks away from Alonzo when she tells him that she loves Charlie and that she still wants him to leave at the end of the month.

Dennis displays more stillness when she listens to Charlie's "Sweet November" poem, and then tears before she kisses him, although director Robert Ellis Miller captures this from an odd angle. In the climactic farewell scene Dennis is strangely devoid of tears. She mostly uses stillness again to look at Anthony Newley with Sara's resolve and sadness. Sara's attitude to Gordon as her new December is also devoid of emotion, and she gives no indication to him of the pain she felt from having to let Charlie go.

Charlie and Sara "meet cute" in the way she asks for his help on the driving test, resulting in *him* being caught for cheating. His antagonism towards her is the first obstacle to be overcome in their romance, which is accomplished by presenting Sara as a lovable kook. It is interesting that Charlie is presented as a romantic prospect in light of Newley's effeminate

82 • THE FILMS   *Sweet November* (1968)

Poster for *Sweet November* (1968).

British manner, particularly in the way he places his hands in his waistcoat pockets. Newley also occasionally over-gesticulates, which may be in reaction to Dennis' gesturing. But he supplies emotion when he looks away from the camera when told by Alonzo about Sara, and tenderness in the farewell scene.

Such emotion makes Charlie's character, a supposed playboy who only agrees to be Sara's November to sleep with her, somewhat problematic. Since Sara presumably sleeps with him from day one, his conquest is rather easy, so his decision to stay on after a week can be read as him wanting more sex, or perhaps actually falling in love with her and wanting other things.

Sara's impact on Charlie is demonstrated when he follows up on her initial criticisms of him — why his company fails to employ the handicapped and why they do not make seven-sided boxes. He also does the television repair for Henry Jensen when Clem Batchman visits, which is one of Sara's apartment management jobs. Later Charlie sends Sara a seven-sided box to demonstrate how much she means to him. And then there are the love poems he writes to her.

Sara's kookiness is suggested by her wearing a large white hat inside the testing room, but not outside. Her wardrobe otherwise demonstrates her odd style, e.g., headscarves, pinafores, knee-high boots, and a green, yellow and brown blanket kaftan. The romantic poem that Charlie writes for her and about her defines her character and reads: "A girl I know, she he is partly mad/Yet beyond that smile she is partly sad/She is partly calm, she is partly wild/But she is mostly woman/ No/She is mostly child."

Sara's refusal to accept romance on the date aligns her with a spinster/teacher who keeps filing cabinet records of her monthly therapy visitors. However, her apparent sexual generosity is an ambiguous trait. The implication is that she has sex with her monthly guests, as she sleeps in the same bed with Charlie and lets him kiss her on the first day. Sara makes a comment about Charlie: "If he keeps up that behavior he will always be Pinocchio and never a real boy." This alludes to the adolescent sensibility of their relationship, or at least her view of it. When Charlie tells Sara that he loves her, he says it is the first time he has been in love in his life. She does not reciprocate the sentiment in the moment, and she expresses her opinion that he should marry someone else.

Sara feeding pigeons in the park reflects Dennis' real-life love of animals, something which had also been underlined in *The Fox*. The rye crisps she feeds them suggests both her love of the birds and her spinster/teacher persona. This persona had also been utilized for her character in *Up the Down Staircase*, with her love for animals transposed to caring for children.

Sara analyzes Charlie with "an advanced case of Hurry Hurry Ding Ding." Her therapy to "loosen him up," apart from making him stop work, is to change his wardrobe and give him recreation, like sight-seeing, crosswords, and flying a toy airplane. She also limits his diet to apples and doesn't allow him to wear his watch. When Clem appears, he observes Charlie's main therapy to be poetry writing, and Charlie expresses his desire to initially write blank verse before Sara encourages him to write romantic poems.

The second poem that Charlie reads to Sara uses the film's title and reads as follows:

> Sweet November/They say you're wintry and grey/And yet this love that you bring is sweeter than Spring and warmer than May/Come December when our November is through/We'll face the winter and smile/You know that I'll be staying with you/When we remember November's sunshine we won't mind December's rain/For us it will be like sweet November again.

Charlie keeps changing his mind about what he wants to write poems about, and later we see that he has a pile of them that Sara describes as being "wisenheimer." Her disapproval of the last one is voiced while she paints a canvas, which might seem to be her own form of therapeutic relaxation. However, Charlie's criticism of her painting causes her to stop.

Charlie sees Sara's pill collection, he later asks Clem and then Alonzo about it. This after observing that she is "looking tired." He tells Clem that Sara "get colds" and has "quick tiredness, little trembles, and uneven breathing in her sleep." This leads Alonzo to admit that "she is sick" and "temporary," and has a malady that is rare and incurable. However, the narrative ends at the beginning of December, so we don't see Sara deteriorate any further.

The screenplay offers some genuine wit. When Sara takes Charlie to lunch at the open-air hot dog wagon in the park, she sees him taking out money to pay. She tells him, "Please don't do that. Please be my guest. After all, it's the least I can do." He replies, "Nonsense, I'll pay," and she comments, "Good." Another funny exchange occurs regarding the fruit Sara paints. Charlie comments, "This fruit is rotten." Sara tells him, "I like to refer to it as bruised." To this he replies, "I don't mind the bruises; it's the open wounds."

When Charlies speaks of wanting to write blank verse, he tells Sara, "To hell with it" after she scolds him for wanting to write the easiest kind. She responds with, "And you call yourself a poet." He answers, "The hell with it — with a hey nonny-nonny."

The scene in which Sara paints while criticizes his latest wisenheimer poem offers an ironic exchange. She tells him, "You're a good sport, Charlie. You take criticism so well. Much better than I ever expected. You can tell a person by the way they take criticism."

When Charlie criticizes her painting of a brick wall and sky with "More blue, Sara," she looks at him in stillness and then sits back, stopping her painting after he puts blue paint on her brick wall. She then tells him, "That's very good, Charlie. That's very fine. A brick wall is red. No one writes 'No Handball Playing' in the sky."

Charlie expresses his jealousy over Clem's appearance after Sara asks Clem where is staying, and he tells her a hotel. When she tells him, "You can't," Charlie says, "He can." When Charlie attempts to put three dates back on the tearaway page calendar, Sara catches him and asks, "What are you doing?" Because she shines a torch on his face, he replies, "I'm being blinded."

Other amusing dialogue includes Charlie telling Sara, "I don't understand why you can't have two successive terms. It would be very American of you." (When Charlie repeats "very American," Newley employs an American accent). After Alonzo tells Clem and Carol at the Thanksgiving bridal shower that animals thrive on vegetables, Sara replies, "You never saw a skinny gorilla."

Miller employs visuals to make or underscore a point. For instance, he has the camera rise after Charlie kisses Sara on his first night to suggest that they have sex, while the blue sky seen through the skylight changes to orange to suggest the coming of day.

Unfortunately, the score is often cloying when it employs a singing chorus, and overplays intended comic moments (for example, when Charlie returns with gifts after not attending the Thanksgiving bridal shower). However, the music also supplies emotion for the farewell scene.

The film's pressbook reports that Dennis wore twenty-eight pairs of knee-high boots, and that for the scene where Sara and Charlie eat hot dogs, the actors had to consume twenty-five of them. Newley had never eaten them before and said at the end of the sequence, "I nibbled the last few as though they were sticks of dynamite."

On September 4, 1964, *The New York Times* reported that the material had been originally written as a play, but that Universal Studios had paid to stop production of the play so that the film version could be made instead.

On the Sandy Dennis Foundation website, Actors Memories page, Theodore Bikel talks about working with her. He called it an interesting experience and found her to be one of the most un-star-like stars in films. She spoke her mind and refused to make herself look glamorous (and resisted the efforts of others to make her so). Bikel felt, however, that Dennis' pairing with Newley was a poor combination. Newley was a stickler for accuracy, whereas she was not. "He refused to see that Sandy's freewheeling line readings and interpretations also gave rise to some very interesting, even inspired, moments. He was merely irritated by them. And by Sandy."

Robert Ellis Miller had previously directed the film version of Dennis' Broadway play *Any Wednesday* (1966), although Jane Fonda had been cast in the movie instead of Dennis. Producer Elliott Kastner would go on to produce the 2001 remake of *Sweet November*.

RELEASE: February 8, 1968, with the taglines, "A girl I know, she is partly mad. Yet behind that smile, she is partly sad. She is partly calm, she is partly wild. But she is mostly woman — No. She is mostly child"; "Why would a sweet girl like this give the key to her apartment to a different man each month?"; and "Sara... She had to be remembered by every man she met. So she divided the calendar into twelve men and gave each a month and a key to her apartment. Charlie's month was November because he belonged to Sara as no one ever would again."

REVIEWS: The film received a critically mixed reaction from *Variety* on December 31, 1967; Renata Adler in *The New York Times* on February 9, 1968; and Clive Hirschhorn in *The Warner Bros. Story*. *Variety* wrote that Dennis was "delightful." Adler said that "her stammer is a bit nerve-racking; but she gradually takes over her part." In *Going Steady*, Pauline Kael called the film "Squishy whimsy." She wrote that Dennis "has exhausted her bag of tricks," and "she doesn't have the range and variety for starring roles."

REMAKE: Remade by director Pat O'Connor in 2001, starring Charlize Theron as Sara Deever and Keanu Reeves as Nelson Moss.

DVD: Released by Warner Bros. on January 22, 2009.

That Cold Day in the Park (1969)

Commonwealth United Entertainment/ Factor-Altman-Mirell Films (Uncredited)

CREW: Robert Altman (Director), Donald Factor, Leon Mirell (Producers), Robert Eggenweiler (Associate Producer), Gillian Freeman (Screenplay, based on the novel by Richard Miles), Laszlo Kovacs (Photography), Johnny Mandel (Music), Danford B. Greene (Editor), Leon Ericksen (Art Director), John H. W. Gusselle (Sound), Phyllis Newman (Makeup), Ilse Richter (Costumes), Salli Bailey (Hair). Color, 113 minutes. Filmed at Panorama Studios, Vancouver, Canada, from October to December 1968.

CAST: Sandy Dennis (Frances Austen), Michael Burns (the Boy), Susanne Benton (Nina), John Garfield Jr. (Nicky), Luana Anders (Sylvia), Edward Greenhalgh (Dr. Charles Stevenson), Doris Hickingham (Mrs. Edory), Frank Wade (Mr. Edory), Alicia Ammon (Mrs. Pitt), Rae Brown (Mrs. Parnell), Lloyd Berry (Mr. Parnell), Linda Sorenson (the Prostitute), Michael Murphy (the Rounder).

SYNOPSIS: Thirty-two-year-old Frances Austen lives in the Vancouver apartment of her deceased mother. She invites the twenty-something Boy, who she sees sitting in the rain, into her apartment. He pretends to be mute and sleeps in her guest room. The Boy leaves to visit his sister but returns repeatedly. Frances is angry when she finds that the Boy is not in his room when she wants him to make love to her. When he next returns she nails the room's window shut. He tells her that he is not attracted to her. Frances picks up Sylvia from a brothel and brings her home for the Boy. However, in a jealous rage, she kills the prostitute. Frances kisses the Boy, who cries, aware that he is now her prisoner.

NOTES: Dennis delivers a relatively restrained performance playing a killer with a controlling nature and an unrequited desire. The film inspires sympathy for her touching, if pathetic, character, who is both victimizer and victim. Robert Altman must be credited for keeping the actress' mannerisms in check for the first time onscreen, so that she presents a more orthodox acting style. This is not to say that she doesn't employ *some* of her usual mannerisms, because she occasionally stutters. She also uses her hand to the forehead, hand to her mouth, and eye-closing techniques while her character is under the influence of hash, but that gives this behavior context. She stutters when she speaks to the Prostitute and asks her to go home with her, which can be contextualized as nervousness. She also closes her eyes when she listens at the door to the assumed sounds of the Boy and Sylvia making love.

Dennis' Frances is a conservative woman who wears her shoulder-length dark brown hair up and in a sculptured fashion. She wears it loose at night in her bedroom, in the morning for breakfast before she has bathed and dressed, after she returns from her day out, and after she returns from picking up Sylvia. It is also telling that she should be putting her hair up when the Boy confronts her about his room's windows being nailed shut.

We see Frances smoke when she is alone in her bedroom, as if it is an act of defiance against her deceased mother, although Frances will smoke in the presence of the Boy in her living room. She also smokes when she is alone in the kitchen eating breakfast, and in front of Charles. Dennis affects an English accent, and a portrait of the Queen on a wall suggests the British connection, as does the cockney accent of the older woman lunch guest.

Frances is another of the actress' spinsters who expresses both maternal and matronly behavior, although she also has a sexual agenda. This is apparent from the way she looks at the Boy in a mirrored reflection in the bathroom when he undresses for the bath. Her way of asking him a question and then controlling him shows her treating the Boy like a child, possibly in the same way Frances treated her "senile" mother. However, he becomes complicit in his treatment by failing to object to it.

Altman sometimes presents Frances in a rather sinister light. When she makes the offer to the Boy to stay in her spare room, Altman films her in shadow like a horror movie monster. Additionally, her sudden scream to frighten the Boy

Poster for *That Cold Day in the Park* (1969).

during their Blind Man's Bluff game can also be interpreted as demonstrating the potential antagonism the hash cookies have released.

When the blindfolded Frances, in shadow, is shown looking for the Boy, she has her hands out like Max Schreck in *Nosferatu* (1922). Frances again seems vampiric when shown half in shadow as she tells the Boy she wants him to make love to her, and her scream of realization that she has been confiding in and kissing a doll is monstrous.

Dennis scores a laugh in the way she points to herself and pulls a face when she tells the Boy it was she who made the pineapple cream cake. She also paints an amusing portrait when Frances is stoned on the hash cookies.

She presents stillness when watching the Boy dance to the music she plays for him, when she looks at him before he puts the blindfold on for their Blind Man's Bluff game, and in listening to the Boy when he speaks to her. The latter is emphasized when Dennis holds the stillness after the Boy has left the room, when she can hear him attempting to take out the nails she has hammered into the window sashes. She also offers a resonant stillness while looking at the Boy after she has stabbed Sylvia, and Altman photographs Dennis from the back of her head for the final scene of Frances' entrapment of the Boy.

Dennis imbues a poetic element to Frances by moving to sit back after she looks for the Boy through the keyhole of the spare room. The fact that Frances has her hair down and wears her green nightgown when she goes to the Boy indicates that she has an agenda. Her final reaction to the Boy when he cries shows her being gentle in her madness, kissing his mouth and face, and repeating, "I want you to make love to me."

The scene where Frances has left toys in the bed to fool her into thinking he is there only works because of Dennis' scream of realization at the end. Before this Dennis uses some stuttering in her monologue when Frances admits to being lonely, clasping her hands all the while. The scream comes when she turns on the bedside lamp after kissing a doll's head, presumably thinking it is the Boy. Her scream is more angry than shocked. This perceived humiliation sets up her revenge upon the Boy. The scene also pays off all the previous representations of Frances as unattractive, and it's hard to believe that the Boy would have responded to her attempted seduction had he been there.

We first see Frances walking through the park, purposefully and humorlessly, ignoring the Boy who sits on the bench. Frances will continue her dour demeanor by wearing a black dress for the lunch with her guests, who are presumably friends of her deceased mother. By continuing to socialize with these elders, Frances appears older than she actually is. Both older women in particular are presented as gargoyles, which prefigures Frances as a murderess and jailer. The pettiness of the women is expressed in the way the older of the two childishly and spitefully takes a seat that the younger woman was about to sit in. This behavior also suggests the relationship Frances may have had with her own mother.

Nina and Nicky's permissive sex and consumption of hash cookies are contrasted with Frances' lack of sex and non-use of drugs. Frances eats the cookies that the Boy brings her, unaware they are laced with hash. The hash cookies that she eats provide an insight into Frances' character when she is uninhibited. Her hair comes loose, and she is both playful and scary when she screams at the Boy to frighten him.

Frances contrasts with the women in the waiting room of Dr. McKenzie, since their clothes and hairstyles read as more contemporary. They also seem far more relaxed, since they discuss men and penis size. Additionally Frances is contrasted with the Prostitute at the bar, whose grotesque beehive hairstyle may be period but reads as comical, as well as another barfly who wears her hair in a more natural, down style in the face of Frances' hair being up yet again. The younger men at the bar also parallel the older men that Frances has been socializing with.

When Frances follows the Prostitute into the restroom, the Prostitute asks if she has any blush-on, which Frances does not. This shows Frances' lack of contemporary makeup. In response to Frances' request for the Prostitute to go home with her, the Prostitute replies, "I'm a working girl but not a pervert." This comment is presumably the Prostitute's conservative stance on lesbianism, even though Frances has told her that she wants her for the Boy.

The Prostitute's surprising rejection of the idea is furthered when she tells the young men in the bar about Frances' proposition. These are men that are presumably strangers to the Prostitute because she has told Frances that she is alone at the bar. This allows the men to laugh at Frances as she leaves the bar, and for them to assume that she is a "dyke." A parallel can also be made between Frances and the two lesbians in the bar where Sylvia is found, and Sylvia herself. All three of the other woman appear in clothes and hairstyles more contemporary than Frances.' While Sylvia accepts Frances' offer, she later expresses a distaste for the idea that Frances might join her and the Boy, because of the lesbian implication.

When the Boy crosses his arms in the white jacket he wears as he sits in the rain, it resembles a straitjacket, which prefigures the entrapment he will suffer. Although we have seen Frances repeatedly looking at the Boy in the park through her window, it is Uncle David's sneeze that makes her think the Boy could catch cold. Her guests' fear of the Boy indicates their conservative nature, and Frances smiles when the younger woman tells her, "You're being sentimental."

The Boy's pretence of not speaking presents him as an ambiguous figure, since he may be a duplicitous opportunist. But he also becomes the victim of a controlling psychotic. Frances' assumption that he cannot speak is natural, given that he does not answer her, since she is unaware that he is doing "the number" that Nina will later comment on.

Nina's revelation that the Boy has been doing his silent number since he was a kid exposes him as a veteran manipulator, but also as someone who may be just as lonely as Frances. Frances is right when she tells him that she can be perceived as talking a lot because he does not talk at all; and this also plays on the stereotype of the lonely spinster who is starved for attention.

The Boy shows an insensitive casualness in entering the houseboat that Nina and Nicky inhabit. Nina's anger at him for not knocking when she and Nicky are making love is a rejection of her brother, which is later leavened by her tender invitation for him to come in. The Boy doesn't seem to take the initial rejection as badly as one might.

He first watches through a window as the couple make love. Then he places the dress he has been given by someone at his parent's house to return to Nina over the window to block his view. While he may no longer be able to see the couple, we can still hear Nina's moans. This voyeurism recalls that of Frances watching the Boy in the mirror when they were in the bathroom together.

When we hear the Boy talking to Nina, it comes as no surprise that he can speak, since we had assumed he was faking with Frances. He tells her that he left Frances because he "got tired of not talking." This frustration can be aligned to Frances' continual talk in trying to get him to answer her. Nicky assumes that the Boy was paid to be the "pick up." After the Boy first describes Frances as "an old lady," he later denies it.

The Boy is more responsive to Frances when they are both stoned. He is close to her when he ties the blindfold around her head, which leads her to kiss him on the cheek. The kiss is shown to be casual and impulsive, due to Frances being drugged, and non-sexual. However, while Frances allows him to find her when he is blindfolded, the Boy fails to do the same for her. Also she had used the sound of the harmonica to lead him to her location, but again the Boy does not reciprocate. Altman concludes the game when Frances removes the blindfold only to find herself alone in the living room.

Frances tells the Boy that she discovered her enjoyment of records after taking a course in music appreciation, and she now commits thirty to sixty minutes a day to listening. This sounds more like a disciplined chore than a spontaneous pleasure. Her smiling and applause at the Boy's dancing to the music she plays indicates that she is not totally devoid of humor, because it is so exuberant and campy. However, it is these qualities that also suggest that he is faking his muteness. The dancing is both funny and seductive to her, since he is naked under the blanket.

We see Frances lock the spare room door, which tells us something is wrong, but the Boy does not notice the door is locked until the next morning. When he does, one would think this should signal how untrustworthy Frances is. But it is only one of many narrative points indicating he should flee that he fails to act upon. This makes the Boy implicit in his own entrapment. Presumably he cannot confront Frances about the locked door if he remains mute, though he does eventually voice his unhappiness by speaking to her in reaction to her nailing the window shut.

Frances tells the Boy of being truant from class when she was a schoolgirl and being caught riding her bike by her "masculine" female English teacher. Frances also says that the teacher was "pretty" and that many of the girls had crushes on her. She does not include herself as one of the infatuated girls, though the implication is there. This may suggest that Frances has lesbian tendencies, although her interest in the Boy's sexuality defines her as heterosexual.

The Boy's return to Frances is indicative of the better lifestyle she appears to offer. He tells Nina that Frances gives him his own room and his own bed, things we presume he does not have in his own house. Nina taking a bath when she visits the Boy in Frances' apartment is explained by her saying that there is no bath in the boathouse, and she is as reluctant to use the one in her parents' house as the Boy is to be there. The Boy is seen smoking a cigar while stoned with Frances, and later he drinks her liquor, which are more signs of Frances' preferred, upmarket lifestyle.

As an employee that Frances has inherited from her mother, Mrs. Parnell is a mother surrogate that we assume Frances at least partially resents. Mrs. Parnell's disapproval of the Boy is apparent when he comes to the door and she tells him to "Hop it." This aligns her with Frances' older friends that we met at her lunch. Mrs. Parnell's disapproval of the Boy continues after Frances lets him in, and Mrs. Parnell stands staring at him. This would seem to be an inappropriate action for an employee. The same can be said of Mrs. Parnell's criticism of the wine Frances has chosen to serve with the cookies, and the cookies as well, which Mrs. Parnell states are burned. Frances points out that Mrs. Parnell is not being asked to eat them, but then Frances apologizes to her for "snapping."

Nina's visit to the Boy at Frances' apartment remains curious. Nina never reveals how it is that she was able to find the exact window of the Boy's room much less the apartment itself. Nina's visit also brings up the possibility of an incestuous attraction between the two. She pretends she has something in her eye to trick the Boy into the bath with her, and she says she has a stiff neck in order to get him to massage her. The expectation of her kissing him, however, remains unfulfilled.

The scene of Frances going to the spare room to seduce the Boy includes her confession that she is lonely (coming after Charles has admitted that he is too). She also states that her mother was lonely and felt that Frances was "little company" for her. Frances admits how old people and their feelings disgust her, and how she finds Charles unattractive, partly because he smells like an old man.

The monologue includes Frances saying, "You are very clever at pretending you don't understand." This implies that she knows the Boy has been faking and makes her implicit in her own humiliation. Frances getting onto the bed without asking permission displays her attitude of entitlement. She tells him, "If you feel you want to make love it's all right. I want you to make love to me." Her stance changes from giving the Boy permission to making a demand. Altman will have the last demand repeated at the film's end for horror impact. The "Please" she adds also makes her seem to be begging, and it is noteworthy that all this occurs in darkness.

In the scene where the Boy is in a restaurant with Nina and Nicky, he makes the comment that Frances "makes a big deal out of sex." While this may be true, we haven't seen any way that he could have come to this conclusion, particularly as he wasn't there to hear her bedside monologue. Him finding the bed made when he returns, with the toys on top of the covers, is evidence that Frances has been in his room and knows of his deceit, yet he still stays with her. Also disturbing should be the fact that the doll's head is detached from its body (this presumably occurred when Frances threw it away from the bed in anger). The fact that she does not mention what has transpired or the Boy's absence warns us that she will do something to retaliate. She runs a bath for him, which we have not seen her do since the first night the Boy was with her. He hears the sounds of her hammering the nails into his room window while he is in the bath.

When the Boy finds the window nailed shut, Altman cuts quick from nail to nail — the only time he uses such fast cutting in the film — and then offers an extreme close-up of the Boy's reaction.

When the Boy goes to Frances and confronts her, both he and she are shown as mirrored reflections in her room. He tells her, "Don't think I can't get out of here. And if you think by keeping me here I'm going to bed with you or anything like that, you're wrong. If I want a girl or anything I'll just go and get one myself. And I might not come back." This speech's bravado ignores the obvious fact that he can't get out. It also seems that he gives Frances a mixed message in using "might" concerning coming back. The speech also acknowledges that she has clearly crossed the line of appropriate behavior, even given the bizarre nature of their relationship. His speaking now alters their relationship's dynamic. Frances tells him that she wants things to stay the way they are, which, of course, is impossible and perhaps evidence of her mental unhinging.

Though she apologizes to the Boy, the expectation initially created that she will let him go is thwarted when she locks him into the room yet again. The fact that she goes out to find a girl for him, however, shows that Frances has heard at least part of what he has told her.

When the Rounder goes after Frances to help her he reveals a humanity that the other men in the bar lack. Frances tells him, "I suppose you think it's peculiar or unusual," in reference to her wanting to hire a prostitute for the Boy, but the Rounder reinforces his non-judgmental attitude when he denies that he thinks those things.

The bar scene offers some humor via a man handing out religious propaganda. He approaches what appear to be two lesbians — one femme and one butch. The butch one tells him to "Get the hell out of here." In response he tells her, "Madame, you do not say 'Get the hell out of here' to the Lord." However, the humor of the situation is soon diluted by the violence she uses to push him into a wall. The aggression of the butch lesbian recalls Frances' earlier story of her masculine teacher, although no one could describe this woman in the bar as pretty.

Further laughs come from the scene in which Sylvia and the Boy are brought together in what we can only assume is the room of Frances' deceased mother. The window in the room creates an expectation of escape, although it lacks a fire escape (like that outside the spare room). When Frances locks them in together, the Boy says, "She's pretty handy with the old key." When Sylvia asks if Frances is watching them, Sylvia yells, "Are you looking at us, lady?" The Boy makes an interesting comment when he tells Sylvia that "[Frances] is just a little mixed up."

Sylvia's aggressive sexuality makes the Boy initially unresponsive to her advances. He is presumably impotent, but the rattling of the bed springs adds more humor. It is not the sound of the rattling that draws Frances back to the room; rather, it is her jealousy as she listens at the door. After she has killed Sylvia, the Boy's flight creates the expectation of his escape, although we know that this is impossible because he is still locked into the apartment.

His hiding place of standing in the hallway may seem a poor one. He is within Frances' view when she emerges from the room where she has killed Sylvia, so that her going straight to him is inevitable. One reading of the Boy's reaction is that he is in shock over the murder, which explains his easy discovery. Frances delivers lines that demonstrate her deluded sense of reality: "You don't have to be afraid. I've told her to go." Interestingly, Frances' last line is "Please" after her repeated "I want you to make love to me." This suggests that even in her madness she still knows she needs the Boy's complicity to achieve her goal.

Altman uses the devices of hand-held camerawork, out-of-focus effects (including out-of-focus objects in the foreground and out-of-focus dissolves), zooms, overlapping dialogue, and odd framing. He often shows Frances in mirrored reflections (sometimes distorted in glass walls) to suggest her duplicity. Equally, the Boy's body is objectified more than that of Frances. He is shown walking around the apartment naked when she is out, which signifies his youth and sensuality for the taking. Frances, on the other hand, is sometimes photographed unflatteringly.

The yellow-green interior color of Frances' apartment is a reflection of the green and brown color scheme of her clothes. It also suggests aging and sickness, as represented by Frances' mother and herself.

The director uses atonal hallucinogenic music for the scene in which Frances is stoned, which adds strangeness and a child-like quality to both Frances and the Boy. Prior to this the score had tended to romanticize her. The atonal music will be repeated in the final scene when Frances goes to the Boy after she has killed Sylvia. It now creates the impression of child-like innocence and creepy horror in the madness of Frances.

Altman distances us from the women in the doctor's waiting room, bathroom and office. He does this by shooting the scenes from an exterior point of view, with the camera behind venetian blinds. The blinds recall the ones on Frances' apartment window that were evident as she gazed at the Boy in the park. Altman will repeat the use of the camera as exterior observer with our view of the windowed entrance to the bar where the Rounder takes Frances to meet Sylvia.

Altman stages the scene in which Charles tells Frances of his feelings for her so that she has her back to him at first. Altman then intercuts their dialogue with the footage of Frances' examination. He presumably does this to parallel the two doctors, but it also spares us Charles' embarrassment at Frances' rejection of him. It might have been more narratively interesting if she had found him appealing, although her voiced "disgust" of older people, and specifically Charles, pinpoints her greater interest in the Boy. When Altman returns to Charles and Frances, she is looking at him. Altman has Dennis look into the camera after Charles leaves, as if Frances is looking towards the spare room where she thinks the Boy is.

Altman uses the ticking of the taxi meter as an aural device in counterpoint to the silence of Frances and Sylvia in the back seat together. He has Dennis walk out of frame after Frances decides to go back to the room where she has left Sylvia and the Boy. Altman holds onto the out-of-focus background shot before cutting to darkness and then the sight of Frances entering the room.

The room is lit so darkly that at first we think Frances lying in the bed means that she has joined Sylvia and the Boy for a threesome. However, the Boy yelling, "What are you doing?" and getting up to turn on the room light lets us see that Frances has stabbed and killed Sylvia.

Altman ends the film with a close-up of the Boy's tear-streaked face as the back of Frances' head moves backward and forward, intermittently blocking the camera's view of him. When her head fully blocks the camera the screen is in darkness. Her repeated line, "I want you to make love to me," sounds like an overdub from the earlier scene in the spare room.

The novel had been published in 1965 and was set in France. The Frances character was middle-aged and referred to as the Madame. The Boy was the Blond and named Mignon. He was a more obvious prostitute who had a black pimp named Yves. The novel has been described as "a Place Pigalle peepshow for tired glands."

In an article dated November 13, 1968, in *The Calgary Herald*, entitled "New Film Company Takes Over Vancouver Studios," Altman describes the film as "a situation created when two totally opposite people are brought together in a world that is continually separating." The article says that the production built a complete twelve-room apartment set, covering six thousand square feet of space and erected in the style of the late 1920s. The set was notable for its lack of corners and being filled with curves: curved hallways, high arches, cylindrical pillars, and huge domes. In Frances' bedroom stands an elaborate walnut dressing table with makeup mirror, consisting of six separate drum-like cabinets in stained varnished and polished like old satin. This piece resembles the dressing tables of royalty in the Royal Suite of the Hotel Vancouver.

In a pressbook article on Dennis, Altman says of working with her: "Directing Sandy has made my job more difficult, for in her performance there has been so much that is exciting. Every take and every retake has been like a new show and I regret at having ever to cut a single moment of it." He added, "A director must never be caught lying to an actor, and with Sandy this goes double."

In his book on Altman, Mitchell Zuckoff reports that the script had first been offered to Ingrid Bergman. She sent Altman a note saying that she was rather insulted by the part. Next it was offered to Vanessa Redgrave, who suggested Dennis. Zuckoff says that during filming Dennis initially objected to the monologue scene because she felt Frances would know that the Boy was not in the bed. However, she agreed to do it for Altman, who believed that it would work. Zuckoff also reports that Jack Nicholson was interested in playing the role of the Boy. Altman turned him down, thinking that he was too old.

Nicholson would have been thirty-one at the time of filming. Michael Burns was twenty-one.

The film served as the inspiration for the Bruce La Bruce Canadian comic adult drama *No Skin Off My Ass* (1993), where a lonely hairdresser watches the title sequence of the film and then visits a local park to invite a down-and-out skinhead to his apartment. He draws the silent man a bath and talks to him as he soaks, and then locks his guest in a bedroom. The next day the skinhead leaves through the window and visits his sister. The skinhead then returns to the hairdresser, and the couple settle into a kinky and happy domesticity.

The production company Commonwealth United Entertainment had previously made *The Three Sisters* (1966). Robert Altman would go on to make *Come Back to the 5 & Dime Jimmy Dean, Jimmy Dean* (1982) with Dennis.

RELEASE: June 8, 1969, with the tagline, "How far will a woman go ... to possess a 19 year-old boy."

REVIEWS: The picture was critically lambasted by *Variety* on May 27, 1969; by Howard Thompson in *The New York Times* on June 9, 1969; by Roger Ebert in the *Chicago Sun-Times* on July 22, 1969; and by Pauline Kael in *5001 Nights at the Movies*. *Variety*, however, would say that "Miss Dennis is strikingly effective." Thompson wrote that she was "like a nasal-voiced computer." Ebert said that she "supplies a convincing portrait."

DVD: Released by Olive Films on February 19, 2013. PAL DVD released in Australia by Force Video on March 15, 2004.

Thank You All Very Much (1969)

Columbia Pictures/Amicus Productions/Palomar Pictures International (Aka *A Touch of Love/ The Millstone*)

CREW: Waris Hussein (Director), Max J. Rosenberg, Milton Subotsky (Producers), Edgar J. Scherick (Executive Producer), Margaret Drabble (Screenplay, based on her novel *The Millstone*), Michael Dress (Music), Peter Suschitzky (Photography), Bill Blunden (Editor), Bernard Sarron (Production Design), Tony Curtis (Art Director), Bob Laurance (Makeup), Bert Ross (Sound), Susie Hill (Hair). Color, 102 minutes. Filmed at Shepperton Studios, Middlesex, England.

CAST: Sandy Dennis (Rosamund Stacey), Ian McKellen (George Matthews), Michael Coles (Joe Hurt), John Standing (Roger Henderson), Peggy Thorpe-Bates (Mrs. Stacey), Deborah Stanford (Beatrice), Roger Hammond (Mike), Eleanor Bron (Lydia Reynolds), Margaret Tyzack (Sister Bennett), Maurice Denham (Doctor Dick Prothero), Rachel Kempson (Sister Harvey), Kenneth Benda (Mr. Stacey). Uncredited: Sarah Whalley (Octavia), Shelagh Fraser (Miss Gurnsey), Raymond Adamson.

SYNOPSIS: In 1967 London, philosophy student Rosamund Stacey is working on her doctorate thesis. She learns that she is pregnant by BBC news announcer George Matthews but does not tell him. She tries to have an abortion but fails. Her friend Lydia moves in with her, and Rosamund has the baby and names her Octavia. The baby has surgery for a congenital heart defect. Rosalind gets her doctorate. Planning to move to Edinburgh, she invites George to see Octavia before he goes overseas.

NOTES: This film is notable for giving Dennis her first mother role, although, ironically, she comes off as another spinster-type woman. However, as with her earlier spinster roles, the character has her own quiet strength, as opposed to being merely a passive victim. Her best scene comes when she screams for forty seconds in order to make a scene so that she may be allowed to see her baby in the hospital (which she has been told is not allowed).

Dennis looks sunnier here than she did in *That Cold Day in the Park*. She is photographed more flatteringly, and her skin has more color. Her hair is the same dark brown

Poster for *Thank You All Very Much* (1969).

color, but it is cut in a bob similar to the flip style she wore in *Up the Down Staircase*. In the film's last scene, George tells Dennis that her hair is turning grey, no doubt due to the strain her character has endured. Dennis employs another English accent here, but with a softer tone.

The actress occasionally stutters, gestures and fiddles with her hair. Her hand-to-her-mouth mannerism can be contextualized by her feeling ill at Lydia's party, and her eyes-closing and lip-biting seem appropriate because of Rosamund's labor pains. Equally, when Rosamund sees Octavia at St. Andrews Hospital for the first time her reaction is to touch her mouth with her hand. Dennis' stuttering falls into place as apparent fear when she telephones the hospital about her labor pains, and also when she is nervous upon meeting George at the chemist's. We see her tears when Rosamund consults with Doctor Prothero.

Rosamund dresses in uncoordinated colors. In the first scene she wears a blue blouse with a yellow skirt, and she sports a green head scarf with blue dress and jacket when she tells Joe she is going to have the baby. In the pub lunch scene with Lydia, Rosalind wears sunglasses inside as she eats, while Lydia does not, which adds to Rosamund's characterization as strangely unconventional.

After Rosamund has the baby, it appears that the wardrobe design gives her better color coordination. She wears her green head scarf with a tan dress as she walks the baby in a pram in the park, and dons a brown jacket over her tan dress while walking in the street with the pram. However, at home Rosamund is back to her uncoordinated self, wearing a blue head scarf with a blue dress and brown jacket.

Director Waris Hussein doesn't give Dennis the long reaction shots supplied by previous directors, except for when Rosamund quiets down after having delivered the baby. Otherwise, she offers a moment of stillness in reaction to seeing George on the television. Her eyes fill with tears when she looks at Dr. Prothero and sees that he is more interested in hearing about her parents than her sick child.

Rosamund can be read as weak and passive when she allows her three friends to visit unannounced, and she generously allows Joe to stroke her knee as he calls her a puritan. Her agreeing with him is ironic, given that she knows she is pregnant but he does not. Since Rosamund also presents as a spinster type, we are surprised that so many men would be pursuing her.

Joe calls her a puritan because she has denied him sex by implying that she is having sex with Roger. She also denies Roger sex by implying she is having it with Joe. Both scenarios are ruses, since Rosamund will tell Lydia that her sex with George was her first. This is apparent from Rosamund's awkward behavior when she is seduced. "Puritan" is also applied to Lydia by Roger at the party after Octavia returns from the hospital, in light of Lydia's rejection of his drunken advances.

Rosamund shows gumption when she tells Joe that she intends to have the baby. When he replies, "All women want to have babies; it gives them a sense of purpose," she answers with the following assertiveness: "What utter rubbish. What stupid reactionary childish masculine rubbish. Don't tell me anyone ever endured the physical discomfort of babies for something as vague and pointless as a sense of purpose."

This eloquent speech alludes to Rosamund's intellect. She smiles in the face of the rudeness of Dr. Morrison's nurse, and then allows a fat woman to push her out of a bus seat. Rosamund endures more humiliation during her examination at the anti-natal clinic, as it's attended by a doctor and five student nurses, one of whom is allowed to clumsily perform the initial examination. The end of this scene has Rosamund speaking the film's title, although clearly she is being ironic.

Rosamund's resolve to have the baby is tested by criticism from Lydia, Joe, Beatrice (who has three children of her own), and Sister Harvey (after Rosamund has had the child, but for adoption remains a viable alternative). Her quiet strength is also demonstrated when she swears at the hospital nurse who tells her that she has been left in the wrong ward. Rosamund tells her, "How the bloody hell can you blame me if one of your colleagues was incompetent enough to put me in the wrong room?!"

Equally, when she is in labor in her own room, she yells to the three nurses who are not paying attention as they talk and drink tea: "For god's sake, somebody come and help me." She also shows a firm decisiveness — without anger — in response to Sister Harvey's suggestion of adoption, despite the fact that the Sister calls her "selfish."

The scene in which Rosamund screams in order to see Octavia begins with Dennis' stillness to express her frustration and anger. With Sister Bennett standing over her, Rosamund refuses to make eye contact with the sister when she tries to reason with her. Only when the Sister pulls at Rosamund to make her leave the nurses' room does Rosamund begin her extended screaming.

In the maternity ward, Rosamund sees how the other women there receive visitors while she does not, so she reads a book instead. The arrival of Lydia and Joe, then, is a surprise to both Rosamund and us. When back at home the baby is crying and it is too early to feed her, she tells Lydia that she can't stand the sound. However, when Rosamund picks up the baby, she stops crying.

The plot point of Rosamund not being allowed to visit Octavia in the hospital is initially used to show Rosamund's willingness to let Sister Bennett control her. We are surprised that Rosamund doesn't assert herself more. It is only when Rosamund returns to make a scene by screaming that we see her determination. The screaming itself may be more aggressive than assertive, but she only does it after her attempts to be more assertive fail to work on the nurses and Sister Bennett. The screaming works only because Dr. Prothero hears it and gives her permission to see the baby. Later, in the ward with Octavia, the doctor practically congratulates Rosamund on her behavior. We also see, when Prothero leads Rosamund through the hospital to find Octavia's ward, how Rosamund smiles to herself in her victory.

The flowers sent by Roger demonstrate his continued interest in Rosamund. So does the later scene where he stops his car in the street to talk to her when he sees her walking the baby. This despite the fact that he is with his fiancée. The later party scene, where Roger makes drunken advances towards Lydia, perhaps demonstrates Roger's interest as being merely that of a philanderer.

The scene in which the hugely pregnant Rosamund watches a movie on television has her strangely fascinated by the sex scene in the movie. Her standing up from sitting on the floor to stretch her back parallels the tame sexual gymnastics on the screen.

Hussein overdoes the music so much in the opening scenes that we expect to find an orchestra playing somewhere. The score quietens down as the film progresses, but he brings it up again for a montage after the baby is born. Additionally, the music makes much of the baby crying when she has a cold.

Rosamund's memory of her seduction by George shows his progression from kissing her hand to her neck then mouth. Although she had been talking all the time he was kissing her, Rosamund then stops and kisses George back. Perhaps out of fear and displeasure she pulls away from him, and only returns when George tells her, "Don't go. Please."

Hussein suggests the sex via a freeze frame of the shot of George lying, clothed, on top of Rosamund, and then showing her in her nightgown. Ian McKellen's George seems as doubtful a heterosexual as Anthony Newley in *Sweet November*, since McKellen's manner appears somewhat effeminate. Some analysts have described George as bisexual, however, he does not say or do anything to confirm this theory.

Hussein ends the film in a strange way. The face of Rosamund is shown in close-up, distorted behind the glass of her front door when she closes it after George leaves. We had previously seen the same distorting glass when Rosamund was at the door to greet her friends at the film's beginning. Then Hussein holds on the door as the distorted close-up of Rosamund walks out of the frame as the last shot.

In her interview with Lenore Nicklin for the *Sydney Morning Herald* on September 19, 1972, Dennis labelled this film her favorite to date. She said, "I think the part was a turning point in my development as an actress." In his article in *The Windsor Star*, dated November 10, 1969, John Laycock proposed that this film showed that she was to the late 1960s what Sophia Loren and Brigitte Bardot and Marilyn Monroe were to various earlier eras — a screen symbol with urgent meaning for her particular period. "Her roles sum up the terror of 'modern' woman — how to get freedom and self-confidence, and then what to do with them."

On the Sandy Dennis Foundation website, Actors Memories page, Ian McKellen is quoted from August 2004 about working on the film and working with her. He reports that he had acted with Margaret Drabble in undergraduate productions at Cambridge, where they had both been directed by Hussein. However, Dennis was cast in the film for commercial reasons, something which he says "on the face of it, could not have been less appropriate," since Rosamund was a "quintessential middle-class English gal."

McKellen says that Sandy started with a hefty disadvantage — her accent — and "confounded us all by delivering the lines in a perfectly credible voice that fitted the character exactly." He comments on her stuttering mannerism by saying that the director and editor cut it out so that her acting was transformed. McKellen would say that Dennis' innate strengths were revealed perhaps more clearly than in any other of her films. He thought her "fresh and original."

The actor also described her as being kind in the face of being saddled with an actor who was a neophyte in front of the camera. Off-camera, they joked together, and she told him about her menagerie of animals and her "hubby" back home in the States. "She never played the star and seemed to enjoy being one of the team, with whom she was popular." On his own website McKellen also commented on Sandy in August 1999: "[She] was eccentric on and offscreen."

Executive producer Edgar J. Scherick would go on to executive produce Sandy's made-for-TV movie *The Man Who Wanted to Live Forever* (1970).

RELEASE: Screened in June 1969 at the Berlin International Film Festival. Released in the United States on August 18, 1969, with the taglines, "She Has a Nice Job. And a Nice Baby. What More Could a Single Girl Want?" "The community is uptight about single girls like Rosamund Stacey. That's THEIR hang up," "Should She Tell Her Parents? Could She Marry Him? Or Should She...? What Would YOU Do?" and "Miss Rosamund Stacey joyfully announces the birth of her baby. With grateful acknowledgements to everyone who helped make it such a beautiful event."

REVIEWS: The film was critically praised by *Variety*; Roger Greenspan in *The New York Times* on August 19, 1969; and Clive Hirschhorn in *The Columbia Story*. *Variety* would say that Dennis' performance was "pin-point accurate." Greenspan wrote that she "is more controlled than I have seen before."

DVD: No American VHS or DVD. PAL DVD released in Britain by Optimum Home Releasing on October 13, 2008.

The Out of Towners (1970)

Paramount Pictures/Jalem Productions

CREW: Arthur Hiller (Director), Paul Nathan (Producer), Neil Simon (Screenplay), Quincy Jones (Music), Andrew Laszlo (Photography), Fred Chulack (Editor), Charles Bailey (Art Director), William Farley (Hair), Clay Lambert (Makeup), Dennis Maitland, Elden Ruberg (Sound), Don Record (Titles). Uncredited: Arthur Jeph Parker (Set Decorator), Forrest T. Butler, Grace Harris (Wardrobe). Color, 93 minutes. Filmed in Massachusetts and New York from April to August 1969.

CAST: Jack Lemmon (George Kellerman), Sandy Dennis (Gwen Kellerman), Sandy Baron (Lenny Moyers, TV Man), Anne Meara (Purse-Snatching Victim in Police Station), Robert Nichols (Mr. Cooper, Boston Airplane Passenger), Ann Prentiss (1st Stewardess), Graham Jarvis (Murray the Mugger), Ron Carey (Barney Polacek, Cab Driver in Boston), Phil Bruns (Police Officer Meyers), Carlos Montalban (Manuel Vargas, United Nations Cuban Delegate), Robert King (Agent in Boston), Johnny Brown (Waiter — Train), Dolph Sweet (Police Sergeant Kovalevski), Jack Crowder (Police Officer), Jon Korkes, Robert Walden (Looters), Richard Libertini (Baggage Man — Boston), Paul Dooley (Hotel Clerk — Day), Anthony Holland (Winkler, Walfdorf Astoria Night Desk Clerk), Billy Dee Williams (Clifford Robinson, Lost & Found — Boston), Bob Bennett (Man in Phone Booth — Boston).

UNCREDITED: Ray Ballard (Attendant), J. French (Cleaning Woman), Maxwell Glanville (Redcap), Hash Howard (Second Hippie), Paul Jabara (First Hippie), Milt Kamen (Counterman), Norma Jean Kron (Flight Attendant #1), Alfred Mazza (Bellhop), Mary Norman (2nd Airline Stewardess), B. Paipert (Sweeper), Ronald Porter (Man in Airport), Philip Suriano (Liquor Store Looter), Arthur Tovey (Man in Diner Car), Meredith Vincent (Washroom Lady), A.P. Westcott (Porter).

SYNOPSIS: Gwen and George Kellerman leave their home town of Twin Oaks, Ohio, to travel to New York City. George has a job interview as the new vice president in charge of sales for his company, Drexel. The trip is a disaster. The couple are rerouted to Boston, their baggage is lost, New York has a transit strike, and their hotel room is given away. They get mugged, kidnapped, and robbed as they sleep in Central Park. They fight with a dog and chased by a horse. Gwen loses her wedding ring, and George breaks a tooth and loses his hearing. They are rescued from a demonstration, and George goes to his interview. He gets the job, but Gwen asks him not take it. On the way home, their plane is highjacked.

NOTES: After two independent productions, Dennis' return to mainstream Hollywood films has her playing second fiddle to Jack Lemmon in what is basically a supporting role. While her character doesn't make much comic impact until the second half of the narrative, her performance suggests the comic ability of her stage work that was barely exploited in her earlier film roles.

It is a bit jarring to hear Dennis' American accent after the British ones she used in *That Cold Day in the Park* and *Thank You All Very Much*, and her accent incorporates an inconsistent New York intonation. Her hair is the same dark brown color it was in *Thank You All Very Much*. She only has one major costume in the narrative, although she wears a brown sweater on the plane back to Boston. The main outfit consists of a blue skirt and jacket, with white coat, white scarf, white gloves, white shoes, and a white handbag. This white color scheme presents Gwen as the more innocent and reasonable of the couple, since George wears a grey suit.

Dennis employs her usual mannerisms of stuttering, smiling, hair-fiddling, pointing, and nodding. Her gesturing is acceptable when she beseeches George to sleep in Central

Poster for *The Out of Towners* (1970). The hyphens are not used in the film's screen title.

Park with, "We have nothing to lose but four cents. Please, George." Dennis also uses her eyes-closing mannerism when George talks to Gwen about the kind of breakfast he wanted her to have, as they eat the stale Cracker Jacks.

She gets a laugh from her delivery of "A man does not stand over you at four o'clock in the morning if he doesn't have a knife, does he?" Also amusing is her head-nodding and smiling when she reassures the whistling-through-his-broken-tooth George that she doesn't hear it.

Dennis' best scenes come when Gwen has lost her wedding ring, displaying her anger at how indifferent George is to it, and in the limousine and in the street afterwards in reaction to the demonstrators. In the limousine she makes Gwen's fear rather funny when she tells George and Manuel "No comprende" in reaction to the protestors interpreting her mouthed "plastics" through the window as "bastards." George tells her to "Calm down, it's just a demonstration," and she replies with, "And then they're going to kill us. Look at their faces."

She is also funny when Gwen is being jostled by the demonstrators in the street after the police bring her out of the limousine. She cries, "I'm blacking out. Somebody help me. I'm blacking out." Then, "Don't pull. Please don't pull. Oh my God, my straps are broken."

The character of George is a control freak with a time schedule, which sets him up for failure. It doesn't help that his character is unlikable. His anger is justified, given the context of what occurs to him, but it grows so large as to become unreasonable. Additionally, Neil Simon's witticisms read as sarcasm and anal-retentiveness. Gwen will describe George as being "sourcastic, whining, irritable, insensitive, and intolerant." George's behavior is perhaps understandable, however, since he works to make precision instruments. Also, the fact that he's up for the vice president job implies that he is a man who is used to being obeyed.

George's overreactions are aimed at people who are mostly trying to help him. This presents people as basically good and George as paranoid. An exception is the image of the savage attempt by passengers to grab luggage from the New York airport carousel, showing just how self-centered people can be. George's stomach ulcer, which his anger aggravates, fails to engender the empathy it might with a more sympathetic character. Also, Lemmon's display of stomach pain, as with the moment where he loses a tooth from eating the toy in the Cracker Jack box, comes off as more comic than real.

That said, Lemmon does occasionally make George funny, particularly in the way he laughs at Gwen's suggestion to sleep under the tree in Central Park at night, and his running about while looking for her the next morning. He is also funny in the sideways glance at the little Spanish boy to suggest the idea George has of searching his pockets; when he kneels to pray in the church in defiance of the order to leave; and in crossing himself as the couple leave the church.

Gwen, on the other hand, is presented at first as George's pacifier. Her stance as an observer is demonstrated by her repeated utterance of "Oh my Gawd," which becomes a narrative running gag. Gwen's assessment of George as being "sourcastic, whining, irritable, insensitive, and intolerant" implies that she thinks she does not behave in any of these ways, although she admits to being sarcastic.

Gwen shows real pain when she cuts her foot walking in Central Park, and perhaps it is easier to empathize with her because she has not behaved as unreasonably as George. It is when Gwen becomes more assertive that the narrative adds dimension to the main characters, since this creates conflict between them rather than having conflict inflicted upon them.

The turning point for Gwen comes when she gets out of the police car the looters have stolen and loses a shoe on the way out. She refuses to get involved with George's paranoid rants, and perhaps for the first time he asks her advice. When he asks her, "Well, what do we do now?" she answers with sarcasm, "Oh well, I'm open for suggestions." Gwen's giving the man in the black cape George's watch — without asking George's permission — is another step. We assume that she knows George would have refused to hand over the watch willingly, so Gwen doing so might have spared George the consequence of his pig-headedness.

When Gwen returns to George the next morning, wearing his shoes and carrying the box of Cracker Jacks, she has demonstrated that she can be a resourceful huntress who also cares about her mate. She is perhaps more angry than assertive when she tells George that she doesn't want to wear his shoes any longer, although the anger is diluted when she apologizes for it.

Gwen is assertive in showing her compassion for the lost Spanish boy in the park and telling George that she plans to stay with him, and letting George go to his interview. Additionally, the climactic scene where Gwen tells George that she hopes that he will not accept the job he has been offered shows her final act of assertiveness

The narrative shifts from the point of view of George and Gwen when we see the looters in the liquor store, when the police chase them on foot, and when Meyers watches the police car being stolen (and George and Gwen kidnapped). An expectation is created when we see George awaken without Gwen after the appearance of the man in the black cape at night. We wonder whether the man has taken her. This expectation is thwarted when we see Gwen returning to George with the box of Cracker Jacks.

Another expectation is created when we see Gwen and George running to each other, with her holding the box of Cracker Jacks. Her smiling adds to the expectation of her being able to feed him. The appearance of Corky will stop Gwen from giving George the box, as he comes between the couple when they get to each other. Their chasing him will result in them salvaging the box and some of the Cracker Jacks. However, one expectation that *is* met comes when George declines the airline dinner offered the couple on their flight back to Boston. We know what happened after they declined the dinner on the Boston to New York flight, and it is George going to get Gwen coffee that has him facing the terrorists who hijack the plane.

The issue of whether George initially took the job is ambiguous, since his boasting about it when he returns to Gwen in the hotel room suggests that he has. It seems that it is only when he hears her wish that he not take it, that he changes his mind and decides against taking the job after all to please Gwen.

Although the narrative carries the unpleasant flavor of schadenfreude, there is still plenty of humor in the dialogue. When the stewardess on the plane tells George, "I imagine we've run into some bad weather," he replies, "You don't have to imagine. Just look out the window." On the train to New York from Boston, George tells Gwen in the dining car, "I was going to take you to one of the best restaurants in the world. Here you are eating peanut butter on white bread with nothing to drink. If you ever get your mouth open again, I wouldn't blame you if you never talked to me." When George tells Gwen, "You can't walk with a bleeding foot," she replies, "Well I would fly but New York is fogged in." The line is made even funnier because of Dennis' hand gesture. Gwen hears the lost Spanish boy crying and points it out to George. George replies, "Maybe it's the man with the black cape and he doesn't like my watch." When George asks Gwen how her wedding ring could have slipped off, she replies, "I haven't had any food. My fingers are thinner."

Director Arthur Hiller uses reduced images under the film's opening credits, and point-of-view and hand-held camerawork. His presentation of the two leads is unconventional, since he introduces them in extreme long shot as they leave their house. He then has the camera behind them in the back seat of the car during the drive to the airport for a medium two-shot, though Dennis can be seen in profile. When we hear George being told of the strikes by a Grand Central Station redcap, there is a simultaneous shot of a man reading the *Daily News* newspaper with the headline "Transit Strike Hits!"

For the scene with the man in the black cape in Central Park, Hiller first shows the man's feet walking, then appearing next to the sleeping George and Gwen. The camera pans up the man's back, and we see that he also wears a hat. He leans down toward the couple before his black cape covers the screen, and we hear Gwen's "Oh my Gawd."

For Gwen's climactic speech about why she hopes George won't take the New York job, Hiller mostly favors Lemmon in close-up listening to Dennis. This is presumably due to Lemmon's perceived greater box-office appeal. Hiller also ends the film rather strangely, providing a close-up of Dennis after George meets the hijackers, then using her aural "Oh my gawd" over a shot of the plane.

Neil Simon's credit reads "A Story by" to show that it is his first original screenplay, as opposed to the previous screen adaptations of his stageplays. Reportedly the story was originally conceived as a one-act play, to be combined with three other tales to comprise the anthology drama *Plaza Suite*. However, when the *Plaza Suite* play was produced in 1968, it only contained the latter three stories because Simon had decided "The Out-of-Towners" tale was better suited to the screen. Simon says that the inspiration for the story came from an incident circa 1967 when he flew to Boston to work on David Merrick's musical *How Now Dow Jones*. "Flying up there, I was caught in a major snowstorm, lost my luggage, spent three hours getting to the hotel on icy streets, a trip which normally was a ten-minute ride."

In an article on the *Turner Classic Movies* website, by Bret Wood, Lemmon reported that he was unsatisfied with the film. He said he loves Neil Simon, that Dennis was quite good in it, and that Hiller was "a ball to work for.... Unfortunately, he's no flaming genius as a filmmaker." Lemmon describes a five-minute sequence which was cut that was better than anything left in, a scene he considered important for character motivation. He offers no further clues to the content of this missing footage, however.

Many of the incidents depicted in the film referenced real-life events going on in New York. There was a transit strike in 1966 and a sanitation strike in 1968. The dilapidated condition and overcrowding on the train the Kellermans take from Boston to New York mirrored the decline of passenger rail service that was occurring throughout the entire country in the late 1960s. The muggings and robberies of the Kellermans mirrored the rising crime rate, and Central Park was portrayed as a haven for crime, which it was becoming known for at the time.

RELEASE: May 28, 1970, with the tagline, "When they take you for an out-of-towner, they really take you."

REVIEWS: The film inspired a critically-mixed reaction in Roger Greenspun of *The New York Times* on May 29, 1970; from *Variety*; and from John Douglas Eames and Robert Abele in *The Paramount Story*. Greenspun wrote that Dennis "exercises, or has imposed upon her, exceptional self-effacing restraint." *Variety* said that she and Lemmon "are superb in comedy characterizations." In her book *When the Lights Go Down*, Pauline Kael wrote that Dennis "rang so many sad-sack variations on 'Oh, my God!' that it was apparent that the movies had been wasting her in snivelling, suffering roles."

DVD: Released by Paramount on November 25, 2003.
REMAKE: Remade as *The Out-of-Towners* by director Sam Weisman in 1999, with Steve Martin.

Mr. Sycamore (1975)

Capricorn Productions/Film Ventures International.

CREW: Pancho Kohner (Director/Producer), Robert O. Kaplan (Executive Producer), George Van Noy (Associate Producer), Ketti Frings, Pancho Kohner (Screenplay, based on the play by Ketti Frings and a story by Robert Ayre), Maurice Jarre (Music), John A. Morrill (Photography), Andrew Herbert, George Van Noy (Editors), Charles French (Art Director), Juliellen Weiss (Costumes), Robert Bau (Makeup), Peggy Shannon (Hair), Craig Felburg, Frances Reid (Sound). Color, 74 minutes. Filmed in 1973 in Venice Beach, Los Angeles.

SONG: "Time Goes By" (Maurice Jarre, Paul Francis Webster), sung by Laura Devon.

CAST: Jason Robards (John Gwilt), Sandy Dennis (Jane Gwilt), Jean Simmons (Estelle Benbow), Robert Easton (Fred Staines), Mark Miller (Rev. Fletcher Dunwoody), Brenda Smith (Daisy Staines), Richard Bull (Dr. Ferfield), Ian Wolfe (Abner/Arnie), David Osterhout (Officer Kelly), Lou Picetti (Humphry), Jerome Thor (Tom Higgins), Curtis Taylor (Harry), Paul Berini, Eddie Lewis (Milkmen), Sydna Scott (Clubwoman), Richard Redd, Ron D'Ippolito (Attendants), Darby Hinton (Frank), Hall Brock (Albert), Tawna Nugent (Albert's Sister), Janine Johnson (Piano Student), Walter Scott (Truck Driver), Lance Cremer (News Boy), Evert Smith (Officer), Don Specter, Wayne Smith (Workmen). Uncredited: Richard Elfman, Josh Gordon (Asylum Attendants).

SYNOPSIS: Mailman John Gwilt digs a hole in his backyard and plants himself, hoping to metamorphose into a tree. His wife Jane goes to see Reverend Fletcher about John's plan, and John takes her home. He learns Arnie has become a tree and visits him in the asylum. John hides from the police in the library with Estelle Benbow. Back home in the hole, he receives a check for twenty-five dollars from *Harpers* magazine for poetry he has sent them. John goes to the park, and Jane finds that a new tree has appeared.

NOTES: Dennis' return to films after six years casts her in a secondary role, playing support to Jason Robards. Her character is presented as the narrative antagonist to Robard's protagonist, even when he is assumed to be mad. This is in contrast to the part played by Jean Simmons, which is smaller than Dennis,' where Simmons is more empathetic towards Robards. However, the narrative does not meet the created expectations of Simmons having a romance with Robards, though Dennis' character is still abandoned by her husband. Her character's ambivalence is demonstrated by a limited tolerance, although the conclusion perhaps suggests a final acceptance of his condition.

Dennis has the same long brown hair we saw her last wearing in *Something Evil*, and here she has it tied back for most of the narrative. However, she wears it loose when we see Jane tell John in the yard that she loves him, and when we see her get out of bed during the tornado. Her wardrobe includes a hat she wears in church, and a headscarf. Jane wears the latter when she is looking for John with the police, when she leaves the house to do charity work, and at the climax when she follows John into the park during the tornado.

The actress uses the mannerisms of stuttering, gesturing, and head-nodding, though they are less distracting here than in her earlier work. She gets a laugh from the way Jane elbows John and nods her head "no" when he gestures to a flower to open its petals while they are in church. She also sings as she holds a prayer book. Dennis' best moment may be when she talks to Solomon, admitting that she has neglected the cat and that she will change. Such a scene recalls her real-life fondness for cats. She is also funny in Jane's jealousy of Estelle when Estelle visits John in the yard.

The film's short running time may explain the appearance of some plot holes due to missing scenes. The review in *Variety* lists a running time of 87 minutes, as opposed to the 74-minute print viewed. John talks to Abner in the asylum garden but doesn't replace him as a tree like expected. John drives the milk truck after the second truck has crashed, whereas before he was only a passenger. We don't see how John gets into the locked library, though the way the police officer climbs in the open window is presumably how John also accomplished it.

Additionally, John and Estelle's escape from the police at the library is not shown. A scene where Jane talks to a group of women in her house has no explanation, although Jane later going out to do charity work is aligned with a women's group. We presume that John seeking refuge in the library with Estelle means they have a backstory relationship, which is not shown. We also don't know how the police think to look in the library for John.

The fey nature of the material, perhaps because it is based on a play, often presents a comic element. There is some wit in the dialogue. When Fred learns that John is cold standing in the yard hole in his pajamas, Fred tells him, "I could loan you my lumber jacket." When Jane tells Fred that John has gone, Fred replies, "Timber!" When John returns from being in the park and is seen by Fred, Fred tells him, "Glad you're out of the woods."

John's desire is leavened by his initial fear and lack of courage. This is apparent from his asking Jane to first go with him and then to stand by him as he metamorphoses. The lack of realism is enhanced by the plot point of the straitjacket and how the nurses seemingly give up trying to take John away after they have mistakenly put the jacket on Fletcher.

Additionally, we see how the flower of a plant opens and closes in reaction to John's gesturing, although the daylight would suggest that the flower would already be open. Later Jane will describe John's gesturing as yoga exercises, with her seemingly unaware of his power to control flowers.

The noises that presumably distract John from his change into a tree at night include Daisy and Frank kissing in a car next door, dogs barking, sirens, church bells, and Solomon meowing. However, the fact that John can sleep standing up would seem to indicate the advanced state of his desire.

Estelle is presented as more aligned with John than Jane. She knows about his desire to become a tree, presumably via gossip, since we don't see him tell her. Her support of his plan is contrasted with Jane's rejection of it, though Jane's loss of a husband no doubt influences her stance. Estelle giving John the fox hunting outfit to wear is more of her alignment with his sense of fantasy, and in John's fantasy in the park the outfit becomes that of a circus ring leader to her bareback horse rider.

John's attraction to Estelle is indicated by the way he touches her arm with the riding crop, and her willingness to dance for him shows her feeling for him. Although they kiss, neither suggest that they are about to have a physical affair and cheat on their respective partners.

The narrative repeatedly takes points away from Jane by having her twice tell him that she wants to support him and then behaving in the opposite fashion. It is interesting that the narrative's expectation of rain is introduced by thunder and lightning, but then the rain is delayed for the moment when John tells Jane that he loves her.

John's second fantasy involving Estelle is also interesting in that in it she asks him to delay becoming a tree because they need more time together. Yet when the real Estelle comes to see John it is to say goodbye because she is going to Greece with her fiancé.

Jane bringing John's mailman jacket rather than a raincoat when it rains may be seen

Mr. Sycamore (1975)

as her subtle attempt to get him back to being a mailman. We see how he discards it (in the same way he will reject Mr. Humphry's offer of a promotion) as an end to his former life.

John's metamorphosis continues with his later inability to eat food or smoke his pipe. He will tell Jane that his new purpose in life is to change from a "plodding aging postman to become a youthful vigorous tree." Jane compares John's desire to become a tree to his past poetry — both make him a "laughing stock." The fact that Estelle then brings John a check for his poetry suggests that his desire to become a tree will also be successful. Estelle calling John "Mr. Sycamore" when she leaves him is the final expression of her belief in him.

A newspaper story appears about John with the headline "Postman seeks mystic transformation." This notoriety results in children coming to see John, where an ice-cream man makes sales, and the children throw things at John. This notoriety is exploited by Fred, who builds a fence to feature advertising (including a sign for an optometrist). It is the tornado that will blow away all this paraphernalia and also allow for John's metamorphosis in the park.

John kissing Jane, and her telling him that she misses him, follows their earlier declarations of love to each other. This is her second attempt to show that she wants to support him but that she cannot, highlighted by the fact of him telling her that he is beginning to take root. He also rejects her request to come inside during the tornado, which will see him finally get out of the yard hole, but only to go to the park. Jane following him shows that she is still concerned about him. At the conclusion she touches the leaves of the tree John has presumably transformed into and then sits by it to further express her caring for him. The fact that Jane does not try to harm the tree is an indication that perhaps she believes it is actually John.

Director Pancho Kohner utilizes hand-held camerawork for the scene in which Fletcher comes for John with a straitjacket. John turning off the room light makes the struggle in darkness farcical, with the payoff revealing Fletcher as the one wearing the jacket. Kohner places a Tarzan yell on the soundtrack for the asylum chase, which reads as unnecessary, comically desperate, and offensive.

The chase between the competing milk trucks seems superfluous and is only paid off when they both retreat from an unseen oncoming train. For this reveal Kohner holds on the screen after the trucks pass by until we see the vehicles head back in the opposite direction and hear the sound of the train. Kohner also uses fast motion for the second part of the chase.

Kohner presents John's fantasy in the park with soft-focus lighting and sun-streaked imagery, with the kiss transitioning the narrative to night. The second fantasy presents Estelle in white, floating in soft focus. Kohner gives Robards long takes when John waits to metamorphose. The first comes when he appears to be distracted by noises, and the second when he receives lots of visitors. Kohner employs slow motion to add an otherworldly quality to John's run to the park, and utilizes a reflection of John in the lake's surface to show his transformation into a tree.

The play was produced on Broadway from November 14 to 28 in 1942 and was subtitled "The Saga of John Gwilt in Eight Verses." It was set in the small town of Smeed, and starred Stuart Erwin as John, Lillian Gish as Jane, and Enid Markey as Estelle. In the play John had read the Ovid fable of Philemon and Baucis, and had been inspired to become a tree by the poetess Estelle. The play included a final scene in which Jane and friends of John sit under the shade of the sycamore tree that John has become. Jane in the play was also more encouraging of John's desire than she is in the film version.

RELEASE: December 12, 1975, with the tagline, "A man's desire to escape ... and finds refuge through metamorphosis."

REVIEWS: The picture was critically lambasted by *Variety* on December 12, 1975; by Leonard Maltin in his *2006 Movie Guide*; and by Jay Robert Nash and Stanley Ralph Ross in *The Motion Picture Guide*. *Variety* said that Dennis "uses her rabbity mannerisms to inject some humor." Nash and Ross wrote that she "is preposterous and posing, [and] her acting tricks pall very quickly."

DVD: No DVD. VHS released by Worldvision Home Video.

God Told Me To (1976)

New World Pictures/The Georgia Company (aka *Demon/God Told Me to Kill/Whispers*)

CREW: Larry Cohen (Director/Producer/Screenplay), Edgar Scherick (Uncredited Producer), Frank Cordell (Music), Paul Glickman (Photography), Arthur Mandelberg, William J. Waters, Christopher Lebenzon, Mike Corey (Editors), Steve Neill (Special Makeup), Halston (Costumes for Miss Raffin), Jeffrey Hayes (Sound). Color, 91 minutes. Filmed in New York and at Pinewood Studios, England, from September to November 1975.

SONG: "Sweet Momma Sweetlove" (Robert O. Ragland, Janelle Webb), performed by George Gentre Griffin, heard in bar.

CAST: Tony Lo Bianco (Lieutenant Detective Peter J. Nicholas), Sandy Dennis (Martha Nicholas), Sylvia Sidney (Elizabeth Mullin), Sam Levene (Everett Lukas), Robert Drivas (David Morten), Mike Kellin (Deputy Commissioner), Richard Lynch (Bernard Phillips), Deborah Raffin (Casey Forster), John Heffernan (Bramwell, aka Callaghan), James Dixon (Squad Detective), Sammy Williams (Harold Gorman), Harry Bellaver (Cookie), Al Fann, (Squad Detective), Lester Rawlins (Logan, Board Chairman), William Roerick (Richards), George Patterson (Zero, aka Joe Brown), Jo Flores Chase (Mrs. Gorman), Walter Steele (Junkie), Alan Cauldwell (Bramwell, aka Callaghan, as a Youth), Robert Nichols (Fletcher), Andy Kaufman (Patrolman Jennings), William Bressant (Police Officer), Bobby Ramsen (Sam, Detective), Peter Hock, Alex Stevens, Harry Madsen, Randy Jurgensen (Squad Detectives), Sherry Steiner (Mrs. Phillips as a Girl), James Dukas (Doorman), Mason Adams (Obstetrician), Armand Dahan (Fruit Vendor), Vida Taylor (Miss Mullin as a Girl), Adrian James (Prostitute), Leila Martin (Nurse Jackson), Michael Pendry (Attendant), Dan Resin, Alexander Clark, Marvin Silbisher (Wall Street Executives), Harry Eno (Medical Examiner). Uncredited: Larry Cohen (Man falling in street during sniper attack/Television interviewer of Mrs. Gorman/Voice of Patrolman Jennings/Man falling from VIP stand in St. Patricks Day parade/Television interviewer on courthouse steps).

SYNOPSIS: In New York City, police Detective Peter Nicholas hears from various murderers that the reason for their crimes is "God told me to." The killers speak of a man identified as Bernard Phillips. He is the son of a woman who claims to have been artificially inseminated by an extraterrestrial force. Nicholas learns that his own mother, Elizabeth Mullins, was also inseminated this way. The detective finds Bernard, who tells him that they are brothers. The hermaphrodite alien wants them to mate so they can start a new species. Nicholas kills Bernard and is arrested for murder, claiming that "God told me to." He is committed to Matteawan State Hospital for the Criminally Insane.

NOTES: Dennis' next film role was another supporting part—this time in a horror title populated by veteran character actors. She only appears in two scenes but receives better billing than Deborah Raffin, who has a larger part but is credited as "guest star." Dennis brings an emotional depth to her role, playing a woman who has been cuckolded but has also suffered three miscarriages, and has had to endure a marriage to a half-alien.

Dennis involves her character with sadness at seeing her estranged husband again, and with compassion for the predicament that his being a Catholic brings (making it impossible

God Told Me To (1976)

Martha Nicholas (Dennis, left) with her estranged husband's new girlfriend, Casey Forster (Deborah Raffin), in *God Told Me To* (1976) (Photofest).

for him to ask her for a divorce). In their scene together, Dennis places her hand gently under Tony Lo Bianco's face to show her empathy for him.

In her second scene, Martha is visited first by Casey and then Peter, so that she gets to play the wife meeting her replacement, with her husband seeing both women together. Dennis smokes and wears a full-length dressing gown, and she uses her trademark mannerisms of head-nodding, gesturing and stuttering.

She continues to play up Martha's sadness, underscoring the pathos of her telling of her multiple miscarriages. Dennis also effectively displays the greater understanding of the older woman, Martha's intuition that Peter is leaving them both, and Martha's silent wish to help Casey, the newly abandoned partner. The soap opera element of the scene is alleviated by Dennis' gravitas, and the viewer becomes aware that she is being wasted in such a minor part. The scene is also enhanced by the apparent madness in Tony Lo Bianco's eyes.

It might have been interesting if Cohen had allowed Dennis some edge, for Martha to have had a natural jealousy of and resentment toward Casey, and also anger at Peter. Perhaps this may have made the scene even more soap opera-ish than it is already, but Martha's existing understanding and forgiveness makes her a bit too saintly to be believed. And she's not even the religious one.

The tone of the film mixes police procedural with horror and its aligned ridiculousness, and a comic-book style of science fiction. This allows for some humor in the narrative. Logan telephones the police to warn them about the officer who has been chosen to kill five people in the St. Patrick's Day parade. Lieutenant Jordan replies, "There'll be five thousand dead drunk, you mean."

Peter asks Everett Lukas to publish the police-suppressed information that all the killers said "God told me to." Lukas tells Peter, "Every priest and rabbi from Statten Island to Yonkers would want to hang me by my mustache for making them read sacrilege over their corn flakes."

As the narrative turns from an investigation into the killings to focus more on Peter's connection to Bernard, it loses some interest. The scene where Peter visits Miss Mullin doesn't have the expected sentimental reunion of estranged mother and son. Her repulsion towards him is influenced by the forced insemination (not that that was his fault) and her virgin-ish attitude towards the pregnancy and birth.

The narrative becomes interesting again when Peter finds Bernard at the climax. Cohen's graphic presentations of the vaginas of Mrs. Phillips and Miss Mullin in their respective flashback memories is paid off when Bernard shows Peter his own vagina. Despite the narrative killings that Bernard is indirectly responsible for, he does inspire sympathy when Peter slaps and strangles him.

Cohen employs expressionist camera angles, hand-held camerawork, slow motion, out-of-focus effects, and a freeze frame for the end. Sepia-coloring is used for the flashback to Mrs. Phillips being found naked on the road by the police officer and her insemination, and color for the memory of Miss Mullins. The alien spacecraft's exterior seen in Miss Mullins' memory is footage of an "eagle" spacecraft from the British science fiction adventure TV show *Space: 1999*, which ran for two seasons from 1975 to 1977. The interior seen in both memory flashbacks is the same show's transporter tubes.

Miss Mullins is first presented by Cohen as a hand opening her room curtain to watch Peter approach the retirement home. She reads as a horror movie monster, which leads up to her character's eventual rejection of him as her son. Interestingly, Sylvia Sidney, playing Miss Mullins, uses Dennis' pointing gesture when she guesses that Peter is her son.

Cohen employs pinpoint lighting over Peter's eyes for the Negro bar scene where he defends himself against Zero, and an extreme close-up of one of Bernard's eyes in the climactic showdown between him and Peter. The shot of Bernard freed from the building debris that we had seen fall on him suggests that he may escape, although this is presumably not the case when Peter is later arrested for his murder.

We do wonder about the departmentalization of the powers of a half-alien who has mastered telepathy but cannot survive strangulation, falling debris and fire. The latter is particularly perplexing since we did not see how Bernard escaped from the fiery furnace previously. Cohen ends with Peter repeating the reason for killing Bernard as "God told me to," with Peter, after the second time, looking directly into the camera.

The score by Frank Cordell recalls the theatrical music style of Bernard Herrmann, who had scored Cohen's earlier film *It's Alive* (1974). Herrmann was hired to score this film and first viewed it the night he died. Cohen dedicated the movie to Herrmann. Cohen reportedly next approached composer Miklos Rozsa, who turned it down, saying, "God told me not to."

In his DVD audio commentary, Cohen says that the idea for the film came from a variation on the tale of Superman, about a human who realizes he has special powers and comes to believe that he is a god. The scenario dictated that the protagonist would have a reverse counterpart as the antagonist.

Cohen advises that the images under the opening credits consist of doctored stock footage taken from a British library, as does the footage used for the interior of the alien spacecraft in the memory flashbacks. Cohen admits that there were pick-up shots filmed for some of Lo Bianco's close-ups when Peter is talking to Harold Gorman. Cohen also employed a double for Lo Bianco for some over-the-shoulder shots, reverses and action scenes. This was necessary because the actor was appearing in an off Broadway play at the time of filming and could not work for Cohen after 6 P.M. Lo Bianco also was unable to return for a month for some needed retakes after he fell and broke a shoulder during the end of the run of his off–Broadway play.

Lo Bianco's casting caused further problems for Cohen. After he had been filming for ten days, the actor wanted to test for the role that Robert De Niro had been fired from in the Mike Nichols film *Bogart Slept Here*. Cohen agreed to shut down production on his film for a week. Lo Bianco told him that if he got the role he would not return to finish Cohen's film.

After being tested, the actor had to wait two weeks for the decision about his casting, so he returned to shooting for Cohen. However, Lo Bianco did not get the part, and Nichols shut down production on *his* film, which would be rewritten and made as *The Goodbye Girl* (1977) by director Herbert Ross. The part that De Niro had abandoned and Lo Bianco had not been given would win Richard Dreyfuss the Best Actor Academy Award.

Cohen reports that Robert Forster was originally cast as Peter, and that he completed two days of filming. However, an issue arose between the actor and the director. Forster insisted on chewing gum for his character, something Cohen thought was inappropriate. Forster agreed to refrain, but would actually hide the gum in his mouth and start chewing when he was three-quarters into a scene. Cohen consequently fired Forster from the film.

Cohen also reports that Geraldine Fitzgerald was cast as Miss Mullin because she resembled the mother of Robert Forster. Once Forster was replaced by Tony Lo Bianco, it was decided that Sylvia Sidney looked more like Lo Bianco's mother. Lo Bianco had worked previously with Cohen in the off Broadway play written by Cohen entitled *Nature of the Crime*. It had been directed by Lonny Chapman and ran at the Bouwerie Lane Theatre from March 23 to April 12, 1970.

Poster for *God Told Me To* (1976).

An article by Earl Wilson that appeared in *The Milwaukee Sentinel* on July 23, 1975, reported that Carol Lynley had been cast in the film, presumably as Casey. Why she left the film is unknown.

Cohen would describe Dennis as a "wonderful actress," someone he was "always a big fan of," and said that he was "lucky to be able to get her." He also describes Martha's speech about her miscarriages in her second scene as a "good little aria" and assumes it was the reason that the actress accepted the part.

The St. Patrick's Day parade was filmed by Cohen before he had secured financing for the picture, and was shot live and without sound. The director would restage a small recreation of the shootings in the parade later in Los Angeles for retakes, using squibs (fake bullet hits). The attack upon Peter by Mrs. Phillips was a deliberate variation on the attack on Martin Balsam in *Psycho*. Cohen also reports that Lo Bianco inadvertently broke one of William Roerick's ribs in the scene where Peter pounds Richard's chest performing CPR.

Cohen says that when Roger Corman's company New World Pictures bought the distribution rights, they changed the film's title to *Demon* in order to associate it with *The Omen*. In the audio commentary the director also makes mention of a sequel, though he is perhaps being comic, since it has yet to be made. He states that it would take place twenty-five years later and we would see Peter contacted by the other aliens who have been waiting for him after his release from the asylum.

RELEASE: November 1976, and re-released March 1977 under the title of *Demon*. The taglines included, "Don't let it control you!" "IT WILL GIVE YOU NIGHTMARES FOREVER," "Conceived In A HELL Beyond Our GALAXY Destined To Rule Our World!" and "Was he a god—the Devil or something even more terrifying..."

REVIEWS: *God Told Me To* garnered a critically mixed reaction from Roger Ebert in the *Chicago Sun-Times* on December 1, 1976; from Elvis Mitchell in *The New York Times* on April 27, 2003; and from John Stanley in *Creature Features*. Dennis' performance is not mentioned in these reviews.

DVD: Released by Blue Underground on August 26, 2003.

Nasty Habits (1977)

Bowden Productions/Brut Productions

CREW: Michael Lindsay-Hogg (Director), Robert Enders (Producer), George Barrie (Executive Producer), Gordon L. T. Scott (Associate Producer), Robert Enders (Screenplay, based on the novel *The Abbess of Crewe* by Muriel Spark), John Cameron (Music), Douglas Slocombe (Photography), Peter Tanner (Editor), Robert Jones (Art Direction), Harry Cordwell (Set Decoration), Richard Mills (Makeup), Helen Lennox (Hair), Enrico Cortese (Makeup, U.S. unit), Phyllis Sangelli (Hair, U.S. unit), Danny Daniel (Sound). Color, 91 minutes. Filmed on location in Pennsylvania and at the EMI Elstree Studios, England.

CAST: Glenda Jackson (Sister Alexandra), Melina Mercouri (Sister Gertrude), Geraldine Page (Sister Walburga), Sandy Dennis (Sister Winifred), Anne Jackson (Sister Mildred), Anne Meara (Sister Geraldine), Susan Penhaligon (Sister Felicity), Edith Evans (Lady Abbess Hildegard), Jerry Stiller (P.R. Priest), Rip Torn (Father Maximilian), Eli Wallach (Monsignor), Suzanne Stone (Bathildis), Peter Bromilow (Baudouin), Shane Rimmer (Officer I.C.), Harry Ditson (Ambrose), Chris Muncke (Gregory), Oliver Maguire (1st Policeman), Alick Hayes (Abbot), Bill Reimbold (Bishop's Secretary), Anthony Forrest (Thomas), Mike Douglas (Himself), Bill Jorgensen (Himself), Jessica Savitch (Herself), Howard K. Smith (Himself). Uncredited: James Berwick, Pam Rose (Nun).

SYNOPSIS: Hildegarde, abbess of a Philadelphia convent, dies before she can sign the paper-

Nasty Habits (1977)

work to name her successor. An election is held, and Sisters Alexandra and Felicity announce their candidacies. Alexandra sets up a system of microphones and cameras to record Felicity's conversations. A break-in by two Jesuit students occurs, and Felicity's love letters to the Jesuit Thomas are found. Alexandra wins the election, and Felicity is ex-communicated. The students blackmail the nuns, and two money drops are arranged. The media exposes the scandal, and Alexandra is called to Rome. She denies any culpability for the recordings, and releases selected transcripts of the tapes.

NOTES: Dennis plays another supporting role in this mild comedy, and she is likable and funny in the sizeable part. As a nun, she wears a habit and glasses. Her character of Winifred speaks and sings in a voice that is louder than necessary to show her gaucheness. She addresses Alexandra as "Alexandria." Although she is described as being a klutz and lamebrained, Winifred is aware enough to avoid becoming a scapegoat. Her courage is demonstrated when she asks for her signed confession back, and to threaten Alexandra with betrayal if it is not returned.

Poster for *Nasty Habits* (1977).

Dennis uses her mannerisms of smiling, stuttering, gesturing and pointing. She is described by Pauline Kael in her review of the film as parodying her own mannerisms. In the scene where Winifred confronts Alexandra's hypocrisy about knowing about the break-in, she appears to exaggerate her stuttering for comic effect. She is also funny in the way she laughs when told by Alexandra that she could eat her up, and when she groans upon learning she was tricked by the money pick-up person (a man in drag).

When Winifred delivers the Jesuit students' hush money, she dresses in odd civilian clothes with mismatched colors: a short skirt, red stockings, high heels, and a hooded, sheer raincoat. When first seen in this garb, she is eating a large slice of pizza on the bus. Dennis' broad performance to demonstrate Winifred's gaucheness extends to her winking at a crossdresser, who turns out to be the pick-up man, in the Wanamaker's ladies room.

In Winifred's second money delivery she dresses as a man, complete with mustache, hat, and trousers, under the same raincoat she wore previously. While at the police station, Winifred smokes. When Winifred asks Alexandra for the return of her signed confession, Winifred sports a band-aid on her upper lip where the fake moustache had been. She tells Alexandra that the police arrest was "the camel that broke the straw's back."

The treatment attempts to score comic effects from seemingly un-nun-like behavior. This includes Geraldine chewing gum and playing football, Felicity having sex with Jesuit Thomas, Alexandra admiring herself in the glass reflection of a cabinet, Walburger and Winifred and Alexandra all smoking, Geraldine sporting a bathing suit as she dives into a swimming pool, and Alexandra wearing makeup for her television newscast.

This behavior extends to the language used by the nuns. When Hildegarde dies before she can sign the succession paperwork, Mildred says, "Oh Christ." Alexandra tells Maximilian and Baudouin, "Your brother Jesuit, Thomas, has taken to screwing our Sister Felicity." At a meal, Bathildis says, "This shit tastes like dog food," and, "It was a put-up job by those mothers," when the police question the nuns about the Jesuit students' break-in. When Alexandra is told that the Jesuit students are blackmailing the sisters, she responds with "Jesus," and when Geraldine is on the telephone with her, Alexandra responds with "Christ."

The screenplay offers some witticisms. Speaking about her ambition to become the new abbess, Alexandra claims, "Unless I fulfil my destiny, my mother's labor pains were pointless." Walburger hears Felicity say, "We'll have a love fest," and she replies, "I must admit Sister Felicity's campaign is rather glamorous." Hearing about how Felicity has been photographed having sex with Thomas, Alexandra comments, "I glanced at the negative. Only the beautiful should make love if they might be photographed."

In a telephone conversation with Gertrude, Alexandra asks her, "How am I to appeal to these nuns' higher instincts?" Gertrude tells her, "Appeal to their lower instincts."

The novel (and film) parallels the Watergate scandal of 1972 involving the break-in at the Democratic National Committee Headquarters and the revelation that President Nixon had a tape-recording system set up in his offices. Alexandra stands in for Nixon, while her feared opponent Felicity takes on the Senator George McGovern role. Walburger and Mildred are presidential Chief of Staff Bob Haldemann and Nixon aide John Ehrlichman. Winifred is White House Counsel John Dean, Gertrude is National Security Advisor and Secretary of State Henry Kissinger, and Geraldine is Vice President Gerald Ford.

Director Michael Lindsay-Hogg uses hand-held camerawork and point of view photography to good effect. He presents lowbrow comedy via Geraldine's bad driving and car crash when she brings Maximilian and Baudouin to the nunnery, and then shows her ripping her habit on one of the car's tailfins. He employs the rather theatrical sound of thunder when Winifred signs her confession, and the sight of penguins at the North Pole when Gertrude's helicopter arrives. Lindsay-Hogg deserves praise for presenting a mostly all-femme environment that recalls *The Women* (1939), where females can be shown to be as mercenary and status-hungry as men who seek power, with the added irony of making the women nuns.

In his book *Luck and Circumstance: A Coming of Age in Hollywood, New York, and Points Beyond*, Lindsay-Hogg says that while he thought he had a brilliant cast, he was not happy with the final film because his cut was not the one that was shown in cinemas.

Glenda Jackson and Geraldine Page both deliver funny performances. Jackson uses a soft, controlled voice to conceal Alexandra's duplicity, and Page's Method mannerisms are well suited to comedy. For instance, Jackson's face immediately changes from smiling to sneering at Winifred as she leaves after demanding her signed confession be returned.

The only false note comes when Jackson recites Felicity's list of abbey crimes, as her thesaurus-enhanced recitation gives the impression of an actor displaying her vocal technique. In her review of the film, Pauline Kael likened this to an actress demonstrating her powers by reading aloud from the telephone directory.

In an interview with Ed Blank on May 30, 1981, which appeared in *The Pittsburgh Press*, Jackson said that the film was one of her favorite comedies, but it was dismissed by most critics and audiences. "I think it's really very good indeed ... marvellous ... it hasn't got an end; we always knew it didn't." Blank says that Jackson especially liked the opportunity to work with other prominent actresses. "That was such a treat because you never get to work with actresses. If you've got the woman's part, that's it usually, there aren't any others."

RELEASE: March 18, 1977, with the tagline, "The Sisters of this convent are devoted. Devoted to money, power and some very nasty habits." The film's poster that shows a nun with a stockinged leg exposed under her habit dress while holding a tape recorder was changed to create an alternate version in which her leg is *not* exposed.

REVIEWS: *Nasty Habits* received critically mixed reviews from Vincent Canby in *The New York Times*, on March 19, 1977; Rex Reed in *The Village Voice*, on March 28 1977; and Pauline Kael in *When the Lights Go Down*. Canby said that Dennis, "mugging outrageously and badly, gives the kind of performance that, 40 years ago, would have sent her to bed without her supper." Reed wrote that she steals the movie: "[She's] klutzy, rabbit-faced, near-moronic and totally lovable." Kael said, "In her first real crack at screen farce, Dennis turns tactlessness and blurting into woozy slapstick; it's a blissful performance — she's such a drip she's creepy."

DVD: Released by Jef Films/Mvd on August 29, 2002.

The Four Seasons (1981)

Universal Pictures

CREW: Alan Alda (Director/Screenplay), Martin Bregman (Producer), Michael Economou (Associate Producer/Editor), Louis A. Stroller (Executive Producer), Victor J. Kemper (Photography), Jack Collis (Production Designer), Jerry Wunderlich (Set Decorator), Jane Greenwood (Costumes), Terry Miles, Lynn Donahue (Makeup), Judy Goodman (Hair), Gary Cunningham (Sound), Sol Tabachnick (Sound, New York Crew), Candy Flanagin, Terry Saunders (Special Effects), Arlene Alda (Vegetable Photographs), Antonio Vivaldi (Music). Color, 103 minutes. Filmed on location in New York, Virginia, Vermont, Charlottesville, Georgia, and the Virgin Islands.

MUSIC/SONG: "The Four Seasons," Berliner Philharmoniker; "Concerto in C for Two Trumphets," Paillard Chamber Orchestra; "Flute Concerto in C Minor" and "Flute Concerto in F" and "Concerto in C Minor" and "Concerto No. 12 in D," I Musici; "Strangers in the Night" (Bert Kaempfert, Charles Singleton, Eddie Snyder), played by the Winter Roadhouse Band.

CAST: Alan Alda (Jack Burroughs), Carol Burnett (Kate Burroughs), Len Cariou (Nick Callan), Sandy Dennis (Anne Callan), Rita Moreno (Claudia Zimmer), Jack Weston (Danny Zimmer), Bess Armstrong (Ginny Newley Callan), Elizabeth Alda (Beth Burroughs), Beatrice Alda (Lisa Callan), Robert Hitt (Room Clerk), Kristi McCarthy (Waitress), David Stackpole (Doctor).

SYNOPSIS: In spring in New York three married couples go to a country home for the weekend. They are Jack Burroughs and his wife Kate, Nick Callan and his wife Anne, and Danny Zimmer and his wife Claudia. By summer Nick has divorced Anne and has a younger

114 • THE FILMS　　　*The Four Seasons* (1981)

Dennis in *The Four Seasons* (1981).

girlfriend, Ginny. The couples sail on a boat. In fall they visit Nick's daughter Lisa and Beth Burroughs, the daughter of Jack and Kate, at the girls' college. They meet Anne, who has also come to visit Lisa. In winter the couples are at a ski resort, and Nick has married Ginny. She is pregnant and walks out on the others in anger. Danny goes in search of her and falls through a hole in the ice. He is rescued, but his car sinks into the ice. The couples walk back in the snow.

NOTES: Dennis' supporting part in this production marked her return to film roles after an absence of four years, although again she only plays a secondary character. It is notable that she was passed over for the leading female role, which was taken by Carol Burnett, who was four years older than Dennis. This may have been due to Burnett's long-time friendship with Alda. However, the fact that Burnett (and also Rita Moreno) was required to appear in a bathing suit, while Dennis' character wears billowy formless dresses, may support the idea that she was not physically suitable to play Burnett's part.

Perhaps because of Alda's background in television, the narrative has the superficial feel of situation comedy. He gives some of the characters reflective moments in which the actors provide subtle responses. Dennis and Len Cariou in particular are good at this. However, the film is ultimately unsatisfying.

Dennis uses her mannerisms of stuttering, smiling, gesturing, pointing, hand to the forehead, and hair-fiddling. Her stuttering may fit the character of Anne as an indecisive person in the Spring scenes, and it is does help her awkwardness and nervous reaction to meeting Ginny in the Fall confrontation.

Dennis' best scene is perhaps when Anne returns to the narrative for Fall and confesses to Kate and Claudia what her life has been like since her divorce from Nick. Alda gives Dennis her only close-up, and her departure has her raising her hand to gesture goodbye as Anne has her back to the other women.

The screenplay portrays Anne as "inert" and obsessive. Alda makes her look vulnerable as she walks alone, as seen by Jack and Nick. This continues when she lies against Nick looking at the brochure of the boat Kate has suggested renting for the summer. The audience has been told of Nick's intention to leave Anne, so her ignorance of this and apparent continuing fondness for Nick enhances her vulnerability. However, Anne's future is shown to be not so bleak as anticipated when Nick finds a magazine to which Anne has contributed photographs of people.

The men cooking lunch may appear to be a reversal of the gender cliché, but there is also an element of competitiveness in it. This competitiveness is continued in the men riding dirt bikes, where they race back to the house. Jack and Nick's bravado is punished when they both crash on the pathway, and the apparently weaker and fearful Danny gets back first and celebrates his unexpected victory by stripping semi-naked.

Danny's competitiveness is demonstrated when he claims that he can make a better Italian meal than Claudia, who is Italian. Claudia announcing that she is Italian will become a running gag in the narrative, culminating in the Fall episode when Danny yells out the window of their hotel room, "This woman is Italian," so that Claudia will no longer have to announce it. The men's competitiveness continues with them arguing over who will pay the lunch bill. Both Danny and Jack's envy of Nick is conveyed by their silent reactions to Ginny fetching ice for Nick from the hotel ice machine.

Jack is shown to be judgmental and less than empathetic towards Nick when Nick tells him that he is unhappy with Anne, since Jack expresses more concern for the abandoned wife. Jack's disapproval of Nick later leads to Kate's accusation that Jack is jealous of him. This comes particularly after Ginny appears in the narrative. Kate's additional accusation that Jack analyzes when he gets angry rather than expresses his anger will later result in Jack breaking crockery and a chair, and throwing the moose head in the fireplace at the Winter cabin.

Jack's disapproval of Nick continues with his resentment towards Nick for not telling him of his affairs before he left Anne. However, Nick makes the point that Jack would not have been supportive anyway. Jack's supposed jealousy of Nick is demonstrated at lunch when Jack eats a desert with Ginny, and in the soccer game, that the couples and the children play. Nick pushes Jack in the game and Jack then tackles Nick, something Kate notices. This leads to Kate's confrontation with Jack, where again she accuses him of being jealous.

Anne is shown to be artistic in her photography but slow to produce it. This slowness will be one of the criticisms Nick expresses of her. He tells Jack that he married her for her stability, but she is "inert." He says, "I've never heard one stimulating idea come out of her mouth." This criticism is underlined by a look exchanged between the men at dinner after Anne talks about her new idea of photographing vegetables together. She says, "I've been thinking about photographing vegetables in combinations. Not just one at a time. But I'm not sure yet."

Nick also criticizes Anne's obsession with details, and Alda shows her walking alone back and forth as she mulls something over. The women's connection is shown in the way both Kate and Claudia express their surprise at how Nick has brought Ginny with him for the Summer vacation. The couples even complain about the sound of Nick and Ginny's lovemaking keeping them awake at night.

Claudia's announcement during the discussion of Nick and Ginny's behavior on the boat that "I wanna feel like them" is paid off by the sight of her and Danny also swimming naked in the sea. However, though this statement appears to align her with Ginny, in the Fall episode she attacks Ginny when the latter accuses Anne of being unreliable. Claudia's resentment of Ginny extends to her criticism of the younger woman's bathing suit and Danny attributing to her some "mystical qualities." Kate reveals her own surprising resentment of Ginny in the kitchen of the Winter cabin when she tells her, "Don't get upset about what you don't understand."

When Nick told Jack about wanting to leave Anne, he denied that it was because he had met someone else. However, Danny's information later relayed to Jack that Nick had multiple affairs while he was married suggests that perhaps Nick did have someone else waiting. We don't know the timing of when he met Ginny versus when he divorced Anne, so we don't know if Ginny is culpable in the affair. However, Claudia's comment is aimed more at Nick as the person who has been unreliable towards Anne, than at Ginny, who takes the force of the criticism. Claudia will highlight this when she tells Nick, "It was you I wanted to make cry."

The scene in the Fall episode where Nick is alone with his daughter Lisa offers a great moment. He tries to get her to smile, but she is determined not to. Lisa's depression over the divorce of her parents also presents her as a reminder of Anne, just as the chipper Beth is a reflection of Kate. Lisa is shown to be homely and wears glasses, and Nick refers to her as looking like the Bride of Frankenstein. Lisa will be shown to kick the soccer ball when it is passed to her in the couples' game, so we see that she is not totally without hope.

The competition between the men continues, with Nick and Jack skiing in the Winter episode. Their race has Nick skiing down a hill first and then asking Jack to follow him. The fact that Jack loses by falling and injuring his leg gets a surprising payoff when it is revealed that Nick is actually hurt worse, though he doesn't immediately know it.

Kate has told Jack in private how she hates the couples' vacations and wants one only with Jack. However, she later tells the others that she wants friends, perhaps because of the guilt she feels over what she said to Ginny. Jack's anger "freak out" comes after he is accused by the others of being "unforgiving, cold and judgmental." After breaking things, he tells them that he expects "closeness, warmth and unconditional acceptance." However, the male competitiveness resumes in the argument between Jack and Nick over who is going to search for Ginny.

The narrative has plenty of humor. In the car ride to the Callan country house, Danny complains that Claudia has brought her work with her and that he hasn't. She replies, "Danny, please. You're a dentist." When Anne tells Kate and Claudia what Nick said of Anne's taking three years to photograph vegetables—"Don't you think that's a little constipated"—Claudia comments, "Well, that depends on the vegetables."

Jack asks if Claudia is seasick on the Summer boat, and she replies, "No, I'm just trying out this new green makeup." At the hotel in the Fall episode Danny asks Jack, "How come everyone thinks I'm paranoid? You've discussed this behind my back, haven't you?" When Danny describes Ginny as guileless and vulnerable, Claudia responds, "She sure took on a lot of mystical qualities once you saw her swimming naked."

However, other efforts fall flat, like the jumping into the lake, the couples crowded into the boat's kitchen all trying to cook at the same time, Jack's dropped pants during his argument with Kate in the Fall hotel, and Danny's Mercedes sinking into the ice at the Winter climax.

The Four Seasons (1981)

Alda's first image is of an adult woman leading pairs of children down the street on a rope. This action is a prefiguring of how the couples' vacations are organized by the Burroughs. Jack is also the character who claims to want to always "get to the heart of things" and thereby usually leads the conversations. This role is reflective of Alda as the film's director, who leads the actors.

After the prologue, in which the major characters are introduced for the drive to the country, Alda uses nature montages to suggest the titular seasons as introductions for each act. Music is also employed for a time transition in the Summer episode when the boat moves to a new anchorage, and over the soccer game in the Winter segment.

Some of the characters' expressions of friendship reads as self-congratulatory and self-conscious; especially in the way the couples kiss each other and appreciate their quips. However, Alda and Burnett's laughter at Kate's effort to read to distract them from Nick and Ginny's lovemaking noises on the Summer boat reads as genuine. Burnett is also funny in her scream in the Fall hotel room, which she suggests Jack copy to indicate that he is angry, and when she laughs at Danny's expressed fear of the elastic of his underwear in the roadhouse scene of the Winter episode.

Alda said in an interview that when he was promoting the film, he brought the clip of Jack and Kate hearing Nick and Ginny making love to *The Tonight Show*. He thought it would be perfect because it was a little risqué. The NBC censor refused to let him show the scene because they said you cannot portray the sex act visually or aurally. Alda found this amusing, since *The Tonight Show* broadcast what he considered burlesque vulgarity. They routinely made jokes about women's breasts, and replayed the film where one of the Ames Brothers throws an axe and hits an Indian in the crotch, and then Johnny Carson would stagger around holding his own crotch.

In his interview on *Inside the Actors Studio*, Alda said that he had a hard time writing the script on a typewriter at home. After six weeks of difficulty he decided to borrow a friend's house by a lake for a week. He followed the advice of Norman Lear, who said to dictate

Poster for *The Four Seasons* (1981).

the script as a good way to get over a block. Alda went out on the lake in a rowboat and dictated scenes by improvising, and finished the script within the week.

He also advised that he rehearsed the cast for three weeks. He thought it was very important that the actors became friends, because he felt that you can't "act" friendship. The most valuable thing they did was to eat and drink together, and Alda encouraged them to tell each other about their lives. All the actors were open to this. By the end of three weeks they were friends, even though some of them had never met before. This fed into the behavior onscreen, "the stuff in between the lines," and he thought that's what made the movie work.

Alda said that listening to the Vivaldi music is what inspired the film. He came up with the idea of seeing only the three couples when they are on vacation, and then concocted the story from there. Alda also admitted that the character of Jack is based on himself, although he did not intentionally write it that way. Other sources say that the inspiration was an actual incident where Alda thought he had judged a friend too harshly. He realized that not only was he wrong, but that friendship goes through "seasons," so he wrote the script based on that notion.

RELEASE: Released May 22, 1981, with the tagline, "Here's to our friends ... and the strength to put up with them."

REVIEWS: *The Four Seasons* received critically mixed reactions from Janet Maslin in *The New York Times* on May 22, 1981; David Denby in *New York Magazine* on June 1, 1981; and Clive Hirshhorn in *The Universal Story*. Denby wrote of Dennis, "[She] has been given such an embarrassingly typical Sandy Dennis role (a vague kook) that she's almost exploited."

DVD: Released by Universal Studios on May 31, 2005.

REMAKE: The film spawned a short-lived CBS television series in 1984, executive produced by Alan Alda and Martin Bregman. It starred Jack Weston as Danny, with Marcia Rodd replacing Rita Moreno as Claudia, as the only one of the married couples from the film. Beatrice and Elizabeth Alda repeated their roles as Beth and Lisa, however There were also new characters played by Tony Roberts, Barbara Babcock, Allan Arbus, and Joanne Kerns.

Come Back to the 5 & Dime Jimmy Dean, Jimmy Dean (1982)

Sandcastle 5 Productions/Viacom Enterprises/Cinecom Pictures

CREW: Robert Altman (Director), Scott Bushnell (Producer/Costumes), Giraud Chester (Executive Producer), Ed Graczyk (Screenplay, based on his play), Pierre Mignot (Photography), Jason Rosenfield (Editor), David Gropman (Production Design), Stephen Altman (Set Decoration), Greg Fauss, Ben Wilson (Costumes), Fidelio Della Bartolomeo (Hair), David Craig Forrest (Makeup). Color, 105 minutes.

SONGS: "Must Jesus Bear the Cross Alone," sung by Allan Nichols; "Keep on Walking" (Allan Nichols, Tom Walls, Jeff Wilson), sung by Jo Ann Harris; "Sincerely" (Harvey Fugua, Alan Freed), and "If It's a Dream" (Stella Unger, Victor Young), and "Seems Like Old Times" (Carmen Lombardo, John Jacob Loeb), and "It May Sound Silly" (Ivory Joe Hunter), and "You'll Never Know Till Monday" (Robert Allen, Al Stillman), and "Are You Looking for a Sweetheart" (Larry Stevens, Harthman Sherwood), and "I'm in the Mood for Love" (Jimmy McHugh, Dorothy Fields), and "The Last Dance" (Sammy Cahn, James Van Heusen), and "Miss You" (Charles Tobias, Henry Tobias, Harry Tobias), and "Answer Me My Love" (Gerhard Winkler, Carl Sigman, Fred Rauch), and "Kid's Stuff" (Bob Perper, Sal Izzo), and "Moon Love" (Mack David, Mack Davis, Andre Kostelanetz, Pyotr Ilvich Tchaikovsky), and "Melody of Love" (Hans Engelman, Tom Glazer), sung by the McGuire Sisters. Uncredited: "Amazing

Come Back to the 5 & Dime (1982)

Grace" (William Walker, John Newton), heard on the radio in the opening scene; "The Eyes of James Dean Are Upon Us," sung to the tune of "The Eyes of Texas" (aka "I've Been Working on the Railroad") by Cher and Karen Black and Marta Heflin and Kathy Bates; "Wives and Lovers" (Burt Bacharah, Hal David), sung by Karen Black.

CAST: Sandy Dennis (Mona), Cher (Sissy), Karen Black (Joanne), Sudie Bond (Juanita), Marta Heflin (Edna Louise Johnston), Kathy Bates (Stella Mae), Mark Patton (Joseph "Joe" Qualley), Caroline Aaron (Martha), Ruth Miller (Clarissa), Gena Ramsel (Sue Ellen), Ann Risley (Phyllis Marie), Dianne Turley Travis (Alice Ann).

SYNOPSIS: On September 30, 1975, an all-female fan club called the Disciples of James Dean meets inside a Woolworth's five-and-dime store in McCarthy, Texas. The club honors the twentieth anniversary of the actor's death. The store is near Marfa, where Dean filmed *Giant* in 1955. The club's leader, Mona, has claimed that her son, Jimmy Dean, is the son of the actual James Dean. Joe comes to the reunion as "Joanne"—he has had a sex change. S/he exposes Sissy's secret that Sissy has had a double mastectomy, and that Joe himself is the real father of the boy. The latter reveal signals the end of the club.

NOTES: Dennis' return to a leading film role comes as the film adaptation of a stage play she also starred in, as opposed to being an original film part. It is her first such part in thirteen years, but it will also be her last. Dennis will only be seen hereafter in supporting film roles and in television guest appearances. However, it is pleasing to see her again playing a leading role after years of television and supporting parts, and she brings tenderness, humor, anger, and pathos to her performance. It is regrettable that director Robert Altman sabotages her eight-and-a-half-minute monologue, which is the character's narrative centerpiece and might have been a tour-de-force for the actress.

The role of Mona is not a romantic role per se, partially because she is playing the mother of an adult child. However, the flashback structure of the narrative does give her a romantic, if covert, interest in Joe. The narrative deprives Mona of Joe as a returning romantic partner, though even in the flashbacks of the past, Mona is shown to deny Joe's feelings towards her. However, the Hollywood milieu of the material, with the idea that Mona is mother of James Dean, adds its own romanticism to the piece.

The casting of Dennis in the leading role was down to Altman, who had previously directed her in *That Cold Day in the Park* and who had directed her in the play. One wonders if Altman had not made the film, whether she would have been chosen for the part given her perceived poor box office at this time. This is also presuming that the play would have been made into a film at all, given that it only enjoyed a moderate run on Broadway.

It is interesting to ponder what other actresses might have been considered for the role had Altman not directed. The production would have needed someone with bigger box-office appeal than Dennis, which wouldn't have been hard to find at the time. The new crop of leading ladies, however, like Meryl Streep, Sissy Spacek, Jessica Lange, and Debra Winger, were too young for the part. Another newcomer, Glenn Close, had played the mother of Robin Williams in the comedy *The World According to Garp* (1982), but to avoid being typecast in older parts she subsequently chose roles that were closer to her real age.

The role of Mona called for an actress who was age appropriate and also willing to play the mother of an adult man. This latter point is said to be the turning point in the career of an actress, since once she plays the mother of an adult child, her days as a romantic leading lady are over. The age-appropriate consideration seems to leave out Barbra Streisand, who doesn't seem right for the part anyway. Equally, Jane Fonda, Goldie Hawn, Sally Field, Diane Keaton, Marsha Mason, Susan Sarandon, and Jill Clayburgh had all yet to play the mother of an adult child. The same goes for Faye Dunaway, even if she hadn't been virtually ostracized by the Hollywood community after her role in *Mommie Dearest* (1981). Older actresses who might have been considered were Anne Bancroft, Ellen Burstyn, Shirley

MacLaine, Gena Rowlands, and Joanne Woodward. Perhaps even Tuesday Weld. But none of these alternate casting choices were to be.

Dennis is generally photographed more attractively here than she was in *The Four Seasons*. However, the golden/white light in the present scenes alternates between making her look beautiful and aged. This alternation can be rationalized by Mona's emotional states and the locale's heat, which results in her appearing hot and sweaty. She looks beautiful in repose, however, particularly when standing next to the counter that holds the mock-up of Reata, the house from *Giant*, and a theatrical mask that lies on its side. She also looks beautiful when Mona stares at Joanne after Joanne has revealed her transformation. Dennis looks less attractive in the blue-lit flashbacks. One close-up of her in flashback proves less than successful when it becomes apparent that she is not the twenty-years-younger self she is meant to be playing.

Dennis speaks in a southern accent and uses her mannerisms of stuttering, hair-fiddling, head-nodding, pointing, gesturing, tongue-poking, and mouth- and face-touching. She even includes a double pointing gesture in one scene when she alternates from one hand to the other. As a touch of self-reference, Altman has Cher's Sissy amusingly mimicking Mona's speech and gestures.

Mona's delusionary neuroticism may provide some context for this mannered behavior. Even her weight can be justified as that of a woman who has given birth, although she has had twenty years to get back in shape.

We see Dennis dancing three times in flashbacks. The first is when Mona dances with Sissy and Joe to the song "Sincerely," though the dancing consists more of poses than big movements. The second time is when it is only Sissy and Mona before Joe enters after he has been beaten up, and the third comes at the end with Sissy and Joanne, who changes back into Joe.

Dennis is funny when laughing at Sissy's announcement that she'll try out as an ice-skater, and uses a laugh to transition to anger when Mona shakes the ladder that Sissy stands on. The narrative also highlights Mona's tenderness towards Edna Louise in particular, whose own vulnerability is demonstrated as a victim of Stella Mae, who thinks of her as dumb. Joanne will also express tenderness towards Edna Louise, although her comment that Edna Louise "glowed brighter than anybody" is inexplicable. In the play, Joanne adds to this idea when Edna asks Joanne, "Am I still glowin'?" and Joanne replies, "Just like a Texas sunrise."

Dennis shows her vulnerability in the way Mona breathes heavily as she reacts emotionally to the news of James Dean coming to Texas, a moment that Altman matches with the McGuire Sisters' song "If It's a Dream." Mona also makes noises before she advises Juanita that her heart "tends to skip a beat now and then" because she suffers from asthma.

She also has a lovely quiet moment of disappointment when she shows Juanita the latest piece she has retrieved from Reata. Juanita tells her, "Some of those you got in the past years are better," and Mona replies with a sad "Oh." She will repeat this "Oh" when she learns that the other women now know that she has lied about Jimmy Dean.

Mona's asthma prevents her from staying in college since the heat of the weather is not good for her. She tells Joe in flashback that she cannot leave the town and go away with him because it is only in McCarthy that she can breathe easily. The issue of Mona's breathing presents her as a character that is sensitive and physically fragile. In an argument with Sissy, Mona will say that she has raised herself above the sensibility of the town. However, her asthma, combined with her feeling upset over the missing Jimmy Dean, leads her to become breathless at one point, as if suffering from a panic attack.

Her fragility will extend to madness in her delusion that she has borne the child of James Dean, since she denies that it was actually Joe to whom she made love. Mona's fragility is also juxtaposed with the anger she expresses. This comes out in the flashback when she learns that Joe has been fired. She objects to Sissy saying "Three cheers for Mona Magdalene" after Mona reminds her that it was she who was allegedly chosen to have James Dean's child. Mona also expresses anger when she attacks Sissy at the climax.

Her anger is also mixed with concern over the whereabouts of Jimmy Dean, which leads to Mona having trouble breathing and her need to sit down and recover. When Mona starts laughing with the women who are laughing *at* her, the expectation is created that her laughter will again transition to anger. However, she initially simply stops laughing when told that they are laughing at her.

Mona's anger is finally released after Sissy tells her that she has been giving Jimmy men's magazines, which he reads behind the comic books Mona has given him. Mona's fury erupts in a physical attack upon Sissy. Once Mona's lie is exposed, Dennis uses a look of reactive shock before Mona admits the truth when she says, "I feel so embarrassed. I feel like such a fool." Mona lets Joanne rest her head on her shoulder and tells her, "I chose you. I loved you." However, Mona's subsequent disappearance from the present-day narrative implies that Mona will not have a future with Joanne.

The 1982 version of the play published by Samuel French shows the changes the film version made, including dropping some dialogue that make the plot points more explicit. The play describes the store as one of the chain of the H.I. Kressmont Company, which has existed since the late 1920s. Joanne references Kressmont when she quotes the highway sign "See the son of James Dean, visit Kressmont's five-and-dime, nine miles ahead." Mona does as well when she tells Joanne, "We were the busiest, most prosperous Kressmont store in all of Texas."

A large blade fan that doesn't work is a feature of the set and referred to in the play's dialogue, but it is not in the film. The play began with the overture to *Giant*, and Juanita takes a telephone call from Stella Mae, who is on the way to the reunion. Mona is described in the stage directions to be in her late thirties, while Dennis was aged forty-four for the stage version and forty-five for the film. In flashback, Mona is seventeen.

The play had Mona entering while holding a paperback copy of *Gone with the Wind*. That book is recalled when Mona tells Juanita that she has been told by Alice Marie in Waco that Mona is like Scarlett O'Hara, and James Dean is her Clark Gable. The piece of Reata she has retrieved comes from the top of the porch roof. Sissy is said to be the same age as Mona and has bleached hair. Cher was age thirty-six for both the stage and film versions, and had black hair. The single outstanding feature about Sissy is said to be her "gigantic" breasts, and they are described as "large to the point of being abnormal ... awesome."

Juanita leaves to buy bread, as opposed to Sissy in the film, who goes for groceries. Mona says that the turned faucets in the restroom don't produce water, and Juanita asks if she turned them all the way. Mona replies she turned them "as far as they'll go." It is only Sissy who says, "You can't turn 'em no further than that," which is different than the film, where the line is said by both Sissy and Juanita.

Sissy refers to Mexicans as "wetbacks." Mona calls Jimmy Dean "retarded in the brain" and a "moron" to Sissy earlier in the play than in the film, where Mona later tells Joanne. Talking about her son this way in the play causes Mona to have an asthma attack, and

122 • THE FILMS *Come Back to the 5 & Dime* (1982)

***Come Back to the 5 & Dime Jimmy Dean, Jimmy Dean* (1982): From left are Joanne (Karen Black), Mona (Dennis), and Sissy (Cher).**

Juanita gives her pills taken from Mona's purse to calm her down. Mona later has another attack after Stella Mae and Edna Louise arrive, and Mona calls out for Jimmy Dean. Sissy claims that Jimmy Dean is not the son of James Dean, specifically when she talks of how she feels Mona was her best friend. Sissy will also claim that Mona's asthma is "phony" too.

Mona accuses Sissy of saying that Jimmy Dean should be locked up in an institution for "crazy people," which seems to go against Sissy's later claim that the boy is normal. Mona is also more specific about her night with James Dean when she tells Juanita, "I dream about it all the time … Me and James Dean all tangled up in each other's arms under the stars … All peaceful an' quiet with only the slightest summer breeze."

Joanne arrives at the store before Stella Mae and Edna Louise. Joanne's age is not given, but Karen Black was age forty-two in the stage version and forty-three for the film. In the play she wears a pant suit, as opposed to the skirt, jacket and blouse Joanne wears in the film. She is looking for sunglasses as one of the lenses in hers is cracked. Joanne tries on sunglasses, she finds in the store and buys a pair. Joanne exits to use the restroom when she hears that Stella Mae and Edna Louise have arrived.

Stella Mae is the same age as Mona and Sissy. Kathy Bates was age thirty-three during the stage version and thirty-four for the film. Edna Louise is said to be younger, but her specific age is not given. Marta Heflin was age thirty-six during the stage version and thirty-seven for the film. Stella Mae enters wearing the club's jacket, which is described in the stage directions as a windbreaker, as opposed to producing it later in the film. Edna Mae has also brought her jacket but can't get it out of the plastic bag she carries.

Act 1 ends with Mona verbalizing her memory of seeing the hurt and bleeding Joe, and Sissy guessing that Joanne is Joe. Act 2 juxtaposes Mona and Sissy and Juanita with Joe in the past, and all the women in the present. Joe says that Lester T called him a "pansy" during the attack and also "Joanne," which prefigures Joanne's name.

In the play, Stella showing off the black-market photograph of James Dean is juxtaposed with Mona in the past showing the club members a more sanitized photograph of Dean with his shirt off that she has obtained. Mona tells the story of how she met James Dean both in the past and the present. Mona in the past shows the matches that she claims Dean touched and says in the present that she finally sold them to get the money for Jimmy Dean's braces.

The play includes a funny exchange that is omitted from the film. When the women are drinking, Joanne asks if there is anything she can mix with the bourbon. Sissy gestures toward the restroom and tells her toilet water, and Joanne replies, "I'll drink it straight."

Since the film's narrative is based on the play, it cannot help but be somewhat theatrical. Characters exit and enter as in a play to allow others to speak privately, and information is teased out and revelations made. Some of the language is stylized southern. For example, when the women subdue Mona after she has attacked Sissy at the climax, Mona says, "I'm wondering just offhand if you think it's possible that you could let go of my wrist for about five seconds." Interestingly, that line is not in the play version.

Characters like Sidney, Lester T, and, most importantly, Jimmy Dean are spoken of but not seen. The latter recalls the symbol of the dog Sheba in William Inge's play *Come Back, Little Sheba*. Mona calling for Jimmy Dean at the door of the store is a repeated motif. It is perhaps fitting that we never see the boy, since his identity is an illusion. This increases the pain of Joanne's situation, since she presumably never meets her own son. This pain is already heightened by the claim made by Mona, but denied by Sissy, that the boy is mentally retarded.

The midway appearance of Joanne operates as a catalytic device. It alters the status quo, since the information she has about Sissy's secret and Joanne/Joe's admission that it was she who made love to Mona and not James Dean will forever change things, making this reunion the last.

Jimmy Dean supposedly stealing Joanne's car is another catalyst that leads to the reveal of Mona's lies about the boy's mental condition and the identity of his father, although the former plot point is not definitely resolved. Mona says that the death of James Dean is what caused Jimmy to be born a moron, since the "shock of his dying jostled my insides."

The phrase "deceiving to the eye" is repeated and recalls a similar idea in Tennessee Williams' *A Streetcar Named Desire*. This refers to the false front of Reata and also the appearance of Joanne. She does not immediately identify herself, and neither is she recognized by the others, although Mona feels there is something familiar about her.

While Mona is painted as deceitful, the others eventually confess that they never believed her claim that she had made love to James Dean. Sissy will say, "We all know it and accepted it for years." This supposed knowledge makes all the prior action seem a contrivance, when it appeared that they believed Mona's tale and were willing to play along with it by coming to the reunion. Why the club hasn't had a meeting in twenty years is not explained, other than the fact of all the members growing up and away from the town, except for Mona and Sissy.

When Mona asks Juanita whether she too knew Mona had lied, Juanita tells her that she didn't see how it was possible. However, Mona's monologue does explain how it might have been possible since she was at the location shoot for *Giant*. While there remains ambiguity as to whether Jimmy Dean is really a "moron," Mona does eventually admit that she had lied about having sex with James Dean.

The characters' reaction to the idea of Joe's sex change ranges from the disgust of Juanita and Mona to the curiosity of Sissy and Stella Mae, and Sissy's greater acceptance. Stella Mae's curiosity about the mechanics of the operation reveals her small-town mentality. When she asks Joanne if she is a hermaphrodite, Joanne replies, "Just tell everyone I'm a freak. Your friends should understand that."

Joe's sexual identity confusion in the flashbacks has him preferring to be with women and enjoying dressing in drag, but still able to love Mona and have sex with her. Mona's claim that she is better than the townspeople extends to Joe, who feels their disapproval. Attitudes toward Joanne are also expressed at the end by Edna Louise and Juanita. Juanita refuses to shake Joanne's hand goodbye. Edna Louise offers hers then withdraws it quickly after Joanne has shaken it, which shows the limits of Edna Louise's tolerance.

Joanne's confrontation over Sissy's deception about the end of her marriage is more narratively pleasing than Sissy's later confrontation with Mona. This is perhaps because Sissy's vanity and preoccupation with her breasts makes her a less sympathetic target than Mona. Equally, Joanne's attack upon Sissy gives Joanne power, while the attack upon Mona takes power away from Joanne because Mona does not embrace Joanne as Jimmy Dean's biological father. We also see that Sissy is more resilient than Mona. Sissy will forgive Joanne and remain friends with her, but Mona does not recover from her attack and does not return to bond with the other two women.

The final reveal that Mona has been lying is less satisfying in terms of character because of its apparent cruelty. Some may think of Mona as the narrative's cruelest character in her deceptions, but she does not see herself as cruel. This is apparent when she comments, "It just makes me sick to my stomach that people can be so cruel." When Mona tells Sissy, "Constantly I find that you tell nothing but lies," the remark could be aimed at herself, since Mona is the most deceitful of the women.

The conclusion does not explain what becomes of Mona. After refusing to join the others in the idea of another reunion in twenty years, she walks out of the main room of the store, but we do not know where she goes. She appears to Joanne in the flashback mirror, repeating the "Deceiving to the eye" phrase and ending it with, "But it's time."

There is some humor in the narrative. In flashback Juanita tells Mona her opinion of Joe: "He is a sick boy and should be treated before he grows up into a Communist." Mona asks Sissy if she has ever dreamt of what it would be like to make love to somebody real famous, like James Dean. Sissy replies, "You really should experiment with some nobody first before you tackle someone as important as he is."

After Sissy tells Juanita that she is better off praying for the poor people in China than her, Juanita replies, "We stopped praying for them. It didn't seem to be doing much good." When Sissy leaves the store after her fight with Mona, she tells Juanita, "I'm going outside to cool off. Ain't that a laugh" (referencing how hot the temperature is). After Sissy claims that Lester T has only left her temporarily for work, Joanne says, "That's a very believable explanation, but unfortunately not accurate."

Altman uses the sounds of a train (described by Mona as "a slowly passing train") and wind for the present-day milieu. He uses stagey aural effects for the arrival of Mona's bus and Joanne's car, and the subsequent stealing of Joanne's car. The sound of thunder is heard during the climactic revelations, and then fainter thunder in the distance indicates the passing of the storm after all the truths have been revealed. Additionally, Altman includes the sound of wind during the end credits which show how the store is now empty and abandoned.

Sissy's line "It aint rained in twenty years" is combined with thunder for the first of the series of flashbacks which are seen in the 5 & dime's counter mirror. Altman darkens the present-day foreground, employing a theatrical device, to present the background memories. Altman has the arrival of Stella Mae bring the narrative back to the present, and later utilizes shots of Mona and Sissy holding hands and circling as another transitional device.

The present-day scenes are lit with a golden glow to perhaps suggest the heat of the day and the dust, and blue lighting highlights the flashbacks. Altman also employs out-of-focus effects, a floating camera which sometimes zooms, overlapping dialogue, and slow motion. He uses a subjective camera for Edna Louise's point of view when she returns in her new dress but thinks she is alone in the store.

After Mona looks at a photograph of the clubs members, we see them posing for it in the flashback mirror. A click and a flash — the photograph being taken — brings us back to the present.

The combination of music on the jukebox and dialogue is occasionally jarring in its aural clutter; however, the songs often work. Examples include the way "If It's a Dream" plays over Mona's reaction to James Dean coming to Texas, and how the song played on the Wurlitzer in the present transitions to its being heard in the past.

During Mona's monologue about how she met James Dean, Altman has her speaking to Joe in the mirror flashback, and then Joe transition to Joanne in the present. His filming of Mona's eight-and-a-half-minute speech is miscalculated and distracting, with songs heard over her talking and the camera straying from Dennis. This stands in opposition to the way he stays on Karen Black for Joanne's shorter speech about meeting Lester T.

Altman reveals Joanne's identity as Joe by matching an image of the hurt and bloodied Joe in the flashback mirror with Joanne standing in the present-day store doorway, and his touching his face matches her doing the same. However, she touches the opposite side of the face to show that the mirror image is a reverse. Altman also adds the song "Miss You" to the moment.

Altman differentiates the three main actresses via hair color. Mona is a brunette, Sissy has black hair, and Joanne is a redhead. Since we see in the flashbacks that Joe had brown hair, we assume that Joanne has dyed her hair or may be wearing a wig. Altman makes no attempt to make the actresses look younger in the flashbacks from twenty years previously.

Cher overacts her youthful character sense in some of the flashbacks, but she is touching when she cries over Sissy's lost breasts. Karen Black strikes some odd poses, which fit with the odd character that Joanne is, and also with the awkwardness of the situation. Her smiling as she speaks to Sissy while confiding in her is a nice touch, as is her shaking as she cries when she hears Mona's claim that Jimmy is a "moron." Black is also funny in her sly smile at hearing Sissy's telling how Lester T has gone away for a job but will return, since Joanne knows Sissy is lying. Kathy Bates gets one good moment when Stella Mae yells, "I'm happy, Godammit!" to Edna Louise, who has accused her of the opposite.

In his 1982 conversation with James Grissom, Tennessee Williams would speak of the film. He said it has many flaws, but watch Dennis' face. "She allows you into her mental processes in a way I've never seen before. She boils and thinks and plots."

Altman had previously demonstrated an interest in James Dean when he made the documentary *The James Dean Story* (1957) with co-director George W. George. In his book on Altman, *Robert Altman Interviews*, David Sterritt quotes the director as saying that the documentary did not work out the way he would have liked, since it developed into a "sentimental, soppy thing." Altman had wanted to make the film not to idealize Dean but to "go the other way."

Altman says that when he was presented with the Ed Graczyk play he reacted with, "I don't want to read it, I don't want to do it, I'm not interested in James Dean." But when he did read it he became interested because he saw it not as being about Dean but about the phenomenon he caused, which was what the documentary was also about. Altman stated that had he not previously made the documentary, the stage play and the film adaptation would have been entirely different pieces of work. Therefore he considered the three as "all one piece of work."

In his interview with Richard Combs in *Monthly Film Bulletin*, Altman recounted his decision to make a film of the play as follows: "I was standing backstage one night and watching the play and realized there were things on those actresses' faces which the audience couldn't see." He then shot the film with the Broadway cast during a six-year period in his career when he was more interested in filming plays than making original movies. The funding ensured that this film would receive cinema and cable television screenings, whereas other titles were made directly for television.

In Boze Hadleigh's book *Hollywood Lesbians*, Dennis says that Altman talked about the idea of Mona being naïve in thinking that a gay James Dean would impregnate her only *after* the film was released. At the time of filming, the notion of Dean being gay wasn't as widely believed. The idea certainly isn't raised in the play.

In her gossip column dated January 28, 1983, Marilyn Beck quoted Cher on potential Academy Award nominations. Apparently a campaign was being waged to secure Dennis a Best Actress nomination and Cher a Best Supporting Actress nod. However, Cher said that her nomination should be for Best Actress. "When you think about it, I did have more lines than she did in the movie."

RELEASE: First screened at the Chicago International Film Festival in October 1982. Released in the United States on November 12, 1982, with the tagline, "A cup of coffee and a side of dreams."

REVIEWS: The film earned critically mixed reactions from Vincent Canby in *The New York Times* on November 12, 1982; Roger Ebert in the *Chicago Sun-Times*; and Pauline Kael in *Taking It All In*. Canby said that Altman "seems to burden Miss Dennis with most of the close-ups, which do nothing but emphasize an already distraught performance." However, Kael wrote that "Mona is Sandy Dennis' most extravagant creation. She's compellingly strange and repressed, yet carnal and, I think, very beautiful."

DVD: Not available on DVD. Video released by Embassy and M.C.E.G./Virgin Vision June 21, 1989.

Another Woman (1988)

Orion Pictures

CREW: Woody Allen (Director, Screenplay), Robert Greenhut (Producer), Jack Rollins, Charles H. Joffe (Executive Producers), Thomas Reilly, Helen Robin (Associate Producers), Sven Nykvist (Photography), Susan E. Morse (Editor), Santo Loquasto (Production Designer), Speed Hopkins (Art Director), George DeTitta Jr. (Set Decorator), Jeffrey Kurland (Costumes), Fern Buchner (Makeup), Romaine Greene (Hair), Frank Graziadei (Sound). Color, 81 minutes. Filmed in New York and New Jersey from November 1987 to January 1988.

Another Woman (1988)

SONGS: "Gymnopédie No. 3" (Erik Satie), performed by Orchestre De La Société Des Concerts Du Conservatoire; "The Bilbao Song" (Kurt Weill and Bertolt Brecht), sung by Bernie Leighton; "Unaccompanied Cello Suite in D Major" (Johann Sebastian Bach), performed by Yo-Yo Ma; "Ecuatorial" (Edgard Varèse), performed by Ensemble Intercontemporain; "Perdido" (Juan Tizol), performed by the Dave Brubeck Quartet; "You'd Be So Nice to Come Home To" (Cole Porter), sung by Jim Hall; "Lovely to Look At" (Jerome Kern, Dorothy Fields, Jimmy McHugh), sung by Bernie Leighton; "A Fine Romance" (Jerome Kern, Dorothy Fields), sung by Erroll Garner; "Make Believe" (Oscar Hammerstein II, Jerome Kern), sung by Erroll Garner; "Symphony No. 4 in G Major" (Gustav Mahler), performed by the New York Philharmonic; "Smiles" (J. Will Callahan, Lee S. Roberts), sung by Teddy Wilson; "On the Sunny Side of the Street" (Jimmy McHugh, Dorothy Fields), sung by Teddy Wilson; "Sonata for Cello and Piano No. 2 BWV 1028" (Johann Sebastian Bach), performed by Mischa Maisky and Martha Argerich; "Roses of Picardy" (Fred E. Weatherly, Haydn Wood), sung by Frankie Carle; "Sonata for Cello and Piano No. 3 BWV 1029" (Johann Sebastian Bach), performed by Mischa Maisky and Martha Argerich.

CAST (in alphabetical order): Philip Bosco (Sam), Betty Buckley (Kathy), Blythe Danner (Lydia), Sandy Dennis (Claire/Dream Marion/Dream Jennifer), Mia Farrow (Hope), Gene Hackman (Larry Lewis), Ian Holm (Dr. Ken Post), John Houseman (Marion's Father), Martha Plimpton (Laura), Gena Rowlands (Marion Post), David Ogden Stiers (Young Marion's Father), Harris Yulin (Paul). Additional cast (in end credits order): Frances Conroy (Lynn), Fred Melamed (Patient's Voice / Engagement Party Guest), Kenneth Welsh (Donald), Bruce Jay Friedman (Mark), Bernie Leighton (Piano Player), Jack Gelber, Paul Sills, John Schenck (Birthday Party Guests), Noel Behn, Gretchen Dahm, Janet Frank, Dana Ivey, Alice Spivak (Engagement Party Guests), Mary Laslo (Clara), Carol Schultz (Young Clara), Dax Munna (Little Paul), Heather Sullivan (Little Marion), Margaret Marx (Young Marion), Jennifer Lynn

The dream Marion (Dennis) and Ken (Ian Holm) in *Another Woman* (1988).

McComb (Young Claire), Caroline McGee (Marion's Mother), Stephen Mailer (Young Paul), Jacques Levy (Jack), Dee Dee Friedman (Waitress), Josh Hamilton (Laura's Boyfriend), Kathryn Grody (Cynthia Frank), John Madden Towey (Waiter), Michael Kirby (Psychiatrist), Fred Sweda (Tom Banks), Jill Whitaker (Eleanor Banks).

SYNOPSIS: Marion Post is a fifty-year-old New York philosophy professor attempting to write a new book. She hears voices coming through the air vent from the apartment next door. She is particularly intrigued by the voice of Hope whose claim that her life is full of deceptions resonates with Marion. Marion has memories and dreams about the conflict in her past. She finds Hope in an antique store, and the women talk. Marion sees her husband Ken with Marion's friend Lydia. She ends her marriage. She decides to change her life by becoming close to her estranged brother Paul and feels at peace.

NOTES: Dennis only appears in three scenes in this film, but even in a supporting role it is a step up in her career after her previous appearances on television. The scene in the bar is perhaps her best, where she uses a direct gaze in her angry confrontation, as well as a pained expression. The gaze additionally displays her character's ability to listen, as her performance in the first part of the dream also demonstrates, since she speaks to Ian Holm's Ken without looking at him while sitting on a bed in front of him.

Dennis' appearance in the dream play as Marion points out the differences in performance between Dennis and Gena Rowlands as the character. Dennis was age fifty-one at the time, so she is playing age appropriate, and her performance is certainly more unconventional and mannered than that of Rowlands, even given the context of the dream as theater. The argumentative tone of the conversation in the dream scene allows Dennis to be funnier, although it is apparent that she is less physically fit than Rowlands. The idea of Dennis playing Marion as the film's protagonist is certainly an intriguing one, although by this time her box office appeal was presumably lower than that of Rowlands.

Dennis sports the same short hair she wore in *The Equalizer* TV show episode, and only has one costume to wear in her scenes. She uses the mannerisms of stuttering, head-nodding, gesturing, hand-to-the-forehead, and smiling. She also fiddles with her clothes during the bar scene, perhaps to emphasize her character's apparent boredom (rather than merely the affectation of an actress). Her Claire seems to be a neurotic, since her accusations that Jack he has not looked at her nor heard what she has said is untrue. In reply, Jack will suggest that Claire is a little drunk, which may also supply some context. Dennis also smokes during the bar scene.

Narration is inserted here (a lazy narrative device) to relay information we cannot otherwise know or perceive. Director Woody Allen also uses flashbacks, noticeably transitioning from Marion looking at unseen photographs, and shows the adult Marion conversing with the young Paul, although as her younger self. Marion appears to remember conversations and events that she was not privy to, such as the younger Father telling the younger Paul that he must take a job in a paper products factory, and Laura and Scott together after they have made love.

Additionally, Marion has a dream in which she sees her concerns dramatized in a play, and she talks to Sam in his suicide scene, where he had originally been alone. Marion's dream play prefigures the argument she has with Ken about their lack of sex life, and lines of Sam from the dream play transition into Marion's memory of giving Sam the theater mask. Marion at lunch with Hope telling her about the lost chance of having a child leads to Marion's memory of Sam finding out she has had an abortion.

The narrative succeeds when it presents scenes of social awkwardness and confrontation. These include Lynn telling Marion how Paul hates her, Kathy's appearance at the engagement party (which occurs just as a toast to the couple is being made), Claire confronting Marion over David, Paul's accusation that Marion is disappointed and embarrassed by him and his writing, Marion confronting Ken about their less active sex life, and Sam learning that Young Marion has had an abortion. The kiss between Marion and Larry in the park as Marion's dramatization of her reading his novel provides the final awkward moment when she retreats from it.

The climactic confrontation between Marion and Ken, during which she tells him how she knows about his affair with Lydia, lacks anger. Marion only assumes that Ken is having the affair, since what she has seen could be interpreted differently, but this assumption provides her with the resolve to end her marriage. This despite Ken's claims that the affair was "passing, never very serious, and utterly foolish." We only learn that the marriage is ending from Marion's later scene with Paul where he points out the irony of he and Lynn staying together while Marion is breaking up with Ken, and from Marion then referring to it in the scene where she hopes that she and Laura can remain friends.

At the engagement party, Larry describes Ken as a "prig and cold and stuffy," which is demonstrated by his apology to Kathy of "I accept your condemnation." This phrase will be repeated by him to Marion after she questions him about their lack of a sex life. Larry also labels Ken as a "snob" for the use of this phrase, since he says Ken handled a difficult moment "too well." However, Ken's affair with Lydia, presumably ignited by a willingness to make love on a living room hardwood floor, shows that Ken can engage in his own form of reckless and sensual behavior. It's just that this behavior is not inspired by Marion. Additionally, he hugs and kisses Marion in the scene where she asks him to hug her. Ken telling her that the reason they are not having sex is due to them going through a less active period may in reality be hiding the fact that his sexual appetites are being fulfilled by Lydia.

Paul will remind Marion that she described his attempt at writing as "overblown, too emotional, maudlin" and "so embarrassing." In Marion's dream, her Father tells the Psychiatrist that he has not given his daughter "enough feeling." Sam will accuse Young Marion of a "lack of feeling" over her having the abortion. In her psychiatric session that Marion listens to, Hope will describe Marion as "sad" and "lost," having "nothing," "can't allow herself to feel," having a "cold, cerebral life" which is also "empty," and being "bright and accomplished" but having "alienated everyone around her."

Marion initially responds to Larry's kisses in the park underpass and at her engagement party before the "wall went up" and she moves away from him. This indicates what Larry describes as her capability of "intense passion" if she "allows herself to feel." Marion also demonstrates a physical affection when she hugs Ken and touches the arm of Cynthia Frank in gratitude for her compliment. Marion also takes Paul's hand after he rests his hand on her shoulder in the scene at his office, and she puts her arm around Laura in their scene in the park after she has told Laura about her intention to divorce Ken. Interestingly, Young Marion is kissed by Sam as she wears the theater mask to suggest a disconnect, though we assume that their relationship is sexual because she is impregnated by him.

Marion's mother is presented as an abstract figure in an extreme long shot walking the grounds of the country house. She is described by Marion as someone who "loved nature, music, poetry. That was her whole existence." Later we will hear Marion's Father confess that he never loved his wife because he did not choose to marry the woman he really loved. This recalls Marion's choice of Ken over Larry Lewis. Marion reads the Rilke poem "Archaic Torso of Apollo," said to be her mother's favorite. She spots her mother's tears on the last lines, which read, "You must change your life." This implies her mother's unhappiness and also perhaps an awareness of the regret of Marion's Father in marrying her.

Marion's mother is suggested to be an arty delusional, and in this she recalls the Geraldine Page mother in Woody Allen's *Interiors* whose exacting standards of perfection turned her daughters into psychological wrecks. Marion, however, is shown to have more strength. One can consider her new reflection as a mid–life crisis as opposed to a total mental breakdown, and Marion will tell Hope that fifty "traumatized" her. Marion's continued insomnia and inability to concentrate to write her new book are also signs of her reflective preoccupation, although she is shown to prefer to listen to the voices of Hope's sessions rather than work on her book.

The plot point about Marion being able to hear the voices in the psychiatrist's office is resolved when Marion finally, informs the psychiatrist. He will tell Marion that the "strange acoustic oddness" has happened before, and he knows what to do about it. He also gives her information about Hope, which one might think is breaching confidentiality.

That Hope has now terminated her treatment and has gone away may suggest that she has served her narrative purpose of curing Marion. This is implied at the end when Marion tells us that "for the first time, in a long time, I felt at peace." There is a more sinister suggestion that the suicide the psychiatrist stated Hope had begun in Marion's dream may take place in real life.

The screenplay has its share of pretentious howlers, like, "I should never have seduced you — intellectually, I mean." And the gnomic question of whether a memory is "something you have or something you've lost." However, it also offers some genuinely funny lines. Marion tells us when she notices the noise disturbance in her flat, "While I'll admit that eavesdropping on the intimate revelations of a psychiatrist's office might be fascinating to some people, it was not exactly what I had in mind when I rented the place." Kathy refers to the things she returns to Ken at the party as "artefacts from more civilized days between us."

Marion's father tells her that he has disposed of her mother's things because "there are times when even a historian shouldn't look at the past." He criticizes Paul's divorce because he can't "stick to anything." Claire tells Marion, "We didn't just drift apart. I withdrew." And in regards to David, she says, "I must have seemed very bland to him after he met you."

Director Woody Allen utilizes some clever staging by having one character talk to another off-camera, who later enters the frame. His most tricky staging device shows the older and younger Marion in the same scene with Sam when he learns she has aborted their child. Allen switches from Sam talking from one Marion to the other via camerawork that conceals and then reveals.

Gena Rowlands' appearance is changed for the film, her blonde hair dyed a red/brown (which recalls Mia Farrow's hair color). Rowlands' hair is worn in severe styles, either tied back in a braid or in a ponytail. Interestingly, for the two scenes in which she wears a ponytail — at Marion's engagement party and during the dramatization of Larry's novel — the hairstyle reflects her restrained sensuality. Marion's wardrobe sees her wearing primarily brown, changing to black after she has broken up with Ken and is able to write again.

Rowlands effectively masks her warmth via hooded eyes and some stiff body language. Despite this, Rowlands is still funny in the conflicted emotions she expresses in response to Larry kissing her at her engagement party, highlighted by her stuttering. Despite the restrictions placed upon Rowlands, she still gives a good performance, demonstrating a lot during her frequent bouts of listening (as the part requires).

Originally Mia Farrow was supposed to have played the part of Marion, but her real-life pregnancy prevented that. Farrow was age forty-three at the time, so she would have been too young to play the fifty-year-old Marion. However, Rowlands was age fifty-eight, so she was older than the character she played. It is reported that Rowlands was allowed to read the entire script in advance in order to decide whether she would take the part. This was unusual, as reportedly Allen only gives actors access the scenes in which they would appear. Of course, Rowlands' character appears in nearly all the scenes in the film.

Another original casting choice that ultimately changed was for the character of Lynn. Mary Steenburgen had been originally cast as Lynn, and scenes had been shot. Then Allen decided to recast the part, and Steenburgen's scenes were all cut. Lynn, as played by Frances Conroy, only has one scene in the existing film.

During filming Farrow was pregnant with Woody Allen's child. She would give birth on December 19, 1987, to a boy they named Satchel Ronan O'Sullivan Farrow. In her 1997 memoir *What Falls Away*, Farrow would report that she began the film when she was seven months pregnant, and that she wore a pillow to replicate her stomach after the December birth of the baby for the January reshoots.

Pauline Kael claims in her review that the film is an homage to Ingmar Bergman's *Wild Strawberries* (1957). Kael says that the basic units of Allen's film are Bergman's scenes. A viewing of *Wild Strawberries* indeed reveals some similarities, as well as some major differences The Bergman film centers on Eberhard Isak Borg, a seventy-eight-year-old doctor and professor living in Stockholm who is to be given a fiftieth jubilee doctorate in Lund. Bergman's film employs narration at the beginning, and introduces Isak's relatives with photographs the way Allen does with Marion. The unmarried Isak has a son, Evald, a daughter-in-law, Marianne, a deceased wife, and a still living mother. Unlike Marion, Isak is unmarried and lives with his housekeeper, Agda. His journey has him driving to the ceremony and reflecting on his life along the way.

Marianne wears her hair in a ponytail that resembles Marion's ponytail, and, like Marion, she smokes. Evald has borrowed money from Isak, as Paul has done from Marion. Marianne tells Isak that Evald both respects and hates him, as Lynn had said of Paul to Marion. Marianne describes Isak as an "inveterate egotist" and reminds him of how he judged her marriage as a failure when she had asked him if she could live with him. Like the criticism that Paul says Marion made of his writing, Isak does not remember what he is accused of.

The modern Sara prefigures Allen's Laura, while the younger Sara is Isak's cousin. Sara is presumably the woman that Isak loved more than his wife, but who was taken away from him by his brother, Sigrid. Berit Alman, the wife of Sten, with whom Isak's car crashes on the road, is a former actress. This prefigures Allen's actress Claire. As Claire will appear in Marion's dream play, Berit will appear in Isak's dream — as a patient he misdiagnoses as being dead.

Sten Alman also appears in the dream as the person who gives Isak the exam that Isak fails. Sten will tell Isak of the charges made by his former wife, Karin, against him. They are accusations of callousness, selfishness and ruthlessness, similar to accusations made against Marion. Sten also tells Isak that the principal of being a doctor is to ask for forgiveness, something that Isak cannot remember.

Eva, the pregnant wife of the Caltex attendant, Henrik Akerman, prefigures Allen's pregnant Hope. Marianne will also reveal herself to be pregnant. Isak visits his ninety-six-year-old mother with Marianne, the way Marion visits her father with Laura. The mother produces a box of toys and photographs, which prefigures the box of photographs that Marion looks at. Bergman uses the device of having the old Isak talk across time to the young Sara twice, and has Isak watching the married Sara and Sigfrid.

In a dream Isak sees how Karin has sex with an unnamed man — on the ground in the woods — which prefigures the discussion of sex on the hardwood floor in Allen's film. Karin describes Isak as "cold" and having a "false magnanimity," and he is told in the dream by Mr. Alman that the punishment is loneliness.

Bergman's film concludes with Isak's feelings of being worried and sad calmed by a memory of his adult-self seeing his father and mother by the lake as his father fishes. His look of happiness transitions Isak from the dream back to him in bed. Allen finishes *his* film via narration, with Marion to telling us that she finally feels at peace.

In Eric Lax's book *Woody Allen: A Biography*, Lax describes a shot Allen wanted for the film that he was unable to get. For the scene in which Marion talks to Young Paul, Allen wanted the camera to come up over the boy in silhouette as Marion walks through fall leaves into view. However, because the shed location was full of the camera and sound crew, the appropriate angle proved difficult to capture. As a result he was frustrated and felt the resultant scene was merely adequate.

Lax reports that Marion's reading of Larry Lewis's novel and the imagined dramatization as memory was not the original edit of the film. It was to finish with the last scene between Marion and Ken. There was also a long dream sequence that was cut that had Marion seeing Hope in the hallway outside her and her husband's bedroom. It is not known whether this room was that of Marion and Ken or Hope and her husband, who is spoken of by Hope but never seen in the narrative. Allen at one time wanted this scene to end the film.

Other excised scenes included one set in an auditorium at the Union Theological Seminary in Manhattan. Another was supposed to be the first shot of Marion, walking out of a neighborhood delicatessen with instant coffee and supplies for her new office, and walking along the street. Accompanying this was to be her voice-over introducing herself and explaining her work.

Lax reports that Allen and his director of photography held initial discussions about two major issues. The first was whether the dreams and flashback scenes should be shot any differently than the real-time narrative. They decided that keeping them the same allowed for a fluid transition from one scene to the next. The second issue was whether the film should be in black and white or color. Lax points out that modern films shot in black and white are generally poorly received at the box office. Allen had shot some of his previous titles in black and white—*Manhattan*, *Stardust Memories*, *Zelig*, and *Broadway Danny Rose*, and he would go on to shoot *Shadows and Fog* and *Celebrity* the same way.

Here Allen decided to go with color when he realized that his location choices were based on color. He felt the dream sequences might have benefited from being in black and white, bringing a sense of unreality. However he also thought that the sense of restraint that black and white gives was not what he wanted for the film. Allen also changed his mind over the color scheme for costumes, initially favoring Marion wearing black, which he thought would be arresting but ultimately distancing.

Allen comments on how Marion turning fifty reflected his own feelings, and that her character was as close to Allen's own personality as any he has created. Lax quotes lines from early drafts of the screenplay that were dropped from the final version. Marion says, "I liked the idea of a child but the personal aspect of it was too much." This is said to reflect Allen's own ambivalence about being a father, something he became when he turned fifty. He is quoted as saying, "It's no accomplishment to have kids. Any fool can do it."

His opinion changed in particular in regards to his attachment to Farrows's two-year-old daughter Dylan, who visited the set of the film, and whose relationship with the director would became one of the controversies surrounding his break with Farrow. Allen said, "Once you have a child, it is so powerful an experience, it's impossible not to put it first."

Another deleted line that reflects this change-of-life attitude is Marion saying, "I was past fifty now and it was time to leave certain notions behind." Before he turned fifty-three, Allen was quoted as saying that he put all his feelings about turning fifty into Marion. "It took me at least a year to get over it" (turning fifty, presumably, not writing the character of Marion).

Lax said that Allen had high hopes for the film being a commercial success and so establish him with a broad audience as a successful writer and director of dramatic films. He saw it as the culmination of a journey that he thought might have taken ten years but had actually taken about twenty-five. This refers to the director's hope of making serious dramas after transitioning from comedies, or of no longer having to insert himself into his dramas for comic relief, as he felt he had to do with *Crimes and Misdemeanors* (1989) to help the film become a commercial success.

Poster for *Another Woman* (1988).

During the filming of *Another Woman*, Allen said that he cautiously felt his goal was within reach. It had all the elements he wanted to project. It was a serious film, thought not necessarily realistic. He had a cameraman he'd liked so much over the years, and what he thought was a tremendous cast. He thought the omens indicated that everything had fallen into place. However, he was wrong.

Lax says that the generally poor initial reception of the film lead to reduced distribution — even in New York. This was after Allen had said he was used to getting anything he wanted in the city. The screenings at what were considered lesser cinemas was due to the fact that the larger ones didn't want the film because they thought, "No, we're going to die with this."

Allen also commented on the "deliberately high-blown" kind of dialogue in the film, which recalls the previous dramas *Interiors* and *September*. He said it was the direction that gave them that personality more than the writing. He thought it may have been the wrong choice, but that was the style he wanted for those films. He felt the writing was not pompous nor solemn, but rather it was the mood of those pictures, the way he staged it and the way he had the actors talk. This style of dialogue would lead to Vincent Canby capping his bad review of the film by commenting, "I just didn't believe that he knew a thing about those people and their world."

Allen himself would lose faith in the film after screening it for friends. Although he was initially pleased, after listening to the main objection that it was cold, he started to change his opinion. "I think I've blown it," he said. He thought he hadn't made it imaginatively enough, and it was not as exciting as it could have been. The characters were cool, but he thought the film could still be "hot as a pistol." Eventually he would say that it was "cold, boring, ball-less. A cure for insomnia." When he screened it again he was falling asleep after the first fifteen minutes. He felt the film was like the title music: wispy and unfocused. He thought there was good acting in it, but he didn't pull it off. Perhaps "a better person could have made it work." Allen also said, "I wasn't good enough to have it rise to the level I wanted."

"It was a great idea for a comedy sacrificed on the altar of art." At a screening for friends of the film, he would tell Lax, "If I had done this right, I would have made two movies—this one and a comic one where I overhear Keaton or Mia and run out and do whatever they want. That would be the one that could make money and be successful, and this is the one they would cut up for guitar picks."

In Lax's book, *Conversations with Woody Allen: His Films, the Movies, and Moviemaking*, Allen says that the film was originally envisioned as a Chaplinesque comedy that he had written five years prior. The story was about a man who lives in a tiny room who overhears an analyst and a woman speaking, and becomes fascinated. He sees that she is beautiful, and he begins to see her without her knowing that he still listens to her sessions. He solves the woman's problems and becomes her dream man, making all the things happen that she wanted to happen. Allen says he dropped the idea because he considered the man's actions as mean and found the idea of eavesdropping distasteful, although he would go on to use the device again in the comedy *Everyone Says I Love You*. He had the idea to change the story to a dramatic one. He made the main character a woman and had her overhear that her husband and her sister were having an affair. Then when she goes home she learns that what she has overheard is true. Allen decided that this made the story too Hitchcockian, so he changed it again.

Mia Farrow was originally cast as Marion, and Dianne Wiest was to play Hope. But things changed with Farrow's pregnancy and Wiest's decision to take time off from acting to adopt a child. The change in casting of the part of Marion is said to have allowed Allen to explore the issue of having children, which was not so significant in the earlier screenplay.

Allen told Lax that for the character of Marion he wanted someone who was physically similar to Farrow, but older, like Liv Ullmann or Bibi Andersson. But he didn't want to cast those actresses since they were so associated with Ingmar Bergman. He originally wanted Jane Alexander to play the part of Lynn and Max von Sydow to play Paul. Allen considers in hindsight that Marion's character came across as colder than he wanted. He also thought that he didn't deal with the character of Ken as well as he could have. He thought he should have made him more passionate and explosive, and less cerebral.

Lax read the first draft of the script, which had a different beginning and ending. Marion talks about the sensation one gets when looking at the stars. At the beginning she recalls what her father said about looking through the Mount Palomar telescope in California when Marion was eight months in the womb. The stars were bright and impossible to count, and they gave you a perspective on the pointlessness of life and human insignificance in the scheme of things. The ending featured the line, "The stars were coming out now, too, although they were harder to see amidst the lights of the city."

Allen originally wrote Marion as a cold person surrounded by nicer people. But as he filmed, he began to question that decision, since he felt it made the character one-dimensional. So he added scenes to give her more depth and make the situation more interesting. These new scenes involved Cynthia Frank thanking Marion for being an inspirational teacher, Laura on the telephone talking to Ken and then Marion, Laura being at her father's house with Marion, and Marion telling Laura in the park how she and Ken are separating. Allen also added the scene where Laura has had sex with her boyfriend and comments to him about Marion, "She's a little judgmental." This became important because later Laura finds out that this is not the case.

There originally was dialogue between Marion and Hope when they are at the art gallery, but it was taken out so that the women are only seen there in a montage of the time they spend together. The dialogue had Marion talking about Sam, but Allen felt that it came out "dreadful." He tried again at the gallery and had the actresses ad-lib, with the idea that Marion might say, "I may want to get back to my art." He would later reshoot the scene in the antique shop, and though Marion mentions that she used to paint water colors, as did Hope, she doesn't say the specific line. Allen considered going back to the gallery again to make more of the idea of their shared interest in art but didn't, since he thought the brief scene shot was all that was needed.

Lax reports that the music under the opening credits of "Gymnopédie No. 3" was momentarily replaced by Schubert's "Death and the Maiden." However, Allen found that the Schubert piece was much too lively, and so he went back to the Erik Satie piece.

In the book by Allen and Stig Bjorkman, *Woody Allen on Woody Allen*, the director said that the film was criticized by audience members who felt that the characters were too old to have the problems they did. However, Allen dismissed this charge by saying that he knew people of that age who had those problems. Allen said that Gena Rowlands was surprised that he had offered her the part of Marion. After she had turned down the role of the mother in *September* because she thought she was wrong for it, she thought he would never offer her anything else. Allen describes her as "one of our great actresses. She has a huge talent and she's completely professional."

Bjorkman says that when viewing *Another Woman* that *Wild Strawberries* comes to mind because they are both an "exploration into an isolated and considerably frozen human being." He asks Allen if he sees a link between the films. Allen said he hadn't, but "I can when you mention it." Allen also comments that he thinks the Hope character is in some way an incarnation of Marion's inner self leading her to where she can find things out. Allen reports that he heard that Michael Caine had warned Gena Rowlands that Allen never used close-ups. Rowlands was then surprised when he did shoot some of her. Allen says, "She has such a good and expressive face, as well."

In the film's pressbook Rowlands says that she was attracted to the part of Marion for many reasons. She thought it was a very complex character and very far removed from anything she had ever played before. Rowlands says that she was immediately intrigued by the script and that she had always wanted to work with Allen. After making the film, the actress would comment that she enjoyed working with the director very much. "I was struck by his seriousness and dedication of his driving artistic expression. It was challenging and invigorating to work with him."

Rowlands also has a quote about Sandy on the Sandy Dennis Foundation website page of Actors' Memories. She says, "Sandy was a marvellous actress. She was so gifted she made every part look easy ... and she didn't choose easy parts. It was a great pleasure to work with her."

In *What Falls Away* Mia Farrow says that she inadvertently provided the pivotal device for the film. A renowned therapist conducted her sessions in the apartment on the other side of her living-room wall. The therapist's patients were acquaintances, including Allen's agent. Farrow told Allen about this phenomena and commented, "Wouldn't it be so cool to get one of those spy listening devices? We could hear what they're saying though the wall." Allen responded disapprovingly with, "Would you want to define yourself as a person who would do that?" She told him that she was only joking, and that in light of his response she felt like a worm.

Farrow began her ten-year professional relationship with Allen in the 1980s with her appearance in the romantic comedy *A Midsummer Night's Sex Comedy*. This long-term partnership would produce thirteen films and recall other actress/director working relationships, such as D.W. Griffith and Lillian Gish, Josef von Sternberg and Marlene Dietrich, George Cukor and Katharine Hepburn, Jules Dassin and Melina Mercouri, Ingmar Bergman and Liv Ullmann, and Claude Chabrol and Stephane Audran. Farrow was Allen's Muse, an actress of perhaps greater range than his former actress partner, Diane Keaton, and both Farrow and Allen would benefit from their collaborations. The true test of Farrow's value is that after their partnership ended, Allen's films would suffer in the leading actress department. Equally, Farrow's later career would not provide her with the same level of opportunity that she experienced with Allen.

In Ian Holm's autobiography *Acting My Life*, he advises that the part of Ken was originally offered to George C. Scott and Ben Gazarra. Scott reportedly refused to even read the script for some reason.

RELEASE: November 18, 1988.
REVIEWS: The film inspired a critically mixed reaction from Vincent Canby in *The New York Times* on October 14, 1988; and Pauline Kael in *Movie Love*. Canby wrote that "the film's best vignette features Dennis as a long-lost friend." Kael would say that Dennis "lets loose with bursts of smudgy, chaotic anger."
DVD: MGM (video and DVD), released on June 5, 2001.

976-Evil (1988)

Cinetel Films (aka *Horrorscope*)
CREW: Robert Englund (Director), Lisa M. Hansen (Producer), Paul Hertzberg (Executive Producer), Rhet Topham, Brian Helgeland (Screenplay), Thomas Chase, Steve Rucker (Music), Paul Elliott (Photography), Stephen Myers (Editor), David Brian Miller (Art Director), Kevin Yagher Productions (Makeup Effects), Nancy Booth (Set Decorator), Susan Reiner (Makeup and Hair), Elizabeth Gower-Gruzinski (Wardrobe), Kevin and Sandra McCarthy (Special Effects), Sheridan Wolf Eldridge (Sound Design). Color, 92 minutes.
SONGS: "I'm a Wild One" (Steve Marston, Jill H. Roberts, Thomas Chase, Steve Rucker),

heard on the radio in Spike's room; "I Want You Tonight" (Steve Marston, Thomas Chase, Steve Rucker), heard on the radio in school bathroom; "The Only Thing I Really Need" (Steve Marston, Thomas Chase, Steve Rucker).

CAST: Stephen Geoffreys (Hoax Arthur Wilmoth), Jim Metzler (Marty Palmer), Maria Rubell (Angella Martinez, school principal), Lezlie Deane (Suzanne "Suzie" Walker), J.J. Cohen (Marcus), Pat [aka Patrick] O'Bryan (Leonard "Spike" Johnson), Sandy Dennis (Mrs. Lucy Wilmoth, aka Aunt Lucy), Darren E. Burrows (Jeff), Gunther Jensen (Airhead), Jim Thiebaud (Rags), Mindy Seeger, Robert Picardo (Mark Dark), Paul Willson (Mr. Michaels), Greg Collins (Mr. Selby), Joanna Keyes (Suzie's Mother), J.J. Johnston (Virgil), Joe Slade (John Doe), Demetre Phillips (Sergeant Bell), Don Bajema (Deputy), Wendy J. Cooke (Gang Girl), Tom McFadden (Minister), Larry Turk (Operator # 1), Cynthia Szigeti (Female Operator), Christopher Metas (Cashier), Roxanne Rogers (Waitress), Bert Hinchman (Coroner), Nay Dorsey (Paramedic # 1), Jim Landis (Paramedic # 2), Ed Corbett (Santa Claus), Quiglley (Aunt Lucy's Parrot). Uncredited: René Assa, James Boutin (Wife), Nick Dongarra (Husband).

SYNOPSIS: Garden City, 1988. Teenager Spike finds a card for a horoscope telephone service, 976-EVIL, hosted by the Master of the Dark. Spike's cousin Hoax also rings the service and finds himself endowed with supernatural powers. Hoax kills Spike's girlfriend, Suzie, attacks the school bullies, and kills his Aunt Lucy. Spike fights with Hoax, and Hoax falls into the hell that has opened up under their house. The Master of the Dark then seeks another conduit.

NOTES: Dennis' appearance in this horror title comes as another supporting role. While she has a number of scenes, her character ultimately makes a relatively minor impact on the narrative. She plays a comic grotesque that recalls her role in the *Alfred Hitchcock Presents* episode "Gigolo." Her character also suffers the same fate of being eaten by cats, though here the presentation makes it more apparent.

Dennis' Lucy is heard before she is seen, and she has a Southern accent, which immediately recalls her Mona from *Come Back to the 5 & Dime Jimmy Dean, Jimmy Dean*. She wears a variety of fright wigs — short and long brunette and blond hairpieces. The blonde wig is seen when Lucy confronts Spike in the kitchen about stealing money, and it is implied that she has worn this wig to bed (or at least to get out of bed). Lucy also wears makeup and spectacles. We only ever see her at home wearing house dresses, so she may be a shut-in, which might explain her eccentricities.

Lucy has a pet parrot and a number of cats. This reflects Dennis' real life fondness for the animals, which was seemingly exploited in the *Alfred Hitchcock Presents* episode and *The Fox*. The plastic we see on Lucy's furniture suggests her controlling nature. The religious preaching coming from the television shows she watches prefigures her religious fanaticism, as do the religious statues in the front yard of the house and the iconography seen inside.

Dennis uses her mannerisms of gesturing and pointing, smiling, and stuttering. She makes Lucy funny in her anger at Hoax and Spike. She mockingly imitates the moan that Hoax emits when Lucy offers him tea, and she cups his chin when Hoax laughs at how Spike stands up to her. Dennis is also funny in the later confrontation with Hoax about her telephone bill. She gets a laugh as she knocks on his open bedroom door before she exits — after Hoax has scolded her for not knocking before she entered.

Dennis reveals Lucy's vulnerability when Spike holds her arms to stop her from searching his pockets for the money he has stolen. She has a moment of reactive stillness to Hoax telling her, "If you value your life, I suggest you leave me alone." Regrettably, Lucy's murder is achieved relatively quickly by Hoax slashing her, although her being a cat lover is paid off in the reveal of her dead body being eaten by her cats.

Spike losing his bike in the poker game sets his character up as the film's protagonist for the first third of the narrative, whereafter Hoax assumes the role of protagonist, albeit one that is also the narrative antagonist. Spike being a biker adds moral ambiguity to his

Dennis as Mrs. Lucy Wilmoth (aka Aunt Lucy) holding one of her cats in *976-Evil* (1988).

character, although, unlike Hoax, his behavior does not cast him in the role of antagonist as well. His wardrobe of leather jacket, tight clothes, slicked-back hair and ponytail suggests he is a bad boy. He also has a heart tattooed on his hand. However, the leather jacket being brown rather than black would seem to dilute his threat. In the film's pressbook, director Robert Englund describes Spike as a James Dean boy.

In his room, Spike listens to the song "I'm a Wild One" on the radio as if it defines him. This song will be repeated, and also shown to apply to Susie as much as Spike, while Susie and Hoax eat pizza at a diner, then again during the poker game. Spike's smoking and drinking beer add to his bad boy image, as does Spike drinking milk from the bottle he takes from Lucy's kitchen and stealing money from her.

However, Spike's rescue of Hoax from the bathroom dunkers shows him performing an act of kindness. His stealing gloves from the Auto Parts shop and then putting them back before he leaves the store also shows that he has a sense of morality. Hoax will subsequently display a similar if rather too-late ambivalence towards revenge upon Suzie when he kills his spider, thinking that will stop Suzie from being hurt.

Suzie as a bad girl is suggested by her appearance, which apes that of Madonna of the 1980s. She has peroxided hair and wears an exposed bra and torn denim jacket, crucifixes, bracelets, finger-less gloves, a short skirt with bare midriff, stockings with suspender belt, and high heels. Suzie also smokes. In the pizza-eating scene with Hoax she tells him that she was wild at school, having been kicked out of a Catholic school. Her spitting out her coke in response to Hoax's joke about the cow demonstrates her lack of manners.

Her being scared of the spider that conveniently appears on the table at the diner seems to dilute her presentation as a tough bad girl. This is somewhat restored when she fights off Marcus' gang, allowing her to leave unharmed. However, her only partly helping Hoax against the gang and then leaving Hoax alone with them reveals her selfishness.

The way Hoax is presented as a nerd stands in opposition to Spike's cool. Hoax lives with his mother, while Spike lives alone. Hoax's tube message device adds to the idea of his nerdiness, as does the clothes we see him wear at school. He attempts to emulate Spike by obtaining his own motorcycle, but crashes it when he rides it away from school after Spike. Hoax also tells Suzie that he doesn't smoke because his mama wouldn't approve of it. He may be outnumbered when he is attacked by Marcus' gang in the school bathroom, and later at the diner, but we don't see Hoax attempt to defend himself.

Leading up to the locker room confrontation between Hoax and Spike, Hoax accuses Spike of thinking him a "wimp." Hoax does not attempt to fight back against Spike's pushing him around in the locker room. This is ironic, since Spike's aggression recalls the treatment Hoax has received from Marcus' gang. This treatment is given the context of Spike's anger over how Hoax has killed Suzie.

Hoax's nerdiness is enhanced by his knowing that the Daddy Long Legs is not actually a spider, as Suzie describes it, and him telling her that he owns a poisonous arachnid. Hoax's reluctance to kill the Daddy Long Legs shows that he possesses some sensitivity. This comes at some cost, however, when his taking it outside leads him to Marcus' gang. Marcus stepping on the Daddy Long Legs shows that boy's lack of sensitivity towards the insect, and towards Hoax by implication.

Hoax' assertiveness is enhanced by his contact with the Master, which helps him stand up to his mother, Marcus' gang, and also Spike. While Hoax does not fight back against Spike in the locker room confrontation, he does comment on Spike spitting on him, telling him that one day he will be standing over Spike and will spit on *him*. This will indeed happen at the film's climax when Hoax is possessed.

Hoax's total transformation is indicated by the Master's voice overlaying Hoax's own, which aligns his new aggressive behavior with that of the Master's. However, the Master apparently has given Hoax the power to enact Hoax's revenge upon those who have hurt him, as opposed to the Master using him for some other plan. What the Master gets out of the arrangement is not clear, apart from the pleasure of seeing people hurt and killed. If the Master is meant to be Satan, one would think that he might have more ambition.

Spike follows the advice of the Master to steal money from Lucy. His second bit of advice is more commentary than instruction, when Master tells him, "When it rains, it pours. You're not in debt anymore." The rhyming of "pours" and "anymore" by the Master is a poetic device he continues with for a time in his subsequent messages to Hoax. However, as the narrative progresses, the messages are no longer rhymed and are more direct remarks to whomever the Master is speaking.

The narrative setting up Marty to be watching Spike from the diner across the road allows for Marty to rescue him from the oncoming car. However, there is no plot payoff to Marty and Spike subsequently eating together at the diner, since we then move to Spike picking up Suzie for his date. This dangling of plot points comes after the apparently disconnected deaths of the man during the opening credits and later the lady in red shoes.

Another plot point that offers no payoff is Marty going to the office of Angella Martinez to ask to see Spike, since we don't see Marty talking to Spike as a result. However, the scene does inform us that Marty is a private investigator. Likewise, Marty and Angella having dinner later can be read as the result of an attraction formed at their first meeting. Additionally, at the dinner Marty tells her about the After Dark Enterprises offices, which then narratively leads Angella to rescue him at the site later. Angella will also appear at the climax, accompanying Marty to the Wilmoth house and becoming a potential victim of the possessed Hoax. Marty's role at the climax, however, will be less significant.

The expectation of violence against Suzie is created when we see her alone in her home lighting her gas oven to heat up a frozen meal. This is in spite of the Master's claim that he wants to help Hoax make her his "prize," and that Hoax will have her by his side. The Master's secondary instruction to Hoax to draw a circle is intended to "punish her sin." The punishment is presumably aimed at Suzie and referring to her betrayal of Hoax by leaving him at the diner with Marcus' gang. The circle Hoax creates recalls the circle of protection Dennis painted in *Something Evil*, although here the circle seems to have the opposite intention.

Hoax says that "we're gonna scare the shit out of her," and will later tell Spike that he only meant to scare Suzie. The telephone off the hook with the receiver on the floor and the spider near it suggests that the voices we hear during the circle spell come from the Master. One voice even says, "She's all yours, Hoax." The multiple spiders that appear in Suzie's meal suggest a supernatural transference of Hoax's spider, even though his spider stays in his room.

The connection between the spiders becomes apparent when Hoax kills *his* spider in an effort to halt the attack upon Suzie. How Hoax knows about the other spiders and what is happening at Suzie's house at the same time is unknown and unexplained. This lack of explanation also applies to how Hoax is transformed both in the school bathroom and later when on the telephone with the Master.

The climax features some surprises, such as the Wilmoth house being frozen in the kitchen, although Lucy's upstairs room is not. Another surprise is the ground collapsing under the house to reveal the underworld beneath it.

Angella becomes the horror movie convention of the Woman in Peril when she looks inside the house. We can let the contrivance pass that she knows which room is Lucy's, since we assume that Angella has not been in the house before. An alternative reading of this is that the room is the first one she finds. We haven't seen Lucy's room before or the geography of the house's first storey to initially recognize the room as hers. However, the cats in it suggest that this is the case, and their presence prefigures Angella's discovery of Lucy's half-eaten body.

The way Angella walks backwards out of the room and into the hallway creates the expectation of more violence against her, continuing her as a Woman in Peril. However, Englund subverts this expectation somewhat by having Hoax appear from the side and in front of her, rather than behind her. Angella's lack of defense against Hoax's advance is a disappointment. The relief that we might feel from her escaping Hoax is complimented by the perverse pleasure we received from seeing her pushed down the staircase, since she is played as such a tiresome and masochistic victim in the scene.

The way Angella is easily rescued by Marty from the cliff overhanging the underworld suggests that neither of them are really Hoax's intended victims, although he does tease them by shaking the pole they walk over in an attempt to get away from the house. The ineffectual nature of Spike's gun in only shooting Hoax's face implies that the climactic battle will not be resolved so easily. However, the narrative will show that Hoax *is* defeated easily.

The screenplay offers some humor. Suzie observes how Spike prefers to play poker rather than see a movie with her, and tells him, "This is a night I'll never forget," generating a mild laugh. This comment seems to forget the sex she had earlier that night with him. The line of telephone operators at the offices that house After Dark Enterprises are shown to be fakes. The operators include a drunken Santa and a fat woman on a sex chat line. Another laugh comes when Hoax brings Marcus the hearts of Jeff and Rags, and asks, "Would it be possible to enter the game with a pair of hearts?"

Lucy's plastic-covered furniture earns a funny payoff after Hoax kills her and blood spatters on the couch. The parrot repeats, "Not on the couch." Hoax kills it, telling the bird, "That's what the plastic's for, asshole." Lucy's murder initially reads as disappointing until the later reveal of the cats eating her corpse. Angella's discovery of her body is teased out by Hoax luring her to Lucy's bedroom by saying that she is sick, the curtain that surrounds the bed, and the sheet that covers Lucy's body.

Director Robert Englund emphasizes the telephone motif from the very onset. Under the opening credits the sound of a dial tone plays, while the title of the film appears number by number to the sound of the digits being dialed. Blackouts divide the images under the credits, and the sight and sounds of three ringing telephones — in a barbershop, in a car, and from a telephone booth — all suggest the importance of telephone calls to the narrative.

As the man we see walking in the street, and for whom it appears the telephones are ringing, approaches the booth, we hear the sound of flies. This prefigures the danger of the telephone, since the man will be electrically shocked and burned when he touches the receiver. The sound of flies will be repeated later when Marty breaks into the office of After Dark Enterprises, and at the climax when Spike confronts Hoax. While the sound suggests death, its source is never revealed. Another sound heard at the climax is wind, associated with the frozen kitchen.

Englund uses subjective camera work for point-of-view shots, and a hand-held camera, expressionist camera angles, and slow motion. He also employs thunder and lightning as ominous signs after Spike has telephoned the horoscope number, and as he enters Lucy's house to steal money. Englund presents the woman in the red shoes in an objectified way to create the expectation that she will become a victim, an expectation which the narrative meets.

The sex scene between Spike and Suzie is presented in an unusual manner. *He* is the object of desire, with his hair now loose and his chest bare, forming a homoerotic presentation of Spike. Spike's hair will be loose not only during the sex scene, but also when he goes to the church for Suzie's funeral and at the film's climax. Englund supplies additional homoeroticism via the strip poker game that Marcus' gang members play. Although there is one girl also present, it is noteworthy that her undressing is interrupted by the appearance of Hoax, and that she only gets down to her underwear.

Equally, Angella is only stripped down to her slip, and then only the top of it is shown, during the possessed Hoax's attempted seduction of her. Also, after kissing her hand, Hoax pushes her down a flight of stairs, which indicates that he doesn't want her as badly as he has said. The Master seems to speak through Hoax when Hoax tells Angella that Spike had never thought Hoax would get this far with her. This suggests that Hoax had a sexual attraction to her, as perhaps so does Spike. However, this idea is not expressed otherwise in the narrative.

There is the suggestion that perhaps Hoax's admiration for his cousin Spike, which includes Hoax watching him have sex through a telescope, may have an incestuous sexual element to it. Englund doesn't show us what Hoax has written in the tube note he sends Spike during Spike's lovemaking, which may add to the idea of Hoax's feelings of attraction for his cousin.

In their sex scene, Suzie kisses Spike, and we see that she has taken the controlling position by being on top of him. The sex remains obscured by clothing, with Spike only bare-chested and Suzie's breasts partially hidden by her wearing his jacket. Spike seems less interested than he should be in Suzie's panties, which she leaves for him, and we can't tell if the sex is completed or whether it stopped when she realized that Hoax was watching. Hoax going to Spike's room after Spike and Suzie has left holds an erotic undercurrent, since he takes a closer look at the chair on which the couple had sex.

However, the idea of a homoerotic interest that Hoax may have in Spike is lessened when we see him touching Suzie's panties, and how the narrative suggests that Suzie is "the girl of Hoax's dreams." His date with her when they eat pizza at a diner continues this idea. Englund employs an amusing edit, cutting from Suzie telling Hoax, "I'm mad; and when I get mad—" to Suzie continuing at the diner with "—I eat."

Hoax's heavy breathing and climactic laughing during the circle spell suggests sexual excitement, although Stephen Geoffrey uses heavy breathing for his performance as Hoax otherwise. His later transformation by the blue glowing light and the sound of electricity also sees Hoax moaning in a sexual way. The glowing blue light will be seen again — inside the house from an outside point of view — after Hoax has killed Lucy.

Englund cuts from Hoax killing his spider to Suzie falling dead, although the next shot of Spike yelling "No" seems unnecessarily clichéd. Hoax's feelings for Spike are returned to in the scene in the school gym locker room when Hoax tells how he killed Suzie. Hoax says that he did it for Spike, because "she was messing up your reputation." Hoax lies that he saw Suzie also dating Marcus and calls her a "Jezebel whore," which suggests his mother's religious judgment.

Englund intercuts between Suzie at home heating food in her gas oven and Hoax on the tele-

Poster for *976-Evil* (1988).

phone with the Master, and continues the intercutting between Suzie and her meal and Hoax in the circle. This will ultimately lead to the supernatural transference of the spiders to Suzie's meal, her death, and Hoax going to her house to see that she is dead.

Although the scenes of Marcus' gang harassing Hoax are tedious, Englund does provide a turn-around payoff when Hoax finally fights back, taking on two of them. Englund otherwise provides a horror ambience and creates empathy for his protagonists, Spike and Hoax. Their locker room confrontation displays a greater empathy for Hoax, despite the fact that he has killed Suzie. This may be due in part to the fact that Stephen Geoffrey as Hoax shows more range than Patrick O'Bryan's Spike.

The film's tone changes after Hoax's transformation and acquisition of his newly-found powers, as the narrative becomes a more traditional horror killing spree involving an avenging monster. Although we see Spike attempt to attend Suzie's funeral service, for which he is too late, he disappears from the narrative before returning to assist Marty and Angella at the climax and to defeat Hoax.

Again in the climactic confrontation, Spike presents as a weaker and less sympathetic character than Hoax, which makes the defeat of Hoax unbelievable. Also, the addition of Marty to the narrative climax creates the expectation of him as a power against Hoax. This proves unfounded, since he's generally ineffective other than being able to rescue Angella from falling into the underworld.

The climax displays an obvious use of green screen special effects when the underworld opens to reveal fiery depths, which is matched by the ground closing up after Hoax falls into the pit after being pushed out the window by Spike. The pressbook advises that a relatively new process for revolutionary special effects, called Introvision, was used for the film. Introvision was a method of front-end projection that employed splitters, counter-mattes and a very large screen. The system projected images of photographs or miniature sets onto this screen in a three-dimensional way so that action appeared to occur in front of or behind objects.

Englund exercises some restraint with the violence. He doesn't show how Hoax removes the hearts of Jeff and Rags. Likewise, he pans away from the murder of Marcus by Hoax. He suggests the gore by the pan over the other toilet stalls, stopping at the one with blood in the toilet bowl and Marcus' hand on the floor. However, there is still some gore. We see the slashing of Jeff's face, Marcus' hand being cut off, and the gunshot wound to Hoax's face. But it is not as excessive as in most slasher films. Equally, Hoax's facial transformation is only mildly repellent, with his oversized right hand presumably the one that held the receiver when he was transformed by the blue light.

In her interview with Jay Sharbutt of the *Los Angeles Times* dated March 21, 1989, Sandy Dennis would say that she did the film for the money but considered her part as "a sort of a cross between Joan Crawford and Blanche Dubois." In the pressbook Englund describes the film as a classic gothic story. "It's an old story, but one that can always be told again and again. [It's] about temptation and envy, about thwarted love and people taken for granted." He said he found the characters equally endearing because they all lived on the wrong side of the tracks. Englund also said that he tried to permeate the story with evil and liked how the evil manifests itself in a thwarted, adolescent mind, and the abuse of religion.

He was nervous at directing Dennis because he considered her a wonderful actress. He tells how for the fish-raining scene, several fish wranglers and Englund were on top of a crane, all hurling dead fish down on her, Stephen Geoffreys and Pat O'Bryan. The night they shot the scene was an incredibly cold one in Los Angeles. Englund was observing this Academy Award–winning actress performing a scene in which she was having a near-orgasmic religious experience, and he was throwing dead fish on her. Englund says that he figured at that point he had broken the ice with her.

The director also tells the story of how problematic the one-hundred-and-fifty tarantula spiders were. He had used a special blue-smoke background, and somehow the creatures got "stoned" from the smoke. They refused to cooperate. Englund led the crew in rousing choruses of yelling and screaming. They tried banging pots and pans together. They tried jumping up and down. But the spiders refused to move. Desperate, he passed out straws to the crew and they all blew on the tarantulas, which forced them to "act."

Stephen Geoffreys was interviewed by JimmyO on April 14, 2009, for the website *Arrow in the Head*. Geoffreys described the film as "kind of hokey," but he said that the biggest kick was working with Dennis. "She was just amazing. Great, great, great actress. When you get to work with somebody who really knows what they are doing, you're really lucky." He says that he used to see her in New York walking down the street when he was going to school. And then a couple of years later he was in a movie with her. "So it was fun."

RELEASE: March 24, 1989, with the taglines, "Revenge is on the line"; "One Number for Hell!"; "Now, horror has a brand new number"; "...it's for you"; "When Spike dialed 976-EVIL, he knew it was an expensive toll call, but he didn't know that he'd have to pay for it with his soul."

REVIEWS: *976-Evil* was critically lambasted by Richard Bernstein in *The New York Times* on March 25, 1989; John Stanley in *Creature Features: The Science Fiction, Fantasy, and Horror Movie Guide*; and John Kenneth Muir in *Horror Films of the 1980s*. Stanley would say that Dennis "is the best thing in the picture." Muir, however, wrote, "Dennis' portrayal is so cartoony, so two-dimensional, so non-stop awful that it literally jolts one right out of the movie."

DVD: Released by Sony Pictures Home Entertainment on August 13, 2002. The VHS version released by Sony Pictures in 2001 included a scene cut for the DVD release. The forty-nine-second missing scene shows Hoax going to the office of Angella and telling her that he has just about finished the filing job she asked him to do. He asks her if there is anything else he can do for her, and she tells him no. The scene suggests that Hoax has a crush on Angella, which later plays in to his possession and attempted seduction of her.

SEQUEL: *976-Evil II*, aka *976-Evil: The Astral Factor* (1992), was directed by Jim Wynorski. The only character that returned from the original film was Patrick "Pat" O'Bryan as Spike.

Parents (1989)

Vestron Pictures/Great American Films Limited Partnership

CREW: Bob Balaban (Director), Bonnie Palef (Producer), Mitchell Cannold, Steven Reuther (Executive Producers), Christopher Hawthorne (Screenplay), Ernest Day, Robin Vidgeon (Photography), Jonathan Elias (Music), Angelo Badalamenti (Orchestral Music), Bill Pankow (Editor), Andris Hausmanis (Art Director), Michael Harris (Set Decorator), Arthur Rowsell (Costumes), Daniel Barrett (Hair), Linda Gill (Makeup). Color, 82 minutes. Filmed in Ontario, Canada, from August 9 to October 9, 1987.

SONGS: "Cerezo Rosa," aka "Cherry Pink and Apple Blossom White" (Mack David, Jacques LaRue, Louiguy), sung by Perez Prado; "Memories Are Made of This" (Terry Gilkyson, Richard Dehr, Frank Miller) sung by Dean Martin; "Purple People Eater" (Sheb Wooley), sung by Sheb Wooley; "Chantilly Lace" (J.P. Richardson), sung by The Big Bopper; "Moments to

Remember" (Robert Allen, Al Stillman), sung by The Four Lads; "Continental Cuisine" (Angelo Badalamenti, Frank Stanton); "Meatloaf Mambo" (Angelo Badalamenti); "Strike It Rich," theme heard coming from a television in the Laemle house; "Robert Hall."

CAST: Randy Quaid (Nick Laemle, aka Dad), Mary Beth Hurt (Lily Laemle, aka Mom), Sandy Dennis (Millie Dew, aka the Social Worker), Bryan Madorsky (Michael Laemle, aka the Boy), Juno Mills-Cockell (Sheila Zellner), Kathryn Grody (Miss Judith Baxter), Deborah Rush (Mrs. Gladys Zellner), Graham Jarvis (Mr. Zellner), Helen Carscallen (Grandmother), Warren Van Evera (Grandfather), Wayne Robson (Lab Attendant), Uriel Byfield (Little Boy), Mariah Balaban (Little Girl), Larry Palef (Announcer).

SYNOPSIS: The Laemle family have moved from Massachusetts to a new suburban town. The son Michael has become afraid of his father Nick and his mother Lily, and has a recurring dream of them with bloodied mouths. Michael is counseled by his school social worker, Millie Drew. Millie brings Michael home one day, but she is killed by someone in the house. Michael's parents admit that they eat people. When Lily tries to stop Nick from killing Michael, he kills her. Nick is killed when the wine cellar falls on him. Michael then goes to live with his grandparents.

NOTES: Dennis appears in another supporting role in this horror title. While she is mostly photographed unflatteringly, she does imbue her character with empathy, and makes the most of a long, bravura scene involving action. The treatment is another where her character is killed, although she will return at the end for a theatrical-style bow with the other main cast members.

As in *976-Evil*, Dennis is first heard before being seen, and this happens twice in the narrative. Her hair is short, as it was in *Another Woman*, and worn with a side part. Her Millie is not styled in the same 1950s period as Miss Baxter and Lily. Dennis' more contemporary hairstyle and clothes and handbag suggest that she is a beatnik. She smokes and uses her mannerisms of stuttering, hair-fiddling, gesturing and laughing. Dennis' best scene is perhaps the extended sequence in which Millie brings Michael home, takes him to the cellar, looks for him in the kitchen and then is attacked when pushed into the pantry.

Dennis delivers a long scream when she sees the body fall into the cellar window, allowing for Balaban's long reverse zoom that leads to the exterior of the house. Dennis also expresses pain in her shortness of breath as she chases Michael in the cellar, her fall onto her arm when she finally pushes open the cellar door, and after she grabs the blade of the knife that has been stabbed into the pantry where she is held prisoner.

Ominous music plays under the opening credits, which gives way to the blare of horns in the song "Cerezo Rosa." Music will also generate mood during the Laemle meals, and the jaunty music in the attack upon Millie adds a comic element.

The narrative does not identify Michael's age, the time frame (though it is clearly the 1950s), or the name of the town to which the Laemle's move. Sources say that Michael is age ten, that the year is 1954, and that the town is in Indiana.

The narrative presents Michael's parents from his point of view as strange and fearful. This view in particular highlights Michael's jealousy of his father towards his mother, and the boy sees his father as a powerful threat. The conflict between father and son will erupt at the climax, when Michael rejects his parents' lifestyle of eating human meat. Interestingly, Nick wants to kill Michael, who has stabbed him, though not fatally. However, Lily tries to protect Michael, although she is unsuccessful. There is also a sexual implication in Nick's murder of Lily, since he kisses her as she dies. Then there's the suggestion that perhaps later he will eat her.

Michael's fear of the dark extends to seeing his parents in their underwear on a white sheet on the living room floor with bloodied mouths. This moment reads as ambiguous,

Dennis as Mille Dew, aka the Social Worker, in *Parents* (1989).

since it may just be another of Michael's nightmares. However, the return to this imagery for a flashback suggests that it may be real, with the climactic revelation that Nick and Lily do eat human meat seeming to confirm the reality of the vision.

Director Bob Balaban will repeatedly return to this vision, revealing more of the bloody figures of Nick and Lily, and that they are eating meat. This later reveal dismisses a possible notion that the reason Nick and Lily are bloodied is because they are vampires. Such a scenario is less believable anyway, since we see both of them in the daylight.

The idea of cannibalism is also suggested by Lily's pleasure in Nick bringing home the laundry bag, after we have seen him cutting into a corpse at the plant's Division of Human Testing. Additionally, Nick and Lily barbequing after the presumed murder of Millie suggests that it is her body they are cooking and then eating for dinner. This is perhaps what leads

Michael to hit Nick with a baseball bat when Nick carries the meat into the house, and stabbing Nick at dinner when he insists Michael eat the meat. The expectation is created that Michael will succumb to his parents' pressure. When he rejects the meat, it is a satisfying misdirect for the expectation and a narrative continuation of Michael's rebellion.

Nick is shown to work in a morgue, later named as the Division of Human Testing. His access to dead men, who it is believed have been poisoned by toxins, implies the cannibalism that Michael's nightmare suggested. This suspected behavior, however, is somewhat tempered by the idea that the meat the couple eat is compromised. The body of Mille would also seem to be compromised, given that we have seen how she smokes. Her shortness of breath when she chases Michael in the cellar suggests that she is otherwise not well, although it could also be from fear after having seen the body fall into the cellar window.

Michael has a fantasy, when he is in the pantry watching his mother cook, of sausages moving down from a high shelf and wrapping themselves around him like a snake. He also has a nightmare of seeing a moving hand in the kitchen sink and blood pouring from the top of the refrigerator.

Nick acknowledges that Michael is scared of him; however, he tells his son that Michael scares him too. Nick feels that Michael doesn't look or act like him, and that he thinks Michael hates him. Nick adds, "I'm not so crazy about you either." Michael's greater dislike for his father than his mother continues the idea of Michael's jealousy and attitude toward Nick as a rival for her affections. This despite the fact that Michael does not behave overly affectionate towards his mother.

Michael's rebellion takes shape when he sees Sheila after his father has told him not to, and then when Michael sneaks into the plant. The latter act is not given any rationale. However, it pays off when Michael sees his father in the Division of Human Testing. The scene creates the expectation of Michael being discovered by his father when Michael hides under the gurney that Nick stands near to cut into a corpse. Nick drops the laundry bag he has brought with him but does not retrieve it. However, when Nick also drops the scissors he has used, Michael takes them. The intention is perhaps for Michael to use them as a weapon. However, this does not become necessary because a noise distracts Nick before he attempts to retrieve the scissors. The noise also allows Michael to escape from the lab when Nick moves away from the gurney to investigate. Nick's fear that the noise means that someone will discover what he has been doing is ironic given the predicament Michael has been in. The plot point of the scissors will be paid off later at the family dinner when Michael drops them and Nick picks them up.

At dinner, after Lily kisses Michael before he leaves to go to bed, Nick asks for a kiss. Michael gives him one, but the fact that Nick has to ask shows the antagonism between the two, which will be paid off at the climax. After Michael finds the amputated leg in the cellar, there is no rationale given for what leads Nick to Michael's room. But we are relieved that at least Nick has not appeared in the cellar, as expected.

The attack upon Millie employs some thriller conventions, like the cellar door that closes and will not open. There is the possibility that Michael has closed the door on her and that perhaps it is simply jammed. However, the shot of the car returning home suggests that it is either Nick or Lily who has closed it on purpose. The gloved person that will push Millie into the pantry, attempt to stab her with a knife through the door, and hit her with a golf club also suggests that it is one of Michael's parents.

The climactic battle between Nick and Michael would seem to be an easy one for Nick to win, although he has been weakened by being stabbed by both Michael and Lily. After

Nick falls down the stairs to the cellar, the expectation is created that he will recover when Michael approaches him. This thriller cliché comes to fruition when Nick suddenly grabs Michael. Michael fights off his father until Nick conveniently gets hit by the falling wine rack. Although this action has no specific cause (such as Michael pushing the rack), it does pay off Nick's earlier fondness for the wine cellar. The red wine from the bottles mixes with Nick's blood.

Balaban downplays the idea of the gas leak and the house being set on fire at the end, employing only a white-out for the transition to Michael's subsequent scene with his grandparents. The closing suggestion that the grandparents are also cannibals (given the suspicious meat sandwich) may be a gothic-flavored continuation of the family's cannibalism. Or it may be simply a paranoid observation made by the victimized protagonist. Even if we choose the first explanation, the fact that Michael refuses to carry on the family tradition would seem to promise an end to it.

The director employs such cinematic techniques as subjective camerawork, point-of-view photography, expressionist camera angles, slow motion and blackouts. He also uses grainy black and white photography for one of a Michael's flashbacks. This flashback also includes superimposed images as Michael runs in slow motion.

Balaban repeats shots of people walking by showing only their feet, and also likes having the camera at below floor level. He transitions from Michael's nightmare sea of blood to a bowl of red liquid in Lily's kitchen the next day. He also repeats the use of extreme close-ups of Michael to show him watching his mother when she is cooking and when he is in the pantry, and his father when Michael is hiding in the plant's Division of Human Testing.

The echoed voices of Michael's parents and Sheila are heard for Michael's walk to the cellar that leads to his discovery of the amputated leg hanging from the ceiling. Balaban includes a heartbeat on the soundtrack when Michael enters the cellar as a conventional thriller scare device. He also has Michael walking backwards to create the expectation (which is ultimately

Poster for *Parents* (1989).

met) of something being in his way. This will be the amputated leg hanging from the ceiling that he walks into.

The period design of the film is impressive, apparent from the choice of source music, clothes, and set decoration. However, all the photographic affectation eventually becomes irritating since it draws attention to technique and away from the narrative. Balaban presents the attack upon Millie as a set piece, complimented as it is by the score, and uses quick cuts and extreme close-ups of Millie's eyes. He also uses what appears to be a circular revolving set on which Nick, Lily and Michael sit at the climax.

In her interview with Jay Sharbutt of the *Los Angeles Times*, dated March 21, 1989, Dennis advises that when Balaban asked her to do the film she read the script but wasn't crazy about doing it. "I thought a lot of the film was pretty obvious to me ... but he talked to me a long time about what he was going to do. I liked him, so I said, 'Yes.'"

Executive Producer Steven Reuther had produced the remake of *Sweet November* (2001).

RELEASE: January 27, 1989, with the tagline, "There's a new name for terror..."
REVIEWS: Critically mixed reactions to the film came from Caryn James in *The New York Times* on January 27, 1989; Roger Ebert in the *Chicago Sun-Times* on April 7 1989; and Pauline Kael in *Movie Love*. Kael wrote, "The scenes with Sandy Dennis go into comedy heaven."
DVD: Released by Geneon [Pioneer] on May 25, 1999.

The Indian Runner (1991)

The Mount Film Group/Miko/NHK Enterprises
CREW: Sean Penn (Director/Screenplay), Don Phillips (Producer), Thom Mount, Stephen K. Bannon, Mark Bisgeier (Executive Producers), Patricia Morrison (Co-Producer), Jack Nitzsche (Music), Anthony B. Richmond (Photography), Jay Cassidy (Editor), Michael Haller (Production Design), Bill Groom (Art Director), Derek Hill (Set Decorator), Jill Ohanneson (Costumes), Frank Bianco (Hair), Hallie D'Amore (Makeup), Mark "Frito" Long (Sound), Gary Elmendorf (Special Effects). Color, 126 minutes. Filmed on location in Plattsmouth and Omaha, Nebraska, from August 27 to October 30, 1990, and January 1991.

SONGS: "Feelin' Alright" (Dave Mason), performed by Traffic; "Comin' Back to Me" (Marty Balin), performed by Jefferson Airplane; "Fresh Air" (Jesse Otis Farrow), performed by Quicksilver Messenger Service; "Couch" (Eric Haller), sung by Eric Haller, Bret Haller and Craig Levitz; "Red Texas Sunset" (Bud McGuire), sung by Paulette Tyler; "Caballito Chontaleno" (Carmino Zapata), performed by Grupos; "Rio Rojo" (Esteli); "Green River" (John C. Fogerty), performed by Creedence Clearwater Revival; "Brothers for Good" (Eric Haller), sung by Eric Haller and Bret Haller; "Summertime" (George Gershwin, Ira Gershwin, Du Bose Heyward), performed by Janis Joplin & Big Brother & the Holding Company; "I Shall Be Released" (Bob Dylan), performed by The Band; "Rio Grande." Uncredited: "The Ballad of John Henry" (Traditional), sung by Mr. Baker to Joe.

CAST: David Morse (Sheriff Joe Roberts), Viggo Mortensen (Frank "Frankie" Roberts), Valeria Golino (Maria), Patricia Arquette (Dorothy, aka Dottie), Jordan Rhodes (Deputy Sheriff Randall), Dennis Hopper (Caesar), Sandy Dennis (Mrs. Roberts, aka Mother), Charles Bronson (Mr. Roberts, aka Father), Enzo Rossi (Raffael), Harry Crews (Mr. Baker), Eileen Ryan (Mrs. Baker), Trevor Endicott (12-year-old Joe Roberts), Brandon Fleck (7-year-old Frank Roberts), Kathy Jensen (Lady at Carwash), Jim Devney (Deputy #1), Dr. Leland J. Olson (Doctor), Annie Pearson (Hotel Manager), Thomas Blair Levin (Clyde), V. Stacy Klein (Lucy), Benicio Del Toro (Miguel), James J. Luxa (Randall's Partner), Adam Nelson (Cellmate), Eddie Katz (Guy on Commode), Kenny Stabler (Indian Runner), Don Shanks (Young Indian Runner), Neal Stark (Circus Midget), Elaine Schoonover (Bearded Lady), Larry Hoefling (Larry), Phil Gould (Man at Del Mar), Chuck Ulmer (Frank's Boss), Joe Martin (Dorothy's Father), Helen

Halmes (Dorothy's Mother), Jimmy Intveld (Kid on Highway). Uncredited: Jill Anderson (Face at the Bar), John Blyth Barrymore (voice), Pete Boughn (Pallbearer), Allison Caine (voice).

SYNOPSIS: In 1968 in Nebraska, Joe Roberts is the Cass County Sheriff. His brother Frank returns from Vietnam but leaves town before seeing their parents. Six months later Mrs. Roberts has died, and Mr. Roberts commits suicide. Frank returns after having been in prison, and is accompanied by his pregnant girlfriend, Dorothy. The couple marry. When Dorothy goes into labor, Frank kills the barman Caesar. Joe goes after Frank to arrest him for murder but lets his brother drive across the state line.

NOTES: Dennis' last film appearance sees her playing another supporting role in Sean Penn's directorial debut. She is only in three short scenes and has few lines. She looks physically heavier than we have previously seen her, with one critic describing her as "shockingly plump." This is perhaps due to weight gain from the chemotherapy Dennis was undergoing at the time of filming. She also wears her short hair brushed off her forehead in a style that is new for her. During her brief appearances she still manages to insert her trademark mannerisms of eye-closing, repetition of words, head-nodding, and smiling.

Dennis is first viewed in a mirrored reflection, and her expression of apparent pain as she moves prefigures the character's illness and death in the narrative. It is suggested that Mrs. Roberts is a religious woman, since she tells Joe to remember his "serenity" as a way for him to assuage his guilt over killing Baker. Her funeral being held at a church also suggests her faith.

The narrative opens with a prologue in which an Indian chases a deer that dies, apparently from exhaustion. The Indian breathes the deer's last breath and is said to feel its peace and stillness. The plot point of the Indian Runner is repeated when Joe and Frank get drunk together at their parents' farm. Frank refers to himself as an Indian Runner who is a "messenger," and describes Joe as a "bear."

Frank has Joe chase him in the cornfield, reversing the idea of the Indian Runner from the prologue. Also unlike in the prologue, the prey is not caught. Joe is perhaps too drunk and Frank too fast to be caught. At the climax, Frank will momentarily stop as he drives on the highway, chased by Joe, when Frank experiences visions of the Indian Runner. Penn also intercuts an image of the Indian Runner in between shots of Frank hitting Caesar with a chair to kill him.

Frank is described as a "hell raiser," which the tattoos over his body seem to indicate. His impulsive behavior extends to him deciding not to see his parents; consequently, he doesn't see his mother before she dies. Frank also beats up a man in his prison cell for apparently little reason, which demonstrates that Frank's impulses can be violent. This has also been suggested by the information that he has hit Dorothy, which led to his incarceration.

Frank steals a car from Jerry's birthday party and eventually burns it up. We also see him presumably stealing money from a gas station, although we aren't shown him attacking an attendant. Frank blows smoke in the face of his landlady when she tells him about the phone call he has received (rather than allowing him to take it). Perhaps this justifies his hostility towards her, as he is rude and then attacks her. In any case, his reaction is unwise and impulse, considering that she may have the power to evict him.

Frank also appears impulsive in his throwing what appears to be coffee onto another worker at the bridge site when he is on the bridge, and in the hide and seek game in the cornfields where he has Joe chase him. When it appears that Dorothy rejects Frank's request for sex, he stares at her and then spits peas at her, before later supposedly fighting with a man at Caesar's bar. Dorothy will describe Frank as "restless." At Caesar's bar he will say, "I get in a violent way," and that the man he fought with looked at him "cross."

Poster for *The Indian Runner* (1991), Dennis' last film appearance.

Maria will comment to Joe about Frank, "He's got a problem." When Frank goes to the police station to tell Joe he wants to collect his car, Frank takes Randall's gun away from him without his knowing. Joe notices that Randall's gun is missing from its holster, and Frank gives it back. Although this action has no plot payoff, it does demonstrate Frank's ability and perhaps his sense of humor. It also may suggest that at this point in the narrative he still has the potential to be good. This moral ambiguity is also apparent from the fearful apology Frank makes in the police car with Joe, and how Frank returns to his construction job for a time.

Frank leaving Dorothy when she goes into labor is more of his impulsive bad behavior. When Joe finds Frank at Caesar's bar, Joe will call Frank a "selfish son of a bitch" and "the angriest man I know." Joe will also tell Frank that he is "weak." Frank's attack upon Caesar and beating him to death is more impulsive behavior. It seems that his going back to his house to be seen by Joe is a deliberate act, as if he wants Joe to follow him and perhaps kill him the way he knows Joe had killed Baker.

Frank, however, does not make himself a sacrifice to Joe by provoking his brother to kill him when he stops on the highway. However, Frank's decision to drive on over the state line represents his final act of impulsivity, since Joe tells us that it means Frank has abandoned his family and newborn son. Though not knowing the fate of Joe is a little frustrating, we can guess that his future will not be rosy.

The screenplay includes a number of dialogue howlers, such as Joe's line in the narration after he has shot Baker: "I tried telling myself I'd done my job; but I didn't believe me." Joe quotes a letter from Frank about his Vietnam buddies: "Guys over here expect their hair to stay dry in the rain." Penn underscores this line with the sound of thunder and rain. Frank and Joe often speak in rhyming dialogue, which reads as twee. Dorothy's apparent sexual rejection of Frank's advance comes after he comments that he has "mosquito bites that need scratching," and that they should "go fiddle with hydraulics."

The scene at Caesar's bar, when Joe finds Frank after he's run away from Dorothy's labor, sees Frank trying to rationalize his bad behavior. He talks about life being a math class and how the math man who keeps saying all the answers makes everyone else angry. Frank also comments that "Gasoline was my favorite smell," and that the world only has two kinds of men — heroes and outlaws.

This nonsense might be contextualized by the idea that Frank has been drinking, although the heroes and outlaws will be matched when Joe comments about there being only the strong and the weak. The heroes and outlaws idea can also be equated with the men as cowboys in the home movie, and at the climax when Joe has the vision of Frank as the cowboy, who is presumably an outlaw.

Sean Penn's overuse of technique is perhaps forgivable for a first-time director, although some of the overwrought performances are another matter. Perhaps it is a given that when an actor directs, the film would feature acting which seems indulgent. Penn's fascination with David Morse's passive yet Method-style acting is perplexing. Morse's habit of staring and smiling at whomever he talks to demonstrates both sensitivity and perhaps an emotional inhibition. This is apparent in the scene where Joe learns that his father has killed himself, and Morse delivers no discernible reaction.

Viggo Mortensen's Frank offers the same lack of reaction when Joe informs him of the death of their mother. Perhaps this behavior is typical of the men of the family, since we don't see their father cry over the death of his wife. However, as Frank has Dorothy to whom he can express affection, so does Joe have Maria and Raffael.

The Indian Runner (1991)

When Frank is drunk (and perhaps stoned), he momentarily cries, which suggests an ability to express emotion, at least while inebriated. Later we see Joe cry tears when he talks to Maria about Frank, and he appears to sob when told on the telephone that Frank has killed Caesar. Frank will sob when he apologizes to Joe after he has come to collect his car the day after the bar fight. Interestingly, neither actor manages to inspire empathy from their crying, perhaps because the display of it is so difficult and abrupt.

Mortensen has a good moment when Frank sees the mirrored reflection of his bloodied face at Caesar's bar after he has killed Caesar, and his expression changes from maniacal to disbelief. However, the blood remaining on his face during the climax overplays Frank's badness, since he looks like a leering horror movie antagonist.

Penn likes to focus on odd people who don't provide any plot payoff. These include the circus midget and the bearded lady at the Delmar Hotel, and the lady at the carwash who follows Joe around and circles his car as he cleans it. This oddness also extends to the near-neurotic smoking that most of the characters seem to do. Marijuana smoking is indulged in by Maria, Dorothy and perhaps Frank. Equally, both Joe and Frank are drinkers.

In the prologue Penn uses quick cuts, slow motion, the sound of a heartbeat or drums, and narration. In the film he also uses shock cuts, expressionist camera angles, out of focus effects, slow motion, and hand-held and subjective camerawork.

Prefiguring devices are also employed. These include Mrs. Baker speaking to Joe on the soundtrack before she is seen to do so, and Mrs. Roberts seen in her house alone when Joe and Frank are driving to see her. Another disassociated effect is the sound of the earth-drilling from the bridge site in the montage of the wedding of Frank and Dorothy. Penn also repeats the sound of the drilling for the scene of Frank's attack on Caesar, as well as the sound of Indian drums and Dorothy's scream during delivery.

Penn has trouble with pacing, apart from indulging some of his actors. He dwells on some scenes too long, which becomes tedious. Examples are the scene when Joe comes to Frank's Delmar Hotel room and the men barely speak but smoke, and the extended coverage of the baby Raffael's attempts to speak.

The scene where Joe and Frank get drunk together at their parents' house also reads as unnecessarily extended and dull, but is redeemed somewhat by the chase in the cornfields. Penn's addition of what sounds like Indian drums echoes the sound effect from the prologue, and presumably expresses Frank's identity as an Indian Runner. Equally plodding is the extended scene at Caesar's bar when Frank has run away from Dorothy's labor and Joe comes after him.

The climax also begins disappointingly with the car chase. Penn tries to beef it up by intercutting to Dorothy graphically giving birth, with an obvious body double for Patricia Arquette. Additionally, the reappearance of the boy Frank, even as Joe's fantasy vision, is a way for Penn to bypass a violent confrontation and supply some figurative and satisfying poetry.

The film is credited as being inspired by Bruce Springsteen's song "Highway Patrolman," which appeared on his 1982 album *Nebraska*. The Springsteen song identifies Joe Roberts as an army sergeant from "Perrineville" barracks number 8, who is now the highway patrolman of the title. It says that his brother Franky "ain't no good." Maria is also named as Joe's wife. Joe is said to have had a wheat farm which suffered because of dropping wheat prices. Franky went into the army in 1965 and came home in 1968.

Joe is called to a roadhouse on the Michigan line about a kid that was bleeding in the head, and Franky is said to have caused it. Joe sees Franky in a Buick at the crossroads and chases him, then stops and watches the car drive to the Canadian border. The song finishes with the repeated idea that Franky "ain't no good" because he turned his back on his family.

Some sources have surmised that the screenplay is an exploration of the differences between Sean Penn and his troubled younger brother Chris, who allegedly battled with alcohol and drug use and was found dead in his home in 2006. Others claim that the brothers in the film reflect the duality in Penn himself. He is the respectable, socially-conscious family man that is married with kids, and the rebellious hellraiser who punches paparazzi. In an article in *Interview Magazine* dated September 1991, Penn answers the question of how much of his own life is in the film, and whether he is the good brother or the bad. "I no longer believe in such absolutes. Nobody is a total prick. There's shades of that in all of us."

In Richard T. Kelly's book *Sean Penn: His Life and Times*, Kelly quotes producer Don Phillips on the casting of Dennis. Phillips states that Dennis was Penn's inspiration for the mother character. Phillips told Penn that Dennis had always been one of his favorite actors, but he understood that she was dying of cancer. Penn met with her in New York, and she agreed to do the part. This was perhaps partly because it was to be filmed in Nebraska, which was her home, and also partly because she would be playing a woman who was dying of cancer.

David Morse is quoted by Kelly as saying, "You could see a fragility about her, she obviously wasn't well. But Sandy Dennis was not a fragile presence. She just had a great core to her, the kind I think you only develop after a lifetime of suffering different things." Morse would also report that she and Mortensen got along very well, and that he wrote a poem about her that was very beautiful.

Mortensen wrote an article for *Focus Features* dated September 7, 2007, entitled "Missing Sandy Dennis," which included the poem he had written for her. The article, sans poem, is also featured on the actor's website, *www.viggo-works.com*, dated 1995. Additionally, there is a photograph by Michael Tighe of him with Dennis sitting in profile in the foreground and Mortensen in the background, presumably from the scene they shot together. She is not looking at him and he is not looking at her, and it appears that, as Frank, he is wearing an army uniform.

Mortensen mentions that the bulk of her role in the film was in an eight-page scene that was cut. The scene had Joe taking Frank to meet his parents. Frank rejects their efforts at hospitality and attempts at small talk, insults them, and storms out of the house. Frank's behavior is especially devastating to his mother, who dies not long after. Mortensen said that Dennis was brilliant and heartbreaking in the scene, but that Penn decided that the film would work better if Frank refuses to see his parents. Mortensen says that after the three days of shooting the scene, she returned to New York and he never saw her again.

The article also includes a brief discussion of her career, and analyzes what happened to it. Mortensen says that she found herself largely marginalized by critics and by those with the power to hire. Within the movie industry she was generally dismissed. If she was remembered at all it was as a "quirky has-been, a benign but overly complicated and totally unbankable actress."

He says that Dennis did not complain about this, other than "very rarely — to wonder out loud how she was going to make ends meet and care for the many stray cats and dogs she had taken in over the years." Mortensen claims that she did not dwell on the past and never claimed to be the victim of injustice, personal or professional, though he believed a case could easily be made for that being so. To him, she was essentially a modest woman with a great gift, one which she enjoyed sharing, as both an actress and a teacher of actors. "[She was] a professional artist in the best sense."

Mortensen's poem describes Dennis modestly celebrating what he thinks she knew was a "goodbye glimpse of home" by eating and drinking. No movie could show how her eyes looked after the scene they had shot was completed. "She limped outside worn out and uncomplaining to squeeze onto the flimsy, rusted seat of a child's swingset for a photo opportunity." Her hands were shaking and she was freed from the sandals she had worn in the scene that made her feet swollen. The morning she left he carried her suitcase from her hotel room and they embraced in the driveway. She refused to let him take her to the airport, and she kissed him on the cheek goodbye before she got in the taxi to leave.

Sean Penn wrote about Dennis in a quote that appears on the Sandy Dennis Foundation website page of Actors' Memories. He says that she "never met an unpredictable instinct she didn't like. She was an actress and woman with beautiful idiosyncrasies and gentleness. There's never been anyone like her. And me and movies miss her a lot.... I was honored to work with her."

Richard T. Kelly reports that Penn had originally titled the film *A Slow Dark Coming* and then *Greetings from the Wasteland*. He came to *The Indian Runner* after finding a book on Native American running by Berkeley anthropology professor Peter Nabokov. Producer Don Phillips could not interest a Hollywood studio in Penn's screenplay, particularly because it was about a man who murders someone and gets away with it. It was thought that if Penn had a star like Robert De Niro or Tom Cruise attached, things might be different.

Penn, however, saw Viggo Mortensen in his supporting role in *Fresh Horses* (1988). He was drawn to the actor's "angularity, a severity to his handsomeness," and thought he would be perfect for the role of Frank. Supposedly during filming, Penn felt that Mortensen's "inherent kindness" was too visible. He had the actor work with a member of the Hells Angels motorcycle club that the director knew in order to acquire an edginess that Penn felt necessary for the character.

The director had seen David Morse in *Inside Moves* (1980). He had wanted to work with him because he felt the actor had a kind of soulful dignity that Penn responded to. Morse had been directed by Sean's father, Leo, in 1985 in an episode of the TV show *St. Elsewhere*, in which the actor was part of the ensemble. Leo had said Sean had written Morse a letter after seeing *Inside Moves* that the actor didn't receive.

Don Phillips was opposed to the casting of Morse because he felt he and Mortensen weren't believable as brothers. Other actors were tested, like Liam Neeson. Penn wrote a special scene for Morse to test with that was not in the screenplay. The actor had to get angry, cry and laugh. The way Morse did it convinced Phillips that he should be cast as Joe.

Richard T. Kelly also reports that Gene Hackman was originally cast as Mr. Roberts, and then Jon Voight was considered after Hackman was no longer attached to the film. Don Phillips thought that the casting of Bronson was a good choice, since his real-life wife, Jill Ireland, had died of cancer. Also, the actor had a son who had died of a drug overdose, paralleling the "bad seed" notion of Mr. Robert's son Frank. Penn asked Bronson to play the part without the mustache the actor had worn in so many movies.

RELEASE: Screened at the Cannes Film Festival in May 1991, and at the Toronto International Film Festival on September 7, 1991. Release in the United States on September 20, 1991, with the tagline, "Frankie and Joe. Two brothers with nothing in common ... except blood."

REVIEWS: The film garnered a critically mixed reaction from *Variety*; from Janet Maslin in *The New York Times* on September 20, 1991; and from Roger Ebert in the *Chicago Sun-Times* on October 4, 1991. Maslin wrote that Dennis is "strangely effective." Ebert said that she is an unexpected casting choice, but she "fits well."

DVD: Released by MGM on December 11, 2001.

Television

The Guiding Light (1956)

(TV series)
CREW: Irna Phillips (Creator and Head Writer); David Lesan, Joe Ainley (Executive Producers).
NOTES: *The Guiding Light*, also known as *Guiding Light*, was a television soap opera that ran from 1937 to 2009 and holds the record as the longest running drama in television history in the *Guinness Book of World Records*. The series had begun as a radio show and then doubled as a television series from 1952.

Sandy originated the part of Alice Holden, playing it from May to June 1956. She was then replaced by Diane Gentner. At this time episodes were only fifteen minutes in duration. The show was filmed live in New York City. Actors played their part twice, since it was broadcast separately for CBS television in the morning and then for CBS radio in the afternoon.

DVD: Not available. The shows from 1956 are believed to be lost forever. Although videotape was invented in 1956 and replaced kinescope filming, the shows only began to be archived in the 1970s.

Naked City (1962)

(TV series). Season 4, Episode 2, "Idylls of a Running Back," Shelle Productions/Screen Gems
CREW: John Peyser (Director), Charles Russell (Producer), Stanley Neufeld (Associate Producer), Herbert B. Leonard (Executive Producer), Leo Davis (Supervising Producer), Ernest Kinnoy (Teleplay), Nelson Riddle (Music), John S. Priestley (Photography), Hugh Chaloupka (Editor), Robert Gundlach (Art Director), Albert Griswold (Set Decorator), Mike Maggi (Makeup). Filmed at the Biograph Studios, Bronx, New York. Black & White, 48 minutes (without commercials).
CAST: Paul Burke (Detective Adam Flint), Horace McMahon (Lieutenant Mike Parker), Harry Bellaver (Detective Frank Arcaro), Nancy Malone (Libby Kingston), Aldo Ray (Elvin Rhodes), Nancy Wickwire (Norma Rhodes), Sandy Dennis (Eleanor Ann Hubber), William Daniels (Harry Culverin), Joe Silver (Mr. Ketton — Assistant District Attorney), Bob Romann (Tony Cavalejo), Coley Wallace (Pixie Gates), Philip Sterling (Officer Schulberg). Uncredited: Richard S. Castellano (Motel Waiter), Lawrence Dobkin (Narrator).
SONG: "Somewhere in the Night" (Billy May), opening theme music.
SYNOPSIS: Pro football star Elvin "Colossus" Rhodes is shot by waitress Eleanor Hubber at the Sheraton Motor Inn after a game at Yankee Stadium. Eleanor gives herself up to the police, claiming that she and Elvin are lovers. Circumstantial evidence seems to support the claim. When Eleanor is questioned by Adam Flint, he sees how she is delusional and that the affair has all been in her imagination.
NOTES: Dennis gets an "And Introducing" credit for her guest appearance on this television show despite the fact of her prior appearance on television in the *Guiding Light* series. She is a brunette, and wears a grey mink jacket over a dress that features a corsage pinned to her left shoulder. This attire is distracting during the initial police interrogation scene. Later it is a

shock to see her in a waitress uniform at the diner when Elvin comes to confront her, since her wearing the mink previously would suggest that she might have a less proletarian job.

Dennis uses her mannerisms in this performance — stuttering, breaking up sentences, repeating words, and gesturing — although she also offers stillness for important emphasis. She makes the character sweet and vulnerable so as to be believable as the apparent victim of a womanizer. At the climactic reveal of her delusional personality, she supplies tears without an obvious display of emotion. There is also the suggestion of madness in her girlish smiles.

She has a moment of lucidity when she admits that Elvin was not in the hotel rooms with her, and here she employs a direct gaze as she speaks to Flint. However, Dennis returns to Eleanor's madness when she says that the pictures she had of him on her walls spoke to her. Before she is taken away, she confronts Elvin, but in her madness she does not recognize him as the man she claims to be in love with. "You're not Elvin Rhodes at all. You look like him but I oughta know. We love each other very much."

When we first see her as Eleanor, Dennis licks her lips as she watches Elvin's football game. For the flashback scene where Eleanor has Elvin autograph her program, he is seen to smile at her before she smiles back at him. That the others who surround Elvin for autographs are boys is telling. She will note the difference to Harry when she shows how Elvin has written "Warmest Personal Regards" on her program and only "Lots of Love" on those of the boys. Dennis uses her stammer when she gives herself up to the police, telling Flint, "I had to shoot him bec ... because, you see, I love him."

The relationship between Eleanor and Harry is suggested by the fact that they hold hands as they walk up the stairs to the subway train after the game. Her hesitancy is revealed when we learn that she has not given him an answer to his marriage proposal. Eleanor's reluctance may be due to Harry being a nondescript type of man, as opposed to the more idealized figure of Elvin that she chooses for her romantic fantasy. Harry's prissiness is suggested by the later scene when he uses an inhaler at the police station for his flu. This earns a laugh when Parker tells Flint, "Get him outta here; he's spreading viruses." The fact of Eleanor creating a fantasy lover in Elvin extends her personality from mere disinterested partner to Harry to a woman who has mental problems, the cause of which is not revealed within the parameters of the episode.

When Eleanor tells Parker about her going to visit Elvin on the night he autographed her program, and then how he took her to dinner, it is presumably meant to be believable. However, perhaps it is a modern viewing of the material that makes it apparent that she is lying. This is despite the attempts made to make Elvin look to be an unattractive romantic partner. This is also suggested by the fact that Elvin is not seen in the flashbacks, which are portrayed from Eleanor's point of view. She is an equally unattractive romantic partner for Elvin, since she seems to have poor self-esteem, suggested by her remark that at first she was surprised that he wanted her.

Flint describes Eleanor as "wide-eyed and vulnerable," and also "a helpless kid and not too bright." The cleaning lady of Eleanor's apartment describes Eleanor as "kind and mousy." Eleanor's efforts to convince others that Elvin is her lover by hiring out-of-state hotel rooms and purchasing the mink jacket would seem to belie the resources she has as a waitress. However, the fact of her going to this trouble is an indication of the depth of her delusion and what she will do to support it.

Director John Peyser intercuts newsreel footage of a football game with recreations, and his treatment generates some humor. A little boy is seen watching with disgust as a man eats a hamburger at the opening game. Aldo Ray scores a laugh from Elvin's "What?!" reaction to Flint telling him that Eleanor has said she had to shoot him because she loves him. Mike Parker earns a laugh when he scolds Flint for interrupting his interrogation of Eleanor. "You know better than to interrupt a confession. These things got rhythms."

Assistant District Attorney Ketton, on the telephone to Parker, has to explain what the slang expression "the whole magilla" means. A newspaper that Flint reads sports the headline "Colossus Falls," which is a pun on Elvin being known as Colossus. Elvin delivers a speech while in the hospital that shows his insight into the public's taste for toppling those they have adored and bringing them down to their level. The teleplay adds a funny button to this scene. In response to Elvin's tirade, Flint says, "There's no need to get excited," and Elvin replies, "Why shouldn't I get excited? I got shot."

The casting of Aldo Ray as Elvin is odd since Ray is obviously in no condition to be playing an athlete. Peyser doesn't help by photographing the actor unflatteringly so that his bloated face makes him look grotesque. The casting may have been made to underscore the supposed idea that Elvin is a cheating husband, but it does not match up with the notion of him as a Colossus hero-king.

Writer Ernest Kinoy would also pen the second *Naked City* episode in which Sandy Dennis would appear, entitled "Carrier." The series was a spin-off of the 1948 film directed by Jules Dassin. The show was a police drama that focused on the lives of the detectives of New York's 65th Precinct and aired from 1958 to 1963. It was created by Stirling Silliphant, and the original thirty-minute running time of the first season was replaced by a one-hour running times for the next three seasons. This change was due to the fact that the show had been cancelled by ABC after the first season and revived in the longer format. The fourth season would be the last in the show's run.

The storyline for the episode was based on an incident that occurred on June 14, 1949. Philadelphia Phillies first baseman Eddie Waitkus was shot in his room at the Edgewater Beach Hotel in Chicago by nineteen-year-old Ruth Ann Steinhagen, a deranged female fan. Perhaps Dennis was cast in the part since she actually resembles Steinhagen. Steinhagen is said to have shot Waitkus with a .22 caliber rifle, though Eleanor uses a .38 revolver in the teleplay.

Steinhagen was found not guilty by reason of insanity and confined to the Kankakee State Mental Hospital. She was diagnosed as schizophrenic and given electric shock therapy. After three years Steinhagen was released as cured, and Waitkus asked that the charge of assault to kill be dropped. Author Bernard Malmoud took the basic elements of the Waitkus story for his book *The Natural*, which was published in 1952. A film version was released in 1984, with Waitkus renamed Roy Hobbs and played by Robert Redford, and Steinhagen renamed Harriet Bird and played by Barbara Hershey.

RELEASE: Broadcast by ABC on September 26, 1962.
REVIEWS: The episode was critically acclaimed by David Cornelius on the website *DVD Talk* on February 3, 2006. He wrote that Dennis "is frightening in the role of the stalker."
DVD: Included in the box set *Naked City—Set 2* by Image Entertainment on November 22, 2005.

Naked City (1963)

(TV series) Season 4, Episode 29 "Carrier," Shelle Productions/Screen Gems

CREW: Director (James Sheldon), Charles Russell (Producer), Herbert T. Leonard (Executive Producer), Stanley Neufeld (Associate Producer), Leo Davis (Supervising Producer), Ernest Kinoy (Teleplay), Nelson Riddle (Music), John S. Priestley, Andrew Laszlo (Photography), Robert Gundlach (Art Director), Charles L. Freeman, Hugh Chaloupka (Editors), Albert Griswald (Set Decorator), Mike Maggi (Makeup). Filmed at the Biograph Studios, Bronx, New York. Black & White, 51 minutes (without commercials).

CAST: Paul Burke (Detective Adam Flint), Horace McMahon (Lieutenant Michael "Mike" Parker), Harry Bellaver (Detective Frank Arcaro), Sandy Dennis (Lorraine Kirchwood), Bruce Gordon (Dr. Sorensteen), Peter Morelli (Alan), Anthony Zerbe (Phil Korshow), Sam Gray (Sol Chaplin), Bibi Osterwald (Grace), John Horn (Freddy Ushont), Donald Melvin (Joey Danahan), Estelle Evans (Crossing Guard). Uncredited: Lawrence Dobkin (Narrator).

SONGS: "Somewhere in the Night" (Billy May), opening theme music; "Inutil Paisagem," aka "Useless Landscape," aka "If You Never Come to Me" (Anton Carlos Jobim), and "Samba de Uma Nota So," aka "One Note Samba" (Antonio Carlos Jobim), both heard in instrumental versions at the dancehall.

SYNOPSIS: Lorraine Kirchwood, a carrier of the deadly infectious disease Van Nortons Sawyers Fever, escapes from the Welfare Island Hospital. The New York police department is notified and a search begun. Lorraine is rescued by Alan, the neighbor of Philip Korshow, who takes her to his apartment. The police track her down when she leaves Alan's apartment. Adam Flint convinces her to go back to the hospital.

NOTES: A blonde Dennis gets to use her arsenal of mannerisms here, which includes eye-closing, eye-rolling, stuttering, broken sentences, teeth-baring, smiling, hand to the forehead, and head-shaking. She appears wearing a head scarf when outside, and notably when she runs from Phil in Freddy's apartment stairway.

Her Lorraine presents as a sheltered child-woman who is both naïve and suspicious of other people, given the environment she has left. She believes that she is not a medical threat to others, although she does hesitate to touch people. This ambiguity is reflected in the moment when Joey reaches out to her and Lorraine looks concerned, but she allows Joey's hand to touch hers. When Alan invites Lorraine into his apartment, she has a stunted response. Though presumably she hesitates due to fear of a strange man, this also indicates an arrested development.

Her eye-closing is seen during Dennis' first appearance, when Lorraine looks out her hospital room window. She repeats it, with eyes rolling to the back of her head, in response to Alan's "Are you all right?" after she has fled from Phil. Dennis moves her mouth when Lorraine walks through Central Park. As there is no audio attached to the movement, we do not know if she is meant to be singing or simply moving her mouth in an odd context.

Dennis has three pivotal scenes to showcase her performance. When Alan initially refuses to retrieve her suitcase from Freddy's apartment, she displays a touching tenderness in beseeching him to get it. When he later confesses that he loves her, he calls her "Lori" and "a very pretty girl." Perhaps it is also Alan's repeating that he wants to "analyze their relationship" that would send anyone running and sends Lorraine off. She repeats "no," and Dennis closes her eyes and offers a strangled cry. When Adam confronts Lorraine at the climax, she again uses eye-closing and hands raised as a gesture of defiance. She also slurs her speech when she deludedly claims that the doctors told her she didn't kill her parents and that she isn't a carrier. However, it seems to be Adam's relating of how Phil has been infected that makes her realize the truth. Dennis presents stillness for the change, although there is an abrupt cut from seeing her hands previously raised to her hands being down.

The teleplay uses a gradual reveal of information, presumably for dramatic effect. When we first see Lorraine in the hospital room, the appearance of an orderly with her lunch suggests that she may be in prison. Such an assumption is furthered by the narration's talk of islands and prisons. The orderly drops a fork and looks afraid of Lorraine when he turns his back on her to pick it up. She eases his fear by picking it up herself and *not* plunging it into him. The toys in Lorraine's room will be explained when we later learn that she came here as a fourteen-year-old child, while her packing one stuffed animal in the suitcase she takes with her to leave suggests her child-like nature.

The fact of her door being unlocked works against the idea of Lorraine as prisoner, as does the fact she passes five nurses on her way out of the grounds and no one attempts to stop her leaving. This is echoed by the behavior of Grace, who Lorraine runs into on the bridge and who it is later revealed to be a laundress at the hospital. It is Adam Flint's interview with Dr. Sorensteen that gives us the context of Lorraine's stay at the hospital. He explains that her being there was on a voluntary basis, since there are no legal grounds for her to be held.

Lorraine's good nature is expressed by her lack of anger when a man runs into her in the street and she laughs in reaction. Joey will describe Lorraine as a "kook" for wanting to buy him a balloon, since, at age eight, he feels he is too old for one. Director James Sheldon emphasizes this point by following Joey's declaration with a shot of Lorraine holding a balloon.

At the dance hall Freddy tells Phil, "You must be getting desperate. She's got a face like a lily." To this Phil replies, "You gonna look at her face?" This comment suggests that Phil has a sexual agenda for Lorraine, although he also seems interested in her suitcase. Freddy's poor opinion of Lorraine's attractiveness is also noteworthy, as we don't get a good look at any other women at the dance hall to make a comparison, and we certainly don't see Freddy with a woman.

Alan being an agoraphobic is a delicious irony, since he comes across as sicker than Lorraine. His initial refusal to get the suitcase that she has left in Freddy's apartment reads as inexplicable before he confesses to his malady. Alan dressed in a tight and sheer t-shirt that makes him appear to be practically semi-naked creates an impression of someone who pays a lot of attention to his body. This can be interpreted as him being another ladies man and therefore the second sexual threat to Lorraine. However, when his disability is revealed, it makes his physical good health ironic.

The teleplay uses the transition of five days to show how long Lorraine has been staying with Alan and also for the first victim of her as a carrier to be found. The fact that the victim is Phil seems like karmic payback. Although he didn't actually hurt Lorraine, we prefer him being a victim rather than Joey, although one could make the argument that the boy was equally manipulative. Phil calls Lorraine a "pig" when he learns she has infected him and also repeats the comment, "She asked for it," as a rationale for pursuing her.

The idea that Alan's agoraphobia should be cured when he has to chase after Lorraine outside his apartment is funny, particularly as it occurs without any struggle. Additionally, the timing of Freddy arriving in front of the apartment building with the police just as Lorraine runs out of the building is fortuitous. Lorraine's fate to live forever in the Welfare Island Hospital is a rather sad one, but what else could be done with her?

Sheldon employs a few visual effects. When Lorraine crosses the road as she walks the city, he uses a subjective camera for her point of view. The view is shown to be wavy, perhaps in light of Lorraine's excitement, and this is paid off when a man stops her from being hit by traffic. When Lorraine lets the lamb at the Children's Zoo suck her finger, it is a disturbing image, and not just because she may be infecting the animal.

An extreme close-up of Phil is used for his advance upon Lorraine in Freddy's apartment to present his apparent threat to her, although, ironically, she will prove to be a greater threat to him. Sheldon doesn't show how Lorraine gets past Phil to get out of the apartment. The next shot is of her exiting the doorway and running down the stairwell. Her escape is topped off by the use of a stunt woman to show Lorraine awkwardly slip down the stairs, the stuntwoman's identity partially obscured by Lorraine's headscarf.

We see Alan lying on his bed after Lorraine has run out on him. The bars on the headboard look like prison bars, an apt metaphor for his agoraphobic imprisonment. When Phil is in the isolation ward and suffering from fever, he drinks water by sucking on a water-soaked cloth. This echoes Lorraine's finger being sucked by the lamb, and his gasps for breath make ugly and disturbing sounds.

Director James Sheldon would go on to direct Dennis again in the 1963 *The Fugitive* TV show episode "The Other Side of the Mountain."

RELEASE: Broadcast by ABC on April 24, 1963.

REVIEWS: The episode was critically acclaimed by the website *The November Sparrow* on May 19, 2009. It wrote, "Sandy Dennis is perfect casting for Lorraine, a person truly out of step with the world. Hopelessly naïve, tentative in every step, Sandy brings much charm to this tabula rasa."

DVD: Not available.

The Fugitive (1963)

(TV show), "The Other Side of the Mountain," A Quinn Martin (QM) Production/United Artists Television

CREW: James Sheldon (Director), Alan A. Armer (Producer), Quinn Martin (Executive Producer), Arthur Weiss (Associate Producer), Alan Caillou, Harry Kronman (Teleplay, from a story by Alan Caillou), Fred Mandel (Photography), Peter Rugolo (Music), Walter Hannemann (Editor), Serge Krizman (Art Director), Sandy Grace (Set Decorator), Walter Schenk (Makeup), Bob Wolfe (Costumes), Lynne Burke (Hair). Filmed at the Samuel Goldwyn Studios, West Hollywood, California, Black & White, 51 minutes.

CAST: David Janssen (Dr. Richard Kimble, the Fugitive), Sandy Dennis (Cassie Bolin), Frank Sutton (Del Jackson), Ruth White (Gram), R.G. Armstrong (Sheriff Bradley), Barry Morse (Lieutenant Philip Gerard), John D. Chandler (Quimby), Hugh Sanders (Leo), Johnny Day (Masters), Paul Birch (Police Captain), Bruce Dern (Deputy Sheriff Jessie Martin). Uncredited: William Conrad (Narrator).

SYNOPSIS: Richard Kimble arrives in the mining town of West Virginia. He meets Cassie Bolin and she guides him to her cabin. Cassie then takes Richard to the mine which has a tunnel that leads to the other side of the mountain and the next city. She asks to go with him, but he refuses. The Sheriff and Richard's hunters find the mine, and Cassie entraps herself with them. When they get out, she decides to leave town.

NOTES: Dennis uses her mannerisms in this performance but also has moments of stillness for the direct expression of honesty. Here she employs stuttering, broken sentences and repetition, pointing and hand-gestures, smiling, head-shaking, tongue-sliding and poking, mouth-touching, and eye twitching. She employs a Southern accent for Cassie, and speaks in hillbilly slang to present a woman who is uneducated. Still, she describes the mine cave as "the dreaming room," and her wish to leave the town shows she has ambition to better herself.

Dennis' Cassie is an androgynous character, dressed mostly in long shirt and pants and wearing a cap. After she takes Richard to Gram's cabin, Cassie wears a ribbon in her hair, partly to keep it out of her face but also to suggest her femininity. Her fighting with Del shows Cassie's spunk and masculine aggressiveness. She jumps on his back. While her punching as she sits on top of him is weak, her biting his hand and then aiming a rifle at him restores her aggressiveness. Her stance in warding off Del also demonstrates Cassie's bravery of spirit as much as it shows her defending what she thinks is her chance to leave the mountain.

Her desire to help Richard may be connected to a romantic longing, but it is also aligned to her wanting him to take her away with him because she cannot leave by herself. In the cave she will tell him, "Takes a lot of gumption to go down there alone." Gram warns her about Richard when he is outside washing up, "You can't hold a fella like that. You can't keep him for a pet like he was a rabbit or something." Cassie replies, "I found him — ain't nobody gonna take him away." Cassie answers while holding Richard's jacket, both caressing it and searching the pockets. Cassie gives Gram her own warning: "You scare him off and I'll sit you down on your skinny old shanks."

Cassie lies to Richard about a truck that she claims she has lent to the one of the hunters, Ames Woodruff. This lie is intended to make Richard stay at the cabin in anticipation of the return of the truck, although he soon realizes the ruse. The reveal occurs after Del's appearance in his jeep, which adds some ambiguity since we think that the jeep is the truck that Cassie has spoken of. There is also no other apparent narrative reason for Del to appear at the cabin, given that he is previously seen with the hunters, apart from the idea of him just "coming by," as Cassie tells Richard he tends to do.

Gram asks Richard to take Cassie with him by saying, "You wouldn't have to be ashamed of her. She can be real handsome in a dress." Cassie will eventually be seen wearing a dress, but only after Richard has finally rejected her in the mine, and she decides she can leave home by herself in the epilogue. Then she wears no hair ribbon but a tucked-in blouse and skirt, and a hat that Gram hands to her. Finally, she tells Grams, "I don't need nobody," rejecting help and going it alone.

When Del appears at the cabin, he replies to Cassie's declaration that Gram is not home with, "She must've just know'd I's coming back." Cassie then tells him, "You see any weasel traps around?" indicating her low opinion of Del. Cassie's beseeching of Richard to take her with him is one of Dennis' two finest moments in the episode because she is relatively free of mannerisms. It helps that her vulnerability is emphasized by the dirt smudged on her face after Cassie's fight with Del. Cassie presents her help as practical, since she tells Richard he can't get past the bloodhounds or out of the mountains on his own.

The Sheriff gets the funniest line in the teleplay after Del says, "She wouldn't even let me past the front door." To this the Sheriff replies, "If I was her I wouldn't either." When the hunters get to Gram's cabin, she is alone and tells them that Cassie went out to pick berries. This is the excuse that Cassie gave to Del for where Gram had gone. To Gram's claim, Philip asks, "Where?" and Grams replies, amusingly, "Anywhere there's berries to be found." Philip's deduction that Richard has been at the cabin comes from the outside wash area, where he sees the dirty water in the basin, wet soap and a dirty towel that is dry. The latter is the real giveaway for Philip, since he says that Richard, being a doctor, would never use a dirty towel.

In the mine, when Cassie asks Richard to take her with him, she tells him, "I wouldn't be in your way and there wouldn't be nothin' I wouldn't do." This latter comment is ambiguous, since it could read as her being either pathetic or brave. Additionally, when she describes herself as "something you coulda pick off a berry bush," we can read this as either her having low self-esteem or self-awareness.

Cassie speaking of the cave they rest in as "the dreaming room" allows for Dennis' second finest moment. She is both lyrical and sad in the knowledge of her frustration over her life and Richard's rejection of her. This is despite his attempts to placate her with the idea that she can go down the mountain alone, which she eventually decides to do in the epilogue. Cassie lets Richard go ahead while she holds off the hunters, and this is again evidence of her bravery, with the insight that she will not be harmed by the Sheriff because she is his kin. Her bravery seemingly becomes self-sacrifice when she knocks down a cave archway and entombs herself with the hunters.

Director James Sheldon plays with the androgyny of Cassie's character by initially suggesting that she is a man. She is first heard by Richard walking, then we see her booted feet. From behind we see that she wears her shirt pulled out of levis and her sleeves are rolled up. The cap she wears hides her shoulder-length hair. When Richard wrestles with Cassie and they roll down the hill, her cap falls off and she is revealed as a woman. There is a laugh from Cassie's reaction to Richard's attack: "Boy, I never seen a man so mean. What are you trying to do? Kill me or something?" It is apparent that a body-double is used for Cassie's climb back up the hill, although there are some continuity problems with how messed her hair is on the walk back to Gram's cabin.

There is a point of view shot from the helicopter of the Sheriff, Jessie, Roy and his dogs when it approaches. This is the only visually interesting piece of camerawork in the episode. When the action moves to the mining caves, the light from the candle that Cassie holds is clearly not the only light source, which becomes obvious after Richard leaves with the candle and Cassie remains well illuminated.

The TV show was created by Roy Huggins and aired for four seasons from September 17, 1963, to August 29, 1967, with one hundred and twenty episodes produced. Richard Kimble was from the fictional town of Stafford, Indiana. In every episode the pre-credit sequence repeated the scene of Richard on the train to death row, seated with Philip, when the train derails and crashes, allowing him to escape. Interestingly, the episode "The Other Side of the Mountain" never has Richard verbalize the nature of his search for the one-armed killer (played by Bill Raisch) of his wife. The TV show would be remade twice. The 1993 feature film *The Fugitive* starred Harrison Ford as Richard Kimble and Tommy Lee Jones as "Samuel" Gerard, while *The Fugitive* was a TV show that ran for one season from 2000 to 2001 and starred Tim Daly as Richard Kimble and Mykelti Williamson as Philip Gerard.

RELEASE: Broadcast on ABC on October 1, 1963.
REVIEWS: None available.
DVD: Included in the box set *The Fugitive Season 1 Volume 1* by Paramount Home Video on August 14, 2007.

Arrest and Trial (1964)

(TV show), Season 1, Episode 19, "Somewhat Lower than the Angels," Revue Studios
CREW: William Claxton (Director), Charles Russell (Producer), Frank P. Rosenberg (Executive Producer), Robert Crean (Teleplay), Ray Fernstrom (Photography), Bronislaw Kaper

Arrest and Trial (1964)

(Theme), Raymond Beal (Art Director), George Ohanian (Editor), John McCarthy, Robert C. Bradfield (Set Decorators), Corson Jowett (Sound), Bud Westmore (Makeup), Larry Germain (Hair). Filmed at Universal Studios, Universal City, California. Black & White, 75 minutes (without commercials).

SONG: "I'll Never Smile Again" (Ruth Lowe), sung by Sandy Dennis.

CAST: Ben Gazarra (Detective Sergeant Nick Anderson), Chuck Connors (Attorney John Egan), John Larch (Deputy District Attorney Jerry Miller), Roger Perry (Detective Sergeant Dan Kirby), John Kerr (Assistant District Attorney Barry Pine), Steve Forrest (Rev. Bill Hewitt), Sandy Dennis (Molly White), Don Galloway (Mitchell Harris), Joe Higgins (Jake Shakespeare), Monica Lewis (Thecla Whitney), Hampton Fancher III (Raymond), Ken Lynch (Detective Lieutenant Tom Handley), Sue Randall (Maris Hewitt), Damian O'Flynn (Judge), Jon Lormer (Vicar), Vic Tayback (Bartender), Elizabeth Harrower (Studio Club Woman).

SYNOPSIS: At the All Night Bowls bowling alley, the Rev. Bill Hewitt rescues Molly White from drunken men. He takes her to the apartment of his sister, Maris. When he returns the next morning he finds Maris dead and Molly gone. Molly telephones Bill from the Santa Monica pier for money, and he brings the police. Molly admits to killing Maris, then denies it, but is charged with murder. When asked to reenact her story at Maris' apartment, she confesses to the murder.

NOTES: Dennis' first full-on murderess (she only *attempted* murder in *Naked City*) allows her to play a duplicitous character less mentally ill and more calculating than the one in "Idylls of a Running Back." Here she uses the mannerisms of stuttering and broken sentences, gasping, blinking, eye-closing, hand-gesturing, finger pointing, tongue-poking, mouth-touching, and hair-fussing. She also employs moments of stillness for emphasis (e.g., when she does not initially react to Bill's asking her to turn herself in to the police). Additionally, Dennis engages in physical action to define her character. She pushes violently past Bill outside the church, she rests under the pier boardwalk and lowers her head, she breaks a window to steal clothes, and, at the episode's climax, she reenacts the scene of the crime.

Her blonde hair has dark roots, perhaps as a character signifier. Her costumes include a one-piece bathing suit, shirt and pants, a prison dress, and a sweater and skirt for the court hearing. Dennis is heard singing "I'll Never Smile Again" off-key when she is in Maris' bathroom, presumably running a bath, and seen smoking at the beach house.

Her best scene in the episode is Molly's speech to Attorney John Egan about her abusive childhood, which culminates in her statement that she "learned to be afraid." Although Dennis uses stuttering and head-rolling, she also sheds tears. She sits in an oddly off-center, casual way during the hearing scene, with her left arm placed on the desk in front of her. The climactic reenactment allows her to contextualize all her nervous mannerisms, given that she is being repeatedly interrupted and flustered by John Egan.

Bill describes Molly to the police as a "drifter," after she had told him on the drive to his place that she had no home. Part of the reason he came to her aid at the bowling alley is that he recognized her as someone that repeatedly came to his church for food. The bartender describes Molly as "trouble," and the two men she was with as "rich kids." A woman at a boarding house states that Molly was evicted for being unsuitable and for never paying rent, and that she borrowed money and didn't pay it back. The woman says, "She was a liar. Not a truthful girl, nor a nice one." A bookseller tells the police that Molly used to sleep in the back room of the store, and that "she has a major talent — a talent for survival." Nick describes Molly as an "untouchable who contaminates," which recalls Dennis' carrier in *Naked City*. Deputy District Attorney Jerry Miller says of Molly, "She's got a record from here to Mount Etna, and she's just as explosive."

After Thecla asks Molly to go with her to Mexico, Molly stands behind her sideways and looks back at the woman suspiciously. Thecla claims to have had two husbands and has spent the night of the murder with Raymond, which is his alibi. However, there is a lesbian suggestion from the way Thecla is presented, and perhaps this is what Molly is suspicious of. Thecla tells Molly that Raymond has described Molly as a "fleer," i.e. one who runs away.

The biggest laugh in the teleplay comes from an exchange between Molly and John Egan after she has asked Bill to leave the room. Talking about Maris, Molly tells John, "I appreciate people who are kind to me." To this he replies, "I know; I just saw you in action." This bit of sarcasm is aimed at Molly's lack of appreciation for Bill's help. Egan also makes the observation that Molly is "a peculiar girl who thrashes around in every direction," referring to her confession then denials. When Assistant District Attorney John Pine says, "She doesn't have a prayer," Egan replies, "That's the one thing she does have," referring to Minister Bill's support.

The issue of the killer's identity, and whether Molly or Raymond is the liar, is what drives the narrative. This is only resolved with the reenactment at the climax. Pine says that Molly can be identified at a pawn shop selling Maris' things, but Raymond remains a suspicious character. The climactic reveal of Molly as the liar and the killer surprisingly comes quietly, after John has guessed it. Her final comments to Bill are as follows: "You wanted innocence from me. I didn't have it anymore. I did once. Maybe if we had met then, I dunno.... Your timing was bad, Reverend." Molly is finally shown to be a compulsive liar with an awareness of her manipulation.

Director William Claxton's car mock-ups are crude here for the driving scenes, which make obvious use of rear projection. However, the lattice fence that Thecla stands behind when questioned by Nick is a nice effect and underscores her own duplicity, since she lies to him about knowing Molly. When Thecla goes back to Molly, she inexplicably yells after her when she sees her running to the beach — something we assume Nick could hear. It turns out that Nick has not heard, and the expectation that Molly has run into the sea to drown herself remains unfulfilled.

Despite Dennis' overuse of performance mannerisms, the episode is most compelling when she is on screen. The scenes in which Bill battles a crisis of faith are less interesting, as are those that feature Raymond. They are both basically passive characters, whereas Molly in an active one.

The show only ran for one season and produced 30 episodes. It debuted on September 15, 1963, and ended on September 5, 1964. Its format followed along the lines of *Dragnet* and was a precursor to *Law & Order*. Set in Los Angeles, the first part of the episode is dedicated to The Arrest, during which a crime is committed and the criminal caught. The second is The Trial, detailing a hearing which covers the defense of the criminal. One criticism of the show was the casting of Chuck Connors as an attorney, since he was associated with westerns (making one wonder how an attorney is *supposed* to behave). Producer Charles Russell also produced *Naked City*. *Arrest and Trial* would be remade by Dick Wolf using actual footage and reenactments of sensational real life crimes; it ran for two seasons, from 2000 to 2002.

RELEASE: Broadcast on ABC on February 2, 1964.
REVIEWS: None available.
DVD: Included in the *Arrest and Trial Part 2* box set by Timeless Media Group, released on March 19, 2008.

Mr. Broadway (1964)

(TV show), Season 1, Episode 7, "Don't Mention My Name in Sheboygan," Talent Associates/Paramount

CREW: Alex Marsh (Director), Larry Arrick (Producer), David Melnick, David Susskind (Executive Producers), Robert Russell (Teleplay), Music (Dave Brubeck), Jack Priestley (Photography), Emanuel Gerard (Art Director), Muriel Gettinger (Costumes), Tone Karnash (Editor), Sam Robert (Set Decorator), Bill Herman (Makeup), Ed Callaghan (Hair), Botany 500 (Mr. Stevens' Wardrobe), Eckstein-Stone (Titles). Filmed at Biograph Studios in New York, Black & White, 60 minutes (with commercials).

CAST: Craig Stevens (Mike Bell), Lani Miyazaki (Toki), Horace McMahon (Hank McClure), Diana Muldaur (Miss Adams, Receptionist), Max Cleyen, Bob Murray, Chester Morris (Orin J. Kelsey), Joan Bennett (Mrs. "Bootsie" Kelsey), Sandy Dennis (Patricia Kelsey), Robert Webber (Roland Hogan).

SYNOPSIS: Roland Hogan plots with twenty-one-year-old Patricia Kelsey to blackmail her father, Orin. They hire Madison Avenue public relations man Mike Bell to supposedly protect Orin from the "Sheboygan" scandal of Orin's wife being a prostitute. Mike meets Patricia at the Sutton Gallery exhibition, and she prevents him from being beaten up by Orin's henchmen. Patricia tells Orin that Mike has kidnapped her. At the pier Orin brings ransom money, and Roland demands it. Roland fights with Mike and is shot by Orin. Patricia confesses to her father of the plan to rob him of his money.

NOTES: Dennis plays another criminal, this time one who blackmails her own father, in this TV guest appearance. Although she begins the episode mannerism-free, she soon resorts to them, although there are some moments where they remain dormant. Dennis employs stutters and word repetition, hand gestures, pointing, head-shakes, smiles, eye-closing, slurred speech, a nasal whine, broken sentences, laughing, whispering, and hair-fussing. She is seen wearing a black band in her blonde hair, as well as her hair up (in the art gallery scene), covered in a scarf, and loose. Dennis drives a car, applies lipstick, dials a telephone, runs during the climax, and screams when Roland is shot. She is also heard in voice-over reading the letter she has written and sent to Mike at the end.

When Patricia tells Mike of her mother's alleged past as a prostitute, Dennis holds her arms crossed over her chest and is reasonably free of affected mannerisms. Perhaps staging the scene with her back to Mike helped. When she tells her father of Mike's alleged blackmail, Patricia sheds tears. She also produces tears when Patricia tells Roland that she wants to call off their plan. The tears here are more apparent, as she is filmed in close-up (rather than in longshot like in the earlier crying scene). Dennis receives another close-up for the scene in which Patricia tells Mike how no one ever loved her.

The teleplay has some wit. Hank tells Mike, "You could sue the pants of him [Orin Kelsey] for something like this." Mike replies, "What do I want with his pants?" When Patricia tells Mike that her father didn't leave her any money in his will, Mike replies, "He's smart. Maybe it's to keep you from putting rat poison in his orange juice." Mike later sums up Patricia's manipulations with, "One minute you're Little Miss Muffet. The next minute you're Mata Hari. Then you flip the switch from Scarlett O'Hara to Joan of Arc to Alice in Wonderland." The Alice in Wonderland crack relates back to Patricia first seen in the park climb over Alice in Wonderland statues when she goes to meet Roland.

Director Alex Marsh uses quick cuts for the scene where Orin advances upon Mike with the fire-poker. Mike throwing the chair into the window is shown from a subjective point of view, as if he is throwing it at the camera. Marsh zooms in on Dennis for the end of the scene where she has pretended to her father that Mike has kidnapped her; and the fight scene in the storeroom between Mike and Roland features some odd angles and one out-of-focus shot of Mike.

The show was created by Garson Kanin. It lasted for one season in 1964 and produced thirteen episodes. Horace McMahon had been in *Naked City*. It's instructive to compare his acting style to Dennis,' given her mannerisms and his more naturalistic approach. Executive Producer David Susskind would go on to produce Dennis' made-for-TV movie *A Hatful of Rain* (1968).

RELEASE: Broadcast by CBS on November 7, 1964.
REVIEWS: None available.
DVD: Not available.

A Hatful of Rain (1968)

Rediffusion Television/Talent Associates
CREW: John Llewellyn Moxley (Director), David Susskind (Producer), Robert Arden, Alan Shayne (Associate Producers), Michael V. Gazzo (Teleplay), Jack Shultes (Editor), Fred Pusey (Set Decoration), Albert Wolsky (Costumes). Color, 120 minutes. Filmed in December 1967 in Stonebridge Park, London, England.
CAST: Sandy Dennis (Celia Pope), Michael Parks (Johnny Pope), Peter Falk (Polo Pope), Herschel Bernardi (John Pope Sr.), Don Stroud (Mother), John P. Ryan (Chuck), Jack Kehoe (Apples), Toni Bull (Putski).
SYNOPSIS: Johnny has become addicted to morphine after a hospital stay. He needs forty dollars a day to support his habit. His older brother Polo tries to protect him by giving him money and concealing his brother's condition from his pregnant wife, Celia. Because of Johnny's inattention, Celia is attracted to Polo. She almost suffers a miscarriage when she learns about Johnny, who eventually admits to his family to being an addict.
NOTES: Dennis' casting in this made-for-TV movie, after appearing as a leading film actress, was viewed as less detrimental to her career than the later made-for-TV movies *The Man Who Wanted to Live Forever* and *Something Evil*. This is because *A Hatful of Rain*, as made by members of the Actors Studio, was considered more prestigious than the conventional made-for-TV movie.

This was a remake of the 1957 film directed by Fred Zinnemann that starred Eva Marie as Celia Pope, Don Murray as Johnny Pope, Anthony Franciosa as Polo Pope, Lloyd Nolan as John Pope Sr., Henry Silva as Mother, Gerald S. O'Loughlin as Chuch, and William Hickey as Apples, but no one credited as Putski. The original film was about a Korean War veteran. David Susskind had previously executive produced the TV show *Mr. Broadway*, which featured Dennis as a guest star in one episode.

RELEASE: Broadcast by ABC on March 3, 1968.
REVIEWS: *A Hatful of Rain* received critically mixed reactions from Jack Gould in *The New York Times* on March 4, 1968; and from *The Pittsburgh Press* on March 10, 1968. Gould wrote that Dennis (and Parks and Falk) "play their roles like so many introverted wooden figures." *The Pittsburgh Press* said, "Michael Parks and Sandy Dennis out-mumble and out-method each other."
DVD: Not available.

A Hatful of Rain (1968)

Still from the made-for-TV *A Hatful of Rain* (1968). In the background stands from left Polo Pope (Peter Falk) and John Pope Sr. (Herschel Bernardi). In the foreground sits Celia Pope (Dennis) by the bedside of her husband, Johnny Pope (Michael Parks).

The Man Who Wanted to Live Forever (1970)

(aka *Only Way Out Is Dead/The Heart Farm*), Palomar Pictures International/Canadian Film Development Corporation

CREW: John Trent (Director), Terence Dene (Producer), Edgar J. Scherick, Henry Denker (Executive Producers), Henry Denker (Teleplay), Dolores Claman (Music), Marc Champion (Photography), M.C. Manne, Ron Wisman (Editors), Jack McAdam (Art Director), Roger Palmer (Costumes), Ken Brooke (Makeup), James Keeler (Hair), Earl Fisset (Set Dresser), John Aldred (Sound). Color, 72 minutes. Filmed in British Columbia and Ontario, Canada, from May 19 to June 28, 1970.

CAST: Sandy Dennis (Dr. Enid Bingham), Stuart Whitman (Dr. McCarter Purvis), Burl Ives (Thomas Maynard "T.M." Trask), Tom Harvey (McBride), Robert Goodier (Dr. Wilfrid Morton), Ron Hartmann (Dr. John Emmett, Administrator), Jack Creley (Dr. George Simmons), Joseph Shaw (Dr. Franz Heinemann), Allen Doremus (Dr. Carl Bryant), Kenneth James (Clinton), Harvey Fisher (Copter Pilot), Robert Warner, James Forrest, Robert Mann (Guards), John S. Davies (Doctor), Clem Hambourg (Pianist), Dr. V.K. Saini, George Pyfrom, Claudia Koropecki (Surgeons). Uncredited: Nina Keogh (Trask's Nurse).

SYNOPSIS: Heart surgeon Dr. McCarter Purvis is hired by T.M. Trask to work in his research center located in the remote Rockie Mountains of Canada. Purvis begins an affair with hematologist Enid Bingham. Purvis and Enid believe that Trask's insistence on the staff signing over the rights to their body parts after their death is to ensure him of donors should he need a heart transplant. Trask has a heart attack, and Purvis is chosen to be the donor. Purvis and Enid flee to the mountains and escape from Trask's pursuing helicopters to safety.

NOTES: Dennis agreeing to make a conventional made-for-TV movie may seem a demotion for an actress associated with leading film roles. This was at a time when there was a definite industry demarcation between actors that worked in film and those that worked in television. The fact that her character has a romantic and sexual relationship in the narrative somewhat redeems the choice of material, even if she plays a supporting role to Stuart Whitman (despite her receiving top-billing). Within the limitations of playing the girlfriend of the protagonist, she delivers a performance that any competent actress could. She remains forgettable in a thriller that is equally forgettable.

Here Dennis' brown hair is longer than we have previously seen it, with it reaching her elbows; and the times when she has it tied back or loose may be an indication of her character's activity. When we see her in the lab, it is worn tied back. However, it hangs loose when she walks with Purvis outside the center and after they have made love in her apartment, which is suggested by both of them wearing matching bathrobes.

Enid's wardrobe may be at least partially determined by the cold weather. However, it is interesting that on the date with Purvis, she wears a long blouse and pants and initially has her hair tied back. For the concert, however, she has her hair in a ponytail and wears a short black dress. For the skiing scenes she initially wears black pants, a blue jacket, a beanie and comically giant, round, yellow-tinted goggles. Why her goggles are different from those that Whitman wears is not explained, and his are rectangular and more flattering. When Enid is in the open car with Purvis, she wears a brown head-scarf, and for the climactic ski scene she change into white overalls.

Dennis uses the mannerisms of eye-closing, head-nodding, and some stuttering. The latter is perhaps given context from her fear when talking to Purvis about something being amiss with her test studies. The fact that Enid has had a nervous breakdown in the past provides more context for Dennis' mannerisms, although the narrative only involves this plot point at the conclusion. We also see Enid smoking when Purvis is on the telephone with Morton. Since this occurs after having sex, it can be comically viewed as a late post-coital convention. Dennis also occasionally pulls faces for reactions.

Trask's bank of six video monitors with which he keeps tabs on the Center, suggests his controlling nature. This is further demonstrated by his watching Purvis and Enid talking in the lab, and then later the couple in her apartment. Trask again uses his video monitors to watch Purvis talking to Morton. The expectation of Purvis and Enid being caught when they go to Emmett's office is created first by the shot of the nurse, who has overheard them, and then by intercutting between the recital and the building's security guard. There is some ambiguity attached to whether the nurse has actually heard Purvis and Enid's plan, since she isn't shown to acknowledge it, and there is no plot payoff. The narrative ups the ante for the office search by locating Trask's files in a secret safe with a wired alarm.

Interestingly, revealing what the files say is left until later when Purvis and Enid look at the printed photographs she has taken, as opposed to her offering an analysis on the spot. The security guard is added as a second source of intercutting to raise the tension even higher. When the guard finds Purvis and Enid in the office, it fulfills one of the expectations, although only momentarily because Purvis is clever enough to make up a plausible excuse.

Trask's secret agenda is suggested by his appearing with a cane, which implies that he is sick. This plays out when Enid finds in his medical records that he has a weak heart, and also when Trask suffers a second heart attack. He has a bank of four monitors in his sick room so that he can watch the conversation between Purvis and Emmett, and later watch the helicopter pursuit of Purvis and Enid.

The fact that Enid's car radio can pick up Trask talking to his helicopters is pure narrative convenience. And it is unbelievable that the pursuing helicopter's occupants fail to see Purvis and Enid jumping from their car before it drives off a cliff into the river below. This contrivance merely eats up some running time as the helicopter flies in close to the car to report that the couple are not in it, although it does give Purvis and Enid more time to

Poster for the 1970 made-for-TV movie *The Man Who Wanted to Live Forever* (aka *The Heart Farm*).

get away. Trask also fails to see the escape on his video monitors, which can now view events from the helicopter.

Purvis and Enid walk through the woods to where they left their skiing equipment when they were on the mountain before. The idea that they can just lie still in the snow and stay hidden from the helicopter is another dramatic contrivance. It is as much a contrivance as the idea that Trask would just let them get away once they were over the property line.

A further contrivance is that the occupants of the first helicopter could have survived the crash, considering the fire that erupted, and we are told only that the co-pilot, Corey, is injured. However, the survival of the pilot Clinton is needed for Trask to finally get his donor heart, with Trask insisting that Clinton is injured to justify killing him for the heart. An unintentional laugh arises when McBride tells Trask that the couple will never make it over the property line, and Trask replies about Purvis, "The man has spirit and heart."

Director John Trent uses a helicopter's point of view for the opening arrival at the Trask building, and for the climactic helicopter chase. The sight of a beating heart for Morton's surgery is rather shocking. The operation scene lasts for three minutes, a rather long time. Trent, however, breaks up the procedure with shots of the supporting machinery, and reaction shots of Trask and Enid. Trent provides a romantic view of Purvis and Enid skiing together as a couple who move in parallel motion when first seen in the snow on their scouting trip. This image is repeated for the film's conclusion.

While his use of a musical score is often obtrusive, Trent effectively employs fast cuts for the fight sequence in the lab between Purvis and Emmett. The scene is enhanced by the lights being off. Trent also uses quick cutting during the climactic helicopter pursuit. The use of these fast edits at the climax in particular heightens the tension by raising the question of whether Purvis and Enid have been shot. The tension continues with a view of Purvis and Enid lying still in the snow. The last image of the couple skiing in long shot finally reveals that they have survived the shootings.

RELEASE: Broadcast in Canada on November 20, 1970, and in the United States on ABC television on December 15, 1970. A tagline for the film under the title *The Heart Farm* was "1000 miles from civilization, but its terror reaches out to the world."

REVIEWS: The telefilm was critically acclaimed by Jacob Siskind in *The Montreal Gazette* on November 21, 1970; and by Michael Karol in *The ABC Movie of the Week Companion: A Loving Tribute to the Classic Series*. Siskind wrote that Dennis "is a hematologist who seems ready to burst into tears at the drop of a hypodermic." Karol said that she gives a "rare non-eccentric and effective performance."

DVD: No DVD. VHS released by Ray Bren Productions and Designer Skin. No dates available.

Something Evil (1972)

CBS Television Network Productions/Primetime Entertainment, Belford Productions (uncredited).

CREW: Steven Spielberg (Director), Alan Jay Factor (Producer), Harvey Lembeck, David Knapp (Associate Producers), Robert Clouse (Teleplay), Wladimir Selinsky (Music), Bill Butler (Photography), Allan Jacobs (Editor), E. Albert Heschong (Production Design), Sandy Grace (Set Decorator), Stephen Lodge, Agnes Lyon (Costumes), Ken Chase (Makeup), Gloria Montemayor (Hair), Brandes, Berke & Associates (Special Optical Effects). Color, 74 minutes. Filmed at Studio City and Walt Disney's Golden Oak Ranch, California.

SONG: "Apple Bar Candy Song" (Charlie Marie Gordon), sung by Laurie Hagen, an auditioning singer, and Irene during the dubbing session.

CAST: Sandy Dennis (Marjorie "Marge" Worden), Darren McGavin (Paul Worden), Jeff Corey (Gehrmann), Johnny Whitaker (Stevie Worden), John Rubinstein (Ernest Lincoln), Ralph Bellamy (Harry Lincoln), David Knapp (John), Laurie Hagen (Beth), Herb Armstrong (Mr. Schiller), Margaret Avery (Irene), Norman Bartold (Mr. Hackett), Sheila Bartold (Mrs. Hackett), Lois Battle (Mrs. Faraday), Bella Bruck (Mrs. Gehrmann), Lynn Cartwright (Secretary), John J. Fox (Sound Man), Alan Frost (Alan), Carl Gottlieb (Party Guest), John Hudkins (McDermott), Crane Jackson (Neighbor), Michael Macready, Paul Micale (Mr. Faraday), Margaret Muse (Mrs. Schiller), John Nolan, Connie Hunter Ragaway (Singer), Elizabeth Rogers, Steven Spielberg (Party Guests), Bruno VeSota (Neighbor), Debbie and Sandy Lempert (Laurie).

SYNOPSIS: New York advertising executive Paul Worden and his artist wife Marjorie move into a farmhouse with their son Stevie and daughter Laurie. After mysterious happenings, Marjorie comes to believe that the house is haunted. She attempts suicide but is saved by the caretaker, Gehrmann. Stevie behaves as if possessed. Marjorie exorcises the demon by keeping the boy in a circle of protection she has painted in the children's room. The Wordens then move out of the farmhouse.

NOTES: This made-for-TV movie is Dennis' second and continues the notion that her days as a leading film actress were over. She plays another mother in this role, the parent of older children than those in *Thank You All Very Much*. Dennis is photographed in lots of close-ups, presumably as favored television coverage.

It helps that her character is more the protagonist than she was in *The Man Who Wanted to Live Forever*. Marjorie begins as a congenial wife and mother. Her being an artist suggests that her belief in the idea of the house being possessed by a devil is the fancy of a creative and non-rational person. Additionally, being a *female* artist adds to the stereotype of the emotional person who can lapse into hysteria when something misunderstood presents itself. The progression of her emotional distress allows Dennis to create an empathetic performance with sincerity and expressions of anger.

She has the same long brown hair she sported in *The Man Who Wanted to Live Forever*, and wears it at various times loose, in plaits, and tied back. For a dinner scene between Marjorie and Paul, she wears a low-cut black dress, which is a style we have not seen her don before in her films. Her wardrobe also features a lot of the color red. Marjorie has a red nightgown, and red cardigan and stockings. The color red also appears in the cracked car windshield before the crash, and as the color of the contents of the barn jar.

Dennis uses the mannerisms of hair-fiddling, stuttering, and head-nodding, although they become less noticeable when the narrative stakes are raised. We hear her laugh in response to a story Harry tells Marjorie of a grape-eating and kissing keyhole devil. She screams when she sees the red goo in the barn jar and then finds one later in the kitchen cupboard. She has tears in her eyes when she telephones Paul to tell him that she has hit Stevie, and when she tells the children that she cannot trust herself to help them anymore.

Marjorie asserts herself by telling Paul that she doesn't like how their caretaker is slaughtering chickens for supernatural protection, and also when she tells Paul that she wants them to leave the house the day after the incident when the wind appeared in the children's room. It is noteworthy that it is she and not Paul who is the one to investigate the sound of the baby crying at night, although perhaps being female and a mother makes her more sensitive to the sound.

Dennis shows Marjorie's strength when she tells Paul that she is leaving the house, her conviction mixed with anger. Director Steven Spielberg ends the scene with a close-up on her after Paul has told Marjorie, "We'll go back to the city and live happily ever after." She cries, and her look expresses her anxiety over the situation, and also suggests that she knows that the family were not happy in the city before. Marjorie yells at Stevie to stop playing with a spider on a string, thinking that it is annoying Lauren, though the girl doesn't appear upset. She yells again when she follows Stevie into the nestled archway and calls out his name, and her anger when she chases and catches him will result in the plot point of her hitting him — revealed in an oblique way. The expectation is that Marjory will hit Stevie when she catches him and repeats, "I told you to stay in the yard." But we don't see her hit him. We only hear her tell Paul on the telephone, "I have done something terrible," and Paul sees Stevie's bruises and the bloodied nose. Marjorie doesn't directly tell Paul that she has hit Stevie, but her apology to Paul implies that she has. The apology shows Dennis being sincere in her guilt but also retaining some anger in her frustration. She is shown in close-up as a distorted reflection in a hand mirror after she throws a devil sculpture and smashes a dressing table mirror in her bedroom.

A prologue shows McDermott in the barn repeating, "Ye shall be taken." He falls out of the barn window in the loft to his presumed death. Marjorie mirrors this action when she attempts suicide by jumping out the same window. The wind in the barn suggests the evil presence, a presence that appears again when Stevie and later Marjorie go into the barn, and when Marjorie attempts suicide.

The mobile that moves on its own above Stevie's bed echoes the evil wind. Its presence perhaps explains why Marjorie is seen to have slept with the boy in her living room rather than the children's room. After we see Stevie follow a toad into the barn, Marjorie reads from Lincoln's devil book that the devil can materialize as a toad. Stevie mentioning the jars in the barn will be paid off when Marjorie sees the pulsating red liquid in one of them.

The wind in the children's room after Marjorie has escaped the barn suggests more of the evil presence. Her putting herself and the children in the circle of protection acknowledges her belief in the wind being a supernatural presence. There is also wind in the nestled archway into which Marjorie follows Stevie, and her long hair getting caught in some branches is a nice touch.

There is some ambiguity behind Harry's sympathy for Marjorie's plight, since we don't know if he has another agenda for the family to leave the house. Suspicion arises perhaps from the fact that Harry has the books on devils in the first place, and because Ralph Bellamy, who plays Harry, also played the devil-worshipping Dr. Sapirstein in *Rosemary's Baby* (1968). This ambiguity is furthered by his confession to Marjorie that he is not as hard of hearing as he has led people to believe, which shows him to be duplicitous. However, the devil's seeming killing of Harry for presumably attempting to help Marjorie is an indication that Harry is not in league with the demon after all. The fact that we see the devil attack Harry when Marjorie is calling him is surely not a coincidence. The issue of Harry is resolved when Ernest tells Marjory that Harry has been attacked but is not dead, although we don't see Harry again in the narrative.

Harry has told Marjorie that "love is more powerful than pentacles," which suggests that her maternal instinct can defeat the devil. It also implies that her power would be stronger if she bonded with Paul, though the problem is that Paul is not empathetic to her plight. Only after Paul is shown the eyes in the film footage does he believe Marjorie's story. It is noteworthy that the devil seemingly prefers to battle with her while the wind keeps Paul out of the children's room, and only the disappearance of the devil's presence allows Paul back in.

Something Evil (1972)　　　　TELEVISION • 175

This publicity photo from the made-for-TV movie *Something Evil*, 1971, features Marjorie "Marge" Worden (Dennis) and her husband Paul (Darren McGavin, standing). Seated is their neighbor, Harry Lincoln (Ralph Bellamy).

Marjorie hearing the baby crying in the daytime and in the house is a progression of the devil's harassment, culminating in her finding that the noise comes from a jar of the red pulsating goo in a kitchen cupboard. Why Marjorie doesn't retrieve the key to the children's bedroom she has hidden in order to open the door, rather than attempting to break it down with Paul and Gehrmann, is a mystery. However, the wind in the room suggests the devil's presence. We think that Stevie is raised in the air until we see that his height is explained by him sitting on the top bunk of a bunkbed. Lauren's rescue appears to be made easier by the fact that she is sitting in the circle of protection when Paul goes to her.

The narrative ends on an image of the farmhouse after the Wordens have driven away. The image changes to the painting that Marjorie had initially created, with the devil symbol in the closing credits recalling the devil sculpture she had thrown into her dressing table mirror.

Paul earns a laugh when Marjorie tells him that "I feel that something or someone is trying to possess me," and he replies, "Yeah. Me." Otherwise the treatment is lacking in humor — apart from the unintentional sort.

Spielberg opens with an extreme close-up of eyes. He will continue with out-of-focus effects, slow motion, jump cuts, quick cuts, expressionist camera angles, and hand-held camerawork. His overuse of odd camera angles actually becomes comic during the climactic possession and heightens the ridiculousness of this tale of the supernatural.

The director cuts from a shot of Marjorie drinking from a cup to an extreme close-up of the children in the corn-eating competition at the Lincolns' house party. He uses repeated reverses for Marjorie trying to open the barn door, so that it appears she is pushing against herself holding the door shut. He also employs quick intercutting between Stevie throwing a basketball against the outside wall of the house and Marjory throwing down clay to break the clay circles she has made.

The movie is said to have been made to capitalize on the success of the novel *The Exorcist*, by William Peter Blatty, which had yet to be released as a movie. That film would be released June 19, 1973. *Something Evil* was the first made-for-TV movie made by producer Alan Jay Factor, who also played the part of Alan. Associate Producer David Knapp played the part of John.

RELEASE: Broadcast by CBS on January 29, 1972.

REVIEWS: *Something Evil* earned a critically mixed reaction from Dave Kaufman in *Daily Variety*, who wrote that Dennis "begins her performance on a high level and never wavers. There is no shading for real impact."

DVD: Not available.

Police Story (1978)

"Day of Terror ... Night of Fear," David Gerber Productions/Columbia Pictures Television

CREW: E. Arthur Kean (Director/Teleplay), Mel Swope, Larry Brody (Producers), David Gerber (Executive Producer), Arthur David Hilton (Associate Producer), Richard Shores (Music), Jerry Goldsmith (Music Theme), Emmett Bergholz (Photography), Ronald LaVine (Editor), Ross Bellah, Robert Peterson (Art Directors), Lloyd A. Linnean (Set Decorator), Ben Lane (Makeup), Harold Harrison (Special Effects). Color, 90 minutes (without commercials). Filmed at Warner Bros. Studios, Hollywood, in October 1977.

CAST: Chad Everett (Officer Ron Tice), Sandy Dennis (Sharon Bristol), Bruce Davison

(Victor Joe Vero), Tom Simcox (Sergeant Duvall), Michael Baseleon (Sergeant Boller), Malcolm Atterbury (Alfred Weiser), Ward Costello (Deputy Chief Franklin J. Hosford), Andy Romano (Lieutenant Celano), Sheila Larken (Virginia "Ginny" Hosford), Warren Oates (Clark "Richey" Neptune), Graham Brown (Eustis McCoy), Jack Dodson (Osburn "Ozzie" Parker), David Zooey Hall (Nick Volusia), Erin Gray (Laurie Tice), Irene Tedrow (Mrs. Weiser), Howard Honig (Dr. Taylor), Clete Roberts (Canton Mackay), Barry Cahill (Leon Rigby), David Brooks (Berlin), William Steven Shaw (Officer Goshen), Ken Magee (Taft), Albert Able (Scully), Toni Crupi (Hauser), Terry Jastrow (Bernasconi), Wayne Heffley (Hartley), Ron Stokes (Gunther), Tom Gagen (Officer Johnson), John Dresden (Butler), Richard Wieand (Worley), Kyle Richards (Viki Jo Vero).

SYNOPSIS: Small-time crooks Richey Neptune and Victor Joe Vero rob a bank and take the employees of Farrell's Tours hostage. They use Sharon Bristol to talk on the telephone with the police hostage negotiator, Ron Tice. Coffee man Eustis McCoy is shot by Richey. The robbers eventually come out of the office, holding Ginny Hosford at gunpoint. Victor Joe gives himself up, and releases Sharon and Alfred Weiser. Richey releases Ginny and surrenders to the SWAT team.

NOTES: This generic episode of a police drama has Dennis in a supporting role as a guest star, although she is not billed as such. While she gives a good performance, it is confined to the limitations of the genre and is a performance that perhaps any competent actress could give. Her appearance here may be viewed as an even bigger step down from film roles than her prior made-for-TV movies. The fact that it is a two-part episode redeems it slightly, since its length can be likened to a made-for-TV movie. In fact, a promo for the show describes it as a "movie." Dennis' appearance is indicative of her apparent fall from grace as a movie star and of her lack of film offers.

It is interesting to consider who else was a guest star in the episode and to compare their status in films at the time. Chad Everett receives top billing, though he had mainly worked in television and film supporting roles at the time, playing the lead in only two films. Warren Oates earns a guest star credit, and had achieved a succession of leading film roles in the 1970s after slaving in supporting television and film roles for fifteen years. After his appearance here, however, Oates would only play one more leading film role, and was otherwise seen in supporting roles and on television. Billed below Dennis is Bruce Davison, who had previously appeared in four leading film roles, though he had also done television guest appearances and made-for-TV movies. Davison would go on to play the lead in three films. Neither Everett nor Oates were Academy Award winners nor even nominees, but Davison would go on to receive a Best Supporting Actor nomination in 1991.

Dennis' first appearance shows only the back of her head, as Sharon talks to Mr. Weiser about his upcoming trip to Rome. It is only after a scene between Mr. Parker and Eustis that we get a frontal shot of her, still talking to Weiser. She has longer hair than the last time she was seen, in *Nasty Habits*, and her character wears glasses. Sharon wears a white dress and jacket over a tan-colored blouse, and stockings.

She is assumed to be a spinster after she later tells Richey that she is thirty-five years old and has no husband or boyfriend. Dr. Taylor describes her as "plain looking" and someone "who hasn't had much to do with men." Richey himself will continue this attitude towards Sharon when he calls her "dried up." Sharon will also tell Richey that she has difficulty meeting people on a personal level. She says, "I stumble over my words and I drop things, so I tend to look foolish at times." This self-characterization justifies Dennis' stuttering mannerisms.

In her performance she will also employ the mannerisms of head-nodding, smiling, gesturing and pointing. Her repeated gestures include hands clasped together and held to her chest, and a hand to her forehead, chest, mouth and neck. Richey puts his hand on her arm to thank Sharon for warning him not to go to Canada, telling her, "That's sweet of you." She motions for him to remove it to show that she is not comfortable with him touching her.

Dennis' best scene is perhaps when she becomes angry with Richey after he has killed Eustis. She refuses to shoot Richie with his own gun twice, and tells him that she doesn't believe him anymore. This attitude of Sharon's stands in contrast to her romantic interest in Richey suggested earlier (rationalized as supposed Stockholm syndrome).

Sharon being the telephone liaison with Ron separates her from the other hostages, which allows Richey to ask her about her personal life. One redeeming aspect of her performance is that Dennis is not presented as an emotional hysteric. This stands in stark contrast to the hysteric that Ginny is shown to be, although Ginny would seem to be threatened more than Sharon. Sharon's lack of hysteria can also be contextualized by the way she is shown to bond with Richey.

The bonding is established when she tells Richey how she relates her life working in the office with his experience of being in jail, and she tells him that she wants him to get away safely. When Sharon uses "we" when talking to Ron about the robbers, Dr. Taylor analyzes it as the result of someone suffering from Stockholm syndrome. Taylor opines that Richey has shown her more attention than she has ever had before, which makes her cooperative and emotionally involved with the robbers. The Stockholm syndrome plot point is furthered after Sharon is safe at the end, and she tells Parker, "I acted like a stranger. I didn't even know myself." However, her coming out of the syndrome is presumably suggested by her change of heart about Richey after he has killed Eustis.

The narrative creates the expectation of the Farrell's Tours office invasion by intercutting scenes set there with the bank hold-up for no immediate reason. We also see that the people at Farrell's hear the gunshots and police sirens. Another narrative expectation comes at the climax when Richey appears to surrender, and the created expectation of his trying something desperate is not met. The narrative also shifts from the bank robbery and office invasion as a central plot concern when it presents Ron Tice at home in bed with his wife on his day off, as the domestic situation of a policeman before he is called in to work. Ron also telephones his wife when he is on a break from the negotiations, and their level of intimacy is demonstrated when she tells him, "You ain't much but you're all I've got."

There is an interesting moment when Weiser tells the other hostages that he refuses to go along with any attempted escape plan that may endanger his life, warning that he will alert the robbers to such a plan. This presents Weiser as being more of a coward than the others. Such cowardice will be borne out after Weiser realizes that Ginny is related to the Chief, and Weiser thinks he can use her to obtain his freedom. This point is expressed in an amusing exchange between Weiser and Eustis. Weiser says, "I've got to get out of here," and Eustis replies, "We've all got to get out of here." Weiser's wife appearing at the site does not help to provide empathy for Weiser because of his cowardice, unlike the way Viki Jo is used to make Victor Joe seem sympathetic. Weiser further demonstrates his cowardice when he alerts Richey to Parker trying to escape, and finally when he tells Richey about the connection between Ginny and Chief Hosford. After Weiser is safe and reunited with his wife, he expresses shame over his behavior, but Ron forgives him, claiming that he acted human.

Victor Joe's hesitance to shoot Parker is more evidence of his greater humanity. However, his telephoning Ron behind Richey's back can be viewed as duplicitous. This is something which is confirmed later when Victor Joe separates himself with Sharon and Weiser in the elevator from Richey and Ginny, who have alighted. Still, Victor Joe's actions are to help the hostages more than harm them.

The narrative shows some depth when one of the sergeants informs Deputy Chief Hosford that the negotiation delaying tactic allows for "positive transference of feelings" between the robbers and the hostages. This would theoretically make it harder for the robbers to kill people they have come to know. There is also some depth in Sharon's bonding with Richey, adding a dimension to her character that the other hostages do not have.

One disappointing plot point is how Eustis become the token African American who is punished. It is he who is slugged when the robbers first invade the office, and he is the only one of the hostages to be killed. Thankfully, when Ron is interviewed by Canton Mackay at the end, he points out that one man was lost — which means, despite the rescue of the others and the capture of the robbers, there is "nothing to celebrate."

The plot point of Ginny being the daughter-in-law of Chief Hosford is teased out in regards to who has knowledge of it. Dr. Taylor comments on the idea that the robbers are unaware of the information with, "If someone tips the balance it could be a slaughterhouse in there." The TV news broadcast that the robbers watch gives the Chief's name, but only the other hostages make the connection. When Richey suggests they kill Ginny, it is because she has a husband and child and not because he knows of her connection to the Chief. Presumably the childless Sharon is someone the police would be less concerned about.

The teleplay includes some humor, particularly in the dialogue. After Ron has the power in the office reconnected, he tells Richey, "Now you know I keep my word." Richie replies, "Big deal. You threw a switch."

When Chief Hosford offers to go into the office for the face-to-face meeting, the Sergeant tells him that his being Ginny's father-in-law and the Deputy Chief puts him in "direct conflict" with himself. In response, Hosford says, "Sergeant, you are in conflict with me."

Otherwise, there is some repetition of the details of the hostage demands. The deadlines being extended dilute the dramatic effect, although they are perhaps necessary to lengthen the episode into two parts. Additionally, Richey going up and down the stairs to the roof at the climax is repetitious.

Director E. Arthur Kean favors quick cuts and short scenes. Police radio broadcasts are heard as we get a helicopter view of the city, though it is not shown who is listening to the broadcasts. Kean zooms in on Weiser for dramatic impact on two occasions. He also, amusingly, stands Richey next to a life-size cut-out of a smiling woman in the office, which is presumably something used for advertising.

Kean delays the reveal of the death of Eustis, since we are not shown him being shot. He only suggests the death by the sight of Eustis' outstretched, lifeless arm. Kean reveals Richey as the shooter via a pan up from the pointed gun to Richey's face, and ends on a freeze frame of Ron.

Police Story was a crime drama that covered both the professional and personal lives of the men and women of the Los Angeles Police Department. It was created by former policeman Joseph Wambaugh and ran for five seasons, from September 25, 1973, to May 28, 1978. The running time for episodes was usually sixty minutes with commercials.

The episode was covered in an uncredited article in *The Phoenix* dated March 7, 1978. A variation on the article appeared in the *Waycross Journal-Herald* on March 15, 1978, and was credited to Jerry Buck. Buck states that the episode was originally entitled "The Mouth Marines," referring to the police negotiators, and was changed a couple of weeks before airtime, for reasons unknown.

Bruce Davison is quoted in the article as saying that he had fun because his manager's office was in the same building in which he filmed. The bank his character robbed was a bank that would never cash his checks because he didn't have an account there. Davison says that he sought out the role because he wanted to work with Warren Oates. "He's my favorite actor. I find him interesting and dangerous and vulnerable all at once."

RELEASE: Broadcast by NBC on March 4, 1978.

REVIEWS: The episode garnered mixed critical reaction from Jerry Buck in the *Waycross Journal-Herald* on March 15, 1978; and Bernie Harrison in *The Washington Star* on August 20, 1978. Harrison wrote that "Everett, Warren Oates, Bruce Davison, and Sandy Dennis give it a good try."

DVD: Not available.

Perfect Gentlemen (1978)

Paramount Television/Bud Austin Productions

CREW: Jackie Cooper (Director/Producer), Bud Austin (Executive Producer), Nora Ephron (Teleplay), Dominic Frontiere (Music), William K. Jurgensen (Photography), Jerry Dronsky (Editor), Lyle R. Wheeler (Production Design), Jim Claytor (Art Director), Rick Gentz (Set Decorator), Hallie Smith-Simmons (Makeup), Lynn Del Kail (Hair), Shirlee Strahm (Women's Wardrobe), Joe Roveto (Men's Wardrobe). Color, 90 minutes. Filmed in Hollywood from October 27 to November 1977.

CAST: Lauren Bacall (Mrs. Lizzie Martin), Ruth Gordon (Mrs. Cavagnaro), Sandy Dennis (Sophie Rosenman), Lisa Pelikan (Annie Cavagnaro), Robert Alda (Ed Martin), Stephen Pearlman (Murray Rosenman), Steve Allie Collura (Vinnie Cavagnaro), Dick O'Neill (Mr. Appleton), Ken Olfson (Desk Clerk), Rick Garcia (Nick Auletta), Robert Kya-Hill (Johnson), Shane Sinutko (Jacob Rosenman), William H. Bassett (Wade Shelton, Southern Man), Laurie Hagen (Mrs. Wade Shelton, Southern Woman), Ralph Manza (Frankie Fox), Erik Stern (Jackie Brockhurst), Selma Archerd (Hotel Supervisor), Jeff Maxwell (Hotel Doorman), Larry Watson (Chauffeur), Steve Bluestein (Bellboy), George Zateslo (Policeman #1), Frederick Rule (Policeman #2), Martin Gish (Policeman #3), Joseph Benti (Newscaster), Barbara Simpson (Reporter), Tony Matranga (Guard #1), Johnny Oliver (Guard #2), Cy Wong (Guard #3), Julie Kalcheim (Amy Rosenman), Tony Crupi (Thur). Uncredited: Jackie Cooper (Man at the Lido Entrance and in Elevator).

SYNOPSIS: Sophie Rosenman, Annie Cavagnaro and Lizzie Martin are all wives of men in the Palm Springs Wyndham Institute for Men. The women steal the money Lizzie's husband Ed has arranged as bribe money for his pardon. Annie's mother-in-law, Mrs. Cavagnaro, opens the safe of the hotel where the money is to be delivered. The women frame Nick Auletta for the robbery, the man who had framed Annie's husband, Vinnie. Nick is arrested. Mrs. Cavagnaro leaves for Rome, and the other women divide up the money.

NOTES: Dennis' return to made-for-TV movies sees her playing a part that is more sizeable than her secondary one in *Police Story*. She receives third billing, under Lauren Bacall and Ruth Gordon, but her character of Sophie is actually a major instigator of the narrative. She introduces herself to the Lisa Pelikan character and to Bacall. It is she who suggests that Bacall steal the money that she has agreed to deliver for her husband, and it is she who organizes the edited tape recording used to indicate that the robbers are male.

Dennis wears the same long hair she sported in the *Police Story* episode, and wears glasses only for the scene where Sophie works on the accounting books at home. She is photographed more attractively here. At one point Sophie describes Bacall's Lizzie as the group's strategist and herself as make-up and costumes, which provides context for the grey wig she dons to disguise herself as her mother-in-law. At one point Sophie and Lizzie shop for men's clothes, which they will wear during the robbery.

Sophie wears a ski mask for the robbery, and a man's suit and tie. This is the second time Dennis has been seen in drag, after her similar appearance in *Nasty Habits*. When Sophie shows Lizzie her male outfit, she also wears a hat, which she will not use in the robbery, with her hair tucked up under it.

Dennis displays her familiar mannerisms of tongue-poking, head-shaking, stuttering, smiling, gesturing, pointing, and eye-rolling. The scene in Lizzie's home steam room, however, has her disappointingly pulling faces, only partially justified as her reaction to the heat.

Sophie is shown to be the mother of two children. She is presented as a lesser sexual presence than the younger Annie in the scene when the women first meet their husbands in prison. Her husband Murray touches Sophie's face, whereas Aninie's husband Vinnie kisses Annie. However, Dennis looks beautiful wearing a blue dress with purple top, heels, and loose hair when Sophie and Lizzie meet Annie at the Parkhurst Towers Hotel.

Dennis' best scenes require her to make small speeches, the first regarding the McDonalds moving to the same street as Sophie's delicatessen. The second comes when she tells Lizzie and Annie that if she was on a plane and noticed that a wing was missing, she would rather go down with the crashing plane than speak up about the wing. Sophie equates this stance with her wanting to stay on with the failing deli rather than use the cut of the stolen money to do anything extravagant. This stance is hardly surprising given that she has two children to raise alone. Rather than go to Rome, like Mrs. Cavagnaro, or leave her husband, like Lizzie, Sophie only wants to buy a new washing machine, a new counter for the deli and paint the truck.

The narrative introduces Lizzie, Sophie and Annie according to their financial differences. Lizzie travels to the motel in a chauffeured limousine, Sophie drives the Rosenman's Deli truck, and Annie is on a Roadways bus. The scene in the elevator where Lizzie points a gun at the bellboy in front of Sophie and Annie is telling. It demonstrates Lizzie's gangster connections but also her overreaction to what the bellboy says. He simply asks the women, "Are you girls here to visit relatives?" This is an act that reads as innocent interest, although perhaps his use of the word "girls" may be construed as condescending.

Annie's bursting into tears may also be an overreaction and demonstrates her sensitivity to the idea of her husband being incarcerated. However, Lizzie's demand that the boy apologizes to Annie tops it. The scene is interesting in that this behavior occurs before it is clear that the Wyndham Institute is a prison, and that the women are wives of prisoners. Annie's penchant for crying is identified as her criminal strength, for her crying will be used during the robbery to get the hotel's security guards into the office so that they can be controlled by Sophie and Lizzie.

The narrative is slow to get to the action. After the initial establishment of the characters as wives of prisoners, the decision to steal the money is not made until two thirds of the way in. The revelations of Annie's pregnancy and Ed's affair smacks of soap opera. Additionally, the prison picnic and softball game are little more than filler.

Ruth Gordon doesn't appear until twenty minutes in. This is particularly odd, since Gordon receives billing over Dennis and Lisa Pelikan, and then she disappears for another thirty minutes. Later she disappears yet again and only reappears in the last fifteen minutes for the heist. This makes Gordon's role a decidedly supporting one in relation to the other three women.

The made-for-TV movie *Perfect Gentlemen* (1978) stars (from left) Lauren Bacall, Ruth Gordon, Dennis, and Lisa Pelikan. Note that all the women wear male drag in this publicity shot.

Sophie aims a gun at Annie's head during the robbery to present her as another supposed hostage. This is a way to clear Annie of any apparent involvement and also to help stop the male guards from trying to do anything in case Annie will be hurt. This pretence continues with Annie staying in the hotel after the robbery rather than going with the other women.

Sophie's van not starting for the getaway is a tired cliché. However, the expectation of the women being caught after we see police cars arriving at the hotel is not met. Instead, Mrs. Cavagnaro asks the police to help her start her car, which allows the women to escape.

Why Nick's apartment is broken into and the U.S. bag taken is not immediately apparent, and only later explained when some money is left there after the robbery. This operates as a means to show that the union money is recovered and also illustrate Annie's revenge upon Nick for framing Vinnie. The latter point is somewhat short-sighted, since arresting Nick doesn't immediately help Vinnie get out of jail. There is also the possibility that Nick may want to inflict a payback upon Vinnie if he ends up in the same prison.

Teleplay writer Nora Ephron's attempt at humor sometimes falls flat. Sophie's line at the end of the elevator scene — "Who was that masked man? — is only mildly funny, as is Sophie telling Annie that Murray "withheld withholding tax." Additionally, the following exchange between Sophie and Annie is, at best, mildly amusing:

SOPHIE: Do you drink?
ANNIE: No.
SOPHIE: Neither do I. Let's have a drink.

An exchange between Annie and Mrs. Cavagnaro gives Mrs. Cavagnaro the funnier line: "Your father-in-law once got sent up to Sing Sing. I could never figure how it got that oriental name." Additionally, Mrs. Cavagnaro speaks of associates Benny the Tooth, Sidney the Horse, Lester the Snake, and Frankie the Fox, the latter being her partner for her trip to Rome. Sophie's story about the McDonalds that moved down the street from her delicatessen begins with Sophie telling Annie, "I was killed by a hamburger."

Director Jackie Cooper includes a spiffy disco music theme, but his use of music is otherwise obtrusive. He favors repeated aerial views. He has Dennis and Lisa Pelikan employ a comic stare in reaction to Bacall's Lizzie pointing a gun at the bellboy, and offers a freeze-frame of Sophie in a grey wig as a transition dissolve.

There is a montage of Sophie, Annie and Lizzie traveling to the prison, and Cooper uses effective shorthand to show Lizzie delivering the suitcase. We see her arrive at the hotel in her limousine, the room number 1703, hear a knock on the door, and then see Lizzie leaving the hotel without the suitcase. Cooper employs more shorthand in resolving the appearance of the Southern couple during the robbery by showing Mrs. Cavagnaro pointing a gun at them and cutting to the couple tied up.

In a self-referential touch, Mrs. Cavagnaro watches the family comedy *Skippy* (1931) on television in her hotel room, which starred Cooper as a child. And Cooper himself makes a cameo appearance in the film. Ruth Gordon sports dyed-black hair to play an Italian mama but doesn't attempt an Italian accent. Equally, as Annie, Lisa Pelikan's pregnancy bump becomes less apparent as the narrative progresses. Cooper ends on a freeze-frame image of Lizzie, Sophie and Annie laughing together at the gun cigarette lighter, and offers recap images from the film under the closing credits. In his autobiography, *Please Don't Shoot My Dog*, Cooper says that the film had a two-hour running time, although he may be including commercials in this time.

In an article in *The Dispatch* that appeared on March 10, 1978, Lauren Bacall was asked why she agreed to make her first made-for-TV film. "It's a good script," she answered "There are not too many of those around. It's got humor with drama." Bacall also said that Jackie Cooper was "fantastic—always prepared, knowing exactly what he wanted, and a pleasure to work with."

RELEASE: Broadcast March 14, 1978, on CBS.

REVIEWS: The film was critically lambasted by John J. O'Connor in *The New York Times* on March 14, 1978; by James Wolcott in *The Village Voice* on March 20, 1978; and by Molly Haskell in New *York Magazine* on April 10, 1978. O'Connor wrote that "Miss Dennis, who could give Katharine Hepburn stiff competition in the trick of tear-filled eyes, makes the most unlikely of delicatessen owners." Wolcott said that she "as pure Golda is up to her old tics." Haskell wrote, "Sandy Dennis is oddly affecting."

AWARDS: Nominated for the Edgar Allan Poe Best Television Feature Award.

DVD: Not available.

Wilson's Reward (1980)

CREW: Patrick O'Neal (Director), Robert Halmi Sr. (Producer), Bernard Eismann (Teleplay, based on the short story "Vessel of Wrath" by W. Somerset Maugham), Dick York (Music), Peter Politanoff (Art Director). Filmed on the island of Bonaire in the Netherland Antilles.

CAST: Sandy Dennis (Martha James), Gerald S. O'Loughlin (Ginger Ted Wilson), Fred Morsell (Governor Van Den Hoag), Rosemarie Vis (Young Girl), Lois Dia Donales (Wilson's Mate). Uncredited: Wilfred Depal (Houseboy), Mark Soper (Reverend James).

SYNOPSIS: Martha James is a missionary living in the West Indies in the 1920s. She travels to an outlying island to treat an appendicitis case and finds Ginger Ted on board the boat on which she returns. He is a boatman for hire and has the reputation of being a drunken womanizer. The boat breaks down en route, and they are forced to spend the night on a small island. When they hear of a cholera epidemic, Martha persuades Ted to accompany her as she travels the islands to render treatment. He returns as a non-drinking missionary, now engaged to Martha.

NOTES: This made-for-TV movie brought with it the same level of prestige as *A Hatful of Rain*, making it a step above the average made-for-TV movies *The Man Who Wanted to Live Forever*, *Something Evil*, and *Perfect Gentlemen*. Additionally, the fact that Dennis plays the leading role makes it rather special in her television canon. Therefore, it is doubly unfortunate that it is not available for viewing.

In an interview printed in the *Daily News*, dated June 20, 1980, Gerald O'Loughlin said that he was delighted to accept the role because it was a rare chance for him to play a romantic lead. He also liked the idea of playing a drunk, because in real life he was a reformed drinker. The actor also said that he was comfortable with the team since the director was a classmate from the Neighborhood Playhouse and because of his former eight-year relationship with Dennis, although it was a little strange at first doing the romantic scenes.

RELEASE: Broadcast June 21, 1980, by Liberty Mutual.
REVIEWS: *Wilson's Reward* garnered mixed critical reaction from John J. O'Connor in *The New York Times* on June 27, 1980, who made no mention of Dennis' performance.
PRIOR PRODUCTIONS: Previously made as the British film *The Beachcomber*, aka *The Vessel of Wrath* (1938). Directed by Erich Pommer, the earlier film was co-produced by Charles Laughton, who starred as Ginger Ted alongside Elsa Lanchester as Martha Jones. The story was also adapted, as "The Vessel of Wrath," for an episode of the British TV show *W. Somerset Maugham* broadcast in 1970.
DVD: Not available.

Young People's Specials (1985)

"The Trouble with Mother," Paulist Productions
CREW: Tom G. Robertson (Director, Producer, Teleplay), Ellwood Keiser (Producer).
CAST: Sandy Dennis (Patricia Benson), Jennifer Ginsberg (Laurie Benson), Amy Palmer (Judy Benson), Robert Elkins (Herb Benson).
SYNOPSIS: Patricia Benson is a mother who is challenged by her thirteen-year-old daughter Laurie to defend her traditional role of housewife against the modern feminist ideal of being a career woman.
NOTES: Paulist Productions was established to make the religious TV show *Insight*, which ran for fifteen seasons from 1960 to 1984, and other religious titles. *Young People's Specials* was a family TV show that ran for two seasons from 1984 to 1985. The website for actor Robert Elkins claims that the episode was filmed in Cincinnati. A still exists of Dennis with Jennifer Ginsburg sitting at what looks like a kitchen table. Her hair is shorter than it had been in *Come Back to the 5 & Dime Jimmy Dean, Jimmy Dean*, which was her last appearance on film or television.
RELEASE: Unknown, although the news snippet attached to the back of the still of Jennifer Ginsburg and Sandy is dated March 18, 1979.
REVIEWS: None available.
DVD: Not available.

This shot from "The Trouble with Mother" episode of the TV show *Young People's Specials* (1985) shows Laurie Benson (Jennifer Ginsberg, left) sitting at a table with her mother Patricia Benson (Dennis).

The Execution (1985)

Comworld Productions/Newland/Raynor Productions

CREW: Paul Wendkos (Director), Milton T. Raynor, Oliver Crawford (Producers), John Newland (Executive Producer), William Wood, Oliver Crawford (Teleplay, based on the novel by Oliver Crawford), Georges Delerue (Music), Michael Margulies (Photography), Steven Cohen (Editor), Jack Senter (Art Director), Ethel Robins Richards (Set Decorator), Jim Kessler (Men's Costumes), Mina Mittelman (Women's Costumes), Nick Pagliaro, Peter Altobelli (Makeup), Don Sheldon, Jean Austin (Hair). Color, 90 minutes.

SONGS: "Piano Sonata No. 14" aka "Moonlight Sonata" (Ludwig van Beethoven), heard in flashback during Marysia's torture.

CAST: Loretta Swit (Marysia Walenka), Rip Torn (Walter Grossman/Wilhelm Gehbert), Jessica Walter (Gertrude Simon), Barbara Barrie (Sophie Langbein), Sandy Dennis (Elsa Spahn), Valerie Harper (Hannah Epstein), Martin E. Brooks (Martin Renner), Michael Lerner (Sidney Ferraro, Assistant District Attorney), Allan Miller (Ted Simon), Alan Oppenheimer (Max Langbein), John Randolph (Judge), Peter White (Gil Spahn), Rita Zohar (Worker at the '38 Club), R.J. Adams (Investigative Reporter), Jered Barclay, Barbara Beckley, Bill Dearth, Burke Denis, Jeanne Dougherty, Ariane Gogny, Cantor Avshalom Katz, Michael Kearns, Catherine Schreiber, Robert Hooks (Alton Reese). Uncredited: Cynthia Lea Clark (Waitress).

SYNOPSIS: In Los Angeles in 1970, five women friends meet regularly on Wednesday nights to play mah-jong. They are all survivors of Birkenau. Their camp tormentor, Wilhelm Gehbert, now owns a Malibu restaurant. Since he has escaped punishment, the women plan to kill him and draw lots to determine who shall be the executioner. Marysia Walenka is chosen, and she attempts to kill him but fails. It is reported on the news that Gehbert is dead, and the women jointly admit their culpability. The police receive a confession from Martin Renner, however, who is the real killer.

NOTES: Dennis' return to made-for-TV movies sees her in a supporting role in this ineffectual melodrama that pays lip service to the tragedy that was the Holocaust. She has little of substance to do here. She does a lot of standing around and listening, and receives few opportunities that allow her to rise above the material.

However, Dennis does have some moments. She effectively displays shock when she sees her torturer on television and then tells her friends about it; she is the only one of the female conspirators to read aloud from Marysia's confession; and she reacts in close-up when Marysia is chosen to be the killer. Dennis also displays stillness and resolve in her response to Gil's reaction to Elsa's confession. However, she can't do much with the last scene she has with Gil, where she is going to the police to confess, and he tells her that he doesn't know who she is anymore. Here she gesticulates wildly, and the closest Dennis comes to displaying emotion is when Elsa touches Gil's face.

Dennis' fifth billing indicates her box office fall from grace. She is credited below Loretta Swit, better known as a television actor rather than a film star, whose top billing comes from her playing the lead role. It can also be rationalized because of Swit's then-concurrent appearance on the TV show *M*A*S*H*. Swit was only a few months younger than Dennis, but the idea that Dennis could have played Swit's part is presumably inconceivable because of the perception that she is less physically desirable than Swit, at least in how she is presented here.

Three other actors also received billing above Dennis. Rip Torn had appeared in five leading film roles but had slipped to playing supporting parts at this time. Though both had made films, and Barbara Barrie had played one leading role, she and Jessica Walter were better known as actors who guest starred on TV shows. Billed *after* Dennis, Valerie Harper was also an actress primarily known for her television work.

Dennis' hair here is shorter than in *Come Back to the 5 & Dime Jimmy Dean, Jimmy Dean*, matching the shorter style she wore for the *Young People's Special*. In one scene she has her hair tied back in a ponytail, which is an unusual look for her. Her Elsa also wears glasses. Dennis is generally photographed unflatteringly here, with perhaps the trauma of her past a the reason behind this.

Dennis employs her mannerisms of gesturing, stuttering, eye closing, lip-biting, and the hand on the forehead. Ironically, while Dennis doesn't use her pointing mannerism here, Michael Lerner as Ferraro does. Dennis adopts a German accent for the character of Elsa, and her gesturing perhaps can be attributed to her being Jewish, like in *Perfect Gentlemen*, where she also played a Jewess.

Elsa is the instigator of the action, since she spots Walter on television, then tells the other women, and finally goes to his restaurant with Marysia. However, the narrative soon casts Marysia as the main protagonist. Marysia goes back to the restaurant to see if he has the scar that Gehbert had, and then she is the one who draws the task killing Gehbert. Elsa then merely becomes one of the four women that confess to Gehbert's murder.

Elsa's inability to bear children is an affliction presumably common to all the women victims. The sexually injured Marysia overcomes her inability to make love with a man when she does so with Gehbert, believing him to be Walter. This gives context to her excessive smiling at herself in a mirror before she tells him, "I'm so happy." However, the appearance of Walter's parrot sets off Marysia's memory and changes her happiness to horror at the irony that the man who has helped her overcome her trauma is the same man who had

The stars of the made-for-TV movie *The Execution* (1985). Clockwise from left: Valerie Harper, Barbara Barrie, Jessica Walter, Dennis, and Loretta Swit (seated).

caused it in the first place. Marysia's devastating realization is shown via a double image of her crying as she stands in front of the same mirror.

The playing of "Moonlight Sonata" during Gehbert's torture of Marysia is perhaps a sign of his supposed refinement and appreciation of music. The screaming of the parrot suggests his perversity and sadism, as well as the pain of Marysia. However, the fact that Gehbert has a pet bird attests to the idea that he *can* develop some emotional attachment.

Walter leaving repeated telephone messages for Marysia also suggests an obsessive and possessive nature, as does his coming to her boutique at night after he has gleaned the address from her restaurant credit card payment.

An expectation is created with the appearance of the gun in Marysia's boutique and her reaching for it while being kissed by Gehbert. However, she grabs her keys instead to go to the bathroom and call her own shop in order to create an excuse to get away from him. One actually feels a strange empathy for Gehbert in this situation, despite our knowledge of his war atrocities.

The scene at the Kristallnacht '38 club reads as filler, with a speaker addressing the attendants clearly being someone preaching to the converted and telling them things they already know. All five women are at the club meeting, and Sophie is chosen to "memorialize the event" by banging a drum that has a Star of David on it while the group chants "Never Again."

Gehbert slapping Marysia is the first present-day assault on her, which will be followed by his attempt to strangle her. His shaking as he holds a gun on her may initially indicate his expression of "compassion" for Marysia, since he tells how he thinks he showed too much compassion in his experiments at the camp. However, it is later revealed that he has been physically weakened by the gunshot wound. There is also the question of whether Marysia has actually killed Gehbert, although we see him stop moving after she smothers him with the pillow. This ambiguity is seemingly resolved when Gertrude sees on the television a news report of his murder. It is only at the climactic revelation that we see that Gehbert was actually killed by Martin Renner during a follow-up pillow smothering.

When Ted walks out on Gertrude after she tells him of their multiple-confession plan, she responds with the howler, "I'm too much woman for you. I always have been." This comes after he calls her a whore for supposedly having slept with Gehbert. The three husbands' individual responses to their wives' confessions — all false, by the way — vary, but that of Gil is the most cryptic. He tells Elsa that he doesn't believe her, but he doesn't explain why.

Elsa earns a different fate than the other married women, Gertrude and Sophie. Gil cannot accept her decision to make the confession and leaves her because of it. He also doesn't return after the women are released from prison, although at this point they don't appear to be legally exonerated of the conspiracy charge. At the last mah-jong meeting, Elsa says she now plans to take classes to occupy herself, since she appears to be newly single.

Director Paul Wendkos uses a TV-style introduction for the actresses as the woman arrive at the house for the mah-jong game, with their names attached to their screen appearance. Elsa arrives having been driven by her husband, as opposed to Marysia and Sophie and Hannah, who arrive alone and drive themselves. While this may show the other women as being more independent, it also presents Elsa as a married woman with a romantic interest. This notion will be explored for the character of Marysia, who uses herself to attract Walter in order to see if he has Gehbert's identifying scar.

Wendkos reveals the women's camp prisoner tattoos to indicate their shared experience, though the narrative will tell little else of their time there. He employs zooms and quick cuts between Walter and Marysia when Walter introduces himself at the restaurant lunch to Marysia and Elsa, and blue lighting for Marysia's flashback of being tortured by Gehbert. Wendkos uses a subjective camera when Gehbert aims his gun at Marysia, and also for Renner's point of view behind a billowing curtain as he watched Marysia and Gehbert struggle, Marysia smothering Gehbert, and himself retrieving her gun from the bushes where Gehbert had thrown it.

Wendkos can't redeem the narrative cliché of Gehbert resuming consciousness as he lies on the floor to grab Marysia when she leans over him to retrieve the gun. However, he ends with Marysia's bracelet left by Ferraro among the mah-jong tiles, and uses this image under the end credits. The suggestion is that the women will never again play mah-jong together, since what has transpired has changed their dynamic forever.

Having the five actresses affect accents becomes troublesome, particularly when Valerie Harper's New York intonation keeps slipping into her speech. This issue is topped by the four of them playing Jews and therefore over-gesticulating, though Swit as the Pole does her own share of gesticulating.

Also problematic is Swit. Her changing hairstyles identify her as the movie's star; however, while her performance is not bad, she fails to engender the sympathy required to lift the material into the tragic dimension it needs. Since the characters are written as one-dimensional historical constructs with a political agenda, it is up to the actors to enliven them. Only Rip Torn is successful in inspiring some empathy for Gehbert (despite him being the narrative antagonist who is seduced then rejected, shot, smothered twice and eventually murdered).

Loretta Swit was interviewed by John Anderson for *The Vindicator*, November 12, 1984. When she was asked about concentration camp survivors, tears welled up in her eyes, her voice broke, and she supposedly extended her arm as if gripping an imaginary support. She said she had visited Auschwitz five or six years back.

Valerie Harper would tell Charles Witbeck in *The Times-News* on January 7, 1985, about her character of Hannah. "Hannah never married because of her camp experience. In camp she lacked control, and once out she vowed never to become dependent again. That makes sense." In an interview with Ron Weiskind published in the *Pittsburgh Post-Gazette* on January 14, 1985, Harper said to research her role she spoke to survivors of concentration camps and read a lot of material, much of which surprised her.

To the question of the morality of the women wanting to kill their former tormentor, Harper responded with the following: "Does it accomplish anything? These women — their friendships will never be the same again. Paul wanted a sad ending so that we didn't say, 'Hooray, the Nazis dead.'"

REVIEWS: The telefilm earned a critically drubbing from Bob D. Matteo in *The Mount Airy News* on January 11, 1985; from Judy Flander in the *Lakeland Ledger* on January 14, 1985; and from Faye Zuckerman in *St. Joseph News-Press* on July 7, 1986. Dennis' performance was not mentioned specifically, but Matteo wrote that "the performances of the leading actresses are stilted and heavy-handed [and] boast the worst collection of German/Eastern European accents you may ever hear in one movie."

AWARDS: Nominated for Outstanding Achievement in Costuming.

DVD: PAL DVD released by Consolidated on December 18, 2003. Video released by StarMaker on date unknown.

The Love Boat (1985)

Season 9, Episode 9, "Roommates/Heartbreaker/Out of the Blue," Aaron Spelling Productions/Douglas S. Kramer Company/The Love Boat Company

CREW: Richard A. Wells (Director), Dennis Hammer, William Bickley, Michael Warren (Producers), Douglas S. Kramer, Aaron Spelling (Executive Producers), Paula A. Roth (Teleplay, "Roommates"), John Collins (Teleplay, "Heartbreaker"), Joan Brooker, Nancy Eddo (Teleplay,

"Out of the Blue"), Larry Warwick (Art Director), Nolan Miller (Costumes). Color, 60 minutes. Filmed at Warners Hollywood Studios.

CAST: Gavin MacLeod (Captain Merrill Stubing), Bernie Kopell (Doctor Adam Bricker), Fred Grandy (Ship's Purser "Gopher" Smith), Ted Lange (Bartender Isaac Washington), Patricia Klous (Cruise Director Judy McCoy), the Love Boat Mermaids (Themselves), Ted McGinley (Ashley Covington Evans), Deborah Bartlett (Susie), Tori Brenno (Maria), Macarena (Sheila), Diana Canova (Christine Bradley), Jeff Conaway (Andy Jackson), Sandy Dennis (Gina Caldwell), Nanci Lynn Hammond (Jane), Teri Hatcher (Amy), Debra Johnson (Patti), Harvey Korman (Cabot Fairfield), Toni Lamond (Mrs. Burton), Andrea Moen (Starlight), Warren Munson (Edgar Fairchild), Beth Myatt (Mary Beth), Jill Whelan (Vicki Stubing).

SYNOPSIS: In "Roommates," Slovenly Vicki Stubing and neatnik Judy McCoy become roommates and make an odd couple. In "Heartbreaker," Christine Bradley pretends to be in love with a heart-transplant recipient. In "Out of the Blue," Gina Caldwell pursues multi-millionaire Cabot Fairfield, who promises to make people's wildest dreams come true.

NOTES: Dennis' guest appearance on this TV show represents a further career step down — lower than made-for-TV movies and the TV show guest appearances that followed. This is because guest appearances on this show were made by those considered to be faded film stars or actors who were already associated with television rather than film. The perception of the show being of lowbrow quality was underlined by its use of a laugh track. Perhaps one can accept that Dennis wanted to work with comedian Harvey Korman, who appears in the episode with her, or that she simply accepted the job as the best that was offered to her at the time. Whatever her reasoning, it appears to be a misstep that she would recover from.

The romantic comedy TV show was created by Jeraldine Saunders. It was set on a cruise liner and ran for nine seasons from 1977 to 1986, featuring storylines in which passengers and crew had romantic and allegedly funny adventures. The show format followed three storylines simultaneously. One was comic and focused on a member of the crew; the second, highlighting the interaction between a crew member and a passenger, was of a more romantic nature; and the third was dramatic and focused on one or a group of passengers. The three episodes were written by three different writers.

RELEASE: Broadcast on December 7, 1985, by the American Broadcasting Company (ABC).
REVIEWS: None available.
DVD: Not available.

Alfred Hitchcock Presents (1985)

Season 1, Episode 10, "Gigolo," Universal/MCA/Michael Sloan Productions (Uncredited)
CREW: Thomas Carter (Director), Alan Barnette (Producer), Christopher Crowe (Executive Producer), Daniel Sackheim (Associate Producer), Steve DeJarnatt (Teleplay, based on a story by Arthur Williams), Ernest Gold (Music), Mario Di Leo (Photography), Heather MacDougall (Editing), Bill Malley (Production Designer), Mary Ann Brienza (Set Decorator), Sharon Day (Costumes), Hank Garfield (Sound). Color, 24 minutes. Filmed in Toronto, Canada, in September 1985.

SONGS: "Funeral March of a Marionette" (Charles Gounod), opening theme music; "This Could Be the Night," "Nowhere Fast" (Jim Steinman); "Libiamo ne' lieti calici," aka "The Drinking Song" from *La Traviata* (Giuseppi Verdi, Francesco Maria Piave); "Let Me Call You Sweetheart" (Leo Friedman, Beth Slater Whitson), sung by Brad Davis; "Just a Gigolo" (Leonello Casucci, Irving Caesar).

CAST: Sandy Dennis (Sylvia Locke, aka Mrs. Arthur Kreshner), Brad Davis (Arthur Kreshner), Virginia Capers (Ruth), Billy Ray Sharkey (Man), Tina Challey (Molly), Alfred Hitchcock (Host).

SYNOPSIS: Arthur Kreshner is in debt and has twenty-four hours to pay back some hoods.

He is newly married to the wealthy Sylvia Locke, who populates her mansion with cats. Arthur sees where Sylvia hides her diamonds. He smothers her with a pillow and feeds her ground-up body to the cats. A cat pushes a boom box into Arthur's bath, and he is electrocuted. The maid, Ruth, takes the diamonds.

NOTES: Dennis is top-billed for this TV show guest appearance, although she is the secondary character in the narrative. Brad Davis was an actor who was still earning leading film roles, though he was not Oscar nominated like Dennis had been. Davis's character is both protagonist and antagonist, and he appears before and after Dennis' participation. Given the thumbnail nature of the material, Dennis gives a broadly comic performance that is both funny and empathetic.

Her appearance on the show is perhaps a step up from *The Love Boat*, which some consider the nadir of her career. This is because a guest appearance on an anthology mystery series carries more prestige than an appearance on a situation comedy or a police procedural. A perusal of the calibre of other guests on the new series indicates actors that range from fading film stars to new actors to actors that were more associated with television work than film. Dennis appears to be the only actor among the group who had been Oscar nominated. Guest stars on the original series included many former Oscar winners, like Bette Davis, and future Oscar winners like Joanne Woodward. This indicates the lesser prestige of the new series compared to the original, but it is also a further reminder of Dennis' career decline. The perception is based on her not having appeared in a film for three years and her not appearing in another for three more (and even then in a supporting rather than leading role).

Dennis plays Sylvia Locke, who marries the titular "Gigolo" Arthur Kreshner (Brad Davis) in this *Alfred Hitchcock Presents* episode.

In the episode Dennis' hair is shorter than it was last seen in *The Execution*, and her wardrobe adds to the idea of her character being an eccentric. She is first seen in a dressing gown with hair-ribbon and feather boa, dancing, and her subsequent outfits will nearly all feature hair-ribbons and boas. The exception is what she wears during the pool scene, which is a bathing cap, nose-plug, and bathing suit (although Dennis' body is not revealed in the suit). She also sports a sun umbrella when Sylvia is in her backyard, and has feathers on her slippers to match her feather boa.

Her Sylvia speaks with a Southern accent and a lisp, and uses funny baby talk and sometimes a girlish whispering voice. She also walks with a wiggle. Dennis uses her gesturing mannerisms, including the pointing gesture, as well as smiling. However, her stuttering is not apparent here, perhaps because Sylvia doesn't get to say much in the narrative. She also delivers some wild laughter in the scene with Sylvia and Arthur in bed before he kills her.

Sylvia has a love interest, even though Arthur only intends to exploit her. In the murder scene she initially turns away from his attempt to kiss her, telling him, "You married me for my diamonds." She will hug him when he claims that this is not true, though we don't see the couple kiss. Her wild grabbing of Arthur and her cackle suggest that perhaps she may be a wild lover, or perhaps it is the expression of her previous frustration. Only a backstory, which the narrative does not provide, could confirm which.

Sylvia's fondness for cats is a narrative point that mirrors Dennis' real-life penchant. Sylvia has seventeen cats. She is also seemingly forgiving of Arthur's meanness towards the cats, changing from a look of disapproval to smiling when he blows a kiss at her after he kicks the cat under the breakfast table. Equally, she does not comment when she sees Arthur throw a cat into the swimming pool. However, these acts create the expectation of karmic payback, which is indeed on its way.

Arthur gazing at the fish in the fish tank at the bar The Garage presents Arthur as a predator to weaker creatures (Sylvia being one of said creatures). Arthur's look of greasy hair, thin moustache, and leather jacket and pants portrays him as sleazy and cheap, traits that Sylvia is presumably willing to overlook.

When the car chases him in the street, a cat also jumps at Arthur from a ledge, prefiguring the trouble he will soon have with cats. The narrative does not provide any time frame for when Arthur marries Sylvia or how he has met her. We assume the marriage has occurred after the warning from the hoods and within the twenty-four hours he has been given to pay back his debt.

Sylvia is introduced by the sight of her hand putting on the record to which she will dance. The gardenia in her mouth as she dances to opera, and the feather boa and hairribbon she wears, present her as eccentric. Sylvia is also seen as juvenile in her use of baby talk, partially contextualized by her happiness as a newlywed, and also the swimming ring she uses to float in the pool.

The narrative offers the proposition that the murdered Sylvia has been reborn as a cat, or that the cats have supernatural powers. This is opposed to the logical conclusion that Ruth, the maid, is the one who taunts Arthur by playing the record Sylvia had previously played, and turning on the blender herself. The idea of Sylvia being reborn as a cat is underscored when Arthur sees a cat holding a gardenia in its mouth — just as Sylvia had done. The supernatural element endures with the wet cat returning after Arthur had stuffed it in a sack and thrown it in the pool (although it is conceivable that Ruth has rescued it).

Ruth's appearance after Arthur is killed furthers the idea that she has orchestrated his death, although we have seen that it was the cat that pushed the boom box into his bath. Her laughter and clothes (she wears dress clothes rather than her maid uniform) underscore this notion. Ruth talking to herself, and speaking of what she will do with the wealth she is appropriating, creates an expectation that she too will be punished for her opportunism. However, this proves not to be the case. The implication is that the cats are aligned with her, or at least prefer Ruth to Arthur. The alignment is suggested by her stating that the cat who pushed the boom box into Arthur's bath was working with her.

Director Thomas Carter employs the sound of thunder at the dinner scene between Sylvia and Arthur, and at Ruth's leaving for the night, to instill a sense of foreboding. He also includes reaction shots of the cats screaming when Arthur smothers Sylvia. Her death is suggested by the resistant movement of her feet ceasing and the slow-motion fall of her feather boa off the bed.

Subjective camerawork is employed twice—first when Arthur approaches the record player and the cat sitting next to it, and second when Arthur moves toward the table upon which the cat and the blender sit. This second instance also features the Hitchcockian technique of alternate points of view, with Arthur's advance seen from the point of view of the cat, and the cat seen from Arthur's point of view. Slow motion is again used for the opening of the secret door, and later when the cat pushes the boom box into Arthur's bath. A cat scream is heard (though the cat is not seen) when Arthur walks through the tunnel.

Carter employs music to good effect, even returning to specific songs to make a point. He utilizes the opera music twice, once to show that Sylvia likes it and the other to suggest her return. He plays "Nowhere Fast" for the chase at the beginning and then again when Arthur is in the bath, as if it is music he likes. Carter has "Just a Gigolo" playing over the scene where Arthur sits by the pool where Sylvia is swimming, and then for the end after Arthur is killed—as if this encapsulates Ruth's point of view. He ends the episode with an echo on Ruth's laughter at Arthur's fate and her good fortune.

Brad Davis' performance is questionable in terms of the limited vocal range he gives Arthur, since he always sounds insincere. He is attractive enough to be a hustler, but the character is written as so unlikable that it might have been more interesting had the viewer at least some empathy with him. This might have made Arthur's death more interesting, and his character less of a one-note villain.

Carter does score points by presenting Sylvia as somewhat grotesque and clinging in her attraction to Arthur, but we don't feel the entrapment that we presumably are meant to over his situation. This might have created a feeling of hope when he does away with her, which is later dashed when he is defeated by the cats and Ruth.

In *The Alfred Hitchcock Presents Companion*, Martin Grams and Patrik Wikstrom report that there was no real cat dropped into the pool, as presented in the episode, and all the cat action was supervised by the American Humane Society. The cats were all trained by the California Company Birds & Animals Unlimited.

"Gigolo" was a credited remake of an episode from the original show entitled "Arthur." That episode came during season five of the original series and was directed by Hitchcock himself. It aired on September 27, 1959. However, the remake has little in common with the original. In "Arthur" it is the title character who is a wealthy man, a successful New Zealand chicken farmer (played by Englishman Laurence Harvey). In the episode he strangles his former fiancée, Helen Braithwaite (Hazel Court), who has returned to him after leaving him for another man a year prior. Arthur strangles her the way he strangles his chickens, and then hides the body. The police suspect him of murder, but since they can't find Helen's body, they lack the evidence to prosecute him.

The original episode offers more character depth than the supposed remake, and it is also partly filmed in an unusual style, with Arthur addressing the audience directly. This style presents the episode as a flashback and therefore predetermines that Arthur will not be punished for his crime (this in spite of the police repeatedly searching the farm for Helen's body, and Arthur "bringing things to a head" by running away to spend three days in a cave). Even the police's attempted bluff in telling Arthur that they found the body doesn't work, since he knows that is not possible.

Arthur seems fond of the chickens he raises, as suggested by the one he holds when we first see him. This mirrors the cats that Sylvia has as pets. However, Arthur's agenda is quickly established when we see him strangle the chicken he holds. Although we don't literally see the strangulation (unlike Helen's later strangulation), the scream of the dying bird equates to Helen's similar scream.

It is implied that Arthur's character has improved after Helen left him. He has refocused his attention on the farm, which he has now made successful. He has told us that Helen leaving him has made him withdraw from other people. He feels that Helen left him because she is an opportunist who found Stanley Braithwaite, whom Arthur considers better for her. He describes Stanley as a gambler, which suggests that Helen is not going to a stable environment, but she prefers to call him a financier.

Helen tells Arthur that she agreed to marry him because she was afraid at the time that there might not be anything better. Ironically, she returns because her marriage to Stanley has not worked out. She tells Arthur that she has nowhere else to go and no money. Adding to Arthur's dislike of the returned Helen is her careless behavior. She leaves the dinner dishes in the sink rather than washing them, drops cigarette butts in a table ornament in place of an ashtray, and accidentally knocks over and breaks the coffee pot. His murder of Helen is, in his twisted mind, a gift. He had apparently told her that if she was ever in trouble she could count on him, and Arthur feels he cannot go back on his word. At one point Helen tells him, "I'd rather be dead." He replies that the least he can do for her — for old time's sake — is to grant her wish.

What the two episodes have in common is the use of a grinder. Arthur has what he calls a hammer mill in his barn, which grinds the ingredients of the chicken feed. It is implied that the reason the police cannot find Helen's body is because he has run her through the grinder and fed her to the chickens. Unlike in "Gigolo," we don't see Arthur feeding anything into the machine. Helen, however, is the special ingredient that Arthur leaves off the list of ingredients he gives to Sergeant John Theron to feed his own chickens.

The original anthology series ran for ten seasons from 1955 to 1965. Seasons eight to ten changed the episodes' running time from twenty-six to fifty minutes, with the series renamed *The Alfred Hitchcock Hour*. The remake series was known as *The New Alfred Hitchcock Presents*, though in the "Gigolo" credits it is *Alfred Hitchcock Presents*. The new series ran for four seasons, from 1985 to 1989, and featured both original works and updates of the first series' episodes.

The opening and closing comments by Alfred Hitchcock that appeared in the original series were re-used in the new series but in a colorized version. The opening and closing for "Gigolo" was taken from the original episode "Apex" from Season 7 (Episode 24), which was broadcast on March 20, 1962. "Gigolo" was entitled "Arthur" while in production.

RELEASE: Broadcast on December 15, 1985, by the National Broadcasting Company (NBC).
REVIEWS: None available.
DVD: Not available.

The Equalizer (1986)

Season 1, Episode 14, "Out of the Past," Universal/MCA
CREW: Richard Compton (Director), Coleman Luck (Co-Producer), Daniel Lieberstein, Peter A. Runfolo (Co-Producers, New York), James McAdams, Joel Surnow (Executive Producers), Michael Sloan, Richard Lindheim (Creators), Cyrus Nowrasteh (Teleplay), Stewart Copeland (Music), William Steiner (Photography), Marc Laub, Michael R. Miller, Norman

Hollyn (Editors), Richard Bianchi (Production Designer), Linda Wayne (Costumes), Joe Cuervo (Makeup), Masarone (Hair). Color, 46 minutes. Filmed in New York.

CAST: Edward Woodward (Robert McCall), Sandy Dennis (Kay Wesley, nee McCall), Stephen McHattie (Eddie Washburn), Barry Primus (Walter Wesley), Brad Dourif (Fenn), Sylvia Miles (Lily, aka Mother), James Gammon (Michael Cub), Hector Osorio (Captain Dutton), Derek Smith (Punk), Dan Moran (Pizza Employee), Jasmine Guy (Gloria), Leonie Norton (Gretchen), Gloria I. Miguel (Bag Lady).

SYNOPSIS: Eddie Washburn is released on parole after an eight-year prison sentence for his involvement in a robbery at the brokerage office of Walter Wesley. Eddie stalks Walter, who had testified against Eddie, although Walter was part of the robbery. Walter's wife, Kay, contacts her ex-husband, Robert McCall for protection. Eddie kills his parole officer. He brandishes a gun at Walter, and Robert shoots Eddie dead.

NOTES: Dennis' guest appearance on this TV show recalls the appearances she made early in her career in police procedural shows like *Naked City*, *The Fugitive*, *Arrest and Trial*, and *Mr. Broadway*. However, while those appearances were made as her career was just beginning, here her career was in decline. This show seemed to have some prestige since the calibre of its guest stars included other Oscar-nominated actors of the past, like Shirley Knight, and future Oscar winners like Olympia Dukakis and Kevin Spacey.

Dennis is the top-billed guest star, although she plays a secondary character and has less screen time than Stephen McHattie and Barry Primus. The show has some elements that make it slightly more interesting than the standard procedural, including the exotic percussive score by Stewart Copeland, which seems to feature whale sounds. Dennis gives a good dramatic performance, supplying presence, emotion and humor.

Her hair is the same length as in the *Alfred Hitchcock Presents* episode, though its color looks lighter. She also wears it parted on the side, as opposed to the center part she previously sported. Dennis looks thinner than in her previous appearances. Her Kay is an upper-middle-class wife of a broker who is successful enough to be able to afford a brownstone. The marriage is Kay's second. Her first was to Robert McCall, and they had two children, a son and daughter, apparently now deceased. Kay's wealth is indicated by her wardrobe, which includes a mink coat and the shoulder pads that were fashionable in the 1980s. She is also seen in a nightgown in the nighttime scene where it is discovered that Eddie has been in the house.

Dennis uses her mannerisms of stuttering, head-nodding, gesturing, pointing, eye-closing, and tongue-poking. She underplays her character's swearing when she says, "Damn you to hell," with her husband later describing her as "headstrong" and even "unreasonable." Robert will comment that he has seen her angry many times, which is only borne out by a few tart comments rather than overt displays.

Dennis brings emotion and tears to the scene where Kay confronts Robert about her perception that he is not helping her, and how she loves Walter. She also sheds tears when she looks at the photographs on Robert's mantelpiece, presumably since they are of her son, Scott. Kay hugs Robert to say goodbye to him in the episode's epilogue.

The narrative presents Eddie and Fenn as lowlifes who resort to hiring prostitutes for Eddie's welcome home party. They are lowlifes, however, with a certain income, enabling them to afford women who seem a cut above street trade. Eddie's coughing suggests an AIDS-like illness, though AIDS is not mentioned specifically in the narrative. However, there may be some connection between the disease and Eddie's impulsive behavior. Later Fenn will tell Robert and Walter that Eddie is dying from something in the lungs that he caught in prison. His being shot by Robert at the climax is an ironic acceleration of Eddie's death.

Eddie stabs Billy, the arms salesman, with a knife that he considers buying, partly because Eddie can't afford the five hundred dollars Billy wants for a gun. Eddie's quick temper is also evident when he blows up at the pizzeria employee after the man refuses to let Eddie use the employee toilet. He smashes the man's face into a pizza on a table, which holds some irony. He also displays temperament when he initially walks out on the meeting between Robert and Walter in the pub at the climax, and when he returns and shoots Fenn.

Eddie running into Walter in the street may initially seem like a coincidence. Given that we see Eddie stalking Walter later, we can rethink the accidental meeting as intentional. The shock of a cat scream is used as a fake scare in the Wesley house after Walter tells Kay about Eddie. Kay having a cat recalls the cats surrounding other characters played by Dennis, as well as feeding into her real-life fondness for the animals.

Robert's appearance one-third of the way into the narrative seems like a long delay for the entrance of the show's star. Kay approaching Robert rather than first consulting Walter will lead to a funny payoff of resistance, though eventually Walter accedes to Robert's involvement. Robert tells Kay, "Perhaps we should talk to your husband about this," and Compton cuts to Walter telling Kay, "Absolutely not." Kay's seeking Robert's help before checking with Walter may also be a sign of her being "headstrong," as Walter later describes her.

Cub's manhandling of Eddie at the bar may seem excessive, including the slap he delivers, but the scene is interesting in that Robert doesn't have to say anything. Also, the slap follows Eddie's stabbing of Billy in the treatment's first display of violence, and is the first retribution dealt to Eddie as the narrative antagonist. Later we will see Eddie shoot Cub and then Fenn, and Eddie attacked by the Bag Lady and then shot by Robert. The Bag Lady's self-defense creates the expectation that Eddie will shoot her, too, which fortunately does not happen.

The climax is somewhat disappointing, since Eddie seems to be defeated too quickly and doesn't even try to shoot Walter as revenge. Perhaps we are meant to think that Robert is such a good security man that he stops Eddie before this can occur. However, it reads more like a too-easy solution to the set-up. Equally, Fenn's killing feels rather arbitrary, although it is assumed that he must suffer because he has been assisting Eddie. We also don't see Walter telling Kay about his real involvement in the robbery, so it appears that he escapes any lasting payback.

The dialogue is full of clichés. When Eddie telephones Walter, he tells him, "My time is over but yours has just begun," referring to the bad time Eddie had in prison. Kay tells Walter after seeing he has a gun, "You're not the kind of man who could kill anyone." He replies, "I hope to hell you're wrong." Robert's ad that Kay retrieves from the newspaper Security Notices reads "Odds against you? Need help? Call The Equalizer." How Robert has been tagged as The Equalizer is not explained in this episode, though it's a clear metaphor.

Kay tells Robert, "You were never there when we were married. Why should I expect it now?" She later voices a variation on her arrogant accusation when she tells Robert, "I come to you for help and I end up with a fool leading a fool." Kay considering Walter arrogant and a fool leads to some ironic humor when Walter tells Robert that he cannot tell Kay the truth about himself because "she's always held me in high esteem." Robert responds that Kay has an "unfathomable depth of understanding."

After some quick cuts and fancy camerawork under the opening credits, director Richard Compton's coverage thankfully becomes more traditional. However, he does employ point of view shots, the occasional odd camera angle, and some hand-held camerawork. Compton has Eddie experience an aural memory of prison after he stabs Billy, and another when the Bag Lady comes after him, to suggest that prison has left Eddie traumatized.

Edward Woodward appears in the opening credits standing in front of a parked car in the dark. He resembles a vampire, which creates the expectation that he will deliver a staccato performance. However, the emotion he brings to the scene where he speaks to Kay about the death of their daughter puts paid for that notion. Robert's persona as a tough guy is somewhat diminished by him wearing spectacles at times, but he does speak in a terse manner at the climax. His saying goodbye to Kay at the window offers some poignancy. Stephen McHattie's performance reads as a bit Method-y, though perhaps the idea of his being sick provides it some context. However, Compton reigns in Brad Dourif, who otherwise can be just as excessive in performance, perhaps as a balance to McHattie. The action–crime drama TV show ran for four seasons from 1985 to 1989.

RELEASE: Broadcast January 15, 1986, by Columbia Broadcasting System (CBS).

REVIEWS: No reviews of the show available. However, Dennis' performance was commented on by Neotrinity on the website *Filmscoremonthly.com*. Neotrinity doubts that she was the first choice for the part she played, given her "highly esteemed and accomplished career." However, he felt that her casting was astute and "an unalloyed triumph as she impressively (with superb subtlety) imbues Kay with a poise, stylishly-dressed sophistication and supple inner strength every inch the (um) Equal of her ex."

DVD: Featured on the DVD *The Equalizer* Season 1, released by Universal Studios on February 12, 2008.

Appendix: Theater Credits

Casts are listed in the order presented in *The New York Times* review when cited.

The Reluctant Debutante

A comedy by William Douglas Home.
CREW: Walt Witcover (Director), Martin Reiss (Scenic Design).
CAST: Ruth Chatterton (Sheila Broadbent), Arthur Treacher (Jimmy Broadbent), Sandy Dennis (Jane Broadbent), Peter Craig (David Hoylake-Johnston), Ralph Purdom (David Bulloch), Helen-Jean Arthur (Clarissa Crosswaite), Harriet MacGibbon (Mabel Crosswaite), Ruth Estler.
SEASON: July 1956 at the Westport Country Playhouse, Connecticut.

The Lady from the Sea

A drama by Henrik Ibsen.
CREW: William Gyimes (Director/Producer).
CAST: Christiane Felsmann (Eillida Wangel), Donald Hotton (Lyngstrand), (Sandy Dennis (Hilde), Helen Quarrier (Bolette), Alan Ansara, Bernard Pollock, Donald Marye, Alex Reed.
SEASON: December 1956 at the Tempo Playhouse, Off Broadway, New York.

Bus Stop

A comedy by William Inge
CREW: Unknown.
CAST: Barbara Baxley, Sandy Dennis (Elma Duckworth).
SEASON: Exact dates in 1957 unknown at the Royal Poinciana Playhouse, Florida.

The Dark at the Top of the Stairs

A drama by William Inge
CREW: Elia Kazan (Director and Producer), Arnold Saint-Subber (Producer), Ben Edwards (Scenic Design), Lucinda Ballard (Costumes), Jean Rosenthal (Lighting).
CAST: Pat Hingle (Rubin Flood), Teresa Wright (Cora Flood), Charles Saari (Sonny Flood), Jonathan Shawn (Boy Offstage), Judith Robinson (Reenie Flood), Evans Evans (Flirt Conroy),

Frank Overton (Morris Lacey), Eileen Heckart (Lottie Lacey), Timmy Everett (Sammy Goldenbaum), Carl Reindel (Punky Givens), Anthony Ray (Chauffer).
  SEASON: December 5, 1957, to January 17, 1959, at the Music Box Theatre, New York.
  NOTES: Sandy Dennis was the second understudy for Reenie Flood and Flirt Conroy. Tuesday Weld was the first. Dennis also played Reenie Flood in the play's national tour, which headlined Barbara Baxley, Audrey Christie and George L. Smith. The tour ran from January 21 to May 30, 1959, and included stops in Delaware, Ohio, Missouri, Chicago, Wisconsin, and Florida.

The Diary of Anne Frank

A drama by Frances Goodrich and Albert Hackett based on the writings of Anne Frank.
  CREW: Cliff Clothren (Director).
  CAST: Sandy Dennis (Anne Frank), William Putch (Otto Frank), June Prud'homme (Mrs. Frank), Margot Stevenson (Mrs. Van Daan), Don Douglas (Mr. Van Daan), Charles Leslie (Peter), John Eames (Mr. Dussel), Jay Lanin, Elena Rafael, Sara Whanger.
  SEASON: July 1959 at the Totem Hole Playhouse, Pennsylvania.

The Glass Menagerie

A drama by Tennessee Williams.
  CREW: William Putch (Director), Benko (Scenic Design), Roger Titus (Lighting).
  CAST: Nancy Andrews (Amanda Wingfield), Doug Robinson (Tom Wingfield), Sandy Dennis (Laura Wingfield), Charles Leslie (Jim O'Connor).
  SEASON: September 1959 at the Totem Hole Playhouse, Pennsylvania.

Burning Bright

A drama by John Steinbeck
  CREW: Matt Cimber (Director), Robert M. Cavallo (Producer), Sheldon Haber (Scenic Design and Lighting), Mary Ann Reed (Costumes).
  CAST: Philip Keneally (Joe Saul), Leon B. Stevens (Friend Ed), Sandy Dennis (Mordeen), Clifford David (Victor).
  SEASON: From October 16, 1959, at the Theatre East, Off Broadway. A revival.

Motel

A drama by Thomas W. Phipps
  CREW: Unknown.
  CAST: Siobhan McKenna, Richard Easton, George Mathews, Joe Ponazecki, Sandy Dennis.
  SEASON: January 1960 at the Wilbur Theatre, Boston.

Port Royal

A drama by Henry de Montherlant, translated by Jonathan Griffin.
CREW: Herbert Berghof (Director), Balllou (Scenic Design), Kathe Berl (Costumes), Lee Watson (Lighting).
CAST: Sandy Dennis (Sister Gabrielle), Jenny Egan (Sister Chaterine de Sainte Flavle), Joan Matthiessen (Sister Helene), Olga Bellin (Sister Marie Francoise de L'Eucharistie), Uta Hagen (Sister Angelique de Saint Jean), Betty Sinclair (Mother Catherine-Agnes de Saint Paul), Olive Dunbar (Mother Madeliene de Saint Agnes), R.J. Harris (Sister Gabrielle's Father), Phillip Bourneuf (M. de Beaumont de Perefixe), Grant Reddick (Official of the Church), William Bogert (Civil Lieutenant), Joe Ponazecki (A Police Officer).
SEASON: April 24 and May 1, 1960, at the Grace Protestant Episcopal Church, Off Broadway, New York.

Face of a Hero

A drama by Robert L. Joseph, based on the novel by Pierre Boulle.
CREW: Alexander Mackendrick (Director), Lester Osterman, Jr. (Producer), Ben Edwards (Scenic Design and Lighting), Ann Roth (Costumes).
CAST: Roy Poole (Raphael Knox), Frank Conroy (Phillip Milliard), Guy Sorel (Otto Litchfield), James Donald (Simon De Grange), Jack Lemmon (David Poole), Mary Farrell (Rhoda Grant), Russell Collins (Victor Bishop), Ellen Holly (Elizabeth Falk), Edward Asner (Perry Cates), Albert Dekker (Leo Fuller), Carlton Colyer (Gordon), George Grizzard (Harold Rutland, Jr.), Sandy Dennis (Millicent Bishop), Betsy Blair (Catherine Poole), Kip McArdle (Rosamund Killie), Edwin Sherin (Jonathan Spring), Lynn Hamilton (Cleaning Woman), Joseph Palma (Judge).
SEASON: October 20, 1960, to November 19, 1960, at the Eugene O'Neill Theater, New York.

The Complaisant Lover

A drama by Graham Greene.
CREW: Glen Byam Shaw (Director), Irene Mayer Selznick (Producer), H.M. Tennent, Donald Albery and F. E. S. Plays (Associate Producers), Motley (Scenic Design and Costumes), Paul Morrison (Lighting).
CAST: Michael Redgrave (Victor Rhodes), George Turner (William Howard), Richard Johnson (Clive Root), Sandy Dennis (Ann Howard), Christine Thomas (Margaret Howard), Googie Withers (Mary Rhodes), Nicholas Hammond (Robin Rhodes), Gene Wilder (Hotel Valet), Bert Nelson (Dr. Van Droog).
SEASON: November 1, 1961, to January 27, 1962, at the Ethel Barrymore Theatre, New York.

A Thousand Clowns

A comedy by Herb Gardner.
CREW: Fred Coe (Director and Producer), Arthur Cantor (Producer), George Jenkins (Scenic Design and Lighting), Ruth Morley (Costumes).
CAST: Jason Robards, Jr. (Murray Burns), Barry Gordon (Nick Burns), William Daniels

(Albert Amundson), Sandy Dennis (Sandra Markowitz), A. Larry Haines (Arnold Burns), Gene Saks (Leo Herman).
SEASON: April 5, 1962, to April 13, 1963, at the Eugene O'Neill Theater, New York.

Any Wednesday

A comedy by Murie Resnick
CREW: Henry Kaplan (Director), George W. George and Frank Granat and Howard Erskine and Peter S. Katz and Edward Specter Productions (Producers), Robert Randolph (Scenic Design), Theoni V. Aldredge (Costumes), Tharon Musser (Lighting).
CAST: Don Porter (John Cleves), Sandy Dennis (Ellen Gordon), Gene Hackman (Cass Henderson), Rosemary Murphy (Dorothy Cleves).
SEASON: February 18, 1964, to February 12, 1966, at the Music Box Theatre, then February 15 to June 26 1966 at the George Abbott Theatre, New York.
NOTES: Sandy Dennis was replaced in the role of Ellen by Barbara Cook from February 22, 1965.

The Three Sisters

A drama by Anton Chekhov
CREW: Lee Strasberg (Director), Will Steven Armstrong (Scenic Design), Theoni V. Aldredge and Ray Diffen (Costumes), Feder (Lighting).
CAST: Kim Stanley (Masha), Nan Martin (Olga), Sandy Dennis (Irina), Luther Adler (Chebutykin), Robert Loggia (Solyony), James Olsen (Tuzenbach), Tamara Daykarhanova (Anfisa), Salem Ludwig (Ferapont), Brooks Morton (Orderly), Janice Mars (Maid), George C. Scott (Vershinin), Gerald Hiken (Andrei), Albert Paulsen (Kulygin), Barbara Baxley (Natalya), John Harkins (Fedotik), David Paulsen (Rode).
SEASON: May 13 to 22, 1965, at the Aldwych Theatre, London.

Daphne in Cottage D

A drama by Stephen Levi
CREW: Martin Fried (Director), Robert Leder and Michael Prods (Producers), Porter Van Zandt (Associate Producer), Joe Mielziner (Scenic Design and Lighting), Theoni V. Aldredge (Costumes).
CAST: Sandy Dennis (Daphne), William Daniels (Joseph).
SEASON: October 15, 1967, to November 18, 1967, at the Longacre Theatre, New York.

Bus Stop

A comedy by William Inge
CREW: Unknown.
CAST: Sandy Dennis (Cherie), Ben Piazza.
SEASON: From August 13, 1970, for six weeks at the Ivanhoe Theater, Chicago.

How the Other Half Lives

A comedy by Ayckbourn
CREW: Gene Saks (Director), Michael Myerberg and Peter Bridge and Eddie Kulukundis (Producers), Lawrence Shubert Lawrence, Jr. (Associate Producer), David Mitchell (Scenic Design), Winn Morton (Costumes), Peggy Clark (Lighting).
CAST: Bernice Massi (Fiona Foster), Sandy Dennis (Teresa Phillips), Phil Silvers (Frank Foster), Richard Mulligan (Bob Phillips), Tom Aldredge (William Detweiler), Jeanne Hepple (Mary Detweiler).
SEASON: March 29, 1971, to June 26, 1971, at the Royale Theater, New York.

And Miss Reardon Drinks a Little

A drama by Paul Zindel
CREW: Melvin Bernhardt (Director).
CAST: Sandy Dennis (Anna Reardon), Estelle Parsons (Catherine Reardon).
SEASON: From July 3, 1971, to August 1971 Sandy Dennis toured with the play in Boston, Connecticut, and Maine. Salome Jens took over the role of Catherine from July 29 in Connecticut, and M'el Dowd and Walter Wanderman was also in the cast.
NOTES: Dennis also appeared in the play in a tour from January to July 1972 and that covered Chicago, Florida and New York at the Hyde Park Playhouse. Also in the cast were Barbara Baxley and Betty Garrett as alternate Catherine's, and Frank Savino.

Let Me Hear You Smile

A comedy by Lenora Thuna and Harry Cauley
CREW: Harry Cauley (Director), Michael Macrae and Barclay Macrae (Producers), Peter Larkin (Scenic Design), Carrie F. Robbins (Costumes), Neil Peter Jampolis (Lighting).
CAST: Sandy Dennis (Hannah Heywood), James Broderick (Neil Heywood), Paul B. Price (Willy Farmer).
SEASON: Only one performance being January 16, 1973, at the Biltmore Theatre, New York.

---

6 Rms Riv Vu

A comedy by Bob Randall.
CREW: Jerry Adler (Director).
CAST: Leonard Nimoy (Paul Friedman), Sandy Dennis (Anne Miller), John J. Martin (Eddie), Barbara Idelson (Pregnant Woman), Dana Gladstone (Larry), Carol Fox Prescott (Janet Friedman), Richard Miller. Randy Robbins (Richard Miller).
SEASON: March 1973 at the Parker Playhouse, the Royal Poinciana Playhouse, and the Coconut Playhouse, Florida.

A Streetcar Named Desire

A drama by Tennessee Williams.
CREW: George Keathley (Director).

CAST: Sandy Dennis (Blanche Dubois), David Wilson, James Broderick (Mitch).
SEASON: July 5 to August 26, 1973, at the Ivanhoe Theater, Chicago.

Born Yesterday

A comedy by Garson Kanin.
CREW: Stephen Porter (Director).
CAST: Gary Merrill (Harry Brock), Billie Dawn (Sandy Dennis), Peter Brandon (Paul Verrall), Eugene Stuckmann, Robert R. Wait.
SEASON: February 1974 at the Royal Poinciana Playhouse, Florida. March 7 to 17, 1974, at the Pellman Theater, Milwaukee.
NOTE: Sandy Dennis repeated the performance in July at the Ogunquit Playhouse in Maine and at the Westport Country Playhouse in Connecticut.

Separate Tables

A drama by Terrence Rattigan
CREW: George Keathley (Director).
CAST: Sandy Dennis (Anne Shankland/Sybil Railton-Bell), James Broderick, Delphi Lawrence.
SEASON: May 6 to June 30 at the Ivanhoe Theater, Chicago.

Absurd Person Singular

A comedy by Alan Ayckbourn
CREW: Eric Thompson (Director), The Theatre Guild and The John F. Kennedy Center for the Performing Arts (Producers), Michael Codron (Associate Producer), Edward Burbidge (Scenic Design), Levino Verna (Costumes), Thomas Skelton (Lighting).
CAST: Carole Shelley (Jane), Larry Blyden (Sidney), Richard Kiley (Ronald), Geraldine Page (Marion), Sandy Dennis (Eva), Tony Roberts (Geoffrey).
SEASON: October 8, 1974, to March 6, 1976, at the Music Box Theatre, New York.
NOTES: Sandy Dennis was replaced in the role of Eva by Carol Lynley from June 26, 1975, and then by Betsy von Furstenberg from January 12, 1976.

Cat on a Hot Tin Roof

A drama by Tennessee Williams.
CREW: Unknown.
CAST: Sandy Dennis (Maggie), David Selby (Brick), Ronald Bishop.
SEASON: Summer tour in 1975. Locations included New York, Maine, Connecticut and Illinois.

Same Time, Next Year

A comedy by Bernard Slade
CREW: Gene Saks (Director), Morton Gottlieb and Dasha Epstein and Edward L. Schuman

and Palladium Productions (Producers), Ben Rosenberg and Warren Crane (Associate Producers), William Ritman (Scenic Design), Jane Greenwood (Costumes), Tharon Muser (Lighting).
CAST: Sandy Dennis (Doris), Ted Bissell and Don Murray (George).
SEASON: The play which ran at the Brooks Atkinson Theatre from March 14, 1975, to May 15, 1978, and then May 16 to September 3, 1978, at the Ambassador Theater, New York.
NOTES: Sandy replaced Ellen Burstyn in the role of Doris, and Ted Bissell and Don Murray replaced Charles Grodin. Burstyn and Grodin had originated the roles. Dennis' run in the play differs according to sources. Some say it was March 8 to May 30, 1977; others say it was from June 21 1976 for eleven months, or that Dennis did the play until February 1977. Ted Bessell is said to have replaced Charles Grodin on December 1, 1975, and Don Murray replaced Bessell on March 8, 1977.

The Royal Family

A comedy by George S. Kaufman and Edna Ferber.
CREW: Unknown.
CAST: Sandy Dennis (Julie Cavendish), Cathleen Nesbitt.
SEASON: June 20 to September 3, 1977, summer tour which covered locations in New Jersey, Pennsylvania, Massachusetts, Connecticut, Maine,
NOTES: From August 15 to 20, 1977, at the Ogunquit Playhouse in Maine Gale Sondergaard replaced Cathleen Nesbitt.

Fallen Angels

A comedy by Noel Coward.
CREW: Unknown.
CAST: Sandy Dennis, Jean Marsh.
SEASON: January 30 to February 4, 1978, at the Royal Poinciana Playhouse in Florida and February 13 to March 5 at the Paper Mill Playhouse, New Jersey.

The Little Foxes

A drama by Lillian Hellman.
CREW: Unknown.
CAST: Sandy Dennis, Geraldine Page, Rip Torn.
SEASON: March 22 to April 2, 1978, at the Paper Mill Playhouse, New Jersey.

Eccentricities of a Nightingale

A drama by Tennessee Williams.
CREW: Michael Flanagan (Director).
CAST: Sandy Dennis, Perry King, Nan Martin.
SEASON: February 1979 at the Long Beach Auditorium, California.

Same Time, Next Year

A comedy by Bernard Slade.
CREW: Unknown.
CAST: Sandy Dennis, Charles Kimbrough.
SEASONS: August 14 to 25, 1979, at the John Drew Theater, East Hampton, New York, August 27 to September 1 at the Ogunquit Playhouse in Maine, and October 20 to November 3 at the Fox Theater, Los Angeles.
NOTE: Dennis also did the play from November 20 to December 21, 1980, at the Stage West Theatre in Winnipeg, Canada, opposite Ted Follows.

The Supporting Cast

A comedy by George Furth
CREW: Gene Saks (Director), Terry Allen Kramer and James M. Nederlander and 20th Century–Fox (Producers), William Ritman (Scenic Design), Jane Greenwood (Costumes), Richard Nelson (Lighting).
CAST: Hope Lange (Ellen), Betty Garrett (Mae), Sandy Dennis (Sally), Jack Gilford (Arnold), Joyce Van Patten (Florrie).
SEASON: August 6, 1981, to September 5, 1981, at the Biltmore Theatre, New York.
NOTE: Dennis toured with the production in the summer of 1982. It played from June 28 to July 3 at the Westport Country Playhouse with co-stars Petty Cosgrove, Barbara Rush and June Dayton and credited director Tom Troupe. The tour continued at different venues from July to August 21.

Come Back to the 5 & Dime, Jimmy Dean, Jimmy Dean

A drama by Ed Graczyk
CREW: Robert Altman (Director), Dan Fisher and Joseph Clapsaddle and Joel Brykman and Jacl Lawrence (Producers), David Gropman (Scenic Design), Scott Bushell (Costumes), Paul Gallo (Lighting), Richard Fitzgerald (Sound).
CAST: Sudie Bond (Juanita), Cher (Sissy), Sandy Dennis (Mona), Mark Patton (Joe), Gena Ramsel (Sue Ellen), Kathy Bates (Stella Mae), Marta Heflin (Edna Louise), Ann Risley (Martha), Dianne Turley Travis (Alice Ann), Ruth Miller (Clarissa), Karen Black (Joanne).
SEASON: February 18, 1982, to April 4, 1982, at the Martin Beck Theatre, New York.

Buried Inside Extra

A drama by Thomas Babe.
CREW: Joseph Papp (Director and Producer), Mike Boak (Scenic Design), Theoni V. Aldredge (Costumes), Ralph K. Holmes (Lighting).
CAST: Hal Holbrook (Jake L. Bowsky), Dixie Carter (Liz Conlon), Vincent Gardenia (Wild Bill Culhane), William Converse-Roberts (Don Kane), Sandy Dennis (Sophia Bowsky).
SEASON: May 4 to May 29, 1983, at the Joseph Papp Public Theater/Martinson Hall, Off Broadway, New York.

NOTE: The production also went to London and was performed from June 17, 1983, for six weeks at the Royal Court.

The Supporting Cast

A comedy by George Furth.
CREW: Unknown.
CAST: Sandy Dennis, others unknown.
SEASON: September 11 to 13, 1983, at Stage West, Calgary, Canada.

84 Charing Cross Road

A drama by Helene Hanff.
CREW: William Fisher (Director), Lee Livingstone (Scenic Design).
CAST: Sandy Dennis (Helene Hanff), Donal Donnely.
SEASON: January to February 1984 at Stage West, Calgary, Canada.

Agnes of God

A drama by John Pielmeier.
CREW: Frank Marino (Director), Steven Perry (Scenic Design), Barbara Blackwood (Costumes), John Culbert (Lighting).
CAST: Geraldine Page (Sister Miriam Ruth), Sandy Dennis (Dr. Martha Livingstone), Deidre O'Connell (Agnes).
SEASON: June 25 to 30, 1985, at the Westport Country Playhouse, Connecticut.

'night, Mother

A drama by Marsha Norman.
CREW: Burry Fredrik (Director).
CAST: Sandy Dennis (Jessie Cates), Eileen Heckart (Thelma).
SEASON: September 10 to 15, 1985, at the Westport Country Playhouse, Connecticut.

A Coupla White Chicks Sitting Around

A comedy by John Ford Noonan.
CREW: Unknown.
CAST: Sandy Dennis (Maude Mix), Elizabeth Ashley.
SEASON: Tour from March 11, 1986, to May 11, 1986, and covered Missouri, Maryland, New York and Florida.

And Miss Reardon Drinks a Little

A drama by Paul Zindel.
CREW: Larry Arrick (Director).
CAST: Sandy Dennis, Anne Meara.
SEASON: August 11 to 16, 1986, at the Cape Playhouse and August 18 to 23, 1986, at the Westport Country Playhouse, Connecticut.

The Odd Couple

A comedy by Neil Simon.
CREW: Unknown.
CAST: Sandy Dennis, Jo Anne Worley.
SEASON: November 1986 in Detroit.
NOTE: Dennis would star as Florence with Stella Stevens as Olive Madison from March 10 to May 10, 1987, at the Stage West Theatre in Calgary, Canada. Kaye Ballard would join Dennis from August 18 to September 4, 1988, in the play at the Pocono Playhouse, Pennsylvania. Co-stars were George Miserlis, Ovidio Vargas, Mary Sharmat, Jeanne McCarthy, Holly McNeill and Myvanwy Jenn. The set was by Michael Smith, costumes by Betsy Ellen Deedrick, and the director was Judith Haskell. The production also played from September 7 to 25, 1988, at the Bucks County Playhouse, Philadelphia.

Bibliography

Albee, Edward. Interviewed by Frank J. Avella for *A Delicate Balance* DVD. 3DD/Fremantle Media, 2004.
Alda, Alan. *Inside the Actors Studio*. Viewed on *YouTube*, September 14, 2012.
_____. Interview from *Archive of American Television*. Viewed on *YouTube*, September 14, 2012.
_____. *Never Have Your Dog Stuffed and Other Things I've Learned*. New York: Random House, 2006.
_____. *Things I Overheard While Talking to Myself*. New York: Random House, 2008.
Allen, Jennifer. "Cher and Altman on Broadway." *New York Magazine*, February 1, 1982, retrieved June 18, 2012, from http://books.google.com.au/books.
Allen, Woody, and Stig Bjorkman. *Woody Allen on Woody Allen*. New York: Grove Press, 2005.
Allen, Woody, and Linda Sunshine. *The Illustrated Woody Allen Reader*. New York: Knopf, 1993.
Allon, Yoram, Del Cullen, and Hannah Patterson. *Contemporary North American Film Directors: A Wallflower Critical Guide*. New York: Wallflower Press, 2002.
_____, _____, and _____. *The Wallflower Critical Guide to Contemporary British and Irish Film Directors*. New York: Wallflower Press, 2002.
Als, Hilton. "The Improbable Elizabeth Taylor." March 24, 2011. *The New Yorker*, retrieved August 21, 2012, from http://www.newyorker.com.
Altman, Robert, and David Sterritt. *Robert Altman: Interviews*. Jackson: University Press of Mississippi, 2000.
Amburn, Ellis. *The Sexiest Man Alive: A Biography of Warren Beatty*. New York: Harper, 2002.
Anderson, Jack. "Barbara Loden Replaces Sandy Dennis in 'Dean.'" *The New York Times*, February 19, 1980, retrieved October 4, 2012, from http://query.nytimes.com.
Anderson, John. "Loretta Swit Gets Nod on Conference." *The Vindicator*, November 12, 1984, retrieved October 10, 2012, from http://news.google.com/newspapers.
"Any Wednesday's Sandy." *Look*, vol. 28, no. 12, 1964: 100–104.
Archer, Eugene. "Kook's Tour of 'A Thousand Clowns' with Miss Harris." *The New York Times*, June 14, 1964, retrieved June 2, 2012, from http://query.nytimes.com/mem/archive.
Armetz, Aljean. "Death of a Bare Stage Play." *The Sarasota Herald-Tribune*, September 5, 1979, retrieved June 16, 2012, from http://news.google.com/newspapers.
Armstrong, Rick. *Robert Altman: Critical Essays*. Jefferson, NC: McFarland, 2005.
Atkinson, Brooks. "The Play in Review." *The New York Times*, November 14, 1942, retrieved August 29, 2012, from http://query.nytimes.com/mem/archive.
Bailey, Peter J. *The Reluctant Film Art of Woody Allen*. Lexington: University Press of Kentucky, 2010.
Barker, Deborah, and Kathryn McKee. *American Cinema and the Southern Imaginary (The New Southern Studies)*. Athens: University of Georgia Press, 2011.
Barker, Dennis E. "Four Seasons' on location in St. John." *The Virgin Islands Daily News*, May 30, 1980, retrieved June 17, 2012, from http://news.google.com/newspapers.
Barnes, Clive. "Stage." *The New York Times*, January 17, 1963, retrieved June 12, 2012, from http://query.nytimes.com/mem/archive.
_____. "Stage." *The New York Times*, October 9, 1974, retrieved June 13, 2012, from http://query.nytimes.com/mem/archive.
Barratt, Mark. *Ian McKellen: An Unofficial Biography*. London: Virgin Books, 2005.
Barsanti, Chris. *Filmology*. Avon, MA: Adams Media, 2010.
Baskin, Ellen. *Enser's Filmed Books and Plays: A List of Books and Plays from Which Films Have Been Made, 1928–2001 (Enser's Filmed Books and Plays)*. Farnham, England: Ashgate Publishing Limited, 2003.

Baxter, John. *Hollywood in the Sixties*. New York: A.S. Barnes & Co., 1972.
_____. *Woody Allen: A Biography*. New York: HarperCollins, 1998.
Beamer, Wayne. "Q&A: Matt Ogens, Director of 'Confessions of a Superhero.'" *Comics Alliance*, November 8, 2007, retrieved June 30, 2012, from http://www.comicsalliance.com.
Beath, Warren, and Paula Wheeldon. *James Dean in Death: A Popular Encyclopedia of a Celebrity Phenomenon*. Jefferson, NC: McFarland, 2005.
Beaufort, John. "Animated Trio of One-Acters — and Some Not-So-Private Lives; Buried Inside Extra Play by Thomas Babe. Directed by Joseph Papp." *The Christian Science Monitor*, May 16, 1983, retrieved June 20, 2012, from http://www.csmonitor.com.
_____. "Transatlantic Salute; Britain Is Bustin' Out All Over — in New York." *The Christian Science Monitor*, May 23, 1983, retrieved June 20, 2012, from http://www.csmonitor.com.
Beck, Marilyn. "Cher Covets Oscar." *Ottawa Citizen*, January 28, 1983, retrieved October 4, 2012, from http://news.google.com/newspapers.
_____. "Valerie Perrine Perfect for Lead in 'Same Time.'" *The Miami News*, August 5, 1976, retrieved June 14, 2012, from http://news.google.com/newspapers.
Bennett, Colin. "Nauseating, So Give Me the Sentiment." *The Age*, October 26, 1970, retrieved August 2, 2012, from http://news.google.com/newspapers.
Bergan, Ronald. "Nora Ephron Obituary." *The Guardian*, June 27, 2012, retrieved September 11, 2012, from http://www.guardian.co.uk.
Bergman, Ingmar. *Smultronstället*, aka *Wild Strawberries*. Svensk Filmindustri (SF), 1957.
Bills, Joe, and David Loehr. *James Dean Collectors Guide*. L-W Book Sales, 1999.
Biskind, Peter. *Star: How Warren Beatty Seduced America*. New York: Simon & Schuster, 2011.
Blake, Richard A. *Woody Allen: Profane and Sacred*. Lanham, MD: Scarecrow Press, 1995.
Blakely, Thomas. "Sandy Dennis Smiles Away Troubled Role." *The Pittsburgh Press*, October 1, 1969, retrieved August 2, 2012, from http://news.google.com/newspapers.
Blank, Ed. "Glenda: A Special Talent." *The Pittsburgh Press*, May 30, 1981, retrieved September 9, 2012, from http://news.google.com/newspapers.
_____. "Love or Hate Her Style. One of a Kind: That's Sandy Dennis." *The Pittsburgh Press*, March 21, 1982, retrieved May 28, 2012, from http://news.google.com/newspapers.
_____. "Sandy Dennis' Effort Fails to Save N.Y. Play." *The Pittsburgh Press*, May 14, 1983, retrieved June 20, 2012, from http://news.google.com/newspapers.
Blau, Eleanor. "Broadway." *The New York Times*, March 4, 1983, retrieved June 20, 2012, from http://www.nytimes.com.
Bonderoff, Jason. *Alan Alda Unauthorized*. New York: Signet, 1982.
Bordman, Gerald. *American Theatre: A Chronicle of Comedy and Drama, Volume 4*. Oxford: Oxford University Press, 1994.
_____, and Thomas S. Hischak. *The Oxford Companion to American Theatre*. Oxford University Press, 2004.
Bosworth, Patricia. *Jane Fonda: The Private Life of a Public Woman*. Boston: Houghton Mifflin Harcourt, 2011.
Bottoms, Stephen. *The Cambridge Companion to Edward Albee (Cambridge Companions to Literature)*. Cambridge: Cambridge University Press, 2005.
Bowie, Stephen. "An Interview with Gerald S. O'Loughlin." *The Classic TV History Blog*, August 26, 2011, retrieved May 16, 2012, from http://classictvhistory.wordpress.com/tag/sandy-dennis.
Boyle, Hal. "Portrait of a Nice Blonde." *St Josephs New-Press*, August 31, 1966, retrieved May 29, 2012, from http://news.google.com/newspapers.
Bret, David. *Elizabeth Taylor: The Lady, the Lover, the Legend, 1932–2011*. Vancouver, Canada: Greystone Books, 2011.
Brode, Douglas. *The Films of Woody Allen*. Secaucus, NJ: Carol Publishing Group, 1991.
Brooks, Tim, and Earl F. Marsh. *The Complete Directory to Prime Time Network and Cable TV Shows, 1946–Present*. New York: Ballantine Books, 2007.
Brown, Jared. *Alan J. Pakula: His Films and His Life*. New York: Back Stage Books, 2005.
Buck, Jerry. "Bernardi to Try New Medium, TV." *Toledo Blade*, February 28, 1968, retrieved July 21, 2012, from http://news.google.com/newspapers.
_____. "TV Film Role Offers Actor Sweet Revenge." *Waycross Journal-Herald*, March 15, 1978, retrieved September 13, 2012, from http://news.google.com/newspapers.
Buckley, Michael. "Sandy Dennis Remembered." *TheaterWeek*, vol. 5, no.33, 1992: 33–35.
Burn, Michael. "A Rare Theatrical Jewel." *The Calgary Herald*, January 25, 1984, retrieved July 7, 2012, from http://news.google.com/newspapers.

Callan, Michael Feeney. *Robert Redford: The Biography*. New York: Knopf, 2011.
Calta, Louis. "Summer Theaters Get Out S.R.O. Sign." *The New York Times*, July 3, 1975, retrieved June 14, 2012, from http://query.nytimes.com/mem/archive.
Canby, Vincent. "Canada Is Luring Movie Producers." *The New York Times*, March 4, 1967, retrieved June 11, 2012, from http://query.nytimes.com/mem/archive.
Cardullo, Bert. *Stage and Screen: Adaptation Theory from 1916 to 2000*. New York: Continuum, 2011.
Casper, Drew. *Hollywood Film, 1963–1976: Years of Revolution and Reaction*. Hoboken, NJ: John Wiley & Sons, 2011.
CBS Radio Mystery Theater. DVD Audio. Vintage Reproductions.
Clooney, Nick. *The Movies That Changed Us: Reflections on the Screen*. New York: Simon and Schuster, 2003.
Coleman, Fred. "Film Festival in Moscow Promises a Few Fireworks." *The Day*, July 3, 1967, retrieved on June 10, 2012, from http://news.google.com/newspapers.
Collier, James F. *The Hiding Place*. World Wide Pictures, 1975.
Combs, Richard. "Come Back to the 5 & Dime Jimmy Dean, Jimmy Dean." *Monthly Film Bulletin*, vol. 50, no. 596, 1983: 231–232.
_____. "Lives of Performers: A Discussion with Robert Altman." *Monthly Film Bulletin*, vol. 50, no. 596, 1983: 233.
Considine, Shaun. *Bette & Joan: The Divine Feud*. New York: E.P.Dutton, 1989.
Cooper, Jackie. *Please Don't Shoot My Dog: The Autobiography Of Jackie Cooper*. Berkley, CA: Morrow, 1955.
Coplon, Jeff, and Cher. *The First Time*. New York: Pocket Books, 1999.
Corliss, Richard. "The Lively Adventures of Play TV." *Film Comment*, vol. 19, no. 1, 1983: 51–57.
Corry, John. "Broadway." *The New York Times*, July 9, 1976, retrieved June 15, 2012, from http://query.nytimes.com/mem/archive.
Counsell, Colin. *Signs of Performance: An Introduction to Twentieth Century Theatre*. New York: Routledge, 1996
Crane, Leila. "At Westport Playhouse." *The Hour*, September 12, 1985, retrieved June 21, 2012, from http://news.google.com/newspapers.
_____. "*'night, Mother* Opens." *The Hour*, September 9, 1985, retrieved June 21, 2012, from http://news.google.com/newspapers.
Craske, Bill. "The Indian Runner." *Senses of Cinema*, June 13, 2001, retrieved November 20, 2012, from http://sensesofcinema.com.
Crawford, Cheryl. *One Naked Individual*. New York: Bobbs-Merrill Company, 1977.
Crosby, Joan. "*Evil* Big Scare Film." *The Pittsburgh Press*, January 20, 1972, retrieved August 6, 2012, from http://news.google.com/newspapers.
Cukor, George. *Heller in Pink Tights*. Paramount Pictures, 1960.
Dalton, David. *James Dean, the Mutant King: A Biography*. Chicago: Chicago Review Press, 2001.
Dambrofsky, Gwen. "Sandy Dennis Rebounds After Movie Dry Spell." *The Leader-Post*, April 6, 1984, retrieved June 14, 2012, from http://news.google.com/newspapers.
Daniel, Kerry Lee. "A Fox, 29 Cats, a Movie Star, and an Epiphany." *Western North Carolina Woman*, retrieved December 17, 2012, from http://www.wncwoman.com.
Daniels, Lee A. "Obituaries." *The New York Times*, March 5, 1992, retrieved May 17, 2012, from http://www.nytimes.com/1992/03/05/obituaries.
Darren, Alison. *Lesbian Film Guide*. New York: Continuum, 2000.
Daugherty, Herschel. *Alfred Hitchcock Presents*. Season 3, Episode 16: "Sylvia." Shamley Productions, 1958.
Dawson, Nick. *Dennis Hopper: Interviews (Conversations with Filmmakers)*. Jackson: University Press of Mississippi, 2012.
DeCaro, Frank. *The Dead Celebrity Cookbook: A Resurrection of Recipes from More Than 145 Stars of Stage and Screen*. Deerfield Beach, FL: HCI, 2011.
Delatiner, Barbara. "All the Summer's a Stage." *The New York Times*, June 24, 1979, retrieved June 14, 2012, from http://query.nytimes.com/mem/archive.
Denby, David. "Movies: Here's to Cheese!" *New York Magazine*, June 1 1981, retrieved October 24, 2012, from http://books.google.com.au/books.
Dennis, Christopher, and Bonnie Dennis. DVD audio commentary on *Confessions of a Superhero*. Virgil Films and Entertainment, 2008.
Dennis, Sandy, and Louise Ladd. *Sandy Dennis: A Personal Memoir*. Kingston, RI: Papier-Mache Press, 1997.

Derry, Charles. *The Suspense Thriller: Films in the Shadow of Alfred Hitchcock.* Jefferson, NC: McFarland, 2001.
De Vries, Hilary. *After Midnight: The Life and Death of Brad Davis.* New York: Pocket Books, 1998.
Dobes, J.M. "Nora Ephron's Greatest Hits." *Examiner.com*, June 26, 2012, retrieved September 18, 2012, from http://www.examiner.com.
Dolan, Marc. *Bruce Springsteen and the Promise of Rock 'n' Roll.* New York: W.W. Norton & Company, 2012.
Donahue, Deirdre. "Even with the Coca-Cola Kid, Things Aren't Going Better for Eric Roberts — Just Ask Him." *People*, September 9, 1985, retrieved June 19, 2012, from http://www.people.com/people/archive/article.
Drake, David. "Interviews." *Broadway.com*, August 20, 2007, retrieved August 1, 2012, from http://www.broadway.com.
Drew, Bernard L. "Actress Sandy Dennis Arrives in Two Movies." *The Evening News*, March 23, 1968, retrieved July 16, 2012, from http://news.google.com/newspapers.
Drew, Mike. "Far from Perfect 'Gentlemen.'" *The Milwaukee Journal*, March 14, 1978, retrieved September 18, 2012, from http://news.google.com/newspapers.
Drucker, Mort, and Larry Siegel. "Who in Heck Is Virginia Woolfe?" *Mad*, no. 109, March 1967: 4–10.
_____, and Stan Hart. "In the Out Exit." *Mad*, no. 118, April 1968: 4–10.
Duke, Alan. "Hollywood Crackdown Nabs Faux Superheroes." *CNN Entertainment*, June 3, 2012, retrieved June 30, 2012, from http://articles.cnn.com.
Eames, John Douglas, and Robert Abele. *The Paramount Story.* New York: Simon & Schuster, 2004.
Ebert, Roger. *I Hated, Hated, Hated This Movie.* Kansas City, MO: Andrews McMeel Publishing, 2000.
_____. *Roger Ebert's Four Star Reviews, 1967–2007.* Kansas City, MO: Andrews McMeel Publishing, 2008.
Epstein, Rob, and Jeffrey Friedman. *The Celluloid Closet.* Arte/Brillstein-Grey Entertainment/Channel Four Films/Home Box Office/Sony Pictures Classics/Telling Pictures/Zweites Deutsches Fernsehen, 1995.
Epstein, Rob, et al. *The Celluloid Closet (Special Edition).* Filmmakers Commentary. Sony Pictures Home Entertainment, 2001.
Erickson, Hal. *Encyclopedia of Television Law Shows: Factual and Fictional Series About Judges, Lawyers and the Courtroom, 1948–2008.* Jefferson, NC: McFarland, 2009.
Erskine, Thomas L, and James M. Welsh. *Video Versions: Film Adaptations of Plays on Video.* Westport, CT: Greenwood, 2000.
Evans, Everett. "In TUTS Show, Jo Anne Worley Finds She Really Has a 'Gypsy' in Her Soul." *Houston Chronicle Archives*, July 12 1987, retrieved August 1, 2012, from http://www.chron.com/CDA/archives.
Farrow, Mia. *What Falls Away: A Memoir.* New York: Nan A. Talese, 1997.
Fay, Francis X. Jr. "Sandy Dennis Dies of Cancer at 54." *The Hour*, March 4, 1992, retrieved May 31, 2012, from http://news.google.com/newspapers.
Film Reference: Theatre, Film and Television Biographies. Retrieved May 15, 2012, from http://www.filMr.eference.com/film/40/Sandy-Dennis.
Finstad, Suzanne. *Natasha: The Biography of Natalie Wood.* New York: Three Rivers Press, 2002.
_____. *Warren Beatty: A Private Man.* New York: Harmony, 2005.
Fish, Tim. "The Four Seasons." *Daily News*, June 19, 1981, retrieved September 24, 2012, from http://news.google.com/newspapers.
Flander, Judy. "Torn Ideal Villain in 'The Execution.'" *Ocala Star-Banner*, July 7, 1986.
_____. "A Well-Acted 'Execution' Movie." *Lakeland Ledger*, January 14, 1985, retrieved June 21, 2012, from http://news.google.com/newspapers.
Flatley, Guy. "For Film Makers, Horror Stories Are a Supernatural." *The New York Times*, July 16, 1976, retrieved August 6, 2012, from http://www.nytimes.com.
Flautz, John. "Ballard, Dennis Perfect in 'Odd Couple' Theater Reviews." *The Morning Call*, August 18, 1988, retrieved June 22, 2012, from http://articles.mcall.com.
Fonda, Jane. *My Life So Far.* New York: Random House, 2006.
Foster, Jodie. *Tales from the Darkside.* Season 4, Episode 15, "Do Not Open This Box." Laurel Productions/JayGee Productions, 1988.
Fowler, Jimmy. "Arts." *Dallas Observer*, September 7, 2000, retrieved June 26, 2012, from http://www.dallasobserver.com.
Fox, Julian. *Woody: Movies from Manhattan.* London: B.T. Batsford, 1996.
"*Fox, The* Pictorial." *Playboy*, vol. 14, no. 10, 1967: 81–85.
Frankel, Haskel. "Square Deal at the Round Table." *The New York Times*, June 26, 1977, retrieved June 15, 2012, from http://query.nytimes.com/mem/archive.

Friedman, Lester D., and Brent Notbohm. *Steven Spielberg: Interviews (Conversations with Filmmakers)*. Jackson: University Press of Mississippi, 2000.
Garvin, Alan. "What in the World!" *Rome News-Tribune*, August 21, 1966, retrieved May 31, 2012, from http://news.google.com/newspapers.
Gaver, Jack. "Play 'Clowns' Way to Screen." *The Pittsburgh Press*, February 5, 1966, retrieved June 2, 2012, from http://news.google.com/newspapers.
Gelb, Arthur. "Theatre." *The New York Times*, April 26, 1960, retrieved May 20, 2012, from http://query.nytimes.com/mem/archive.
Gent, George. "TV." *The New York Times*, January 20, 1968, retrieved June 26, 2012, from http://query.nytimes.com/mem/archive.
Gibson, David. "There's No Mush About This 'Weepie.'" *Evening Times*, November 14, 1969, retrieved August 2, 2012, from http://news.google.com/newspapers.
Gibson, Joy Leslie. *Ian McKellen*. London: Weidenfeld and Nicholson, 1986.
Girgus, Sam B. *The Films of Woody Allen (Cambridge Film Classics)*. Cambridge: Cambridge University Press, 2002.
Goldin, J. David. "The CBS Radio Mystery Theatre." Retrieved July 12, 2012, from http://radiogoldindex.com.
Gussow, Mel. *Edward Albee: A Singular Journey*. Winona, MN: Applause Books, 2000.
Graczyk, Ed. *Come Back to the 5 & Dime Jimmy Dean, Jimmy Dean*. New York: Samuel French, 1982.
Graham, Sheilah. "Comedy Brings Lemmon, Sandy Dennis to Liberty." *Youngstown Vindicator*, July 7, 1970, retrieved August 9, 2012, from http://news.google.com/newspapers.
_____. "Sandy Dennis Top Crybaby." *The Pittsburgh Press*, December 11, 1966, retrieved from http://news.google.com/newspapers.
_____. "Sandy Stingy on Clothes." *The Pittsburgh Press*, December 17, 1967, retrieved June 11, 2012, from http://news.google.com/newspapers.
Grams, Martin, and Patrik Wikstrom. *The Alfred Hitchcock Presents Companion*. OTR Publishing, 2001.
Grape, Nancy. "Two Fine Actresses Light Up Stage in Ogunquit's 'The Royal Family.'" *The Lewiston Evening Journal*, August 16, 1977, retrieved June 15, 2012, from http://news.google.com/newspapers.
Grauman, Walter. *The Fugitive*. Season 1, Episode 22–23, "Angels Travel on Lonely Roads: Parts 1 and 2." Quinn Martin Productions/United Artists Television, 1964.
_____. *The New Breed*. Season 1, Episode 6, "Till Death Do Us Part." Selmur Productions/Quinn Martin Productions, 1961.
Greiff, Louis K. *D.H. Lawrence: Fifty Years on Film*. Carbondale, IL: Southern Illinois University Press, 2006.
Grissom, James. "Sandy Dennis: A Willful Intent to Grow." *Follies of God*, retrieved December 17, 2012, from http://jamesgrissom.blogspot.com.au.
Gussow, Mel. "Along the Straw Hat Trail." *The New York Times*, July 22, 1977, retrieved June 15, 2012, from http://query.nytimes.com/mem/archive.
_____. "The Stage." *The New York Times*, August 7, 1981, retrieved June 17, 2012, from http://theater.nytimes.com/mem/theater/treview.
Hadleigh, Boze. *Celebrity Diss and Tell: Stars Talk About Each Other*. Riverside, NJ: Andrews McMeel Publishing, 2005.
_____. *Hollywood Lesbians*. New York: Barricade Books, 1994.
Hall, Carla. "'Equalizer' Has Produced Compelling Hero." *Eugene Register-Guard*, February 11 1987, retrieved October 12, 2012, from http://news.google.com/newspapers.
Hallowell, John. "Movies/Glamor gets the gate as the 'uglies' come into their own." May 24 1968. *Life Magazine*. Retrieved October 24 2012 from http://books.google.com.au/books.
Hamill, Brian, Derrick Tseng, and Charles Champlin. *Woody Allen at Work: The Photographs of Brian Hamill*. New York: H.N. Abrams, 1995.
Hanauer, Joan. "'The Execution'—a Bizarre Thriller." *The Modesto Bee*, January 14 1985, retrieved June 22, 2012, from http://news.google.com/newspapers.
Harrison, Bernie. "The Movies." *The Washington Star*, August 20, 1978, retrieved from *Lakeland Ledger* on September 13, 2012, from http://news.google.com/newspapers.
Haskell, Molly. *From Reverence to Rape: The Treatment of Women in the Movies*. New York: Penguin Books, 1974.
_____. "Movies." *New York Magazine*, April 10, 1978, retrieved October 24, 2012, from http://books.google.com.au/books.
Heymann, C. David. *Liz: An Intimate Biography of Elizabeth Taylor*. New York: Atria Books, 2011.

Hillel, Aron. "Caped Crusaders Crash L.A. City Hall." *Neon Tommy*, August 31, 2012, retrieved June 30, 2012, from http://www.neontommy.com.
Hiller, Arthur. *Alfred Hitchcock Presents*. Season 3, Episode 33, "Post Mortem." Shamley Productions, 1958.
Hirsch, Foster. *Love, Sex, Death, and the Meaning of Life: The Films of Woody Allen*. Cambridge, MA: Da Capo Press, 2001.
_____. *A Method to Their Madness: The History of the Actors Studio*. Cambridge, MA: Da Capo Press, 2001.
Hirschhorn, Clive. *The Columbia Story*. London: Hamlyn, 2001.
_____. *The Universal Story: The Complete History of the Studio and All Its Films*. London: Hamlyn, 2001.
_____. *The Warner Bros. Story: The Complete History of Hollywood's Great Studio, with Every Warner Bros. Feature Film Described and Illustrated*. New York: Crown Publishers, 1987.
Hischak, Thomas S. *American Theatre: A Chronicle of Comedy and Drama, 1969–2000*. Oxford: Oxford University Press, 2001.
Hitchcock, Alfred. *Alfred Hitchcock Presents*. Season 5, Episode 1, "Arthur." Shamley Productions, 1959.
Hoban, Russell. "The Antic Arts: The New Ingenue." *Holiday*, vol. 37, no. 3, 1965: 131, 134–136, 183–184.
Hofler, Robert. *The Man Who Invented Rock Hudson: The Pretty Boys and Dirty Deals of Henry Wilson*. Cambridge, MA: Da Capo, 2006.
Holm, Ian. *Acting My Life*. New York: Bantam, 2004.
Hoover, Bob. "Good Cast Is Wasted in Gory 'Parents.'" *Pittsburgh Post-Gazette*, June 2 1989, retrieved November 9, 2012, from http://news.google.com/newspapers.
Hopper, Hedda. "Sandy Dennis Is Wanted for 'Any Wednesday' Role." *The News and Courier*, April 14, 1965, retrieved June 21, 2012, from http://news.google.com/newspapers.
Horn, Barbara L. *Edward Albee: A Research and Production Sourcebook (Modern Dramatists Research and Production Sourcebooks)*. Westport, CT: Praeger, 2003.
Horowitz, Susan. *Queens of Comedy: Lucille Ball, Phyllis Diller, Carol Burnett, Joan Rivers, and the New Generation of Funny Women (Studies in Humor and Gender)*. New York: Routledge, 1997.
Hosle, Vittorio. *Woody Allen: An Essay on the Nature of the Comical*. Notre Dame, IN: University of Notre Dame Press, 2007.
Howell, Chauncey. "The Day It Rained More Than a Handful." *The New York Times*, March 3 1968, retrieved June 21, 2012, from http://query.nytimes.com/mem/archive.
Hutchings, David. "Sandy Dennis: The Queen of Artfully Oddball Roles Finds Peace as a Cat-Crazed Recluse." *People*, March 13, 1989, retrieved June 1, 2012, from http://www.people.com/people/archive.
Inge, William. "New Scenarist's Views." *The New York Times*, October 8, 1961, retrieved May 29, 2012, from http://query.nytimes.com/mem/archive.
Jackson, Kathi. *Steven Spielberg: A Biography*. Westport, CT: Greenwood, 2007.
James, David. "Showtime." *The Press-Courier*, August 16, 1981, retrieved September 19, 2012, from http://news.google.com/newspapers.
Kabatchnik, Amnon. *Blood on the Stage, 1950- 1975: Milestone Plays of Crime, Mystery, and Detection*. Plymouth, UK: Scarecrow Press, 2011.
Kael, Pauline. *5001 Nights at the Movies*. New York: Holt, Rinehart and Winston, 1984.
_____. *Going Steady*. New York: Warner Books, 1970.
_____. *I Lost It at the Movies*. Boston: Atlantic Monthly Press/Little, Brown and Company, 1965.
_____. *Movie Love*. New York: Dutton, 1991.
_____. *When the Lights Go Down*. New York: Holt, Rinehart and Winston, 1980.
Kagan, Norman. *American Skeptic: Robert Altman's Genre-Commentary Films*. Pierian Press, 1982.
Kapsis, Robert E., and Kathie Coblentz. *Woody Allen: Interviews (Conversations with Filmmakers Series)*. Jackson: University Press of Mississippi, 2006.
Karlin, Lynn. "The Only Perfect Relationship in This Fickle World." *New York Magazine*, March 24, 1975, retrieved October 24, 2012, from http://books.google.com.au/books.
Karol, Michael. *The ABC Movie of the Week Companion: A Loving Tribute to the Classic Series*. iUniverse, 2008.
Karp, Alan. *Films of Robert Altman*. Lanham, MD: Rowman & Littlefield, 1981.
Kashner, Sam, and Nancy Schoenberger. *Furious Love: Elizabeth Taylor, Richard Burton, and the Marriage of the Century*. New York: Harper Paperbacks, 2011.
Kass, Judith M. *Robert Altman: American Innovator*. New York: Popular Library, 1978.
Katselas, Milton. *Butterflies Are Free*. Frankovich Productions/Columbia Pictures, 1972.
Kazan, Elia. *Kazan on Directing*. New York: Vintage, 2010.

_____. *A Life*. Cambridge, MA: Da Capo Press, 1997.
Kelley, Bill. "Guest Cast, Plot Makes Intriguing Equalizer." *Sun-Sentinel*, January 15, 1986, retrieved October 12, 2012, from http://articles.sun-sentinel.com.
Kelly, Kevin. "Eric Roberts Has Mass Appeal." *Boston Globe*, October 4, 1981, retrieved June 19, 2012, from http://pqasb.pqarchiver.com/boston/access.
_____. "Stage." *Boston Globe*, March 3, 1982, retrieved June 19, 2012, from http://pqasb.pqarchiver.com/boston/access.
Kelly, Richard T. *Sean Penn: His Life and Times*. Edinburgh: Canongate, 2005.
Kerr, Walter. "I Love Sandy Dennis But..." *The New York Times*, November 5, 1967, retrieved June 11, 2012, from http://query.nytimes.com/mem/archive.
_____. "Q. Mr. Ayckbourn Is Sex Funny? A. It Depends. With Me..." *The New York Times*, October 20, 1974, retrieved June 13, 2012, from http://query.nytimes.com/mem/archive.
_____. "Stage View." *The New York Times*, October 20, 1974, retrieved June 13, 2012, from http://query.nytimes.com/mem/archive.
_____. "Stage View." *The New York Times*, August 16, 1981, retrieved June 18, 2012, from http://theater.nytimes.com/mem/theater/treview.
Keyser, Les. *Hollywood in the Seventies*. New York: A.S. Barnes & Company, 1981.
Keyssar, Helene. *Robert Altman's America*. Oxford: Oxford University Press, 1991.
Killen, Tom. "Sandy Dennis, Personal Singular." *After Dark*, vol. 8, no. 11, 1976: 62–65.
King, Kimball. *Woody Allen: A Casebook (Casebooks on Modern Dramatists)*. New York: Routledge, 2001.
King, Paul. "Nobody — Not Even Actors — Knows What Will Happen Next." *Edmonton Journal*, April 27, 1974, retrieved June 22, 2012, from http://news.google.com/newspapers.
King, Seth S. "What's Doing in Chicago." *The New York Times*, May 19, 1974, retrieved June 13, 2012, from http://query.nytimes.com/mem/archive.
Kirkpatrick, Rob. *Magic in the Night: The Words and Music of Bruce Springsteen*. New York: St. Martin's Griffin, 2009.
Koblenz, Eleanor. "Dennis Enjoying 'White Chicks' Role." *Schenectady Gazette*, April 14, 1986, retrieved June 21, 2012, from http://news.google.com/newspapers.
Kohner. Pancho. *Lupita Tovar: The Sweetheart of Mexico*. Xlibris Corporation, 2011.
Kolin, Philip C. *Conversations with Edward Albee*. Jackson: University of Mississippi Press, 1988.
Kolker, Robert. *A Cinema of Loneliness: Penn, Stone, Kubrick, Scorsese, Spielberg, Altman*. Oxford: Oxford University Press, 2000.
Koprince, Susan. *Understanding Neil Simon (Understanding Contemporary American Literature)*. Columbia, SC: University of South Carolina Press, 2002.
Koresky, Michael. "Old Haunts." *Reverse Shot*. Retrieved August 26, 2012, from http://reverseshot.com/article/something_evil.
Korman, Harvey. "The Love Boat." Archive of American Television. Viewed on *YouTube*, October 7, 2012.
Krampner, Jon. *Female Brando: The Legend of Kim Stanley*. New York: Back Stage Books, 2006.
Kroll, Gerry. "Resurrection." *The Advocate*, February 6 1996, retrieved October 24, 2012, from http://books.google.com.au/books.
Kupecek, Linda. "Shoot Alberta." *Cinema Canada*, April 1984, retrieved July 8, 2012, from cinemacanada.athabascau.ca.
Lackmann, Ron. *Mercedes McCambridge: A Biography and Filmography*. Jefferson, NC: McFarland, 2005.
Lambert, Gavin. *Natalie Wood*. New York: Back Stage Books, 2005.
Landazuri, Margarita. "Who's Afraid of Virginia Woolf?" *Turner Classic Movies*. Retrieved July 5, 2012, from http://www.tcm.com.
Lawler, Sylvia. "'Execution' Draws Controversy." *Sunday Call-Chronicle*, January 13, 1985, retrieved June 21, 2012, from http://pqasb.pqarchiver.com.
Lawson, Carol. "Broadway." *The New York Times*, March 28 1980, retrieved October 4, 2012, from http://query.nytimes.com.
Lax, Eric. *Conversations with Woody Allen: His Films, the Movies, and Moviemaking*. New York: Knopf, 2009.
_____. *Woody Allen: A Biography*. Cambridge, MA: Da Capo Press, 2000.
Laycock, John. "Annoyed Thanks to Sandy Dennis." *The Windsor Star*, November 10 1969, retrieved August 2, 2012, from http://news.google.com/newspapers.
Lee, Luaine. "Life Has Been Wild for Jo Anne Worley." *Ocala Star-Banner*, June 16 1987, retrieved August 1, 2012, from http://news.google.com/newspapers.
Lee, Sander H. *Woody Allen's Angst: Philosophical Commentaries on His Serious Films*. Jefferson, NC: McFarland, 1997.

_____. *Eighteen Woody Allen Films Analyzed: Anguish, God and Existentialism.* Jefferson, NC: McFarland, 2002.
Lehman, Ernest. "He Was Very Afraid." *Talk,* April 2000: 150–155, 183.
Lemmon, Chris. *A Twist of Lemmon: A Tribute to My Father.* New York: Applause Books, 2008.
Levin, Bernard. "So Much Promise Fades into Such a Lot of Gloom." *Daily Mail,* May 14, 1965.
Lindsay-Hogg, Michael. *Luck and Circumstance: A Coming of Age in Hollywood, New York, and Points Beyond.* New York: Alfred A. Knopf, 2011.
Little, Deborah. "The New Film." *Pittsburgh Post-Gazette,* May 13, 1968, retrieved July 21, 2012, from http://news.google.com/newspapers.
Logan, Joshua. *Bus Stop.* Twentieth Century–Fox, 1956.
Lord, M.G. *The Accidental Feminist: How Elizabeth Taylor Raised Our Consciousness and We Were Too Distracted by Her Beauty to Notice.* New York: Walker & Company, 2012.
Lowry, Cynthia. "'Hatful of Rain' Had Strong Punch." *Gettysburg Times,* March 5, 1968, retrieved July 21, 2012, from http://news.google.com/newspapers.
Lucas, John Meredyth. *The Fugitive.* Season 4, Episode 19, "The Breaking of the Habit." Quinn Martin Productions (QM)/United Artists Television. 1967.
Lustig, Bill, and Larry Cohen. DVD audio commentary, March 2003. *God Told Me To.* Blue Underground, 2003.
Maltin, Leonard. *Leonard Maltin's 2006 Movie Guide.* New York: Plume, 2005.
Mann, Daniel. *Hot Spell.* Paramount/Wallis-Hazen, 1958.
Mann, Delbert. *The Philco Television Playhouse.* Season 4, Episode 1, "Segment." Showcase Productions, 1952.
Mann, William J. *How to Be a Movie Star: Elizabeth Taylor in Hollywood.* New York: Mariner Books, 2010.
Marshall, Cheryl. "Sandy Dennis Highlights Chilling Drama's Action." *Youngstown Vindicator,* August 22, 1969, retrieved July 28, 2012, from http://news.google.com/newspapers.
Mate, Rudolphe. *Miracle in the Rain.* Warner Bros., 1956.
Matteo, Bob D. "Awkward 'Execution' Punishes Viewers." *The Mount Airy News,* January 11, 1985, retrieved June 21, 2012, from http://news.google.com/newspapers.
McBride, Joseph. *Steven Spielberg: A Biography.* Jackson: University Press of Mississippi, 2011.
McGilligan, Patrick. *Robert Altman: Jumping Off the Cliff.* New York: St. Martin's Press, 1989.
McNulty, Charles. "The Other Side of Summer; The light and the Darkness; Female Brando: The Legend of Kim Stanley by Jon Krampner." *Los Angeles Times,* June 4, 2006, retrieved June 25, 2012, from http://pqasb.pqarchiver.com/latimes.
Monahan, Kaspar. "Sandy Dennis in Second Bid for an Oscar." *The Pittsburgh Press,* June 28, 1967, retrieved July 13, 2012, from http://news.google.com/newspapers.
Moorehouse, Rebecca. "Oscar Holder Sandy Dennis." *Sarasota Journal,* March 3, 1971, retrieved July 21, 2012, from http://news.google.com/newspapers.
Morehouse, Ward. "Actress Strays from Nebraska." *The Pittsburgh Press,* April 29, 1962, retrieved May 20, 2012, from http://news.google.com/newspapers.
Moritz, Terri. "'Thank You Very Much' is Conventional Drama." *Youngstown Vindicator,* September 25, 1969, retrieved August 2, 2012, from http://news.google.com/newspapers.
Mortensen, Viggo. " Missing Sandy Dennis." Retrieved June 22, 2012, from http://www.viggo-works.com.
Moseley, Roy. *Bette Davis.* Lexington: University Press of Kentucky, 2003.
Muir, Florabel. "Sandy Dennis Prefers Cold Weather for Acting." *The News and Courier,* October 9, 1968, retrieved June 12, 2012, from http://news.google.com/newspapers.
_____. "Warners 'Sweet November' Filmed on Historic Brooklyn Background." *The News and Courier,* May 6, 1967, retrieved July 21, 2012, from http://news.google.com/newspapers.
Muir, John Kenneth. *Horror Films of the 1970s.* Jefferson, NC: McFarland, 2007.
Munn, Michael. *Gene Hackman.* London: Robert Hale, 1997.
_____. *Richard Burton: Prince of Players.* New York: Skyhorse Publishing, 2008.
Mussellwhite, Bill. *The Calgary Herald,* January 7, 1974, retrieved June 22 2012 from http://news.google.com/newspapers.
Nash, Jay Robert, and Stanley Ralph Ross. *The Motion Picture Guide.* Chicago: Cinebooks, 1986.
Nemirow, Martin. "Motel." *The Harvard Crimson,* January 12, 1960, retrieved May 20, 2012, from http://www.thecrimson.com.
"News of the Theater." *The New York Times,* October 10, 1981, retrieved June 19, 2012, from http://www.nytimes.com.
Nichols, Mary P. *Deconstructing Woody: Art, Love, and Life in the Films of Woody Allen.* New York: Rowman & Littlefield, 1998.

Nichols, Mike. "Interview on NBC News — Today, July 29, 1966." Special Feature on DVD of *Who's Afraid of Virginia Woolf?* DVD Special Edition. Warner Home Video, 2006.
Nicklin, Lenore. "Miss Dennis Takes a Relaxed Look Back." *Sydney Morning Herald*, September 19, 1972, retrieved June 1, 2012, from http://news.google.com/newspapers.
_____. "A Touch of Love — and Then Millstone…" *The Sydney Morning Herald*, December 7, 1970, retrieved August 2, 2012, from http://news.google.com/newspapers.
O, Jimmy. "Interview: Stephen Geoffreys." *Arrow in the Head*, April 14, 2009, retrieved November 2, 2012, from http://www.joblo.com/horror-movies/news/interview-stephen-geoffreys.
O'Brien, Daniel. *Robert Altman: Hollywood Survivor*. New York: Continuum, 1995.
O'Connor, John J. "TV." *The New York Times*, March 14, 1978, retrieved June 15, 2012, from http://query.nytimes.com/mem/archive.
_____. "TV." *The New York Times*, June 27, 1980, retrieved June 16, 2012, from http://query.nytimes.com/mem/archive.
O'Connor, Pat. *Sweet November*. Warner Bros./Bel-Air Entertainment/3 Arts Entertainment, 2001.
Ogens, Matthew. *Confessions of a Superhero*. Hate Kills Man (HKM)/Hunting Lane Films/Ogens/Smokeshow Films, 2007.
Oliver, Edith. "The Current Cinema." *The New Yorker*, July 2, 1966: 64–65.
Oppenheimer, Peer J. "Sandy Dennis: The Star Who Lives with Fear." *Herald-Journal*, May 17, 1968, retrieved June 11, 2012, from http://news.google.com/newspapers.
Parish, James Robert. *Good Dames: Virtue in the Cinema*. New York: A.S. Barnes, 1973.
Parker, Jerry. "Whatever Happened to Sandy Dennis?" *The Tuscaloosa News*, April 15, 1973, retrieved May 19, 2012, from http://news.google.com/newspapers.
Paseman, Lloyd. "'Another Woman' Features Fine Ensemble Work." *Eugene Register-Guard*, March 31 1989, retrieved October 23, 2012, from http://news.google.com/newspapers.
Payton, Gordon, and Martin Grams, Jr. *The CBS Radio Mystery Theater: An Episode Guide and Handbook to Nine Years of Broadcasting, 1974–1982*. Jefferson, NC: McFarland, 2004.
Penn, Frank. "Joan of Arc Grilled … Again." *Ottawa Citizen*, January 10, 1974, retrieved June 22, 2012, from http://news.google.com/newspapers.
Petrucelli, Alan W. "TV Chatter." *Record-Journal*, September 22, 1985, retrieved October 10, 2012, from http://news.google.com/newspapers.
Pitts, Michael R. *Charles Bronson: The 95 Films and the 156 Television Appearances*. Jefferson, NC: McFarland, 2004.
Plecki, Gerard. *Robert Altman (Twayne Filmmakers Series)*. Boston: Twayne Publishers, 1985.
Portman, Jamie. "For Dennis, Oscar's an Ogre." *Ottawa Citizen*, January 3, 1984, retrieved July 7, 2012, from http://news.google.com/newspapers.
_____. "Sandy Dennis Trying to Escape the Web of Typecasting." *The Windsor Star*, February 2, 1984, retrieved July 8, 2012, from http://news.google.com/newspapers.
Purcell, Chris. "A Lack of Execution." *The Sydney Morning Herald*, April 26, 1987, retrieved June 21, 2012, from http://news.google.com/newspapers.
Quirk, Lawrence J. *The Films of Warren Beatty*. New York: Citadel, 1991.
_____. *Totally Uninhibited: The Life and Wild Times of Cher*. Quill, 1993.
Raidy, William A. "Sandy Dennis Has the Plain Facts." *The Pittsburgh Press*, October 24, 1976, retrieved May 19, 2012, from http://news.google.com/newspapers.
Reed, Rex. "A Lotta Things I Wanted More and Didn't Get." *The New York Times*, June 19, 1966, retrieved May 28, 2012, from http://query.nytimes.com/mem/archive.
_____. "'Nasty Habits' Is Hilarious Heavenly Hash." *The Village Voice*, March 28 1977, retrieved September 8, 2012, from http://news.google.com/newspapers.
Rice, Charlie. "The Star Who Lost Her Petticoat." *This Week Magazine, The Hartford Times*, July 21, 1962: 4.
Rich, Frank. "Stage." *The New York Times*, February 19, 1982, retrieved June 18, 2012, from http://www.nytimes.com/1982/02/19/theater.
_____. "Theater." *The New York Times*, May 5, 1983, retrieved June 20, 2012, from http://www.nytimes.com.
Riese, Randall. *The Unabridged James Dean: His Life and Legacy from A to Z*. Contemporary Books, 1991.
Robertson, Ed. *The Fugitive Recaptured: The 30th Anniversary Companion to a Television Classic*. Beverly Hills, CA: Pomegranate Press, 1993.
Rosin, James. "James Sheldon." *Classic Images*, December 28, 2011, retrieved June 4, 2012, from http://www.classicimages.com/articles.

Rothenberg, Fred. "In Movies, the Execution Is Better Than Love Affair." *Toledo Blade*, January 14, 1985, retrieved June 21, 2012, from http://news.google.com/newspapers.
Rubython, Thom. *And God Created Burton*. London: Myrtle, 2011.
Rulli, Martin, and Dennis Davern. *Goodbye Natalie, Goodbye Splendour*. E-reads.com, 2010.
Russo, Vito. *The Celluloid Closet: Homosexuality in the Movies*. New York: Joanna Cotler Books, 1981.
Salloum, Vicki. "Sandy Dennis Has Her Own Ideas." *Palm Beach Daily News*, January 15, 1976, retrieved August 9, 2012, from http://news.google.com/newspapers.
Sandy Dennis Foundation. Retrieved May 15, 2012, from http://www.sandydennis.org.
"Sandy Dennis: The Star in the $7 Dress." *Time*, vol. 90, no. 9, 1967: 54–57.
Sarris, Andrew. "In Berlin, a Festival or a Funeral?" *The New York Times*, July 20, 1969. Retrieved August 2, 2012, from http://www.nytimes.com.
Schaefer, George. *A Doll's House*. National Broadcasting Company (NBC), 1959.
Schemering, Christopher. *Guiding Light: A 50th Anniversary Celebration*. New York: Ballantine Books, 1986.
Scheuer, Philip K. "The Man Who Does Everything." *The Milwaukee Journal*, August 13, 1967, retrieved July 21, 2012, from http://news.google.com/newspapers.
Schickel, Richard. *Elia Kazan: A Biography*. New York: Harper Perennial, 2006.
_____. "Life Movie Review: Viva the Down Staircase." *Life*, July 7 1967, retrieved November 1, 2012, from http://books.google.com.au/books.
_____. *Woody Allen: A Life in Film*. Lanham, MD: Ivan R Dee, 2004.
Schickel, Richard, and George Perry. *Bette Davis: Larger Than Life*. Philadelphia: Running Press, 2009.
Schoell, William, and Lawrence J. Quirk. *The Sundance Kid: A Life of Robert Redford*. Lanham, MD: Taylor Trade Publishing, 2006.
Scott Royce, Brenda. *Lauren Bacall: A Bio-Bibliography (Bio-Bibliographies in the Performing Arts)*. Westport, CT: Greenwood, 1992.
Self, Robert T. *Robert Altman's Subliminal Reality*. Minneapolis, MN: University of Minnesota Press, 2002.
Sellers, Robert. *Hellraisers: The Life and Inebriated Times of Richard Burton, Richard Harris, Peter O'Toole, and Oliver Reed*. New York: Thomas Dunne Books, 2009.
Sharbutt, Jay. "The Changing Scenes of Sandy Dennis." *Los Angeles Times*, March 21, 1989, retrieved November 9, 2012, from http://articles.latimes.com.
Shearer, Lloyd. "Sandy Dennis: What Will Hollywood Do to Her?" *St. Petersburgh Times*, August 29, 1965, retrieved May 20, 2012, from http://news.google.com/newspapers.
Shearer, Stephen Michael. *Patricia Neal: An Unquiet Life*. Lexington, KY: The University Press of Kentucky, 2011.
Shemanski, Frances. "1977 Summer Theater Straw Hat Directory." *The New York Times*, June 19, 1977, retrieved June 15, 2012, from http://query.nytimes.com/mem/archive.
Sherman, George. *Naked City*. Season 4, Episode 16, "Her Life in Moving Pictures." Shelle Productions/Screen Gems, 1963.
Shipman, David. *The Great Stars: The International Years*. London: Angus & Robertson, 1972.
Sikorski, Fran. "At the Playhouse." *The Redding Pilot*, July 1, 1982, retrieved June 18, 2012, from http://news.google.com/newspapers.
_____. "At Westport: Agnes of God." *The Ridgefield Press*, June 28, 1984, retrieved June 20, 2012, from http://news.google.com/newspapers.
_____. "On Broadway." *The Reading Pilot*, March 4, 1982, retrieved June 19, 2012, from http://news.google.com/newspapers.
_____. "A Theatrical Reunion." *The Ridgefield Press*, September 12, 1985, retrieved June 21, 2012, from http://news.google.com/newspapers.
Sikov, Edward. *Dark Victory: The Life of Bette Davis*. New York: Holt Paperbacks, 2008.
Silet, Charles L.P. *The Films of Woody Allen: Critical Essays*. Lanham, MD: Scarecrow Press, 2006.
Simon, John. "Movies. With Malice Towards Nuns." *New York Magazine*, March 28 1977, retrieved October 24, 2012, from http://books.google.com.au/books.
_____. "Theater." *New York Magazine*, August 24 1981, retrieved October 24, 2012, from http://books.google.com.au/books.
_____. "Theater. The Dean's September." *New York Magazine*, March 1, 1982, retrieved June 18, 2012, from http://books.google.com.au/books.
Simon, Neil. *Rewrites: A Memoir*. New York: Simon & Schuster, 1998.
Sinnott, John. "The Out-of-Towners" DVD review. *DVDTalk*, November 25, 2003, retrieved August 9, 2012, from http://www.dvdtalk.com.

Skinner, Jane. "Actress Sandy Dennis: She Travels by Train, Likes Cats and Dogs." *Palm Beach Daily News*, March 4, 1973, retrieved July 24, 2012, from http://news.google.com/newspapers.

Skinner Sawyers, June. *Racing in the Street: The Bruce Springsteen Reader*. New York: Penguin Books, 2004.

Skoble, Aeon J., and Mark T. Conard. *Woody Allen and Philosophy: You Mean My Whole Fallacy Is Wrong?* Chicago: Open Court, 2004.

Smight, Jack. *No Way to Treat a Lady*. Paramount, 1968.

Smith, Liz. "Love Has Many Faces in New York." *Sarasota Herald-Tribune*, January 23, 1984, retrieved June 17, 2012, from http://news.google.com/newspapers.

———. *Toledo Blade*, October 19, 1981, retrieved June 19, 2012, from http://news.google.com/newspapers.

Smith, Michael. "Burning Bright." *The Village Voice*, October 21, 1959, retrieved May 20, 2012, from http://news.google.com/newspapers.

Soderbergh, Steven, with Mike Nichols. DVD audio commentary on *Who's Afraid of Virginia Woolf?* DVD Special Edition. Warner Home Video, 2006.

Somerset-Ward, Richard. *An American Theatre: The Story of Westport Country Playhouse, 1931–2005*. New Haven, CT: Yale University Press, 2005.

Stang, Joanna. "Sweet Success: From Lincoln, Neb., to Broadway, NY., in Several Uneasy Lessons." *The New York Times*, March 1, 1964, retrieved May 20, 2012, from http://query.nytimes.com/mem/archive.

Stanley, John. *Creature Features: The Science Fiction, Fantasy, and Horror Movie Guide*. New York: Berkley Trade, 2000.

Stern, Keith. *Queers in History: The Comprehensive Encyclopedia of Historical Gays, Lesbians and Bisexuals*. Dallas: BenBella Books, 2009.

Sterritt, David. *Robert Altman: Interviews (Conversations with Filmmakers)*. Jackson, MS: University Press of Mississippi, 2000.

Stevens, George Jr. *Alfred Hitchcock Presents*. "Coming, Mama." Shamley Productions, 1961.

Stevens, Robert. *Suspense*. Season 2, Episode 8. "The Murderer." Columbia Broadcasting System, 1949.

———. *Suspense*. Season 2, Episode 38. "Photo Finish." Columbia Broadcasting System, 1950.

———. *Suspense*. Season 3, Episode 30. "Telephone Call." Columbia Broadcasting System, 1951.

Stolley, Richard B. "Bonnie Koloc's Manhattan Transfer." *New York Magazine*, May 16 1983, retrieved November 1, 2012, from http://books.google.com.au/books.

Stratton, David. "The Pain of Mid-Life Retrospect." *The Sydney Morning Herald*, May 25 1989, retrieved October 23, 2012, from http://news.google.com/newspapers.

Suskind, Jacob. "The Heart Farm Offers Old-Fashioned Thrills." *The Montreal Gazette*, November 21, 1970, retrieved August 15, 2012, from http://news.google.com/newspapers.

Sweeney, Louise. "The Talent Shows, the Cats Don't." *The Christian Science Monitor*, August 20, 1981, retrieved June 17, 2012, from http://www.csmonitor.com.

Tallmer, Jerry. "Theatre." *The Village Voice*, December 12, 1956, retrieved May 20, 2012, from http://news.google.com/newspapers.

Taraborrelli, J. Randy. *Elizabeth*. New York: Grand Central Publishing, 2006.

Taubman, Howard. "Theatre." *The New York Times*, October 21, 1960, retrieved May 20, 2012, from http://query.nytimes.com/mem/archive.

———. "Theatre." *The New York Times*, November 2, 1961, retrieved May 20, 2012, from http://query.nytimes.com/mem/archive.

———. "Theatre." *The New York Times*, April 6, 1962, retrieved May 20, 2012, from http://query.nytimes.com/mem/archive.

———. "Theatre." *The New York Times*, February 19, 1964, retrieved June 1, 2012, from http://query.nytimes.com/mem/archive.

———. "Theatre." *The New York Times*, June 23, 1964, retrieved June 9, 2012, from http://www.nytimes.com/books.

Terrace, Vincent. *Encyclopedia of Television: Series, Pilots, and Specials 1974–1984*. New York: Zoetrope, 1985.

———. *Encyclopedia of Television Shows, 1925 Through 2010*, second edition. Jefferson, NC: McFarland, 2011.

———. *Radio Programs, 1924–1984: A Catalog of More Than 1800 Shows*. Jefferson, NC: McFarland, 2009.

———. *Television Specials: 3,201 Entertainment Spectaculars, 1939 Through 1993*. Jefferson, NC: McFarland, 2007.

Terrill, Marshall, and Peter O. Whitmer. *Steve McQueen: The Life and Legend of a Hollywood Icon*. Chicago: Triumph Books, 2010.

Terry, Clifford. "Sean Penn's 'Indian Runner' A Slow-Motion Marathon." *Chicago Tribune*, October 4 1991, retrieved November 20, 2012, from http://articles.chicagotribune.com.

Thomas, Bob. "Oscar Winners Didn't Show Up." *Owosso-Argus Press*, April 13, 1967, retrieved June 11, 2012, from http://news.google.com/newspapers.
_____. "Sandy Gets 3 Hit Parts in a Row." *Miami News*, June 6, 1967, retrieved June 1, 2012, from http://news.google.com/newspapers.
Thompson, David. *Altman on Altman*. London: Faber & Faber, 2006.
Thompson, Ruth. "O'Neal Moves to Directing Teleplay 'Wilson's Reward.'" *Sarasota Journal*, June 16 1980, retrieved September 19, 2012, from http://news.google.com/newspapers.
Thomson, David. *Bette Davis*. London: Faber & Faber, 2010.
Vespa, Maria. "Sandy Dennis Has a Hit on Her Hands..." *People*, August 23, 1976, retrieved June 14, 2012, from http://www.people.com/people/archive/article.
Viego, Antonio. *Dead Subjects: Toward a Politics of Loss in Latino Studies*. Durham, NC: Duke University Press, 2007.
Virtel, Louis. "Catching Up with George Segal About Mike Nichols and 'Who's Afraid of Virginia Woolf' Rehearsals." *Movieline*, June 11, 2011, retrieved December 1, 2012, from http://movieline.com.
_____. "Which Pop Culture 'Sandy' Should Be the Face of Hurricane Sandy?" *AfterElton*, October 29, 2012, retrieved December 2, 2012, from http://www.afterelton.com.
Wagner, Robert J., with Scott Eyman. *Pieces of My Heart: A Life*. New York: It Books, 2009.
Walker, Alexander. *Elizabeth: The Life of Elizabeth Taylor*. New York: Grove Press, 2001.
Walker, Ann. "Historical Details Sustained Show." *The Leader-Post*, January 11, 1974, retrieved June 21, 2012, from http://news.google.com/newspapers.
Wallach, Allan. "Actor Stays Tuned to Aging Role." *The Pittsburgh Press*, April 27, 1977, retrieved June 14, 2012, from http://news.google.com/newspapers.
Ward, Mike. "The Out-of-Towners" DVD review. *PopMatters*, December 1, 2003, retrieved August 9, 2012, from http://www.popmatters.com.
Warga, Wayne. "Girl with a Good Grip on Chaos." *Life*, vol. 64, no. 6, 1968: 65–67.
Warner Spelling, Cass. *The Brothers Warner*. Warner Sisters, 2008.
Wedding, Daniel. *Movies and Mental Illness: Using Films to Understand Psychopathology*. Kirkland, WA: Hogrefe Publishing, 2009.
Wedman, Les. "Sandy Dennis Is a Movie Star Who Hates Making Movies." *The Sun*, October 16, 1968, retrieved June 12, 2012, from http://news.google.com/newspapers.
Weiler, A.H. "Number of Movies Made Here Sets a Record: 26 in 6 Months." *The New York Times*, July 28, 1969, retrieved June 12, 2012, from http://query.nytimes.com/mem/archive.
Weimann, Frank. *Everything You Always Wanted to Know About Woody Allen: The Ultimate Quiz Book*. SP Books, 1993.
Weiskind, Ron. "Harper Says 'Execution' About Survival." *Pittsburgh Post-Gazette*, January 14, 1985, retrieved June 21, 2012, from http://news.google.com/newspapers.
Weisman, Sam. *The Out-of-Towners*. Paramount/Cherry Alley Productions/Cort/Madden Productions, 1999.
Westgate, Barry. "Another Sniffle-in for Sandy Dennis." *The Edmonton Journal*, August 5, 1969, retrieved June 4, 2012, from http://news.google.com/newspapers.
_____. "Bird Watchers Unite Against Film Company." *The Edmonton Journal*, July 14, 1969, retrieved August 9, 2012, from http://news.google.com/newspapers.
Wexler, Haskell. DVD audio commentary on *Who's Afraid of Virginia Woolf?* DVD Special Edition. Warner Home Video, 2006.
"What's My Line?" Mark Goodson- Bill Todman Productions/NBC. December 19, 1973. Clip viewed on *YouTube* on June 16, 2012.
Williams, Tony. *Hearths of Darkness: The Family in the American Horror Film*. Plainsboro, NJ: Associated University Press, 1996
Wilson, Earl. "Lovely Lynley Lonely? No Men in Her Life." *The Milwaukee Sentinel*, July 23, 1975, retrieved September 4, 2012, from http://news.google.com/newspapers.
_____. "No Fear in 40 for Sandy Dennis." *The Milwaukee Sentinel*, February 26, 1977, retrieved June 1, 2012, from http://news.google.com/newspapers.
_____. "No Permanent Lady for Bessell." *The Milwaukee Sentinel*, September 3, 1976, retrieved June 14, 2012, from http://news.google.com/newspapers.
_____. *Toledo Blade*, March 5, 1980. Retrieved June 17, 2012, from http://news.google.com/newspapers.
Windust, Bretaigne. *Alfred Hitchcock Presents*. Season 4, Episode 26, "Cheap Is Cheap." Shamley Productions, 1959.
Wirz, Julie. "Sandy Dennis at the Palace: This Super Star Is also a Super Lady." *The Hour*, January 22, 1981, retrieved June 13, 2012, from http://news.google.com/newspapers.

Wise, Robert. *Somebody Up There Likes Me*. MGM, 1956.
Wishart, David J. *Encyclopedia of the Great Plains*. Seattle, WA: University of Nebraska Press, 2004.
Witbeck, Charles. "Five Women Plan 'The Execution.'" *The Calgary Herald*, January 11, 1985, retrieved June 21, 2012, from http://news.google.com/newspapers.
Wolcott, James. "Medium Cool: Television and Its Discontents." *The Village Voice*, March 10, 1978, retrieved September 19, 2012, from http://news.google.com/newspapers.
_____. "Movies." *Texas Monthly*, December 1982, retrieved June 19, 2012, from http://books.google.com.au/books.
Wood, Bret. "The Out-of-Towners." *Turner Classic Movies*. Retrieved August 7, 2012, from http://www.tcm.com.
Wood, Robin. *Hollywood from Vietnam to Reagan...and Beyond*. New York: Columbia University Press, 2003.
Wynorski, Jim. *976-Evil II*. Cinetel Films/Grey Matter Entertainment, 1992.
Yankee, Luke. *Just Outside the Spotlight: Growing Up with Eileen Heckart*. New York: Back Stage Books, 2006.
Yurko, J.T. "The Four Seasons." *The Daily Sentinel*, June 28 1981, retrieved September 24, 2012, from http://news.google.com/newspapers.
Zoller Heitz, Matt. "Of Birds and Planes." *The New York Times*, November 2, 2007, retrieved June 22, 2012, from http://movies.nytimes.com.
Zolotow, Sam. "Actors Studio Theater Gives TV Options on 12 Productions." *The New York Times*, October 19, 1964, retrieved June 10, 2012, from http://query.nytimes.com/mem/archive.
_____. "'Daphne' Delayed Until February." *The New York Times*, September 27, 1966, retrieved June 11, 2012, from http://query.nytimes.com/mem/archive.
Zuckerman, Faye. "Characters Bring Far-Fetched 'Execution' Story Alive Tonight." *St. Joseph News-Press*, July 7, 1986, retrieved June 21, 2012, from http://news.google.com/newspapers.
Zuckoff, Mitchell. *Robert Altman: The Oral Biography*. New York: Knopf, 2009.

Index

Absurd Person Singular (play) 28, 29, 31, 204
Alfred Hitchcock Presents (TV series) 3, 41, 137, 190–194, 195, 211, 213, 214, 219, 220
Allen, Woody 42, 128, 130, 131, 132, 133, 134, 209, 210, 213, 214, 215, 216, 218, 219, 220
Altman, Robert 22, 23, 33, 34, 37, 38, 39, 63, 86, 87, 89, 90, 91, 92, 93, 119, 120, 124, 125, 126, 206, 209, 211, 214, 215, 216, 217, 218, 219, 220, 221
Another Woman 15, 42, 126–136, 145
Any Wednesday (play) 13, 15, 16, 20, 21, 26, 34, 85, 202, 209, 214
Arrest and Trial (TV series) 14, 164–166, 195

Bacall, Lauren 33, 180, 182, 183, 218
Balaban, Bob 42, 144, 145, 146, 148, 149
Barrie, Barbara 41, 185, 186, 187
Beatty, Warren 10, 11, 49, 50, 52, 53, 54, 55, 56, 64, 209, 210, 212, 217
Bellamy, Ralph 24, 173, 174, 175
Black, Karen 37, 38, 122, 125, 206
Bogart, Paul 16, 57, 59
Buried Inside Extra (play) 39–40
Burnett, Carol 35, 113, 114, 117, 213
Burns, Michael 22, 85, 93
Burton, Richard 16, 60, 62, 63, 64, 65, 66, 67, 68, 214, 216, 218

Captain Kangaroo (TV series) 31, 32, 33
Cariou, Len 35, 113, 114

Carter, Thomas 41, 190, 192, 193
CBS Radio Mystery Theatre 29–30
Cher 37, 38, 39, 120, 121, 122, 125, 126, 206, 209, 210, 211, 217
Claxton, William 164, 166
Cohen, Larry 30, 106, 107, 108, 109, 110, 216
Come Back to the 5 & Dime Jimmy Dean, Jimmy Dean 2, 3, 22, 34, 37–39, 93, 118–126, 137, 184, 186, 206, 211, 213
Compton, Richard 41, 194, 196, 197
Cooper, Jackie 33, 180, 183, 211
Corey, Jeff 24, 173

Daphne in Cottage D (play) 19, 20, 202
The Dark at the Top of the Stairs (play) 8, 9, 10, 41, 44, 45, 199
Davis, Bette 6, 63, 67, 191, 216, 218, 220
Davis, Brad 41, 190, 191, 193, 212
Davison, Bruce 33, 176, 177, 180
Demon see *God Told Me To*
Dennis, Christopher Lloyd 47
Dennis, Sandy: Academy Award 1, 17, 18, 26, 56, 60, 126, 144, 177; acting mannerisms 1, 2, 8, 16, 21, 25, 26, 28, 31, 46, 47; death from cancer 42–43, 45, 46, 154, 212; lesbianism 35, 43; memoir 44–46; Tony Awards 15, 19, 22

Englund, Robert 42, 136, 138, 140, 141, 142, 143, 144
The Equalizer (TV series) 41, 128, 194–197, 213, 215
Everett, Chad 33, 176, 177, 180

The Execution (TVM) 40, 185–189, 191, 212, 213, 215, 216, 217, 218, 220, 221

Falk, Peter 21, 168, 169
Farrow, Mia 130, 131, 133, 134, 136, 212
Fonda, Jane 15, 54, 56, 85, 119, 210, 212
The Four Seasons 1, 35, 113–118, 120
The Fox 1, 2, 3, 19, 47, 48, 74–80, 83, 137
The Fugitive (TV series) 14, 162–164, 195, 213, 216, 217

Geoffreys, Stephen 42, 137, 143, 144, 217
God Told Me To 30, 31, 106–110
Gordon, Ruth 33, 180, 181, 182, 183
The Guiding Light 8, 157

Hackman, Gene 15, 16, 155
Hadleigh, Boze ("Hollywood Lesbians") 2, 42, 43–44, 68, 72, 80, 126, 213
Harper, Valerie 41, 185, 186, 187, 189, 220
A Hatful of Rain (TVM) 3, 21, 168, 169, 184
Heckart, Eileen 8–9, 18, 25, 28–29, 41, 200, 207, 221
Hiller, Arthur 23, 98, 102, 214
Hogg, Michael Lindsay 32, 110, 112, 216
Holm, Ian 127, 128, 136, 214
Hurt, Mary Beth 145
Hussein, Waris 23, 93, 95, 96, 97

The Indian Runner 42, 149–156
Inge, William 8, 10, 24, 123, 199, 202, 214
Ives, Burl 24, 170

Jackson, Glenda 32, 110, 112, 113

Kazan, Elia 10, 49, 50, 51, 52, 53, 54, 55, 56, 199, 214, 218
Kean, E. Arthur 33, 176, 179
Kohner, Pancho 30, 103, 105, 215
Korman, Harvey 41, 190, 215

Lemmon, Jack 10, 11, 23, 47, 98, 100, 102, 201, 213, 216
Lo Bianco, Tony 30, 106, 107, 109, 110
The Love Boat (TV series) 3, 41, 189–190, 191, 215

The Man Who Wanted to Live Forever (TVM) 24, 97, 168, 170–172, 173, 184
Marsh, Alex 167
McGavin, Darren 24, 173, 175
McKellen, Ian 23, 93, 97, 209, 213
Mercouri, Melina 32, 110, 136
Miller, Robert Ellis 19, 81, 85
Mr. Broadway (TV series) 16, 167–168, 195
Mr. Sycamore 2, 26, 30, 103–106
Morse, David 42, 149, 152, 154, 155
Mortensen, Viggo 42, 149, 152, 153, 154, 155, 216
Moxley, John Llewelleyn 21, 168
Mulligan, Gerry 13–14, 16, 19, 20, 21, 23, 24, 26, 30, 45, 47
Mulligan, Robert 18, 31, 70, 72
Music for a New Year's Night (TV special) 12

Naked City (TV series) 12, 14, 20, 157–159, 159–162, 165, 166, 168, 195, 218
Nasty Habits 1, 32, 33, 110–113, 177, 181
Newley, Anthony 19, 81, 83, 84, 85, 97
Nichols, Mike 16, 18, 22, 62, 63, 64, 65, 66, 67, 68, 217, 219, 220
976-Evil 3, 42, 136–144, 145

Oates, Warren 177, 180
O'Loughlin, Gerald 9, 13, 15, 16, 21, 34, 168, 184

O'Neal, Patrick 34, 183, 220
The Out of Towners 3, 10, 23, 47, 48, 98–103

Page, Geraldine 1, 2, 6, 16, 28, 32, 33, 40, 57, 58, 59, 113, 130, 204, 205, 207
Parents 42, 144–149
Parks, Michael 21, 168, 169
Penn, Sean 42, 150, 152, 154, 155, 215, 219
A Perfect Couple 34
Perfect Gentlemen (TVM) 33, 180–183, 184, 186, 212
Peyser, John 157, 158, 159
Police Story (TV series) 33, 176–180

Quaid, Randy 145

Raffin, Deborah 30, 106, 107
Robards, Jason 12, 13, 15, 30, 103, 105, 201
Roberts, Eric 34–35, 36, 37, 40, 45, 46, 212, 215
Robertson, Tom G. 41, 184
Rowlands, Gena 42, 120, 127, 128, 130, 131, 135, 135–136
Rydell, Mark 19, 74, 76, 78, 79, 80

Same Time, Next Year (play) 30, 31, 33, 34, 35, 44, 204, 206
Segal, George 16, 17, 60, 66, 68, 69, 220
Sheldon, James 160, 161, 162, 164
Simmons, Jean 30, 103
Simon, Neil 42, 98, 100, 102, 208, 215
Something Evil (TVM) 24, 103, 140, 168, 172–176, 184, 215
Spielberg, Steven 24, 172, 173, 176, 213, 214, 215, 216
Splendor in the Grass 10, 11, 49–57
Stanley, Kim 1, 2, 6, 16, 57, 58, 59, 202, 215, 216
Stevens, Craig 167
Strasberg, Lee 7, 16, 18, 202
The Supporting Cast (play) 36, 39, 206, 207
Sweet November 2, 18, 19, 81–85, 97

Swit, Loretta 31, 41, 185, 186, 187, 189, 209

Taylor, Elizabeth 14, 16, 38, 62, 63, 64, 65, 66, 67, 68, 209, 210, 213, 214, 216, 220
Thank You All Very Much 2, 23, 42, 93–98, 173
That Cold Day in the Park 2, 22, 23, 59, 85–93, 98, 119
A Thousand Clowns (play) 12, 13, 14, 15, 20, 26, 44, 201, 209
The Three Sisters 1, 3, 12, 16–18, 20, 57–60, 93
Torn, Rip 33, 41, 110, 185, 186, 189, 205
A Touch of Love see *Thank You All Very Much*
Trent, John 24, 170, 172

Up the Down Staircase 2, 3, 8, 9, 19, 31, 41, 69–73, 74, 83, 95

Vaccaro, Brenda 20, 31, 35, 40

Wells, Richard A. 41, 190
Wendkos, Paul 41, 185, 188, 189
What's My Line? (TV series) 26–27
Whitman, Stuart 24, 170
Who's Afraid of Virginia Woolf? 1, 3, 14, 15, 16, 17, 18, 19, 20, 21, 26, 31, 40, 48, 56, 60–69
Wild Strawberries 131–132, 135
Williams, Tennessee 1, 25, 30, 34, 56, 123, 125, 200, 203, 204, 205
Wilson's Reward (TVM) 3, 9, 34, 183–184, 220
Winters, Shelley 16, 57, 59
Witness to Yesterday (TV series) 27–28
Wood, Natalie 1, 10, 11, 49, 50, 52, 53, 54, 57, 212, 215
Woodward, Edward 41, 195, 197
Woodward, Joanne 6, 8, 43, 44, 120, 191

Young People Specials (TV series) 3, 41, 184, 185, 186

www.ingramcontent.com/pod-product-compliance
Ingram Content Group UK Ltd.
Pitfield, Milton Keynes, MK11 3LW, UK
UKHW050702160426
5217IPUK00038B/1877